TrailBlazer
TODAY'S MOST POPULAR STUDY GUIDES

Last Minute Guide

PHYSICS

for

CBSE XII

Sunder Singh
D.K. Singh

UNICORN BOOKS

Publisher
UNICORN BOOKS
F-2/16, Ansari Road, Daryaganj, New Delhi-110002
E-mail: info@unicornbooks.in • Website: www.unicornbooks.in
☎ 011-23275434, 23262683

Branch : Mumbai
23-25, Zaoba Wadi Thakurdwar, Mumbai-400002
☎ 022-22010941, 022-22053387
E-mail: rapidex@bom5.vsnl.net.in

ISBN 978-81-7806-299-0

Edition: 2015

***Printed at :** Unique Colors, Mayapuri, New Delhi-110064*

Preface

Why should one read 'Last Minute Guide'?

This series has been designed to provide a quick and clutter-free access to all the important concepts of each chapter. These books give the proper exposure needed by a smart student to understand and master each chapter in accordance with the syllabus laid down by the CBSE guidelines without wastage of time.

Efforts have been made to give the outline of each chapter, such as important formulae, rules and fundamentals at the beginning itself, so that the students can revise and brush up the concepts at the last minute as well.

This book is written after extensive research and designed in such a manner that the students can know well in advance the process of writing an answer in the examination.

This format further adds to the students' development by providing *step-by-step marking scheme* of CBSE, which allows the students to learn more about the specific steps, which otherwise most students ignore and, in the process, lose marks on.

This book essentially simplifies the entire process required of a student after studying it in the class:

- Revision of the concepts
- Practice of each concept with examples
- Awareness of the potential trouble areas where marks are lost
- Correct way to properly answer a question

– Publisher

Contents

SYLLABUS & DESIGN OF THE CBSE QUESTION PAPER
PHYSICS-CLASS XII

Time : 3 Hours **Max. Marks : 70**

The weightage of the distribution of marks over different dimensions of the question paper shall be as follows:

A. Weightage to different topics/content units

Unit	Marks
Electrostatics	08
Current Electricity	07
Magnetic Effect of Current and Magnetism	08
Electromagnetic Induction and Alternating Current	08
Electromagnetic Waves	03
Optics	14
Dual Nature of Radiation and Matter	04
Atoms and Nuclei	06
Electronic Devices	07
Communication Systems	05
Total	**70**

B. Weightage to the forms of questions

S. No.	Forms of Questions	Marks for Each Question	No. of Questions	Total Marks
1.	Long Answer (LA)	05	03	15
2.	Short Answer [SA (I)]	02	10	20
3.	Short Answer [SA (II)]/Value Based Question	03	09	27
4.	Very Short Answer (VSA)	01	08	08
	Total	–	**30**	**70**

C. Typology of questions

S. No.	Typology	Weightage in Marks	Weightage in Percentage
1.	Knowledge Based	14	20%
2.	Conceptual Understanding	21	30%
3.	Inferential Type	14	20%
4.	Reasoning Based	11	15%
5.	Skill Based	10	15%
	Total	**70**	**100%**

D. A weightage of around 15 marks has been assigned to the numericals

E. Weightage to the difficulty level of questions

S. No.	Estimated Difficulty Level	Percentage
1.	Easy	15%
2.	Average	70%
3.	Difficult	15%

The question paper will include value based question(s) to the extent of 3 – 5 marks.

UNIT 1

ELECTROSTATICS

(A) ELECTRIC FIELD & POTENTIAL

Important Points to Remember

A.1. Electrostatics deals with the effect of charges at rest.

A.2. Properties of electric charge : Electric charge is

(*i*) conserved

(*ii*) a scalar quantity

(*iii*) quantised i.e. every charge is made of the smallest unit equal to the electronic charge ($q = \pm ne$)

(*iv*) in-varient i.e. its value does not depend upon velocity

(*v*) like charges repel and unlike charges attract each other

A.3. Methods of charging : There are three methods

(*i*) By friction : Two bodies of different materials when rubbed together get oppositely charged

(*ii*) By conduction : The body to be charged is brought in contact of a charged body. The charge is shared in the ratio of the sizes of the bodies.

(*iii*) By induction : The body to be charged is brought near a charged body. The charge appearing on the uncharged body is opposite in nature and its magnitude depends upon the material of uncharged body

$$q_{induced} = -q\left(1 - \frac{1}{K}\right)$$

Where K = dielectric constant of the material of uncharged body.

Note : (*i*) Repulsion is the real test of the presence of charge on a body.

(*ii*) To check the presence of charge and its nature, electroscopes (generally gold leaf electroscope) are used.

A.4. Coulomb's Law :

(*i*) According to Coulomb's law, the electrostatic force of attraction or repulsion between two point charges is directly proportional to the product of the magnitude of two charges and inversely proportional to square of the distance between them.

Mathematically, $F = \frac{1}{4\pi\varepsilon_0}\frac{q_1 q_2}{r^2}$, in vector form $\vec{F} = \frac{1}{4\pi\varepsilon_0}.\frac{q_1 q_2}{r^3}.\vec{r}$

Where ϵ_0 = permitivity of free space = $8.85 \times 10^{-12}\ \frac{C^2}{N-m^2}$

$$\frac{1}{4\pi\varepsilon_0} = 9 \times 10^9\ \frac{N-m^2}{C^2}$$

(*ii*) Forces between two point charges are in accordance with Newton's third law of motion, *i.e.*,

$$\vec{F}_{12} = -\vec{F}_{21}$$

(*iii*) Coulomb's force depends upon the medium in which charges are placed. The max. coulomb force acts in vacuum (or air). In a medium of dielectric constant K the force reduces to the value $\frac{1}{K}$, i.e.

$$F_K = \frac{F_0}{K}$$

(*iv*) Coulomb's law is empirical law.

A.5. Electric Field Intensity :

(*i*) Electric field intensity $\vec{E}$ at a point due to a charge configuration is the force acting on a unit positive charge placed at that point. Generally, it is measured by the force $\vec{F}$ on a small positive test charge q_0 placed at that point divided by the magnitude of the test charge $\vec{E} = \underset{q_0 \to 0}{Lt} \frac{\vec{F}}{q_0}$. The SI unit of electric intensity is NC^{-1}. It is also written as volt per metre (Vm^{-1}).

(*ii*) The direction of electric intensity at a point in the electric field is that in which a positive charge placed at that point tends to move due to the effect of field charge (the charge which produces the electric field) i.e. It is radially outward if the field charge q is positive and radially inward if q is negative.

(*iii*) Electric field intensity due to point charge q at a distance r in air from it given by

$$E = \frac{1}{4\pi \epsilon_0} \cdot \frac{q}{r^2} NC^{-1}$$

(*iv*) The electric force on a charge q placed in an electric field of intensity E is qE. Its direction is shown in the fig. for $+q$ and $-q$

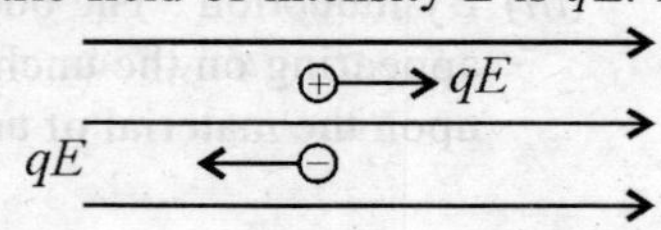

(*v*) Electric field is conservative.

A.6. Electric Potential :

(*i*) At a point is the electric field, electric potential is defined as the work done is bringing unit positive charge from infinity to that point.

$$V = \frac{W}{q_0}$$

It is a scalar quantity and its unit is volt ($V = JC^{-1}$)

(*ii*) Electric potential at a distance r from a point charge q placed in air or vacuum is

$$V = \frac{1}{4\pi \epsilon_0} \cdot \frac{q}{r} \; volt$$ (Imp. for proof)

The potential is positive if field charge q is positive and negative when the field charge q is negative.

(*iii*) Potential due to a number of charges

$$V = \sum_{i=1}^{n} \frac{1}{4\pi \epsilon_0} \cdot \frac{q_i}{r_i}$$

(*iv*) The work done is carrying a charge q from initial point A to final point B is

$$W = q(V_{final} - V_{initial}) = q(V_B - V_A)$$

and V_A and V_B are the potentials at A and B respectively. In this q is taken with sign.

(*v*) Potential decreases in the direction of electric field intensity and its rate of decrease with distance is termed as 'potential gradient'. The relation is

$$E = -\frac{dV}{dr} \qquad \text{(Imp. for proof)}$$

A.7. Potential Energy of a two Charge System :

(*i*) It is defined as the work done is bringing the charges from infinity to their respective points.

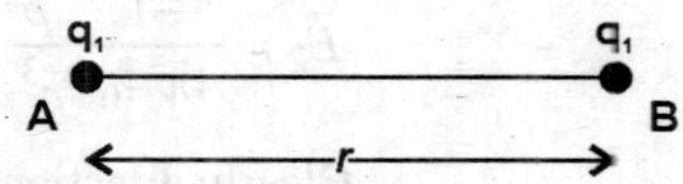

$$U = \frac{1}{4\pi \epsilon_0} \cdot \frac{q_1 q_2}{r}$$

The values of q_1 and q_2 are taken with sign. Negative potential energy indicates attraction and positive potential energy indicates repulsion.

(*ii*) If there are *n* charges in a system then pairs are formed

Number of pairs $= \dfrac{n(n-1)}{2}$

Potential energy (P.E.) of each pair is determined and then total

$$U = \sum_{i=1}^{n} U_i \qquad \text{(added with sign)}$$

A.8. Electric Lines of Force :

(*i*) These are smooth curves, the tangent at a point of which represents the direction of electric field at that point

(*ii*) Properties of electric lines of force are

(*a*) These are continuous but never form closed loops

(*b*) Arbitrarily start from positive charge and end at negative charge

(*c*) Two lines of force can never intersect

(*d*) Relative closeness of the lines represents the magnitude of the field strength.

(*e*) Number of electric lines of force which start or terminate at charge *q* is $\dfrac{q}{\epsilon_0}$

(*f*) For a set of two like charges, there is lateral pressure in between and for a set of unlike charges there is longitudinal contraction in between.

A.9. Equipotential Surface :

(*i*) The potential at every point of such a surface is the same.

(*ii*) Two equipotential surfaces can not intersect.

(*iii*) The direction of electric field intensity is perpendicular to the equipotential surface.

(*iv*) No work is done in moving a charge from one point to another point of the equipotential surface.

A.10. Electric Dipole :

(*i*) The system in which two equal and opposite charges are placed at short distance.

(*ii*) Dipole moment $\vec{p} = q \times 2\vec{l}$

It is a vector quantity directed from negative charge to positive charge. Its unit is C – m.

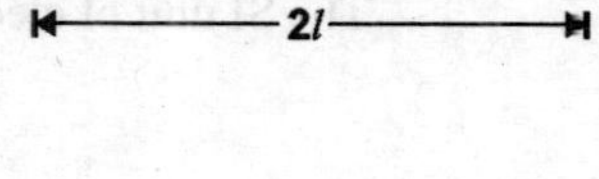

(*iii*) **Electric field intensity due to dipole**

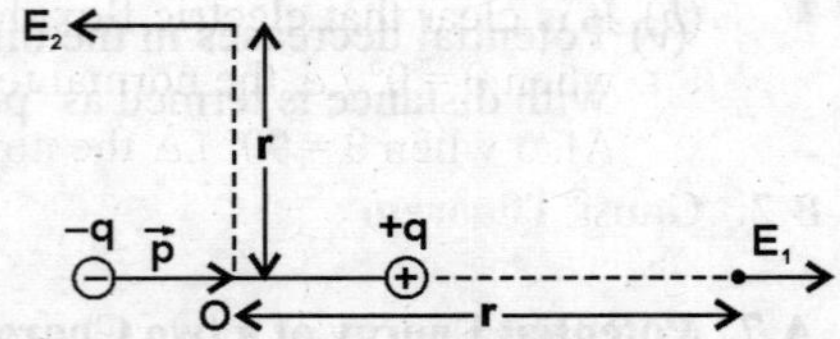

(*a*) **Axial Position** (Imp. for proof)

$$\vec{E}_1 = \frac{1}{4\pi \in_0} . \frac{2\vec{p}}{r^3} \quad \text{when} \quad r >> 2l.$$

Its direction is same as that of $\vec{P}$.

(*b*) **Equatorial Position**

$$\vec{E}_2 = \frac{-1}{4\pi \in_0} . \frac{\vec{p}}{r^3} \quad \text{when} \quad r >> 2l$$

Clearly direction of E_2 is opposite to that of $\vec{P}$.

(c) It is clear that at the same distance

$$\vec{E}_{axial} = -2\vec{E}_{equatorial}$$

(*iv*) **Electric Potential due to dipole**

(*a*) **Axial Position :** At distance *r* from the middle point of the dipole

$$V = \frac{1}{r\pi \in_0} . \frac{p}{r^2} \quad \text{when} \quad r >> 2l$$

(*b*) **Equatorial Line :** The value of potential V = 0

(*v*) **Torque on the electric dipole** (Imp. for proof)

(*a*) The net force experienced by an electric dipole placed in a uniform electric field is zero.

(*b*) An electric dipole placed in a uniform electric field experiences a torque given by:

$$\vec{\tau} = \vec{p} \times \vec{E} \text{ or } \tau = pE \sin\theta$$

Maximum torque acts when $\theta = 90°$ so that $\tau_{max.}$ = PE and for minimum torque, $\theta = 0°$ or 180°

$$\tau_{min.} = 0$$

Note : $\theta = 0$ is the condition of stable equilibrium and $\theta = 180°$ is the condition of unstable equilibrium.

(*vi*) **Work done in rotating the dipole** (Imp. for proof)

The work done in rotating an electric dipole from orientation θ_1 to θ_2 w.r.t. a uniform electric field *E* is:

$$W = -pE(\cos\theta_2 - \cos\theta_1)$$

This work done is stored as *potential energy U* of an electric dipole. Then

$$U = -pE\cos\theta = -\vec{p}.\vec{E}$$

Note : Potential energy is minimum in the condition of stable equilibrium ($\theta = 0$) and is equal to – pE. It is maximum in the condition of unstable equilibrium ($\theta = 180°$) where it is equal to + pE.

(B) GAUSS THEOREM & ITS APPLICATIONS

B.1. Electric Flux :

(*a*) The electric flux ϕ_E passing through an area $\vec{s}$ placed in a uniform electric field $\vec{E}$ is given as:

$$\phi_E = \vec{E}.\vec{s} = Es\cos\theta$$

The SI unit of electric flux is $Nm^2\ C^{-1}$. It is scalar quantity.

(*b*) It is clear that electric flux through a surface placed in the electric field is maximum when $\theta = 0°$ *i.e.* the normal to the surface is in the direction of field lines.
Also when $\theta = 90°$ *i.e.* the normal to the surface is perpendicular to field lines, $\phi_E = 0$

B.2. Gauss Theorem :

(*a*) **Statement :** The total electric flux over a closed surface in free space is $\frac{1}{\varepsilon_0}$ times the net charge enclosed within that surface.

Mathematically, $\phi_E = \oint_S \vec{E}.d\vec{s} = \frac{q}{\varepsilon_0}$, where q = net charge enclosed.

(*b*) (*i*) Gauss theorem is actually a consequence of Coulomb's law and can be derived from it.

(*ii*) Gauss theorem is true only due to the reason that coulomb force law is inverse square law $\left(F \propto \frac{1}{r^2}\right)$.

(*iii*) Coulomb's law can be obtained from Gauss theorem.

B.3. Applications of Gauss Theorem :

Gauss theorem is used to determine electric field intensity due to uniform charge distribution. The cases in syllabus are as follows :

Expression for	Infinite Linear Charge	Infinite Plane Sheet of Charge	Thin Spherical Shell (or Conducting Sphere)
Charge density	$\lambda = \frac{\Delta q}{\Delta l}$	$\sigma = \frac{\Delta q}{\Delta s}$	$\sigma = \frac{q}{4\pi r^2}$
Flux (ϕ)	$\frac{\lambda l}{\epsilon_0}$	$\frac{\sigma s}{\epsilon_0}$	$\frac{\sigma . 4\pi r^2}{\epsilon_0}$
Magnitude of electric Intensity (E)	$\frac{\lambda}{2\pi r \epsilon_0}$ where r = distance from the linear charge	$\frac{\sigma}{\epsilon_0}$	(i) For points on or outside the shell $E = \frac{q}{4\pi \epsilon_0 r^2}$ (ii) Inside the shell $E = 0$
Graph showing variation of *E* with *r*	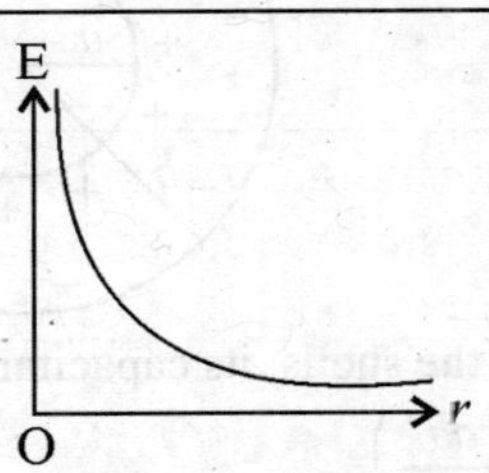	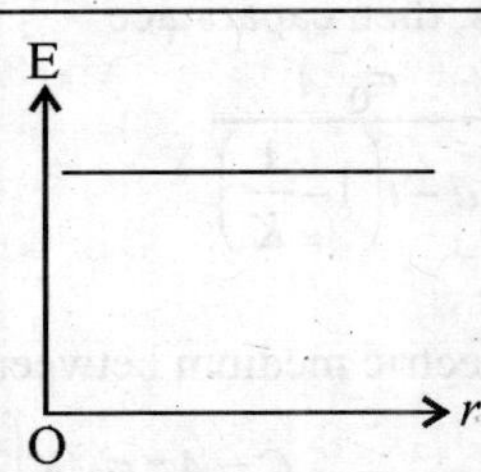	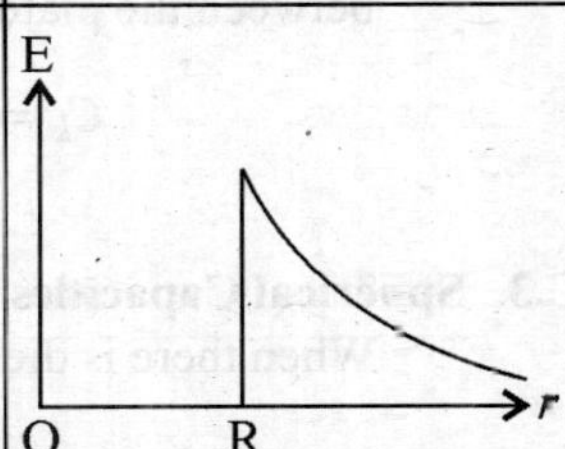

B.4. Electric field intensity due to charged conducting ring at a point on its axis (By use of Coulomb's law) (Imp. for proof)

$$E = \frac{1}{4\pi \in_0} \cdot \frac{q.r}{\left(R^2 + r^2\right)^{\frac{3}{2}}} Nc^{-1}$$

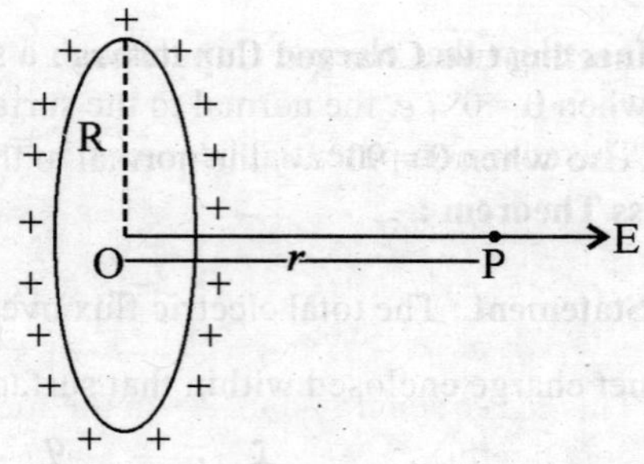

(C) CAPACITORS

C.1. Capacitor :

(*a*) It is a device to store charges and electrostatic potential energy.

(b) Capacitance of a conductor is the ratio of charge stored and the potential attained

$$C = \frac{q}{V}$$

The SI unit of capacitance (C) is farad (F). It is a scalar quantity.

(c) Capacitance of a spherical conductor in air/vacuum

$$C = 4\pi\epsilon_0 R$$

Where R = radius of conductor. In a medium of dielectric constant K, $C_K = KC$

(d) Energy of a charged conductor at potential V

$$U = \frac{1}{2}CV^2 = \frac{q^2}{2C} = \frac{1}{2}qV$$

C.2. Parallel Plate Capacitor : (Important)

(*a*) Capacitance of a capacitor is defined as the ratio of charge on one plate and potential difference between the plates.

(b) If there is medium of dielectric constent K completely filled between the plates, then capacitance

$$C_k = \frac{\in_0 KA}{d}, \; A = \text{plate area}, \; d = \text{plate seperation}$$

When there is air or vacuum between the plates $K = 1$ and

$$C = \frac{\in_0 A}{d}$$

(c) When there is dielectric slab of thickness $t < d$ between the plates, then capacitace

$$C_k = \frac{\in_0 A}{d - t\left(1 - \frac{1}{K}\right)}$$

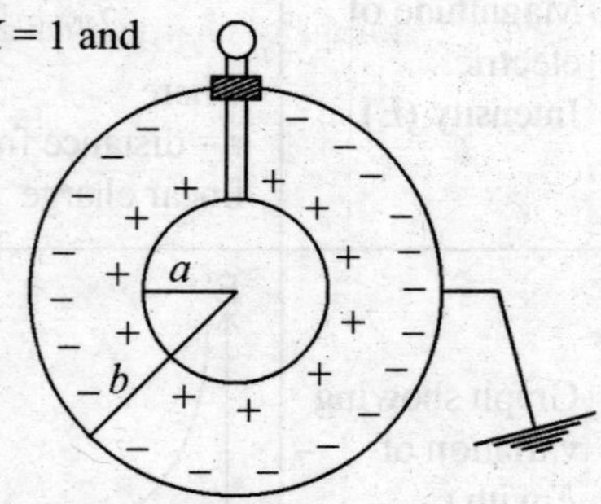

C.3. Spherical Capacities :

When there is dielectric medium between the shells, its capacitance

$$C = 4\pi \in_0 K\left(\frac{ab}{b-a}\right)$$

C.4. Energy of Charged Capacitor : **(Imp. for proof)**

$$U = \frac{1}{2}CV^2 = \frac{qL}{2C} = \frac{1}{2}.q.V$$

The energy is stored in the medium between the plates.

C.5. Connecting two Charged Capacitors :

(*a*) The common potential becomes $V = \frac{q_1 C_1 + q_2 C_2}{C_1 + C_2}$

(b) Loss of energy

$$\Delta U = \frac{1}{2} \cdot \frac{C_1 C_2}{C_1 + C_2} \cdot (V_1 \sim V_2)^2$$

This loss of energy appears in the form of heat etc due to which the connecting wire gets heated.

C.6. Combination of Capacitors :

(*a*) In series $\frac{1}{C} = \sum_{i=1}^{n} \cdot \frac{1}{C_i}$ *i.e.*, $\frac{1}{C} = \frac{1}{C_1} + \frac{1}{C_2} + \frac{1}{C_3} + \ldots$

(*b*) In parallel $C = \sum_{i=1}^{n} C_i$ *i.e.*, $C = C_1 + C_2 + C_3 + \ldots$

C.7. Effect of Introducing Dielectric Slab :

Property	for capacitor without dielectric	for capacitor when slab is introduced	
		Battery connected	Battery disconnected
1. Charge	q	Kq	q
2. Potential	V	V	$\frac{V}{K}$
3. Capacitance	C	KC	KC
4. Electric field	E	E	$\frac{E_0}{K}$
5. Energy	U	KU	$\frac{U}{K}$

C.8. Van de Graff Generator : (Imp.)

It is an electrostatic machine to build up high voltages. It works on the principle of storage of charge on a large spherical conductor.

❑❑❑

VERY SHORT ANSWER TYPE QUESTIONS

(Carrying 1 mark)

Q. 1. Glass rod is rubbed with silk cloth. What changes will occur in the mass of these.

Ans. Glass rod will loose the electrons and will be positively charged. Thus its mass will decrease (equal to mass of lost electrons). The silk cloth will gain the electrons to have negatively charged and its mass will increase.

Q. 2. Calculate the charge carried by 12.5×10^{18} electrons.

Ans. $q = ne = 12.5 \times 10^{18} \times 1.6 \times 10^{-19}$ C = 2.0 C

Q. 3. What is the unit of electrical permittivity of free space (ϵ_0)?

Ans. $C^2N^{-1}m^{-2}$

Q. 4. Does the electric charge vary with the speed of the charged body?

Ans. Charge is invarient

Q. 5. Give two points of distinction between charge and mass.

Ans. (*i*) Charge can be positive, negative or zero. But mass is a positive quantity.
(*ii*) Electric charge is always conserved, but mass is not conserved.

Q. 6. What is the importance of Coulomb's law of electric force in vector form?

Ans. Coulomb's law in vector form establishes that forces between any two point charges are equal and opposite. These forces act along the line joining the charges. Therefore, electrostatic forces are central forces.

Q. 7. If two point charges q_1 and q_2 are such that $q_1q_2 > 0$, what is the nature of force between the two charges?

Ans. $qq_1 > 0$ implies the positive sign with the product of q_1q_2. Therefore, both the charges, *i.e.*, q_1 and q_2 are similarly charged (positive or negative). The force between them is repulsive.

Q. 8. Consider four charged bodies A, B, C and D. Body A repels body B, body A attracts body C and body C repels body D. It is given that body D is positively charged, then what is the nature of charge on body B.

Ans. Body B will be negatively charged.

Q. 9. What is the basic cause of quantization of charge?

Ans. Charge less than that of electronic charge is not possible and only integral number of electrons can be transferred.

Q. 10. What is the relevance of large value of dielectric constant for water?

Ans. Such a large value makes water great solvent.

Q. 11. When is an electric line of force straight?

Ans. Straight lines of force are possible in the field of a single point charge

Q. 12. Two very small charged spheres are suspended by separate non-conducting threads from the same point. If the system is taken in the condition of weightlessness, then what will be the angle between the threads?

Ans. 180°

Q. 13. Two like charges, q_1 and q_2 are placed at points A and B at distance r apart. Can a third charge q_0 placed between A and B remain in equilibrium?

Ans. Yes, the force on q_0 due to q_1 and q_2 will be opposite and can be made equal by suitable adjustment of distance.

Q. 14. There are two (or more) point charges in a region. Are the electric lines of force in the region straight?

Ans. No, most of these will be curved.

Q. 15. An electric dipole rests in unstable equilibrium in an electric field. What is the angle between $\vec{E}$ and $\vec{p}$?

Ans. 180° (note 0° for stable equilibrium).

Q. 16. What is the angle between electric field intensities due to electric dipole in axial and equatorial positions?

Ans. 180°.

Q. 17. Does Coulomb's law obey Newton's third law of motion?

Ans. Yes.

Q. 18. How is force between two charges affected when dielectric constant of the medium in which they are held increases?

Ans. As $F = F_0 / K$, therefore, force decreases when K increases.

Q. 19. What is an ideal dipole?

Ans. The dipole moment $|\vec{p}| = q.2l$

For given value of p, the charge q is large and separation $2l$ between the charges is very small, then dipole is called ideal.

Q. 20. What is the number of electric lines of force starting from +1C charge?

Ans. Number of electric lines of force $= \dfrac{q}{\epsilon_0} = \dfrac{1}{8.85 \times 10^{-12}}$

$$= 1.13 \times 10^{11}$$

Q. 21. Neutral points (where no electric field exists) are obtained in space between the charges q_1 and q_2. How are the nature of these charges related?

Ans. q_1 and q_2 must be like charges.

Q. 22. Electric intensity at the point $(r, 0)$ due to a short dipole placed at the origon with dipole moment directed along positive x-axis is $\vec{E}_1$. If the dipole is rotated anticlockwise by 90°, then electric intensity at the same point is $\vec{E}_2$. How are $\vec{E}_1$ and $\vec{E}_2$ related in magnitude and in direction?

Ans. $|\vec{E}_2| = \dfrac{1}{2}|\vec{E}_1|$

$\vec{E}_1$ is directed along positive x-axis and $\vec{E}_2$ along negative y-axis *i.e.*, $\vec{E}_1$ and $\vec{E}_2$ are perpendicular to each other.

Q. 23. Write down the relation between the electric field and electrical potential at a point.

Ans. $E = -\dfrac{dV}{dr}$ or $V = -\int_{\infty}^{r} \vec{E}.\vec{dr}$

Q. 24. How much work is done in moving a 500μC charge between two points on an equipotential surface?

Ans. Zero.

Q. 25. What is the amount of work done in moving a charge q from the surface of a metal sphere of radius R to its centre?

Ans. Work done is zero because $V_{surface} = V_{centre}$

Q. 26. What would be the work done if a point charge $+q$ is taken from a point A to the point B on the circumference of a circle in the given Fig. 1.1, drawn with another point charge $+q$ at its centre?

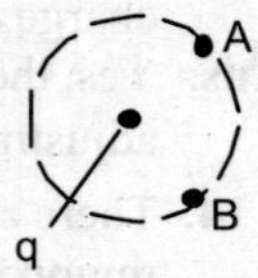

Fig. 1.1

Ans. Work done is zero because $V_A = V_B$.

Q. 27. A hollow metal sphere of radius R carries a charge of + Q. Write an expression for (*i*) the potential at the surface, and (*ii*) at a point inside the sphere.

Ans. (*i*) $V = \dfrac{Q}{4\pi \epsilon_0 R}$ (*ii*) $V = \dfrac{Q}{4\pi \epsilon_0 R}$

Q. 28. A charged particle enters a uniform electric field perpendicular to field lines. What path the particle traces?

Ans. Parabolic path.

Q. 29. Draw two equipotential surfaces due to a point charge.

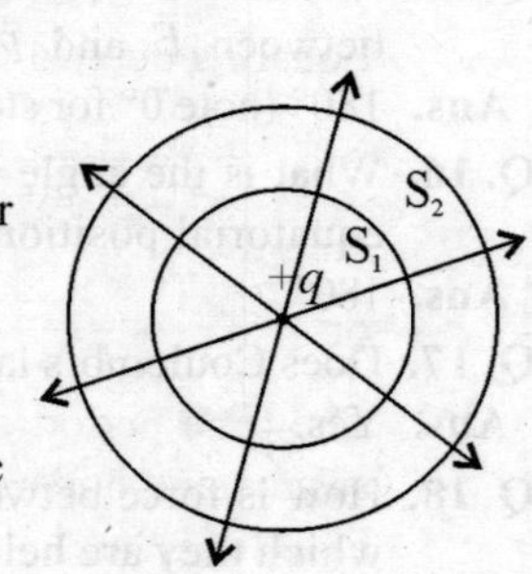

Ans. The equipotential surfaces are S_1 and S_2 which are concentric spheres.

Q. 30. Which of the two electric field and electric potential is continuous across the surface of charged conductor?

Ans. Electric potential is continuous. The electric field intensity is perpendicular to the equipotential surface.

Q. 31. Does the electric potential increase or decrease along the electric line of force?

Ans. Decreases.

Q. 32. When a battery is connected across a capacitor, are the charges on the plates always equal and opposite irrespective of the sizes of the plates?

Ans. Yes, the areas of plates may or may not be equal.

Q. 33. The capacitance of a parallel plate capacitor is C. If area of one plate is reduced to half the size, what will be the new capacitance?

Ans. In formula $C = \dfrac{\epsilon_0 A}{d}$, A is the common area (over laping area).

$$C' = \frac{\epsilon_0 \left(\dfrac{A}{2}\right)}{d} = \frac{1}{2}C.$$

Q. 34. Can there be a potential difference between two conductors of same volume carrying equal positive charges?

Ans. Yes, the conductors may have different shapes of equal volume. Their capacitances will then be different and $V = \dfrac{q}{C}$ will be different.

Q. 35. An air capacitor is given a charge of 2μC raising its potential its potential to 200 V. If on inserting a dielectric medium, its potential falls to 50 V, what is the dielectric constant of the medium?

Ans. $K = \dfrac{V}{V_k} = \dfrac{200}{50} = 4$

SHORT ANSWER TYPE QUESTIONS (SA-I)

(Carrying 2 marks)

Q. 1. Two charges q_1 and q_2 at separation r in vacuum have coulomb force F between them. When the system is placed in a medium of dielectric constant k, then to maintain the same coulomb force, the distance has to change to r'. Find the relation between r and r'.

Ans. In vacuum

$$F = \frac{1}{4\pi \epsilon_0} \cdot \frac{q_1 q_2}{r^2} \quad \text{...(i)}$$

In medium of dielectric constant k,

$$F = \frac{1}{4\pi \epsilon_0 k} \cdot \frac{q_1 q_2}{r'^2} \quad \text{...(ii)}$$

Equating the two values from (i) and (ii),

$$\frac{1}{r^2} = \frac{1}{k.r'^2}$$

or $\quad r'^2 = \frac{r^2}{k} \Rightarrow r' = \frac{r}{\sqrt{k}}$ *Ans.*

Q. 2. The time period of a simple pendulum is T. If the bob and the suspension hook are likely charged, the time period becomes T'. Find the relation between T and T'.

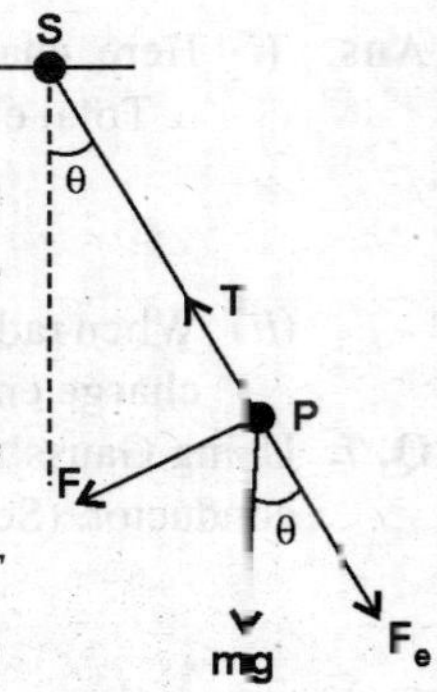

Ans. The force of repulsion F_e on the bob acts along SP. This changes the tension in the thread. Thread being inextensible does not change in length.

The repulsive force being perpendicular to the restoring force F does not contribute to it and hence time period does not change, i.e. $T' = T$. *Ans.*

Q. 3. Prove that at a point where electric field intensity is zero, electric potential need not be zero.

Ans. Let the potential gradient in the region is $\frac{dV}{dr}$

Then electric field intensity

$$E = -\frac{dV}{dr}$$

When $\quad E = 0$, we have

$$\frac{dV}{dr} = 0$$

or $\quad V = \text{Constant}$

i.e. the potential may or may not be zero. *Proved*

Q. 4. Two spherical charged conductors, each of radius R, are at a distance of d ($d > 2R$). They carry charges $+q$ and $-q$. Will the force of attraction between them be $\frac{q^2}{4\pi \epsilon_0 d^2}$?

Ans. No, the force of attraction between two spherical charged conductors will be more than $\frac{q^2}{4\pi \epsilon_0 d^2}$. On account of mutual force of attraction, there will be a redistribution of charges on the spheres as shown in Fig. 1.2. As a result, effective distance between them is reduced and force increases.

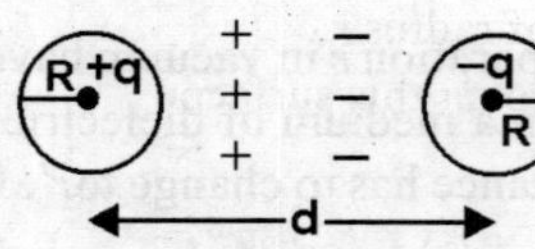

Fig. 1.2

Q. 5. Calculate the potential at a point P due to a charge $4 \times 10^{-7} C$ located 9 cm away.

Ans. As $Q = 4 \times 10^{-7} C$ and $r = 9$ cm $= 0.09$ m.

$$\therefore \text{ Potential,} \quad V = \frac{1}{4\pi \epsilon_0} \cdot \frac{Q}{r} = \frac{9 \times 10^9 \times 4 \times 10^{-7}}{0.09} = 4 \times 10^7 \text{ V } \textit{Ans.}$$

Q. 6. A spherical Gaussian surface encloses a charge of $8.85 \times 10^{-8} C$.

(*i*) Calculate the electric flux passing through the surface.

(*ii*) If the radius of surface is doubled, how would the flux change?

Ans. (*i*) Here, charge $q = 8.85 \times 10^{-8} C$.

$\therefore$ Total electric flux passing through the surface

$$\phi_E = \frac{q}{\epsilon_0} = \frac{8.85 \times 10^{-8}}{8.85 \times 10^{-12}} = 10^4 \text{ Nm}^2\text{C}^{-1} \textit{ Ans.}$$

(*ii*) When radius of the surface is doubled, there would be no change in flux because the charge enclosed remains unchanged.

Q. 7. Using Gauss's law, show that no electric field intensity exists inside a hollow charged conductor. (See Fig. 1.3)

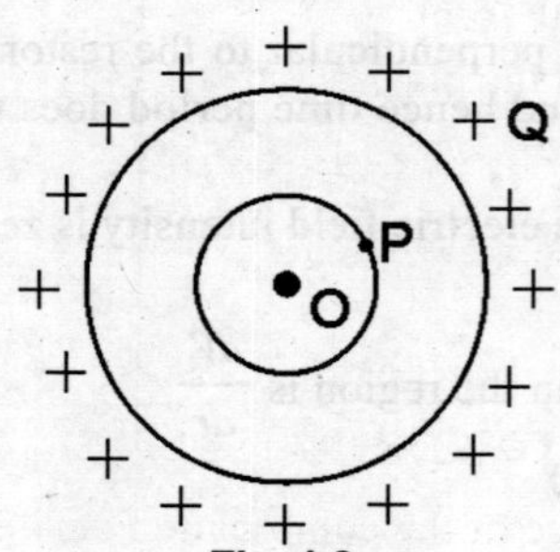

Fig. 1.3

Ans. Let us consider a hollow charged conductor having charge $+Q$, which spreads on its outer surface.

To calculate electric field intensity, $\vec{E}$ at a point P inside the hollow conductor, consider a Gaussian surface. Then, total flux over the Gaussian surface is

$$\phi_E = \oint \vec{E} \cdot \vec{ds} = \frac{1}{\epsilon_0} \text{ (charge enclosed)} = 0$$

$\Rightarrow$ $E = 0$, because no charge is present inside the conductor.

Thus, electric field intensity at all points inside a hollow charged conductor is zero. *Proved*

Q. 8. Apply Gauss's theorem to find an expression for the electric field intensity at any point due to a point charge.

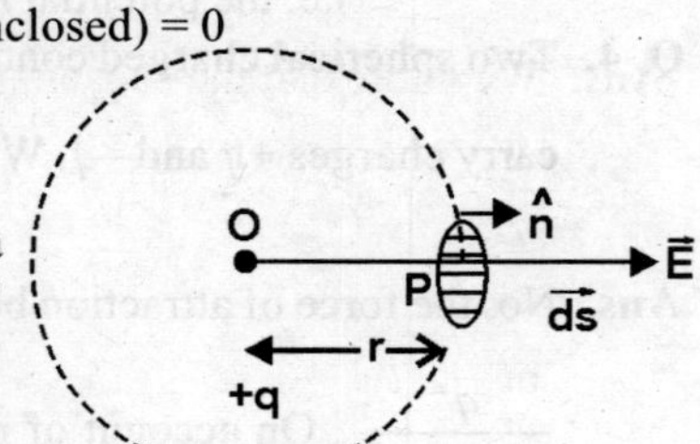

Fig. 1.4

Ans. Let us consider electric field intensity at point P situated at a distance 'r' from a point charge q placed at point O as shown in Fig. 1.4. To apply Gauss's theorem, consider a spherical Gaussian surface of radius r.
Therefore, total electric flux over this surface

$$\phi_E = \oint \vec{E} \cdot ds = \int E ds = E \cdot 4\pi r^2 = \frac{q}{\epsilon_0}$$

$$\Rightarrow \qquad E = \frac{q}{4\pi \epsilon_0 r^2} \quad \textit{Ans.}$$

Q. 9. By what factor does the capacity of a metal sphere increase if its volume is tripled?

Ans. We have $\quad \dfrac{C_2}{C_1} = \dfrac{R_2}{R_1} = \left(\dfrac{V_2}{V_1}\right)^{\frac{1}{3}}$

$$\therefore \qquad C_2 = C_1\left(\frac{V_2}{V_1}\right)^{\frac{1}{3}} = C_1(3)^{1/3} = 1.44\, C_1 \quad \textit{Ans.}$$

Q. 10. An air-filled parallel plate capacitor is to be constructed, which can store 12 μC of charge when operated at 1200 V. What can be the minimum area of capacitor plates? The dielectric strength of the air is 3×10^7 V/m.

Ans. Here, $Q = 12$ μC, $V = 1200$ V, $A = ?$
Dielectric strength $= 3 \times 10^7$ V/m
The electric field between the plates should not exceed 10% of the dielectric strength

i.e., $\quad \in = \dfrac{\sigma}{\epsilon_0} = \dfrac{Q}{A\epsilon_0} = \dfrac{10}{100} \times 3 \times 10^7 \text{ V/m} = 3 \times 10^6 \text{ V/m}$

$$A = \frac{Q}{\epsilon_0 \times 3 \times 10^6} = \frac{12 \times 10^{-6}}{8.85 \times 10^{-12} \times 3 \times 10^6} = 0.45 \text{ m}^2 \quad \textit{Ans.}$$

Q. 11. The equivalent capacitance of the combination between A and B in the given Fig. 1.5 is 15 μF. Find the capacitance of capacitor C.

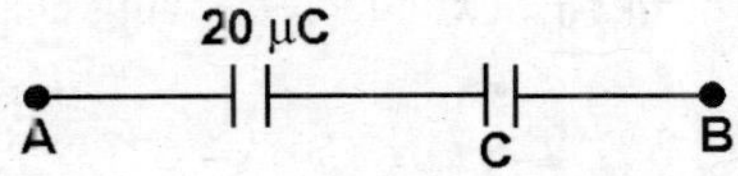

Fig. 1.5

Ans. We know that the capacitance in series, $\dfrac{1}{C} = \dfrac{1}{C_1} + \dfrac{1}{C_2}$

$$\Rightarrow \qquad \frac{1}{C} = \frac{1}{15} - \frac{1}{20} = \frac{4-3}{60} = \frac{1}{60}$$

or $\qquad C = 60$ μF. *Ans.*

SHORT ANSWER TYPE QUESTIONS (SA-II)

(Carrying 3 marks)

Q. 1. Find an expression for the work done is rotating an electric dipole in uniform electric field.

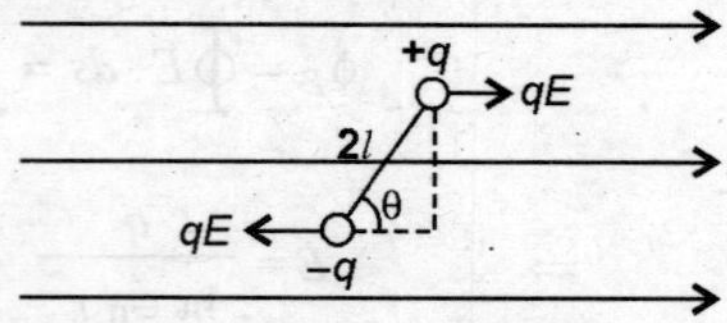

Ans. Let each charge of the dipole is q and distance between the charges is $2l$. Dipole moment

$$p = q \times 2l \qquad \text{...(i)}$$

Let the dipole is placed in electric field of intensity E with dipole moment inclined at angle θ with $\vec{E}$. The forces on the charges of the dipole are qE, qE in opposite directions. Thus they form a couple of moment (torque)

$$\tau = qE \times 2l \sin\theta$$

using (i), $\tau = pE \sin\theta$ ...(ii)

This torque tends to bring the dipole to the position θ = 0. If the dipole is rotated by a small angel $d\theta$ against this torque, the work done

$$dW = \tau \,.\, d\theta = pE \sin\theta \,.\, d\theta$$

Hence the work done in rotating the dipole from $\theta = \theta_1$ to $\theta = \theta_2$ is

$$W = \int_{\theta_1}^{\theta_2} dW = pE \int_{\theta_1}^{\theta_2} \sin\theta . d\theta = pE[-\cos\theta]_{\theta_1}^{\theta_2}$$

or $W = pE(\cos\theta_1 - \cos\theta_2)$ *Ans.*

Q. 2. Tow charge $+25e$ and $-9e$ are placed in air at separation of 40 cm. Where should a third charge q_0 be placed so that it may remain in equilibrium.

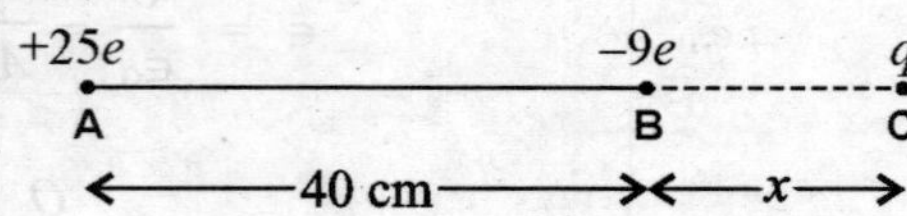

Ans. In case of opposite charges, third charge should be placed beyond the charge of smaller magnitude.

Let BC = x cm

The net force on q_0 due to $+25e$ and $-9e$ is zero. Thus

$$\frac{1}{4\pi \epsilon_0} \cdot \frac{(25e)q_0}{(40+x)^2} - \frac{1}{4\pi \epsilon_0} \cdot \frac{(9e)q_0}{x^2} = 0$$

or $$\frac{25}{(40+x)^2} = \frac{9}{x^2}$$

Taking squaer root,

$$\frac{5}{40+x} = \frac{3}{x}$$

or $5x = 120 + 3x$

or $2x = 120 \Rightarrow x = 60$ cm *Ans.*

Q. 3. n drops of liquid, each at potential V combine to form big drop. Find the potential of this big drop.

Ans. Let the charge on each drop is q then

$$V = \frac{1}{4\pi \in_0} \cdot \frac{q}{r} \quad \text{.. (i)}$$

Where r is the radius of the drop.

The volume of single big drop (radius = R) is equal to the combined volume of n drops

$$\frac{4}{3}\pi R^3 = n \times \frac{4}{3}\pi r^3$$

i.e., $R = n^{1/3} r$

Charge on big drop = $n \cdot q$

Potantial of big drop

$$V' = \frac{1}{4\pi \in_0} \cdot \frac{nq}{R} = \frac{1}{4\pi \in_0} \cdot \frac{n.q}{n^{1/3} r}$$

$$= n^{2/3} \cdot \frac{1}{4\pi \in_0} \cdot \frac{q}{r} = n^{2/3} V \quad \textit{Ans.}$$

Q. 4. In Millikan's experiment, charged oil drop, when subjected to potential difference V falls with some acceleration. If the potential difference between the plates is increased to 2V, the drop moves up with the same acceleration. How much potential difference is required to balance the drop?

Ans. Let the distance between plates is d,

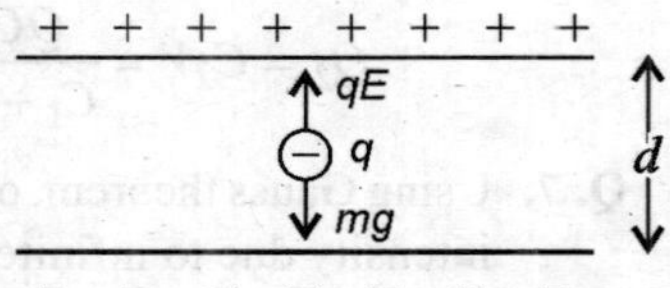

In the first case $mg - qE = ma$

$$\textit{i.e.,} \quad mg - q \cdot \frac{V}{d} = ma \quad \text{...(i)}$$

In the second case

$$q \cdot \frac{2V}{d} - mg = ma \quad \text{...(ii)}$$

Subtracting

$$2mg - 3q\frac{V}{d} = 0 \Rightarrow \frac{mgd}{q} = \frac{3}{2}V \quad \text{...(iii)}$$

Let V' is the potential difference to balance the drop, then

$$q\frac{V'}{d} = mg \quad \text{or} \quad V' = \frac{mgd}{q} \quad \text{..(iv)}$$

From (iii) and (iv)

$$V' = \frac{3}{2}V \quad \textit{Ans.}$$

Q. 5. Derive an expression for the potential at a distance r from a point charge. (Imp.)

Ans. Let charge $+q$ is placed at O. Potential is required at P, where $OP = r$.

On OP produced, we take a point A such that $OA = x$.

If a test charge $+q_0$ is placed at A, force on it is

$$F = \frac{1}{4\pi \in_0} \cdot \frac{qq_0}{x^2}$$

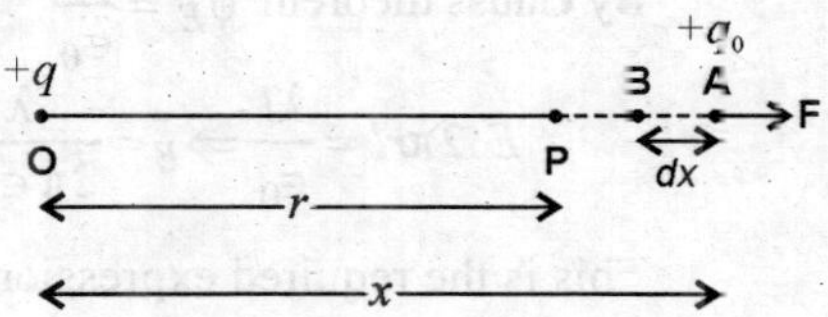

The direction of this force is away from O.

Work done is carrying this test charge from A to B (displacement $= -dx$)

$$dW = F.(-dx)$$

Hence work done in carrying the charge from $x = \infty$ to P $(x = r)$

$$W = \int_{\infty}^{r} dW = -\frac{qq_0}{4\pi \in_0}\int_{\infty}^{r}\frac{1}{x^2}dx = \frac{qq_0}{4\pi \in_0}\left[\frac{1}{x}\right]_{\infty}^{r}$$

$$= \frac{qq_0}{4\pi \in_0}\left(\frac{1}{r} - \frac{1}{\infty}\right) = \frac{1}{4\pi \in_0}.\frac{qq_0}{r}$$

Potential at P is therefore

$$V = \frac{W}{q_0} = \frac{1}{4\pi \in_0}.\frac{q}{r} \quad \textit{Ans.}$$

Q. 6. A conducting sphere A of radius R and carrying charge Q is connected to a neutral sphere B of radius $2R$. How much charge will flow through the connecting wire?

Ans. Capacitances of spheres A and B are respectively

$$C_1 = 4\pi\epsilon_0 R \quad \text{and} \quad C_2 = 4\pi\epsilon_0.(2R) = 2C_1$$

When connected, common potential $V = \dfrac{Q}{C_1 + C_2}$

Charge on sphere B = Charge that flows through the connecting wire

$$Q_2 = C_2 V = \frac{QC_2}{C_1 + C_2} = \frac{Q.2C_1}{C_1 + 2C_1} = \frac{2}{3}Q \quad \textit{Ans.}$$

Q. 7. Using Gauss theorem, obtain an expression for the electric intensity due to infinite linear charge distribution.

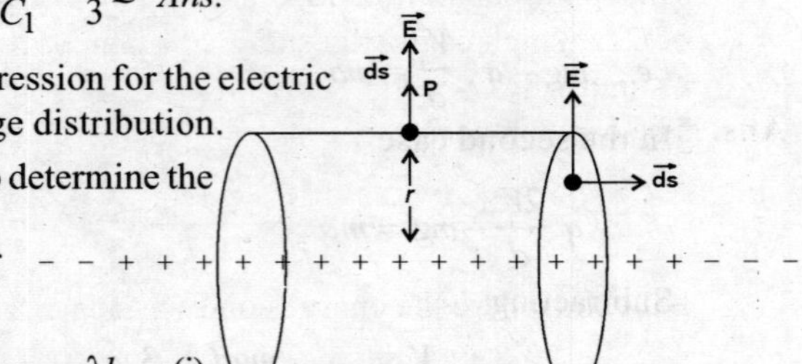

Ans. Let the linear charge density is λ. To determine the electric intensity at P, Gaussian surface is drawn. It is a cylinder of radius r.

Charge enclosed by Gaussian surface $q = \lambda l$ ...(i)

For the surface element surrounding P, the directions of $\vec{E}$ and area vector ds are the same. So that

$$d\phi_E = \vec{E}.\vec{ds} = E.ds \quad \text{...(ii)}$$

For surface element at end surface, $\vec{E}$ and $\vec{ds}$ are perpendicular to each other so that $\vec{E}.\vec{ds} = 0$.

The total electric flux through the closed surface

$$\phi_E = \oint d\phi_E = E\oint ds = E.2\pi rl$$

By Gauss theorem $\phi_E = \dfrac{q}{\in_0}$

$$E.2\pi rl = \frac{\lambda l}{\in_0} \Rightarrow E = \frac{\lambda}{2\pi \in_0 r}$$

This is the required expression.

Q. 8. Four particles, each having a charge 10 μC are placed at the vertices of a square of side 10 cm. Calculate the work done in pulling them apart to infinite separation.

Ans. Potential energy of the system

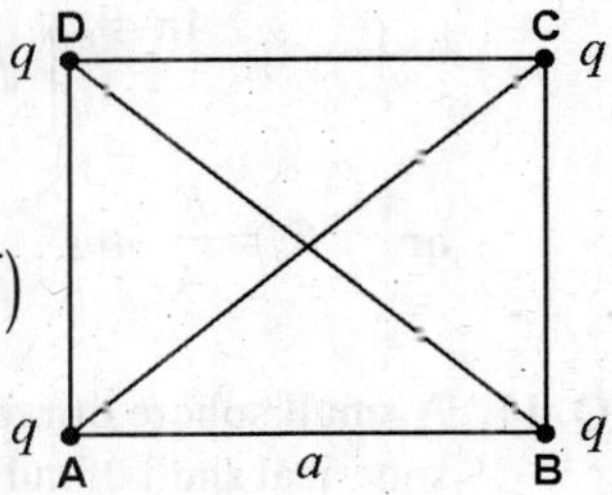

$$U = U_{AB} + U_{AC} + U_{AD} + U_{BC} + U_{BD} + U_{CD}$$

$$= 4 . U_{AB} + 2 . U_{AC}$$

$$= 4 . \frac{1}{4\pi \epsilon_0} . \frac{q^2}{a} + 2 . \frac{1}{4\pi \epsilon_0} . \frac{q^2}{a\sqrt{2}} = \frac{q^2}{4\pi \epsilon_0 a}\left(4+\sqrt{2}\right)$$

At infinite separation P.E. = 0

Thus work done

$$W = \Delta U = \frac{q^2}{4\pi \epsilon_0 r} . \left(4+\sqrt{2}\right)$$

Given $q = 10 \times 10^{-6} C, \ r = 10 \times 10^{-2} m$

$$W = 9 \times 10^9 . \frac{10^{-10}}{10^{-1}} (4 + 1.41)$$

$$= 9 \times 5.41 = 48.7 \text{ J } \textit{Ans.}$$

Q. 9. In the Fig., the variation of charge q with potential difference V for two capacitors C_1 and C_2 is shown. The capacitors have same plate separation but plate area of C_2 is double than that of C_1. Which of the lines in the graph correspond to C_1 and C_2 and why?

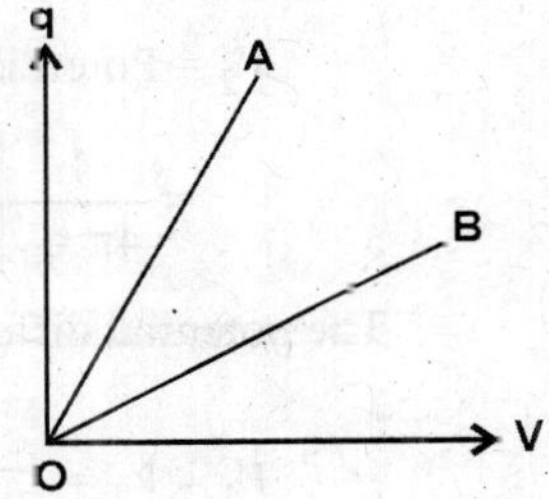

Ans. The capacitances

$$C_1 = \frac{\epsilon_0 A}{d}, \qquad C_2 = \frac{\epsilon_0 2A}{d} = 2C_1$$

If q_1 and q_2 are the charges on two capacitors, then for the same potential difference,

$q_1 = C_1 . V$ and $q_2 = C_2 . V = 2C_1 V = 2q_1$

So that $q_2 = 2q_1 \Rightarrow q_2 > q_1$

From the graph $q_A > q_B$ (for the same potential difference)

Hence, line *A* corresponds to C_2 while line *B* corresponds to C_1. *Ans.*

Q. 10. The Coulomb force between two charges q_1 and q_2 at separation r in air is F. If half of the separation is filled with medium of dielectric constant 9, what will be the value of new Coulomb force?

Ans. In air,

$$F = \frac{1}{4\pi \epsilon_0} . \frac{q_1 q_2}{r^2}$$

When the distnance between the charges is parially filled with dielectric medium,

$$F' = \frac{1}{4\pi \epsilon_0} . \frac{q_1 q_2}{\left[\sqrt{k_1} . r_1 + \sqrt{k_2} . r_2 + ...\right]^2}$$

Here $r_1 = \frac{r}{2}$, $k_1 = 9$, $r_2 = \frac{r}{2}$, $k_2 = 1$

$$F' = \frac{1}{4\pi \epsilon_0} \cdot \frac{q_1 q_2}{\left[\sqrt{9}.\frac{r}{2} + \frac{r}{2}\right]^2} = \frac{1}{4\pi \epsilon_0} \cdot \frac{q_1 q_2}{(2r)^2}$$

or $F' = \frac{F}{4}$ *Ans.*

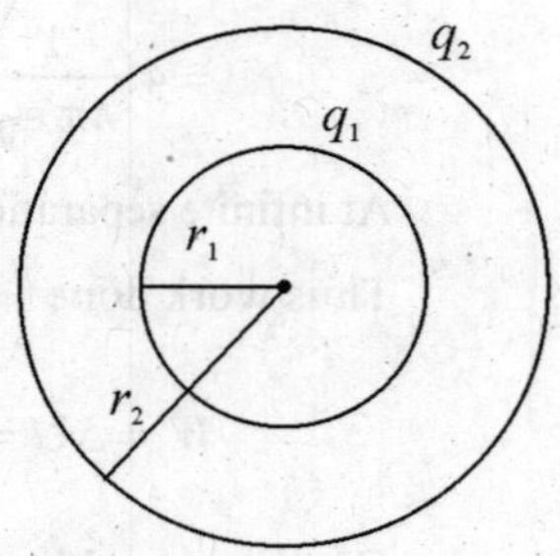

Q. 11. A small sphere of radius r_1 and charge q_1 is enclosed by a spherical shell of radius r_2 and charge q_2. Show that if q_1 is positive, charge will necessarily flow from the sphere to the shell when the two are connected by a wire, no matter what charge q_2 on the shell is.

Ans. Potential of inner sphere

V_1 = Potential due to its own charge q_1 + Potential due to charge q_2

$$= \frac{1}{4\pi \epsilon_0}\left[\frac{q_1}{r_1} + \frac{q_2}{r_2}\right] \quad ...(i)$$

Potential of outer shell

V_2 = Potential due to charge q_1 + Potential due to its own charge q_2

$$= \frac{1}{4\pi \epsilon_0}\left[\frac{q_1}{r_2} + \frac{q_2}{r_2}\right] \quad ...(ii)$$

The potential difference

$$V_1 - V_2 = \frac{q_1}{4\pi \epsilon_0}\left(\frac{1}{r_1} - \frac{1}{r_2}\right)$$

Since $r_1 < r_2$ and q_1 is +ve, $V_1 > V_2$

The charge will therefore flow from sphere which is at higher potential (V_1) to the shell which is at lower potential (V_2). *Proved*

LONG ANSWER TYPE QUESTIONS

(Carrying 5 marks)

Q. 1. What is meant by superposition principle of electric forces? Find an expression for electrostatic force on a charge q_0 due to a number of charges q_1, q_2, q_3, q_4..., etc. present in free space.

Ans. If a number of point charges are present in free space, then each individual force between any two charges is calculated from Coulomb's law. This force is not at all affected due to the presence of other charges. According to the principle of superposition, the total force acting on a particular charge q_0 is the vector sum of the individual forces exterted on the given charge q_0 by all the charges q_1, q_2, q_3, q_4, ..., etc.

Mathematically,

$$\vec{F_0} = \vec{F_{01}} + \vec{F_{02}} + \vec{F_{03}} + ...$$

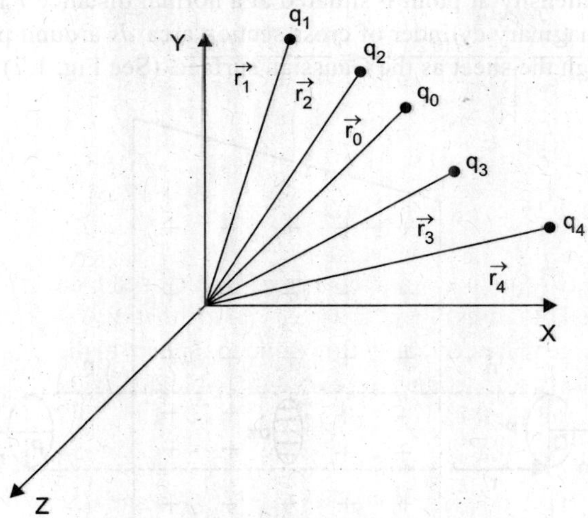

Fig. 1.6

As shown in the above Fig. 1.6, force on charge q_0 due to q_1 will be

$$\vec{F_{01}} = \frac{1}{4\pi \epsilon_0} \cdot \frac{q_0\, q_1}{|\vec{r_0} - \vec{r_1}|^3} (\vec{r}_0 - \vec{r}_1)$$

Similarly,

$$\vec{F_{02}} = \frac{1}{4\pi \epsilon_0} \cdot \frac{q_0\, q_2}{|\vec{r_0} - \vec{r_2}|^3} (\vec{r}_0 - \vec{r}_2)$$

$$\vec{F_{03}} = \frac{1}{4\pi \epsilon_0} \cdot \frac{q_0\, q_3}{|\vec{r_0} - \vec{r_3}|^3} (\vec{r_0} - \vec{r_3}). \text{ ... and so on.}$$

Hence, resultant force experienced by charge q_0 will be

$$\vec{F_0} = \frac{q_0}{4\pi \epsilon_0} \left[\frac{q_1}{|\vec{r_0} - \vec{r_1}|^3} (\vec{r}_0 - \vec{r}_1) + \frac{q_2}{|\vec{r_0} - \vec{r_2}|^3} (\vec{r_0} - \vec{r_2}) + \frac{q_3}{|\vec{r_0} - \vec{r_3}|^3} (\vec{r}_0 - \vec{r}_3) + \text{....for all charges} \right] \quad Ans.$$

Q. 2. **State Gauss's theorem in electrostatics and express it mathematically. Using it, derive an expression for electric field at a point near a thin infinite plane sheet of electric charge. How does this electric field change for a uniformily thick sheet of charge? Imp.)**

OR

State Gauss's theorem. Use it to obtain an expression for the electric field intensity at a point near a uniformly charged infinite plane sheet.

Ans. Gauss's theorem states that total electric flux over a closed surface in free space is $\frac{1}{\epsilon_0}$ times the net charge enclosed within that surface. Mathematically, for a close surface

$$\phi_E = \oint \vec{E}\, \hat{n}\, ds = \frac{1}{\epsilon_0} (q), \text{ where } q = \text{total charge enclosed}$$

Consider an infinite thin plane sheet having a surface density of charge σ. To find electric field intensity at point *P* situated at a normal distance *r* from the sheet, let us consider an imaginary cylinder of cross section area *ds* around point *P* and length 2*r* passing through the sheet as the Gaussian surface. (See Fig. 1.7)

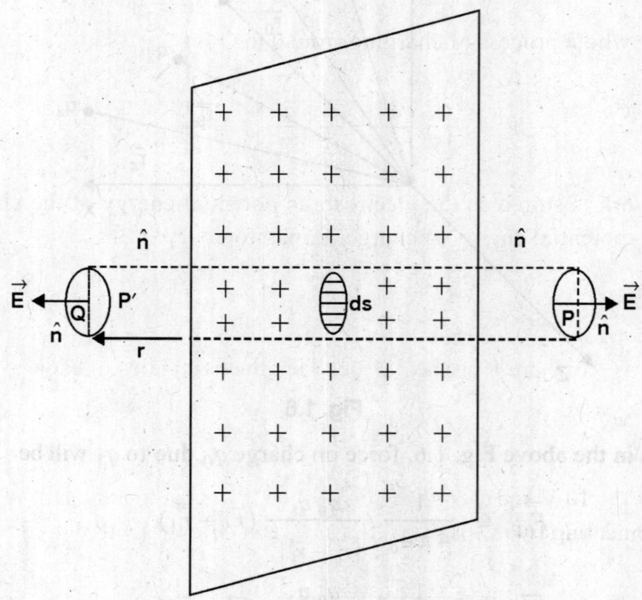

Fig. 1.7

From symmetry consideration, only side faces 1 and 2 of cylinder contribute towards the flux because here $\vec{E}$ and $\hat{n}$ are parallel but curved surface of cylinder does not contribute towards the flux because here $\vec{E}$ and $\hat{n}$ are mutually perpendicular

∴ Total electric flux, $\phi_E = 2\,Eds$ ...(*i*)

According to Gauss's theorem, the total electric flux

$$\phi_E = \frac{1}{\epsilon_0}\text{(charge enclosed)} = \frac{1}{\epsilon}(\sigma\, ds) \quad ...(ii)$$

Comparing equations (*i*) and (*ii*), we get

$$2\,Eds = \frac{\sigma}{\epsilon}ds$$

$$\Rightarrow \quad E = \frac{\sigma}{2\epsilon_0}$$

Thus, electric field intensity is (*i*) directly proportional to the surface charge density σ and (*ii*) is independent of the distance of given point from the sheet.

Q. 3. (*i*) Explain how a capacitor stores energy on charging. Obtain an expression for the energy thus stored.

(*ii*) A battery of 10V is connected to a capacitor of 0.1F. The battery is now removed and the capacitor is then connected to a second uncharged capacitor of same capacitance. Calculate the total energy stored in the system.

Ans. (i) Let a charge on the plate of capacitor be q and its *p.d.* be $\frac{q}{C}$. If an additional charge dq is given to the capacitor plate, work is being done for it, which is given by:

$$dW = \left(\frac{q}{C}\right).dq$$

∴ For the whole process of charging from 0 to Q

$$W = \int_0^Q \frac{q\,dq}{C} = \frac{1}{C}\left[\frac{q^2}{2}\right]_0^Q = \frac{Q^2}{2C}$$

This work is stored as the electrostatic potential energy of the charged capacitor. Hence, potential energy of charged capacitor:

$$U = \frac{Q^2}{2C}$$

But $Q = CV$, where V be the p.d. between the two plates of capacitor, hence,

$$U = \frac{Q^2}{2C} = \frac{1}{2}QV = \frac{1}{2}CV^2$$

(*ii*) Here, $V_1 = 10$ V and $C_1 = 0.1$ F, $C_2 = C_1 = 0.1$ F and $V_2 = 0$

On connecting two capacitors, the common potential will be:

$$V = \frac{C_1V_1 + C_2V_2}{C_1 + C_2} = \frac{0.1\times10 + 0.1\times0}{0.1 + 0.1} = 5\text{ V}$$

∴ Total energy stored in the combined system:

$$U = \frac{1}{2}(C_1 + C_2)V^2 = \frac{1}{2}\times(0.1 + 0.1)\times5^2$$

$$= \frac{1}{2}\times0.2\times25 = 2.5\text{ J } \textit{Ans.}$$

Q. 4. Show mathematically that the electric field intensity due to a short dipole at a distance d along its axis is twice the intensity at the same distance along the equitorial line.

Ans. We know that the electric field intensity at a distance d along the axis of an electric dipole is:

$$E_{\text{axial}} = \frac{1}{4\pi\epsilon_0}\cdot\frac{2pd}{\left(d^2 - a^2\right)^2}$$

and for a short dipole ($a << d$), we have

$$E_{\text{axial}} = \frac{1}{4\pi\epsilon_0}\cdot\frac{2p}{d^3} \quad ...(i)$$

Again electric field intensity at a distance 'd' along the equatorial line of dipole is:

$$E_{\text{equatorial}} = \frac{1}{4\pi\epsilon_0}\cdot\frac{p}{\left(d^2 + a^2\right)^{3/2}}$$

and in case of a short dipole:

$$E_{\text{equatorial}} = \frac{1}{4\pi\epsilon_0}\cdot\frac{p}{d^3} \quad ...(ii)$$

Comparing (*i*) and (*ii*), we get:

$$\frac{E_{\text{axial}}}{E_{\text{equatorial}}} = 2$$

or $$E_{\text{axial}} = 2 \times E_{\text{equatorial}}$$ **Proved**

Q. 5. **Charges of $+2\ \mu C, +2\ \mu C$ and $-2\ \mu C$ are placed at the vertices of an equilateral triangle of side 0.3m each. Find net force experienced by each charge.**

Ans. Here, $AB = BC = 0.3$ m

and $q_A = q_B = +2\ \mu\text{C} = 2 \times 10^{-6}\ C$

and $q_C = -2\ \mu\text{C} = -2 \times 10^{-6}$ C.

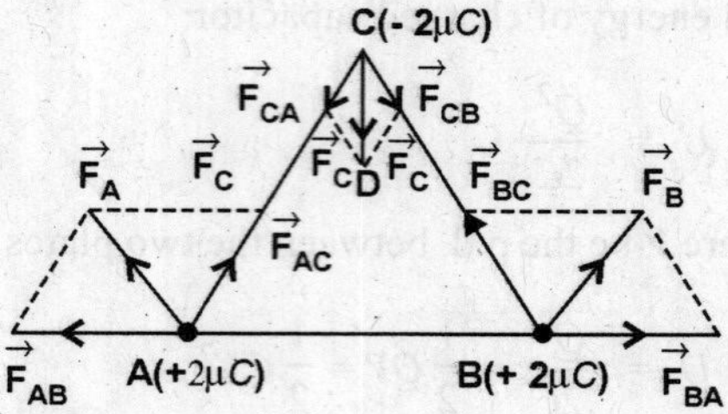

Fig. 1.8

Thus, it is clear that mutual force of attraction/repulsion between any two charges have equal magnitude given by:

$$\vec{F} = |\vec{F}_{AB}| = |\vec{F}_{AC}| = |\vec{F}_{BA}| = |\vec{F}_{BC}| = |\vec{F}_{CA}| = |\vec{F}_{CB}|$$

$$= |\vec{F}_{CA}| = |\vec{F}_{CB}| = \frac{9\times10^9 \times (2\times10^{-6})^2}{(0.3)^2} = 0.4\,N$$

Directions of these forces have been shown in Fig 1.8.

(*i*) As angle between $\vec{F}_{CA}$ and $\vec{F}_{CB}$ is 60°, hence

$$|\vec{F_C}| = 2F_{CA} \cos\left(\frac{60}{2}\right)^{\circ} = 2 \times 0.4 \times \frac{\sqrt{3}}{2}$$

$= .0.69$ N and the force is $\perp$ to *AB* *Ans.*

(*ii*) As angle between $\vec{F}_{AB}$ and $\vec{F}_{AC}$ is 120°, hence

$$|\vec{F}_A| = 2F_{AB} \cos 60° = 2 \times 0.4 \times \frac{1}{2} = 0.4\text{ N}$$

and the force makes an angle 60° from line *AC*. *Ans.*

(*iii*) As in (*ii*) force $|\vec{F}_B| = 0.4$N inclined at an angle of 60° from line *BC*. *Ans.*

Q. 6. **A network of four 10 μF capacitors is connected to a 500 V supply as shown in Fig. 1.9. Determine the following:**

(*i*) An equivalent capacitance of the network

(*ii*) Charge on each capacitor

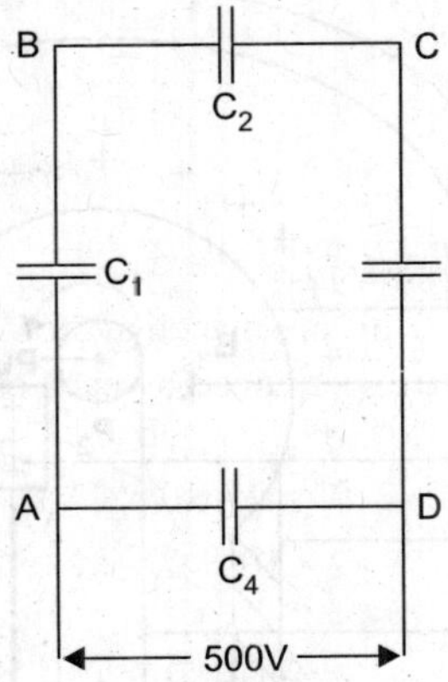

Fig. 1.9

Ans. (*i*) Here, C_1, C_2 and C_3 are joined in series, hence, their combined capacitance C' is given by:

$$\frac{1}{C'} = \frac{1}{C_1}+\frac{1}{C_2}+\frac{1}{C_3} = \frac{1}{10}+\frac{1}{10}+\frac{1}{10} = \frac{3}{10}$$

$$\Rightarrow \quad C' = \frac{10}{3}\ \mu F$$

Now C' is joined in parallel to C_4, hence, resultant capacitance:

$$C = C' + C_4 = \frac{10}{3} + 10 = 13.33\ \mu\text{F}$$

(*ii*) Charge on capacitor C_4, $Q_4 = C_4 V = 10 \times 10^{-6} \times 500 = 5 \times 10^{-3}$ C.

Further, charges on capacitance C_1, C_2 and C_3 are same and given by:

$$Q_1 = Q_2 = Q_3 = C'\,V = \frac{10}{3} \times 10^{-6} \times 500 = 1.67 \times 10^{-3}\ \text{C. } \textit{Ans.}$$

Q. 7. Explain the principle of a Van-de Graff's generator.

Ans. The device is basically an accelerator used to accelerate the positive ions to very high velocities required for annihilation of atoms etc. A labelled diagram of Van-de-Graff's generator is shown in Fig. 1.10.

Principle: Surface density of charge at sharp points of a conductor is extremely high and, hence, charge is continuously being sprayed out from the sharp points. Further, the charge given on to inner surface of the hollow conductor is transferred to its outer surface and is uniformly distributed over it, however large the potential of the outer surface may be.

Construction: *S* is a hollow spherical conducting shell of large radius supported at a suitable height of few metres above the ground by insulating supports. A long endless *V*-belt of insulating rubber is wound around two frictionless pulleys, P_1 and P_2 as shown in Fig. 1.10. The belt can be moved over the pulleys at a high speed by means of an electric motor. B_1 is a spraying comb near the lower end of the belt and is joined to the +ve terminal of an *HT* battery of 5000 – 10000V. B_2 is the collecting comb joined to inner surface of shell *S*. The whole generator is enclosed in a steel chamber filled with nitrogen at high pressure.

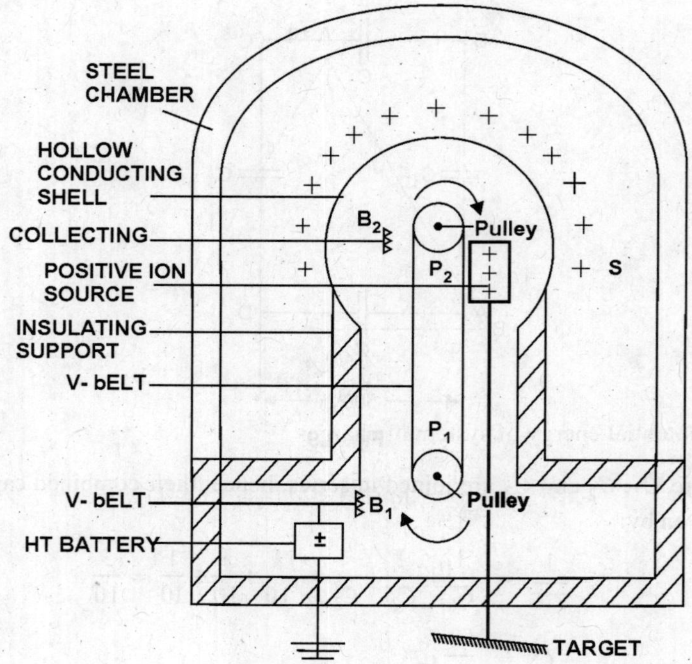

Fig. 1.10

Working: The spraying comb B_1 is given a high positive potential. Due to discharging action of sharp points, a +vely charged electric wind is set-up, which sprays +ve charge on the portion of belt in its neighbourhood.

As the belt moves, it carries the charge upward. As it passes close to collecting comb B_2, a –ve charge is induced on its sharp ends and an equal +ve charge is induced on the farther end of B_2. The –ve charge of comb is discharged due to action if sharp point and it neutralises the *V*-belt too. However, +ve charge induced on farther end of comb B_2 is immediately transferred to spherical shell, *S*.

The whole process is repeated again and again and, in the process, the electric potential of spherical shell may rise to several million volts. The positive ions from the source placed inside *S* are thus at very high potential. There are accelerated to the target kept at negative potential and thus aquire high velocities.

HIGHER ORDER THINKING SKILLS (HOTS)

Q. 1. How many electronic charges form a coulomb of charge?

Ans. Here, charge $q = 1$ C and $e = 1.6 \times 10^{-19}$ C

Let n = number of electronic charges in one coulomb

We have, $q = ne$

or $$n = \frac{q}{e} = \frac{1}{1.6\times10^{-19}} = 6.25 \times 10^{18} \quad \textit{Ans.}$$

Q. 2. Three charges $+q, +2q$ and $-4q$ are placed on the three vertices of an equilateral triangle of each side 0.1m. Calculate the electric potential energy of the system, take $q = 10^{-7}$ C.

Ans. Let *ABC* is an equilateral triangle:

Charge on $A = +q$,

Charge on $B = +2q$ and Charge on $C = -4q$

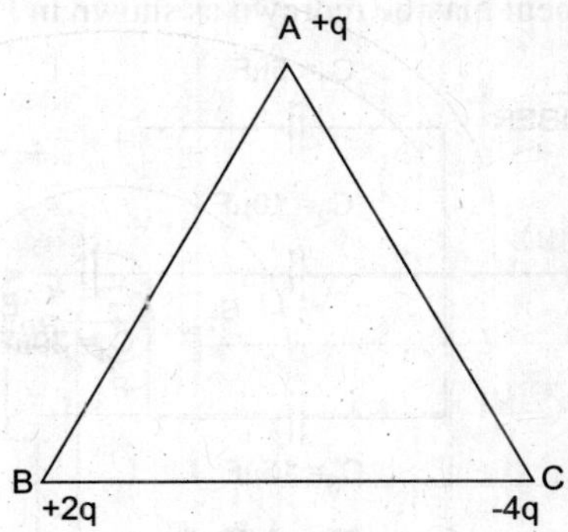

Fig. 1.11

The potential energy of system of charges

$$= \frac{1}{4\pi \epsilon_0} [q\,(2q) + 2q\,(-4q) + (-4q)\,q]$$

$$= -\frac{10q^2}{4\pi \epsilon_0\, r} = \frac{-9\times10^9 \times 10\times\left(10^{-7}\right)^2}{0.1}$$

$= -9 \times 10^{-3}$ J. *Ans.*

Q. 3. Electromagnetic field line cannot be discontinuous. Why?

Ans. An electromagnetic field line of force is a pictorial representation of the electric field. If a line of force had a sudden break, it would indicate the absence of electric field in that region. Therefore, an electric field line cannot have sudden break.

Q. 4. At a point due to point charge, the values of electric field intensity and potential are 32 NC^{-1} and 16 JC^{-1} respectively. Calculate the (*i*) magnitude of the charge and (*ii*) distance of the charge from the point of observation.

Ans. Here, the electric field,

$$E = \frac{Q}{4\pi \epsilon_0\, r^2} = 32 \qquad ...(i)$$

and electric potential,

$$V = \frac{Q}{4\pi \epsilon_0\, r} = 16 \qquad ...(ii)$$

Dividing (ii) by (i),

$$\therefore \quad r = \frac{V}{E} = \frac{16}{32} = 0.5 \text{ m}$$

Putting this value in (ii),

$$\therefore \quad Q = 4\pi \epsilon_0\, rV = \frac{0.5\times16}{9\times10^9} = 0.88 \times 10^{-9} \text{ C } \textit{Ans.}$$

Q. 5. Calculate the equivalent capacitance between the points *A* and *B* in the combination shown in Fig. 1.12.

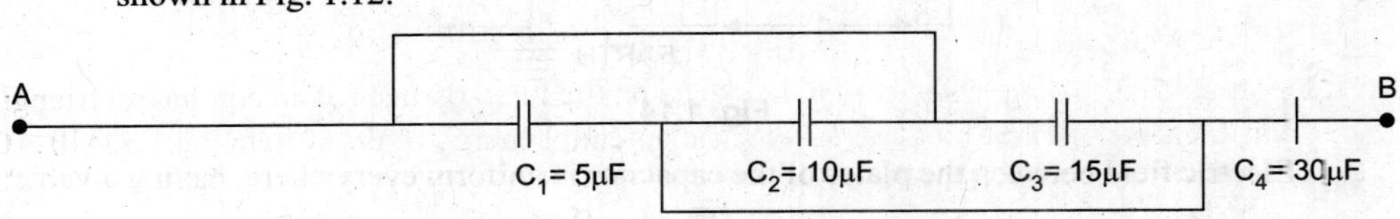

Fig. 1.12

Ans. The capacitor arrangement may be redrawn as shown in Fig. 1.13.

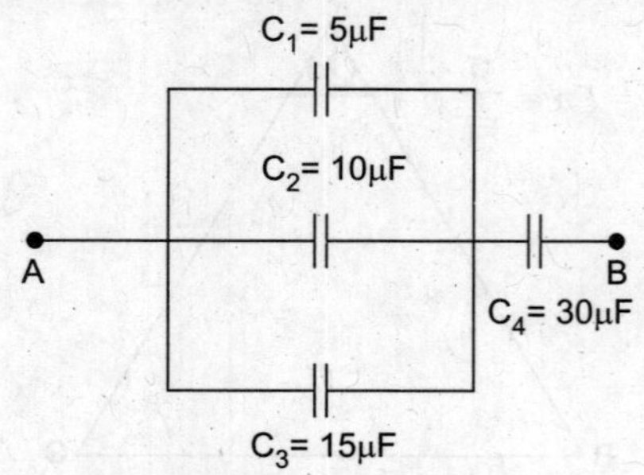

Fig. 1.13

According to this arrangement, C_1, C_2 and C_3 are in parallel. Hence, to their combined capacitance:

$$C' = C_1 + C_2 + C_3$$
$$= 5 + 10 + 15 = 30\mu F$$

As C' and C_4 are series arrangements, then the equivalent capacitance of the whole combination will be:

$$C = \frac{C'C_4}{C'+C_4} = \frac{30 \times 30}{30+30} = \frac{900}{60} = 15\mu F. \ \textit{Ans.}$$

Q. 6. Deduce an expression for the capacitance of a parallel plate capacitor with air as the medium between the two plates. (Imp.)

Ans. Let us consider a parallel plate capacitor connecting two plates, each surface area A, held parallel to each other in air medium such that the separation between the two plates is d. Charges on the two plates are $+Q$ and $-Q$ respectively.

Then, the surface density of charge on either plates is:

$$|\sigma| = \frac{Q}{A} \quad ...(1)$$

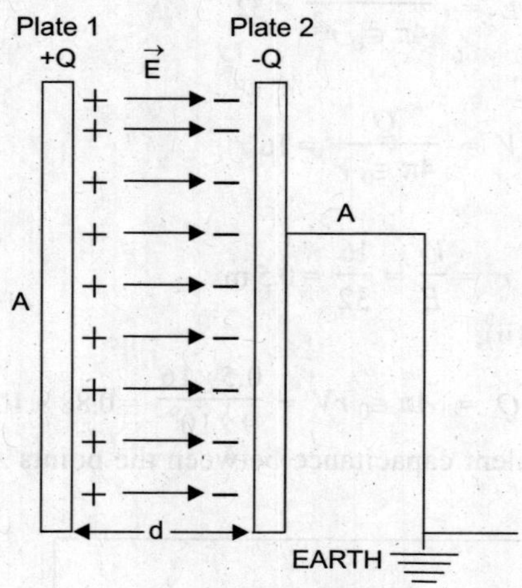

Fig. 1.14

Electric field between the plates of the capacitor is uniform everywhere, having a value:

$$E = E_1 + E_2 = \frac{\sigma}{2\epsilon_0} + \frac{\sigma}{2\epsilon_0} = \frac{\sigma}{\epsilon_0} \quad ...(2)$$

The electric field is directed from +ve plate to the –ve plate. If V be the *p.d.* between the two plates, then

$$V = Ed = \frac{\sigma}{\epsilon_0} d = \frac{Qd}{\epsilon_0 A}$$

or $$V = \frac{Qd}{\epsilon_0 A} \quad ...(3)$$

∴ Capacitance of the parallel plate capacitor

$$C = \frac{Q}{V} = \frac{\epsilon_0 A}{d} \quad \textit{Ans.}$$

Q. 7. An electic flux of $-1000\ Nm^2\ C^{-1}$ passes through a surface of 5.0 m radius centred on the charge.

(*i*) How much electric flux would pass through the surface, if its radius is doubled?

(ii) Find the value of charge causing this flux.

Ans. (*i*) Increase in radius does not affect the electric flux. So, it will remain equal to $-1000\ Nm^2C^{-1}$.

Electric flux through a surface remains same if charge inside the surface is same but size of the surface increases or decreases.

(*ii*) Given $\phi = -1000\ Nm^2\ C^{-1}$, But $\phi = \frac{q}{\epsilon_0}$

$$\therefore \quad q = \phi \epsilon_0 = (-1000)\ (8.85 \times 10^{-12})$$

$$= -8.85 \times 10^{-9}\ C \quad \textit{Ans.}$$

Q. 8. Why is a spherical symmetric surface a convenient choice to prove Gauss's theorem.

Ans. It is a convenient choice because:

(*i*) $\theta = 0$ for all the points on the spherical surface.

$$\therefore \quad \vec{E}.\vec{ds} = Eds \cos\theta = E\,ds \cos 0° = E\,ds$$

(*ii*) $|\vec{E}|$ is constant at all points on the spherical surfaces, so integration expression becomes simple.

(*iii*) It is simple to calculate $\oint ds$ *i.e.*, $4\pi r^2$ in the case of a spherical surface.

❑❑❑

UNIT 2

CURRENT ELECTRICITY

Important Points to Remember

1. Current electricity deals with the flow of electric charges. A flow of electric charges constitutes an electric current.
2. Current carriers – the charged particles which flow in a definite direction and constitute the electric current are called current carriers. e.g.: Electrons in conductors, ions in electrolytes, electrons and holes in semi-conductors.
3. Electric current is defined as the amount of charge flowing through any cross section of the conductor in unit time. $I = Q/t$.
4. Electric current is a scalar quantity.
5. SI unit of electric current is ampere (A).
6. Current flows in an electric circuit only when there is a source of emf and circuit closed.
7. The currents which remain for short duration are called transient currents.
8. 1 ampere = flow of charge of 6.25×10^{18} electrons/second.
9. Current density $\vec{J} = I/A$.
10. Resistor is a component of an electrical circuit offering certain opposition to the flow of current in that circuit.
11. Ohm's law states that the potential difference across the ends of the conductor is directly proportional to the current (I) flowing through it, provided the physical conditions (temperature, pressure, strain, etc.) of the conductor remain unchanged.

$$V \propto I$$
$$V = RI$$

or $$\frac{V}{I} = R, \quad \text{where } R \rightarrow \text{resistance.}$$

12. Resistance $R = \rho l/A$ where ρ is the resistivity of the material of the conductor, l the length and A area of cross section of the conductor. If l is increased n times, new resistance becomes nR. If A is increased n times, new resistance becomes $\frac{1}{n}R$.
13. Resistivity $\rho = m/ne^2\tau$, where m, n, e are mass, number density and charge of electron respectively, τ-relaxation time of electrons. ρ is independent of geometric dimensions.
14. A perfect conductor would have zero resistivity and a perfect insulator would have infinite resistivity. Generally, good electrical conductors are also good thermal conductors.
15. Pure metals are good conductors having low resistivity in the range of $10^{-8} - 10^{-6}$ Ωm. Alloys have somewhat higher resistivity than pure metals.
16. Insulators like rubber, glass, etc. have extremely high resistivity up to an order of 10^{14} Ωm
17. Relaxation time is the average time interval between two successive collisions.
18. Relaxation time decreases with increase in temperature.
19. Reciprocal of resistivity is called the conductivity of the given material. Thus,

Electrical conductivity $$\sigma = \frac{1}{\rho} = \frac{l}{RA}$$

SI unit of electrical conductivity is Sm^{-1}.

20. Conductance of the material G = 1/R.

21. Copper (Cu) wires are used as connecting wires because electrical conductivity of copper (Cu) is high and the electrical resistivity is low.

22. Drift velocity is the average velocity of all electrons in the conductor under the influence of applied electric field. Drift velocity $v_d = (eE/m)\tau$ also $I = neAv_d$.

23. Mobility of a current carrier is the ratio of the drift velocity (V_d) of current carrier to the applied electric field E

i.e., $$\mu = \frac{v_d}{E}$$

24. **Effect of temperature on resistance:** Resistance of a conductor increases with the increase of temperature of conductor $R_T = R_0(1 + \alpha T)$, where α is the temperature coefficient of resistance of the conductor. α is slightly positive for metal conductor, negative for semiconductors and insulators and highly positive for alloys.

25. Semi-conductor diode, liquid electrolyte, transistor, etc. do not obey Ohm's law.

26. **Colour coding :**

Black	Brown	Red	Orange	Yellow	Green	Blue	Violet	Gray	White
0	1	2	3	4	5	6	7	8	9

Tolerance (i) Gold 5% (ii) Silver 10% (iii) No Colour 20%

Example : If colour code on carbon resistor is Red Yellow and Orange with tolerance colour as silver, the resistance of the give resistor is $(24 \times 10^3 \pm 10\%)\Omega$.

27. **Combination of resistors :** $R_{series} = R_1 + R_2 + ...R_n$, $\frac{1}{R_{Parallel}} = \frac{1}{R_1} + \frac{1}{R_2} + ... \frac{1}{R_n}$

28. In series combination of resistors, the effective length of the conductor increases. Hence, resistance increases, because $R \propto l$.

29. In parallel combination of resistors, the effective area of cross section of the conductor increases. Hence, resistance decreases, because $R \propto \frac{1}{A}$.

30. **Cells :** E.M.F. of a cell is defined as the potential difference between its terminals in an open circuit. Terminal potential difference of a cell is defined as the p.d. between its ends in a closed circuit.

31. Internal resistance r of a cell is defined as the opposition offered by the cell to the flow of current. $r = \left(\frac{E}{V} - 1\right)R$ where R is external resistances.

32. Internal resistance of cell depends upon the (*i*) nature of the electrolyte (*ii*) nature of electrodes, (*iii*) distance between the electrodes and (*iv*) immersed area of the electrodes in the electrolyte.

33. **Grouping of cells :**

(i) In series grouping of *n* indentical cells, each of *emf* E and internal resistance *r* circuit current is given $I_s = \frac{nE}{R + nr}$. This combination is usefull when internal resistances of cells are small.

(ii) In parallel grouping of such cells circuit current is given by $I_p = \frac{nE}{r + nR}$. This combination is usefull when internal resistances of cells are large $r >> R$.

(iii) In mixed grouping of *mn* indentical cells, *n* cells are connected in series in each row and *m* such rows are then connected in parallel. The circuit current $I_m = \frac{mnE}{nr + mR}$

Maximum current is obtained when $\frac{nr}{m} = R$ and $(I_m)_{\text{max.}} = \frac{mE}{2r} = \frac{nE}{2R}$.

34. Kirchhoff's Rules :

(i) **Junction Rule :** The algebraic sum of currents meeting at a point is zero. $\sum I = 0$

(ii) **Loop Rule :** The algebraic sum of potential difference around a closed loop is zero $\sum V = 0$

35. Wheatstone bridge is an arrangement of four resistors arranged in four arms of the bridge and is used to determine the unknown resistance in terms of other three resistances. For balanced Wheatstone Bridge, $\frac{P}{Q} = \frac{R}{S}$.

36. Slide Wire Bridge or Metre Bridge is based on Wheatstone bridge and is used to measure unknown resistance. The unknown resistance S is in the right gap, $S = \left(\frac{100 - l}{l}\right)R$.

37. Potentiometer is considered as an ideal voltmeter of infinite resistance.

38. Principle of potentiometer : The potential drop across any portion of the uniform wire is proportional to the length of the portion of the wire provided steady current is maintained in it i.e. $V \alpha I$

39. Potentiometer is used to (i) compare the e.m.f.s of two cells (ii) determine the internal resistance of a cell and (iii) measure small potential differences.

40. Expression for comparison of e.m.f. of two cells by using potentiometer,

$\frac{\varepsilon_1}{\varepsilon_2} = \frac{l_1}{l_2}$ where l_1, l_2 are the balancing lengths of potentiometer wire for e.m.f.s ε_1 and ε_2 of two cells.

41. Expression for the determination of internal resistance of a cell is given by $r = \left(\frac{l_1 - l_2}{l_2}\right)R$.

Where l_1 is the balancing length of potentiometer wire corresponding to e.m.f. of the cell, l_2 that of terminal potential difference of the cell when a resistance R is connected in series with the cell whose internal resistance is to be determined.

42. Expression for determination of potential difference

$V = \varepsilon\left(\frac{\varepsilon}{R + r}\right)\frac{rl}{L}$. Where L is the length of the potentiometer wire, l is balancing length, r is the resistance of potentiometer wire, R is the resistance included in the primary circuit.

43. Joule's law of heating : It states that the amount of heat produced in a conductor is proportional to (i) square of the current flowing through the conductor, (ii) resistance of the conductor and (iii) time for which the current is passed.

Heat produced is given by the relation $H = I^2Rt$.

44. Electric power is defined as the heat produced per unit time in an electric device of resistance R when current is passing through it.

$$\boxed{P = \frac{V^2}{R}}$$

45. Electrical Energy : The electrical energy consumed in a circuit is defined as the total work done in maintaining the current in an electrical circuit for a given time. Electrical energy $= VIt = I^2Rt = (V^2/R)t = Pt$

46. Commercial unit of energy 1 KWh = 3.6×10^6 J.

❑❑❑

VERY SHORT ANSWER TYPE QUESTIONS

(Carrying 1 mark)

Q. 1. A wire of resistivity ρ is stretched to twice its length. What will be its new resistivity?

Ans. Resistivity will remain unchanged at ρ, because resistivity of a material is independent of dimensions of the conductor.

Q. 2. Give reasons why the eletrical conductance of electrolytes is less than that of metals.

Ans. Metals have an exceedingly high number of conduction electrons whose mobility is quite high. In electolytes, number of ions is comparatively less and their mobility too is small.

Q. 3. If the temperature of a good conductor decreases, how does the relaxation time of electrons in the conductor change?

Ans. If the temperature of a good conductor decreases, its resistance decreases.

Since $$R \propto \frac{1}{\tau}$$

or $$\tau \propto \frac{1}{R}$$

so, the time of relaxation increases.

Q. 4. A carbon resistor is marked in coloured bands in the sequence blue, green, orange and gold. What is the resistance and tolerance value of resistance?

Ans. $65 \times 10^3\ \Omega \pm 5\%$

Q. 5. The resistivity of semi-conductors and insulators decreases with increase of temperature. Why?

Ans. As: $\rho_t = \rho_0 (1 + \alpha_r t)$; α_r is negative for semi-conductor and insulator,

hence, $P_t < P_0$

Q. 6. Two wires of equal length, one of copper and other of manganin have the same resistance. Which wire is thicker?

Ans. According to the formula, $R = \dfrac{\rho l}{A}$ for same resistance R and length l, $A \propto \rho$

Hence, manganin wire will be thicker because its resistivity is more than that of the copper wire.

Q. 7. Of metals and alloys, which have greater value of temperature coefficient of resistance?

Ans. Pure metals have a greater value of temperature coefficient of resistance than their alloys.

Q. 8. What are superconductors? Write their two applications.

Ans. As the temperature of certain metals and alloys decreases, their resistance also decreases.

When the temperature reaches a certain critical value called *critical temperature*, the resistance of material completely disappears, *i.e.*, it becomes zero. Then the material behaves as a superconductor.

Thus, superconductors are those material conductors, whose resistance disappears at the critical temperature. The critical temperature is different for different materials. Superconductors are used in (*i*) power transmission and (*ii*) to produce very high-speed computers.

Q. 9. How does the drift velocity of electrons in a metallic conductor vary with increase in temperature?

Ans. Drift velocity is not affected by change of temperature.

Q. 10. What is non-ohmic device? State two examples of it.

Ans. Non-ohmic devices do not strictly obey Ohm's law.
Examples: thyristor and vacuum tubes.

Q. 11. State the condition in which terminal voltage across a cell is equal to its e.m.f.

Ans. Open circuit, *i.e.*, when no current is drawn from a cell.

Q. 12. Draw temperature-resistivity graph for a non-ohmic resistor.

Ans.

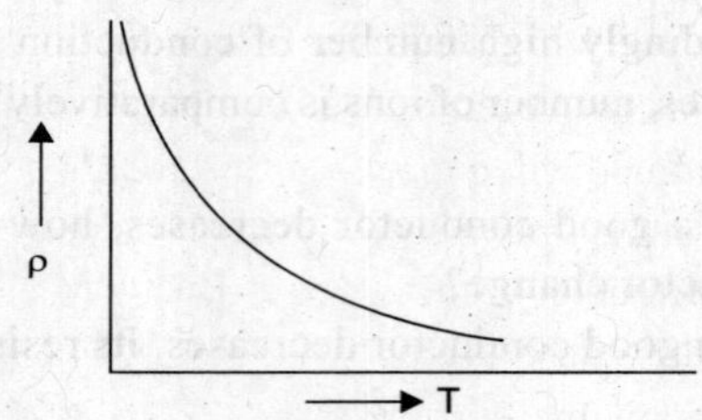

Fig. 2.1

Q. 13. Two electric bulbs P and Q are marked 220 V, 40 W and 220 V, 60 W respectively. Which one has a higher resistance?

Ans. We have, $R = \frac{V^2}{P}$

Hence, $R_1 = \frac{(220)^2}{40} = 1210\ \Omega$

and $R_2 = \frac{(220)^2}{60} = 806.67\ \Omega$

Bulb with lower wattage has higher resistance. *Ans.*

Q. 14. Two heater wires of same dimensions are first connected in series and then in parallel to a source of supply. What will be the ratio of heat produced in two cases?

Ans. Here, $H \propto \frac{1}{R}$

In series, $H_1 \propto \frac{1}{2R}$ ...(*i*)

In parallel, $H_2 \propto \frac{1}{R/2}$ ...(*ii*)

From equations (*i*) & (*ii*), we get

$$\frac{H_1}{H_2} = \frac{1 \times R}{2R \times 2} = \frac{1}{4} \quad \textit{Ans.}$$

Q. 15. How much current will a heater rated 2.5 kW draw when connected to a 250 V electric supply.

Ans. Here, $P = 2.5 \text{ kW} = 2.5 \times 10^3 \text{ W}, \; V = 250 \text{ V}$

We get, $I = \dfrac{P}{V} = \dfrac{2.5\times10^3}{250} = \dfrac{2500}{250} = 10 \text{ A}$ *Ans.*

Q. 16. Show that one ampere is equivalent to a flow of 6.25×10^{18} elementary charges per second.

Ans. We know that, $I = \dfrac{q}{t} = \dfrac{ne}{t}$ $(\because q = ne)$

Where n is the number of electrons.

$\therefore$ $n = \dfrac{It}{e} = \dfrac{1\times1}{1.6\times10^{-19}} = 6.25 \times 10^{18}$ electrons *Proved*

Q. 17. Two bulbs, one of 25 W and other of 200 W are connected in series. As the current passes, one bulb fuses almost instantaneously, which one was fused and why?

Ans. $P \propto \dfrac{1}{R}$, so 25 W bulb will have higher resistance. In series, same current will pass through the bulbs giving higher voltage across 25 W bulb which makes the bulb fuse.

Q. 18. The lights of a car get dimmed when the starter is operated. Give reasons.

Ans. This is because large current is drawn by the starter from the battery.

Q. 19. Why do we prefer a potentiometer to measure e.m.f. of a cell rather than a voltmeter?

Ans. A potentiometer does not draw any current from the cell whose e.m.f. is to be determined, whereas a voltmeter draws some current and as such gives slightly less than actual value of e.m.f. of the cell.

Q. 20. State the characteristics of fuse wire.

Ans. A fuse wire should be of material having (*i*) high resistivity, (*ii*) low melting point and (*iii*) of suitable current rating corresponding to the load in the circuit.

Q. 21. What is the significance of direction of current.

Ans. It gives the direction of flow of charge carriers from positive to negative or negative to positive terminals of an electric source.

Q. 22. Draw temperature-resistivity graph for an ohmic resistor.

Ans. The temperature-resistivity graph is given below.

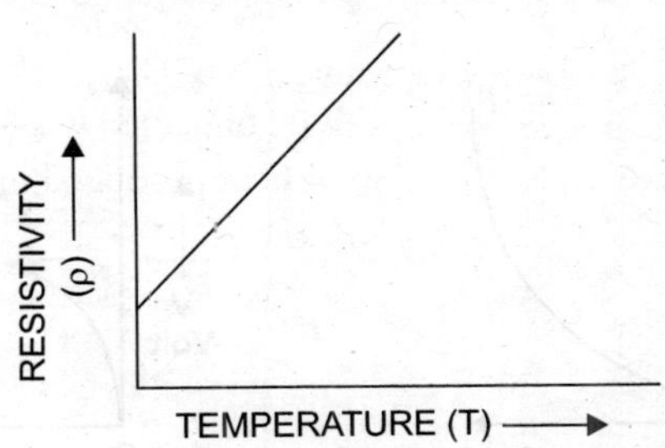

Fig. 2.2

Q. 23. What happens to power dissipation if the value of current passing through a conductor of constant resistance is doubled?

Ans. Power dissipation will become four times because, in this case, $P \propto I^2$.

SHORT ANSWER TYPE QUESTIONS

(Carrying 3 marks)

Q. 1. Two bulbs of same wattage, one having a carbon filament and another having a metallic filament are connected in series to the mains. Which one will glow more?

Ans. Resistance of the carbon filament is more than that of metallic filament. In series combination, there will be same current through them. Since heat produced, $H = I^2 Rt$, therefore, $H \propto R$. Hence, carbon filament bulb will glow more.

Q. 2. A potential difference V is applied to a copper wire of length l and diameter D. What is the effect on the electron drift velocity by (*i*) doubling V, (*ii*) doubling l and (*iii*) doubling D?

Ans. Here, drift velocity, $v_d = \frac{eE\tau}{m} = \frac{eV\tau}{ml}$ $\qquad \left(\because E = \frac{V}{l}\right)$

(*i*) When V is doubled, v_d also becomes double.

(*ii*) When l is doubled, v_d becomes half.

(*iii*) $v_d = \frac{I}{nAe} = \frac{4I}{n\pi D^2 e}$, when D is doubled, v_d becomes $\frac{1}{4}$th.

Q. 3. Draw *V-I* graph for ohmic and non-ohmic materials. Give one example for each.

Ans. *V-I* graph for ohmic material. It is in a straight line passing through the origin.

Example: Copper wire, nichrome

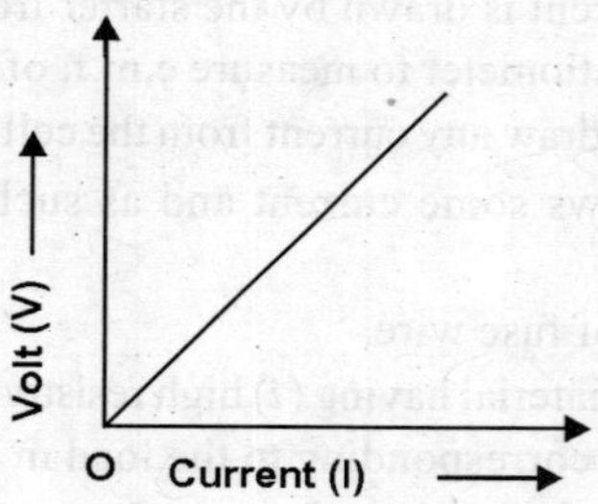

Fig. 2.3

V-I graph for non-ohmic material. It can have any shape other than straight line passing through the origin.

Example: Junction diode, transistor.

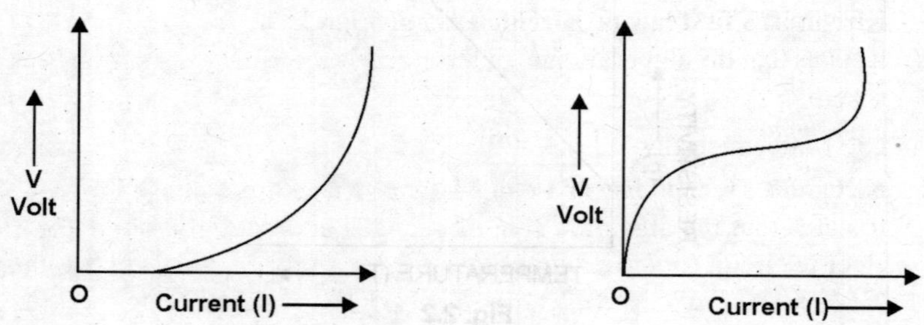

Fig. 2.4

Q. 4. How will you connect three resistances of $R\,\Omega$ each to obtain a total resistance of $\frac{R}{3}\,\Omega$?

Ans. Three resistances should be connected in parallel to get $\frac{R}{3}\,\Omega$ as shown in Fig. 2.5.

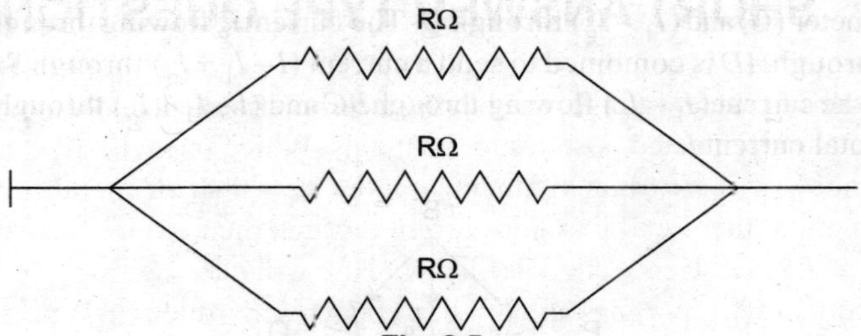

Fig. 2.5

Here, resistances in series,

$$\frac{1}{R'} = \frac{1}{R_1} + \frac{1}{R_2} + \frac{1}{R_3} \qquad (\because R_1 = R_2 = R_3 = R\,\Omega)$$

$$\Rightarrow \qquad \frac{1}{R'} = \frac{1}{R} + \frac{1}{R} + \frac{1}{R}$$

$$\Rightarrow \qquad \frac{1}{R'} = \frac{3}{R} \Rightarrow R' = \frac{R}{3}\Omega.$$

Q. 5. The I-V characteristics of a resistor are observed to deviate from a straight line for higher values of current as shown Fig. 2.6. Why?

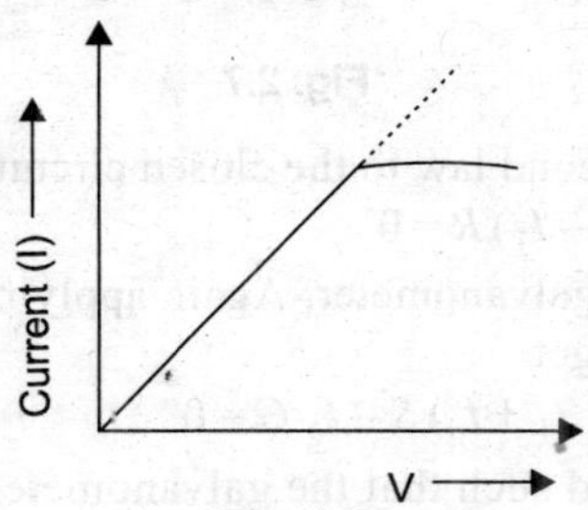

Fig. 2.6

Ans. When high current passes through a resistor (say metallic conductor), large amount of heat ($H = I^2R$) is produced per second. This heat rises the temperature of the resistor. Therefore, the resistance of the resistor starts increasing with increase in temperature (*i.e.*, slope of I-V graph decreases).Thus, the conductor does not obeyOhm's law; when high current passes through the resistor.

Q. 6. State Kirchhoff's laws.

Ans. 1. **Kirchhoff's first law or Kirchhoff's Junction Law.**
It states that the algebraic sum of the currents meeting at a junction in a closed circuit is zero.
i.e., Mathematically, $\boxed{\Sigma I = 0}$

2. **Kirchhoff's second law or Loop's Law or Kirchoff's Voltage Law.**
It states that the algebraic sum of changes in potential around any closed path of electric circuit (or closed loop) involving resistors and cells in the loop is zero.
i.e., $\Sigma \Delta V = 0$

Q. 7. Derive the condition for balance in a Wheatstone's Bridge.

Ans. Wheatstone Bridge: Wheatstone Bridge is being given in Fig. 2.7. The four resistances P, Q, R and S are arranged to form a bridge. Let I be the total current given out by the cell. On reaching point A, it gets divided into two parts. I_1 is flowing through P and $(I - I_1)$ flowing through R. At B, the current I_1 is divided into two parts. I_g through the galvanometer (G) and ($I_1 - I_g$) through Q. The current I_g flowing through the arm BD and ($I - I_1$) through AD is combined to send a current ($I - I_1 + I_g$) through S. On reaching the point C, the current ($I_1 - I_g$) flowing through BC and ($I - I_1 + I_g$) through DC is combined to give total current I.

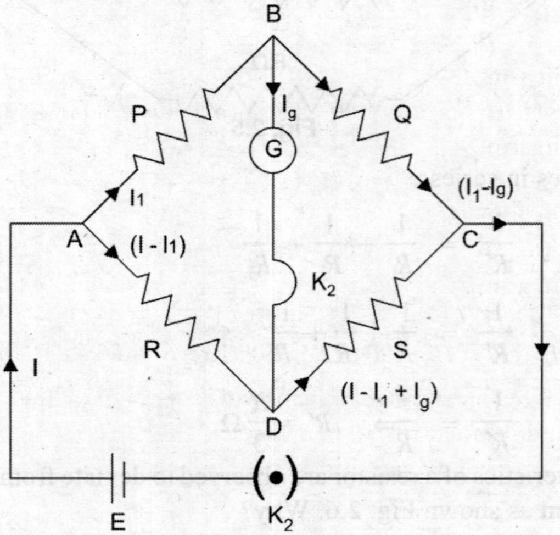

Fig. 2.7

Applying Kirchhoff's second law to the closed circuit $ABDA$, we get

$$I_1 P + I_g G - (I - I_1) R = 0 \quad \text{....(1)}$$

where G is resistance of galvanometer. Again applying Kirchhoff's second law to the closed circuit $BCDB$, we get

$$(I_1 - I_g)Q - (I - I_1 + I_g) S - I_g G = 0 \quad \text{...(2)}$$

The value of R is adjusted such that the galvanometer shows no deflection *i.e.*, $I_g = 0$. Now, since the bridge is balanced, putting $I_g = 0$ in eqn. (1) and (2), we get

$$I_1 P - (I - I_1) R = 0$$

or $\quad I_1 P = (I - I_1) R \quad$ ...(3)

and $\quad I_1 Q - (I - I_1) S = 0$

or $\quad I_1 Q = (I - I_1) S \quad$ ...(4)

Dividing (3) by (4), we get

$$\boxed{\frac{P}{Q} = \frac{R}{S}}$$

which is the balance equation of Wheatstone Bridge.

Q. 8. Compute the ratio of the heat generated in the four arms AB, BC, AD and DC of the given current carrying Wheatstone Bridge (Fig. 2.8).

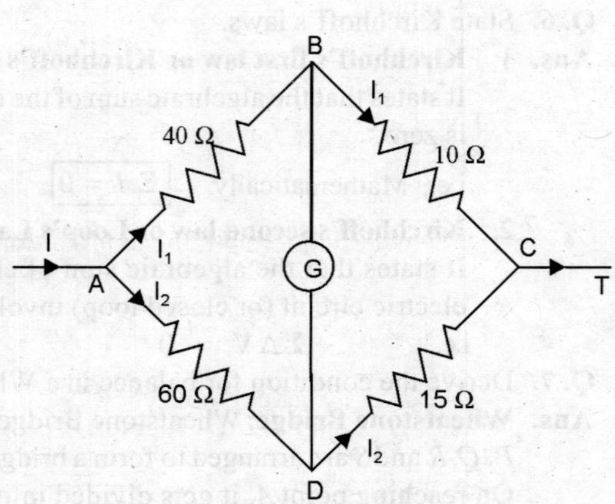

Fig. 2.8

Ans. Here, $\quad P = 40\ \Omega, Q = 10\ \Omega,$
$R = 60\ \Omega$ and $S = 15\ \Omega$

Now, $\quad \frac{P}{Q} = \frac{40}{10} = 4$

and $\frac{R}{S} = \frac{60}{15} = 4$ So $\frac{P}{Q} = \frac{R}{S}$.

It means the Wheatstone Bridge is balanced, *i.e.*, Pot. of B = Pot. of D. Hence no current is flowing in arm BD. Let I_1, I_2 be the currents in arms AB and AD respectively, then P.d. across A and B = P.d. across A and D.

$$I_1 \times 40 = I_2 \times 60$$

or

$$I_1 = 1.5 I_2$$

Heat produced in arm AB,

$$H_1 = I_1^2 \times 40 = (1.5 I_2)^2 \times 40 = 90 I_2^2 \text{ J}$$

Heat produced in arm BC,

$$H_2 = I_1^2 \times 10 = (1.5 I_2)^2 \times 10 = 22.5 I_2^2 \text{ J}$$

Heat produced in arm AD,

$$H_3 = I_2^2 \times 60 = 60 I_2^2 \text{ J}$$

Heat produced in arm DC,

$$H_4 = I_2^2 \times 15 = 15 I_2^2 \text{ J}$$

$\therefore$ $H_1 : H_2 : H_3 : H_4 = 90 : 22.5 : 60 : 15 = 6 : 1.5 : 4 : 1.$ *Ans.*

Q. 9. For what value of load resistance is the power transfer maximum when two identical cells, each of emf E and internal resistance r are connected (*i*) in series (*ii*) in parallel?

Ans. (*i*) When cells are connected in series to the external load resistance R, then effective emf

$$= E + E = 2E$$

Total resistance in the circuit $= R + r + r = R + 2r$

Current in load, $I = \frac{2E}{R + 2r}$

Power delivered to the external load is:

$$P = I^2 R = \left(\frac{2E}{R + 2r}\right)^2 R$$

Power delivered to the external load will be maximum if external resistance = internal resistance of cells,

i.e., $R = 2r$

Then, maximum power, $P_{max} = \left(\frac{2E}{2r + 2r}\right)^2 \times 2r = \frac{E^2}{2r}$ *Ans.*

(*ii*) When cells are connected in parallel to the external load resistance R_1, then effective emf $= E$

Total resistance of the circuit $= R + \frac{r \times r}{r + r} = \left(R + \frac{r}{2}\right)$

Current in load, $I = \frac{E}{\left(R + \frac{r}{2}\right)}$

Power delivered to the external load,

$$P = I^2 R = \left(\frac{E}{R + r/2}\right)^2 R$$

Power is maximum when $R = \frac{r}{2}$

Then, $P_{max} = \left(\frac{E}{r/2 + r/2}\right)^2 \frac{r}{2} = \frac{E^2}{2r}$ *Ans.*

Q. 10. Two cells $\in_1$ and $\in_2$ in the given circuit (Fig. 2.9) have an emf of 5 V and 9 V and internal resistance of 0.3 Ω and 1.2 Ω respectively. Calculate the value of current flowing through the resistance of 3Ω.

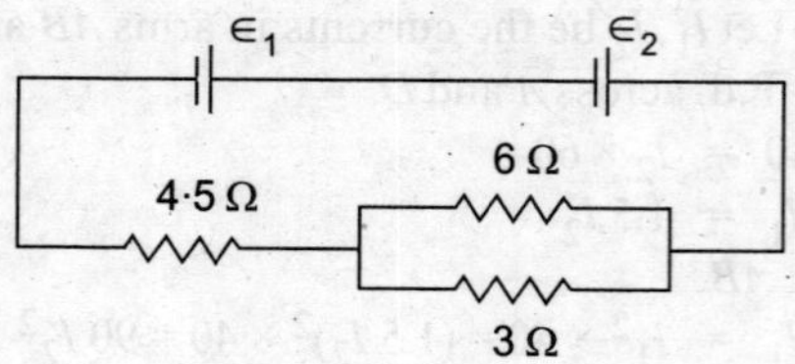

Fig. 2.9

Ans. Here, net emf of circuit

$$\in = \in_2 - \in_1 = 9 - 5 = 4\text{ V}$$

and total resistance of the circuit

$$R = \frac{6\times 3}{6+3} + 4.5 + 0.3 + 1.2 = 8\ \Omega$$

$\therefore$ Main circuit current, $I = \frac{\in}{R} = \frac{4}{8} = 0.5\text{ A}$

If current flowing through 3Ω resistance be I_1, the current flowing through 6Ω resistance will be $(0.5 - I_1)$ and hence,

$$3I_1 = 6\times(0.5 - I_1) \Rightarrow \quad I_1 = 0.33\text{ A } \textit{Ans.}$$

Q. 11. Determine the current through the battery of internal resistance 0.5 Ω for the circuit as shown in Fig. 2.10. How much power will be dissipated in 6 Ω resistance?

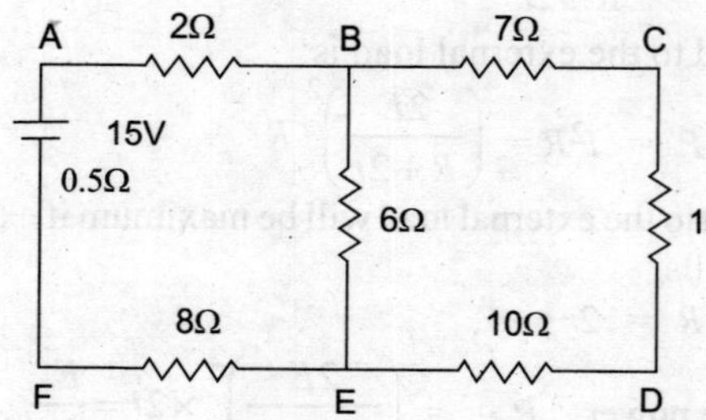

Fig. 2.10

Ans. Resistance of arm $BCDE = 7 + 1 + 10 = 18\ \Omega$ and 6 Ω are in parallel, Their effective resistance,

$$R_p = \frac{18\times 6}{18+6} = \frac{18\times 6}{24} = 4.5\ \Omega$$

Total resistance of the circuit = 2 + 4.5 + 8 + 0.5 = 15 Ω

$\therefore$ Current through circuit, $i = \frac{15}{15} = 1\ \Omega$

Potential diff. across B and $E = i\times R_p = 1\times 4.5 = 4.5$ V

$\therefore$ Power dissipated as heat due to resistance of $6\Omega = \frac{(4.5)^2}{6} = 3.375$ W *Ans.*

Q. 12. Two wires A and B are of same metal, have same area of cross section and have their lengths in the ratio 2:1. What will be the ratio of currents flowing through them when the same potential difference is applied across the length of each of them?

Ans. Here, current, $$I_1 = \frac{V}{R_1} = \frac{VA}{\rho l_1} \quad ...(1)$$

and current, $$I_2 = \frac{VA}{\rho l_2} \quad ...(2)$$

From equations (1) and (2), we get

$$\therefore \quad \frac{I_1}{I_1} = \frac{l_2}{l_1}$$

$$\because \quad \frac{l_1}{l_2} = \frac{2}{1} \text{ or } \frac{l_2}{l_1} = \frac{1}{2}$$

$$\therefore \quad \frac{I_1}{I_2} = \frac{1}{2} \Rightarrow \quad I_1 : I_2 = 1:2$$

Q. 13. A wire of length 2.0 m, diameter 1.0 mm has 50 mΩ resistance. Find the (*i*) resistivity and (*ii*) conductivity of the material of the wire.

Ans. Here, length of wire, $l = 2.0$ m

diameter, $d = 1.0 \text{ mm} = 1.0 \times 10^{-3}$ m

Resistance, $R = 50 \text{ m}\Omega = 50 \times 10^{-3}\ \Omega = 5 \times 10^{-2}\ \Omega$

(*i*) Using, $R = \rho\frac{l}{A}$, we get

Resistivity, $$\rho = \frac{R \times A}{l} = \frac{R \times \pi d^2}{4l}$$

$$= \frac{5\times10^{-2}\times 3.14\times (1.0\times 10^{-3})^2}{4\times2}\ \Omega\text{m}$$

$$= \frac{15.70\times10^{-8}}{8}\ \Omega\text{m} = 1.963 \times 10^{-8}\ \Omega\text{m}$$

(*ii*) Conductivity,

$$\sigma = \frac{1}{\rho} = \frac{1}{1.963\times10^{-8}} = 5.094 \times 10^{7}\ \text{Sm}^{-1}.$$

Q. 14. Why is it dangerous to touch the live wire of the household power supply with sweaty hands than with dry hands?

Ans. Our hands become wet due to sweat, which contains NaCl. NaCl in molten state is a very good conductor of electricity. Therefore, large current may pass through our body, which can be dangerous.

Q. 15. A current of 1.0 mA is flowing through a potentiometer wire of length 4 m and of resistance 4 Ω. Find the potential gradient of potentiometer wire.

Ans. Here, $I = 1.0 \text{ mA} = 10^{-3}$ A

$R = 4\Omega, L = 4$ m

Potential drop across potentiometer wire,

$$V = IR = 10^{-3} \times 4 \times 10^{-3}\ \text{V}$$

$$\therefore \text{ Potential gradient, } k = \frac{V}{L} = \frac{4\times10^{-3}}{4} = 10^{-3}\ \text{V/m}.$$

Q. 16. *V-I* graph for a metallic wire at two different temperatures T_1 and T_2 is shown in the Fig. 2.11. Which of the two temperatures is higher and why?

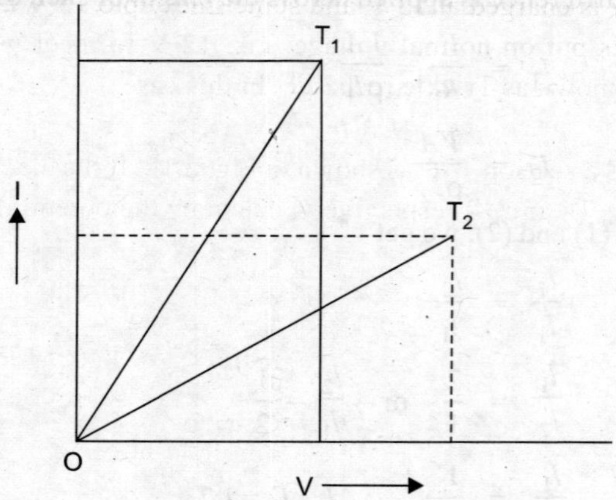

Fig. 2.11

Ans. We know, $R = \frac{V}{I}$ and slope of *I-V* curve $= \frac{1}{R}$

or $$R = \frac{1}{\text{Slope of I} - \text{V graph}}$$

Since slope of the curve OT_2 is smaller than that of the curve OT_1, hence resistance of wire at temperature T_2 is greater than that at temperature T_1. As resistance increases with temperature, so temperature $T_2 > T_1$.

Q. 17. Which of the two has higher resistance: a 1000 W heater or a 100 W tungsten bulb, both marked for 230 V ?

Ans. Resistance of heating element, *R* is given by the relation.

$$P = \frac{V^2}{R} \Rightarrow R = \frac{V^2}{P}$$

Resistance of heater, $R_H = \frac{230 \times 230}{1000} = 52.9\ \Omega$

Resistance of bulb, $R_B = \frac{230 \times 230}{100} = 529\ \Omega$

Thus, resistance of bulb is more than the heater.

HIGHER ORDER THINKING SKILLS (HOTS)

Q. 1. An automobile engine starts easily on a hot day than on a cold day. Why?

Ans. On a hot day, due to high temperature, the internal resistance of the battery electrolyte becomes low and there is less voltage drop in the battery. Thus, a large current is available to start the car easily. On a cold day, due to low temperature, the internal resistance of battery becomes high and, hence, there is a large v oltage drop in the battery. Now the terminal potential difference and, hence, current to the circuit in the car is low. So the car does not start easily.

Q. 2. Why is the terminal voltage across a battery more than its *emf* during recharging?

Ans. When a cell is discharged, it requires slightly more voltage for a quick recharge, *e.g.*, a 12 V battery is charged at 13 V and sometimes upto 15 V also, but once the battery is charged, it is put on normal voltage, *i.e.*, 12 V to meet with internal losses. Such a recharge is known as Trickle recharge. In this case,

$$V = E + Ir$$

Q. 3. A circuit has a section *ABC* as shown in Fig. 2.12. If the electric potentials at points *A*, *B* and *C* are V_1, V_2 and V_3 respectively, calculate the potential at point *O*.

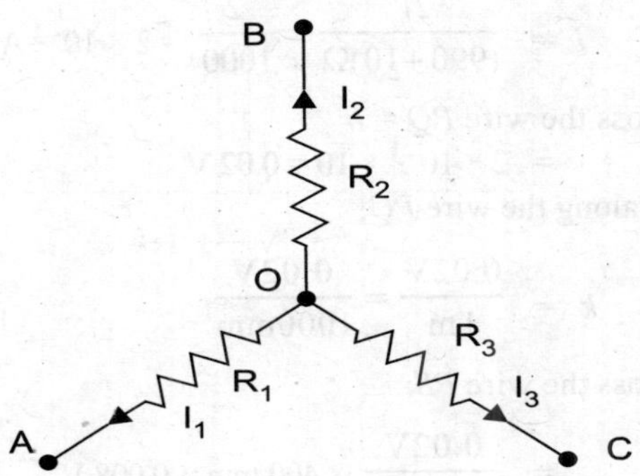

Fig. 2.12

Ans. Applying Kirchhoff's first law at *O*,

$$-I_1 - I_2 - I_3 = 0$$

or $$I_1 + I_2 + I_3 = 0 \quad ...(1)$$

If V_0 is the electric potential at point O:

V_1, V_2 and V_3 are the electrical potentials at *A*, *B* and *C* respectively.

Then, $$V_0 - V_1 = I_1 R_1,\ V_0 - V_2 = I_2 R_2 \text{ and } V_0 - V_3 = I_3 R_3 \quad ...(2)$$

Thus, $$I_1 = \frac{(V_0 - V_1)}{R_1};\quad I_2 = \frac{(V_0 - V_2)}{R_2} \text{ and } I_3 = \frac{(V_0 - V_3)}{R_3}$$

Putting values of I_1, I_2 and I_3 in equation (1), we get:

$$\frac{V_0 - V_1}{R_1} + \frac{V_0 - V_2}{R_2} + \frac{V_0 - V_3}{R_3} = 0$$

or $$V_0\left[\frac{1}{R_1} + \frac{1}{R_2} + \frac{1}{R_3}\right] - \left[\frac{V_1}{R_1} + \frac{V_2}{R_2} + \frac{V_3}{R_3}\right] = 0$$

or $$V_0 = \left[\frac{V_1}{R_1} + \frac{V_2}{R_2} + \frac{V_3}{R_3}\right]\left[\frac{1}{R_1} + \frac{1}{R_2} + \frac{1}{R_3}\right]^{-1}$$

Q. 4. The circuit diagram, Fig. 2.13, shows the set up for measurement of emf generated in a thermocouple connected between *X* and *Y*. The cell *E* of emf 2V has negligible internal resistance. The potentiometer wire of length 1 m has a resistance of 10 Ω. The balance point *S* is found to be 400 mm from point *P*. Calculate the emf generated by the thermocouple.

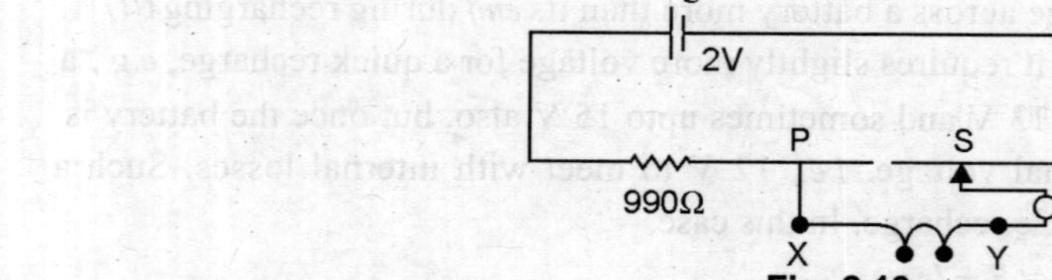

Fig. 2.13

Ans. Resistance of wire *PQ*, $r = 10\ \Omega$

Current through the wire *PQ* is

$$I = \frac{2V}{(990+10)\Omega} = \frac{2}{1000} = 2 \times 10^{-3}\ \text{A}.$$

Potential drop across the wire $PQ = Ir$

$$= 2 \times 10^{-3} \times 10 = 0.02\ \text{V}$$

Potential gradient along the wire *PQ*:

$$k = \frac{0.02\text{V}}{1\ \text{m}} = \frac{0.02\text{V}}{1000\text{mm}}$$

Potential drop across the wire *PS*:

$$= \frac{0.02\text{V}}{1000\text{mm}} \times 400\ \text{mm} = 0.008\ \text{V}$$

Then, emf generated by thermocouple = 0.008V.

Q. 5. **The Wheatstone bridge circuit has resistances in various arms as shown in Fig. 2.14. Calculate the current through the galvanometer.**

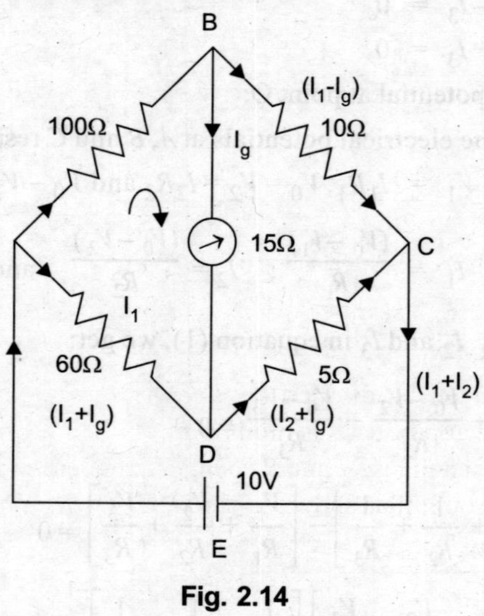

Fig. 2.14

Ans. In the closed loop *ABDA*,

$$100\,I_1 + 15\,I_g - 60\,I_2 = 0$$

or $\quad 20\,I_1 + 3\,I_g - 12\,I_2 = 0 \quad$ ...(*i*)

In the closed loop *BCDB*,

$$10\,(I_1 - I_g) - 5\,(I_2 + I_g) - 15\,I_g = 0$$

or $\quad 10\,I_1 - 30\,I_g - 5\,I_2 = 0$

$$2I_1 - 6I_g - I_2 = 0 \quad ...(ii)$$

In the closed loop *ADCEA,*

$$60I_2 + 5(I_2 + I_g) - 10 = 0$$

$$65I_2 + 5I_g = 10$$

or $$13I_2 + I_g = 2 \quad ...(iii)$$

Solving (*i*), (*ii*) and (*iii*), we get

$$I_g = 4.87 \text{ mA}.$$

Q. 6. What is the equivalent resistance between *A* and *B* in the network of resistances? Find the current through 12 Ω.

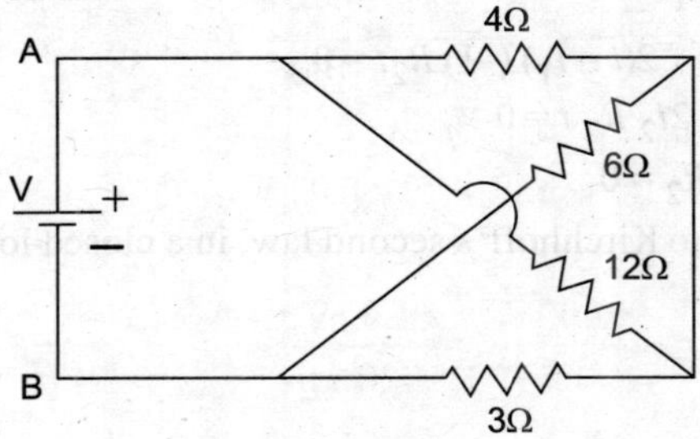

Fig. 2.15

Ans. Here, 4Ω and 12Ω are in parallel. Their combined resistance:

$$= \frac{4\times12}{4+12} = 3\Omega$$

Similarly, 6Ω and 3Ω are in parallel, their combined resistance

$$= \frac{3\times6a}{3+6} = 2\Omega$$

Now the 3Ω and 2Ω, resistances are in series, so the equivalent resistance between *A* and $B = 3 + 2 = 5\Omega$.

Current in the circuit, $I = \frac{10}{2} = 2\text{A}$

Potential difference across $12\Omega = 2 \times 3 = 6\text{V}$

Current through $12\Omega = \frac{6}{12} = \frac{1}{2} A.$

Q. 7. Prove that when a current is divided between two resistances in accordance with Kirchhoff's laws, the heat produced is minimum.

Ans. Let us consider two resistances R_1 and R_2 connected in parallel and the current through the various arms of the circuit as shown in Fig. 2.16.

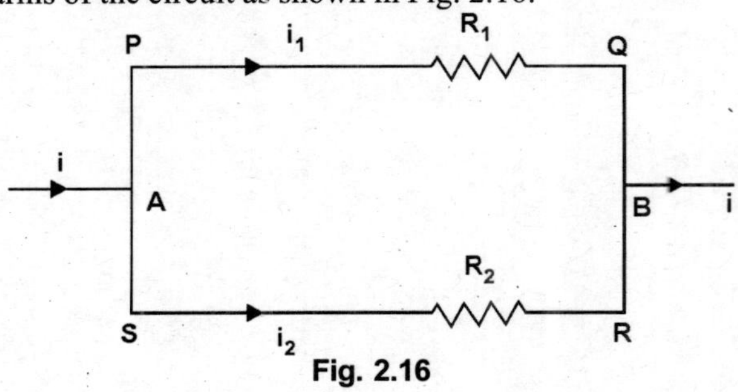

Fig. 2.16

According to Kirchhoff's first law, at junction A,

$$i = i_1 + i_2 \quad \text{or} \quad i_2 = i - i_1 \qquad \text{...}(i)$$

Let H be the heat produced in the circuit in t seconds, then

$$H = i_1^2 R_1 t + i_2^2 R_2 t$$

$$= i_1^2 R_1 t + (i - i_1)^2 R_2 t \qquad \text{From } (i)$$

In case the heat produced in the circuit is minimum, then

$$\frac{dH}{di_1} = 0,$$

Therefore, $2i_1 R_1 t + 2(i - i_1)(-1) R_2 t = 0$

or $2i_1 R_1 t - 2i_2 R_2 t = 0$

or $i_1 R_1 - i_2 R_2 = 0$

which is according to Kirchhoff's second law, in a closed loop.

❑❑❑

UNIT 3

MAGNETIC EFFECTS OF CURRENT AND MAGNETISM

Important Points to Remember

1. Magnetic field is characterized by a magnetic field vector $\vec{B}$.
2. SI unit of magnetic field $\vec{B}$ is tesla (T). It is also referred as Wbm^{-2}. CGS unit of $\vec{B}$ is G (gauss), where $1G = 10^{-4}$ T.
3. A magnetic field can be produced by the following ways:
   (*i*) by a magnet.
   (*ii*) by a current carrying conductor.
   (*iii*) by a moving charge, and
   (*iv*) by changing electric field.
4. According to Biot Savart's law, the magnetic field $d\vec{B}$ induction at a point P due to small current element $d\vec{l}$, carrying current I is given by:

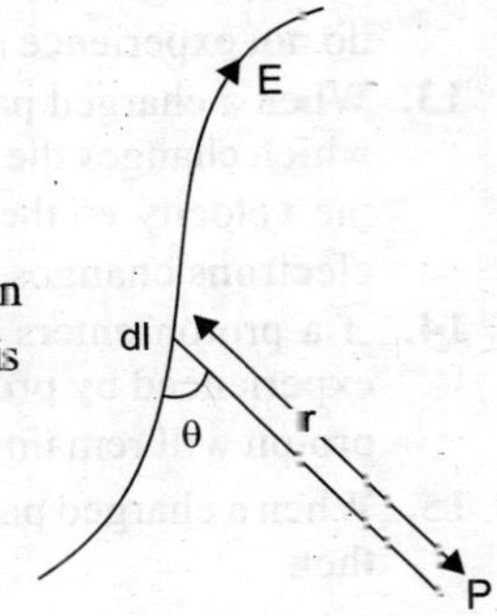

$$d\vec{B} = \frac{\mu_0 I}{4\pi}\left(\frac{\vec{dl} \times \vec{r}}{r^3}\right) = \frac{\mu_0 I}{4\pi}\frac{dl \sin\theta}{r^2}$$

If point lies on the conductor $\theta = 0°$ or $180°$ and $\sin\theta = 0$, then $dB = 0$. Hence, magnetic field induction at any point on the conductor itself is zero.

5. The current element is the source of magnetic field, that is why, the magnetic field is produced due to flow of current in the given wire.
6. The magnitude of magnetic flux density $\vec{B}$ on a given line of induction is generally not constant.
7. **Applications :** (i) Magnetic field at a centre of a current carrying circular coil

$$B = \frac{\mu_0 I}{2a}$$

(ii) Magnetic field at a point on the axis of current carrying coll.

$$B = \frac{\mu_0 N i a^2}{2\left(a^2 + x^2\right)^{3/2}}$$

(N = no. of turns in the coil, a = radius of coil).

8. **Ampere's circuital law :** It states that the line integral of magnetic field around any closed path in vacuum/air is μ_0 times the total current threading the closed path $\oint B.dl = \mu_0 I$.
9. **Applications :**
   (*i*) Magnetic field due to straight infinitely long current carrying straight conductor.

$$B = \frac{\mu_0 I}{2\pi r}$$

(*ii*) Magnetic field due to a straight solenoid carrying current
$B = \mu_0 n I$
n = no. of turns per unit length

(*iii*) Magnetic field due to toroidal solenoid carrying current.

$$B = \frac{\mu_0 N i}{2\pi r}$$

N = Total no. of turns, r = mean radius

10. Inside the copper pipe, the magnetic field is zero, but there is a finite value of the magnetic field outside the copper pipe.

11. Force on a moving charge [Lorentz Force]

(*i*) In magnetic field $\vec{F} = q\left(\vec{V} \times \vec{B}\right)$

(*ii*) In magnetic and electric field $\vec{F} = q\left[\vec{E} + \left(\vec{V} \times \vec{B}\right)\right]$

12. The magnetic force acts only on the moving charge. In a conductor carrying current, the free electrons move towards the positive end of the conductor with some drift velocity, hence, magnetic force acts on them. The positive ions of the conductor being stationary do not experience any magnetic force.

13. When a charged particle moves perpendicular to a magnetic field, it experiences a force which changes the direction of motion of the particle without change in the magnitude of the velocity of the particle. Hence, kinetic energy remains constant but momentum of electrons changes.

14. If a proton enters a strong magnetic field along the field direction ($\theta = 0°$), the force experienced by proton is $F = Bqv \sin\theta = q\upsilon B \sin 0 = 0°$. Therefore, the path of velocity of proton will remain unchanged.

15. When a charged particle moves undeflected in a region where $\vec{E}$ and $\vec{B}$ are both present then

$$\vec{E} = -\vec{V} \times \vec{B}$$

i.e., $\vec{E}$ and $\vec{B}$ are crossed (perpendicular to each other) and velocity

$$v = \frac{E}{B}$$

16. Force on a current carrying conductor in uniform magnetic field
$\vec{F} = i\left(\vec{l} \times \vec{B}\right)$ *and* $\left|\vec{F}\right| = i\,l\,B \sin\theta$
where l = length of conductor
Direction of force can be found using Fleming's left hand rule.

17. Force per unit length between parallel infinitely long current carrying straight conductors.

$$\frac{F}{l} = \mu_0 \frac{i_1 i_2}{2\pi d}$$

(*a*) If currents are in same direction the wires will attract each other.

(*b*) If currents are in opposite directions they will repel each other.

18. 1 Ampere : One ampere is that current, which when flowing through each of the two parallel straight conductors of infinite length and placed in free space at a distance of 1m from each other, produces between them a force of 2×10^{-7} N/*m* of their length.

19. Motion of a charge in

(*a*) Perpendicular magnetic field $\vec{F} = q\,(\vec{v} \times \vec{B})$, $F = qvB \sin 90° = qvB$ (circular path)

(*b*) Parallel or antiparallel field $F = qvB \sin 0°$ (or) $qvB \sin 180° = 0$ (Straight line path)
If $0 < \theta < 90$, the path is helix
$v \cos\theta$ is responsible for linear motion and $v \sin\theta$ is responsible for circular motion
Hence trajectory is a helical path

20. Cyclotron

(*i*) Principle

(*a*) When a charged particle moves at right angle to a uniform magnetic field it describes circular path.

(*b*) an ion can acquire sufficiently large energy with a low ac voltage making it to cross the same electric field repeatedly under a strong magnetic field.

(*ii*) Cyclotron frequency or magnetic resonance frequency

$$v = \frac{qB}{2\pi m}, \ T = \frac{2\pi m}{Bq}, \ \omega = \frac{Bq}{m}$$

(*iii*) Maximum velocity and maximum kinetic energy of charged particle

$$V_m = V_m = \frac{Bqr_m}{m}$$

$$E_m = \frac{B^2 q^2 r_m}{2m}$$

21. Torque experienced by a current loop in a uniform B.

$$\tau = NIBA \sin\theta$$

$$\vec{\tau} = \vec{M} \times \vec{B}$$

Where $M = NIA$

22. Moving coil galvanometer : It is a sensitive instrument used for detecting small electric currents.

Principle : When a current carrying coil is placed in a magnetic field, it experiences a torque. The value of τ depends upon the current. this torque deflects the coil. For deflection θ, we have $I \alpha \theta$ and $I = K\theta$ where $K = \dfrac{NAB}{C}$

Current sensitivity, $I_s = \dfrac{\theta}{I} = \dfrac{NBA}{K}$

Voltage sensitivity, $V_s = \dfrac{\theta}{V} = \dfrac{NBA}{KR}$

Changing $N \Rightarrow$ Current sensitivity changes but Voltage Sensitivity does not change

23. Conversion of galvanometer into ammeter. A galvanometer can be converted into an ammeter of given range by connecting a suitable low resistance S (called shunt) in parallel to the given galvanometer. $S = \left(\dfrac{I_g}{I - I_g}\right) G$

where I_g = full deflection current for galvanometer, I = current to measured by the galvanometer and G = resistance of the galvanometer.

24. A galvanometer can be converted into voltmeter of given range by connecting a suitable high resistance R in series with the galvanometer, whose value is

$$R = \frac{V}{I_g} - G$$

where V = voltage to be measured, I_g = current for full deflection of galvanometer and G = resistance of galvanometer.

25. A shunt is a low resistance which when connected in parallel to the galvanometer, protects it from the strong current.

26. We can increase the range of given ammeter by using a suitable shunt in parallel with the ammeter but we cannot decrease the range of the ammeter.

27. A loop of current acts as a dipole of magnetic moment $\vec{M} = IA\hat{n}$, where I is strength of current through the loop and A is the area enclosed by loop.

28. Work done in rotating a magnetic dipole in a magnetic field from orientation θ_1 to θ_2 is

$$W = MB (\cos\theta_1 - \cos\theta_2)$$

29. Magnetic field due to magnetic dipole

(*a*) at any point on axial line (P)

$$B = \frac{\mu_0 \cdot 2Mr}{4\pi\left(r^2 - l^2\right)^2}$$

(*b*) at any point on equatorial line

$$B = \frac{\mu_0 M}{4\pi\left(r^2 + l^2\right)^{3/2}}$$

Where M = dipole moment, $2l$ = magnetic length of dipole.

30. When a magnet is suspended freely under the combined action of two uniform magnetic fields of intensities F and H acting at 90° to each other, the magnet comes to rest making an angle θ with the direction of H, such that $F = H \tan\theta$.

31. Elements of earth's magnetic field

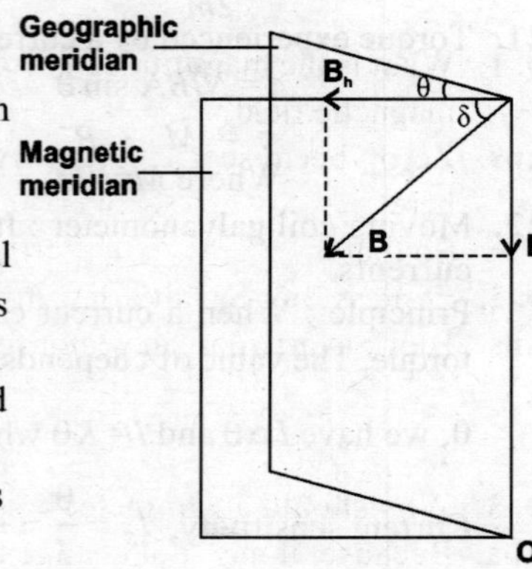

(*a*) Declination (θ)

It is the angle between the magnetic meridian and geographic meridian

(*b*) Inclination (or) Dip (δ)

It is the angle between the direction of total intensity of earth's magnetic field and its horizontal component.

(*c*) Horizontal component of earths magnetic field (B_H)

It is the component of total intensity of earth's magnetic field along the horizontal

$$\tan\delta = \frac{B_v}{B_H}, \quad B = \sqrt{B_v^2 + B_H^2}$$

32. The value of dip at equator is 0° while at poles, it is 90°

33. (*a*) **Intensity of magnetisation**

$$I = \frac{M}{V} = \frac{Magnetic moment}{Volume}$$

$I = \frac{m}{a}$ where m is pole strength

(*b*) **Magnetic induction *B***

$B = \mu_0 (H + I)$

H = strength of the magnetising field

(*c*) **Permeability**

The magnetic permeability of a material may be defined as the ratio of magnetic induction B to the magnetic intensity H

$\mu = B/H$

(*d*) **Magnetic susceptibility** $(\chi_m) = \frac{I}{H}$.

It has no units.

Then, $B = \mu_0$ (H + I)

$\mu_r = 1 + \chi_m$.

34. Hysterisis is the phenomenon of lagging of magnetic induction (B) and intensity of magnetisation (I) behind the magnetic field (H), when a specimen is taken through a cycle of magnetisation.

35. Soft iron is used to make electromagnets, because hysterisis loop for soft iron is narrow. Therefore, energy loss/volume/cycle is small.
36. The magnetic susceptibility of a paramagnetic material varies inversely with temperature.
37. Diamagnetic materials have negative susceptibility.
38. A diamagnetic substance tends to move from stronger parts of magnetic field to weaker parts.

VERY SHORT ANSWER TYPE QUESTIONS

(Carrying 1 mark)

Q. 1. What is the magnitude of force experienced by a stationary charge exposed to a uniform magnetic field?

Ans. Zero, because $F = qvB\sin\theta$

here $v = 0$,

So that $F = 0$

Q. 2. Express Biot-Savart's law in vector form.

Ans. Biot-Savart's law in vector form is:

$$d\vec{B} = \frac{\mu_0}{4\pi}\frac{I(d\vec{l}\times\vec{r})}{r^3}$$

Q. 3. Why should an ammeter have a low resistance?

Ans. Because, it may not change the resistance of the circuit.

Q. 4. What is the magnetic moment associated with a coil of 1 turn, area of cross-section 10^{-4} m^2, carrying a current of 2 A?

Ans. Here, $N = 1$, $I = 2A$ and $A = 10^{-4}$ m^2

We know that $M = NIA = 1 \times 2 \times 10^{-4} = 2 \times 10^{-4}$ Am^2.

Q. 5. A magnetic dipole is situated in the direction of a magnetic field. What is its potential energy? If it is rotated by 180°, then what amount of work will be done?

Ans. We have PE of dipole $= -MB\cos\theta° = -MB$

Work done $= MB(\cos 0° - \cos 180°) = MB(1 + 1) = 2MB$.

Q. 6. Where is the vertical component of earth's magnetic field zero?

Ans. At earth's magnetic equator.

Q. 7. Name the physical quantity whose SI unit is Wbm^{-2}. Is it a scalar or vector quantity?

Ans. Magnetic field $\vec{B}$ is a vector quantity.

Q. 8. Consider Fig. 3.1 where AMB and ANB are semi-circles. What will be the magnetic field at the centre O of the circular loop?

Ans. Zero, because magnetic fields due to AMB and ANB are equal in magnitudes but opposite in directions.

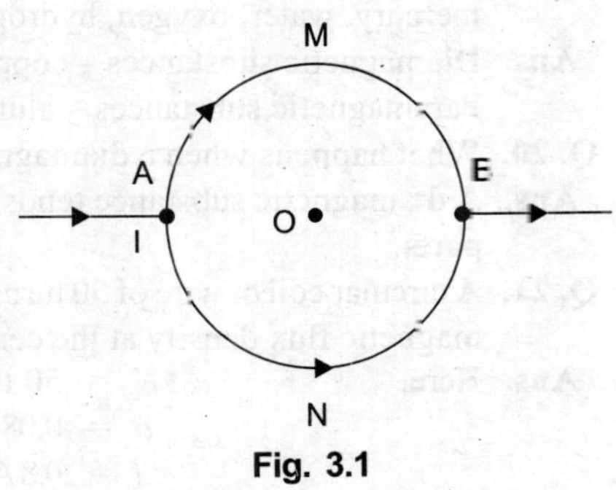

Fig. 3.1

Q. 9. An ammeter and a milliammeter are converted from the same galvanometer. Out of the two, which current measuring instrument has smaller resistance?

Ans. Ammeter has lower resistance than milliammeter as the shunt to be used across galvanometer is of lower resistance for ammeter than that of milliammeter.

Q. 10. What is the basic difference between electric and magnetic fields?

Ans. Electric field is due to a static charge, whereas the magnetic field is due to moving charges. Electric lines of force start at the positive charge and end at the negative charge. Electric lines of force are not continuous but magnetic lines of force are continuous.

Q. 11. Write the SI unit of (*i*) pole strength, (*ii*) magnetic moment of a bar magnet.

Ans. (*i*) NT^{-1} or Am, (*ii*) Am^{-2} or JT^{-1}.

Q. 12. What is the value of the horizontal component of the earth's magnetic field at magnetic poles?

Ans. At magnetic poles, the value of the horizontal component of the earth's magnetic field is zero.

Q. 13. What is the value of dip (*i*) at poles, (*ii*) at equator.

Ans. (*i*) Angle of dip at poles is 90° and
(*ii*) Angle of dip at equator is 0°.

Q. 14. In a certain arrangement, a proton does not get deflected while passing through a magnetic field region. Under what condition is it possible?

Ans. When proton moves parallel or antiparallel to the direction of the magnetic field.

Q. 15. State two factors on which the sensitivity of a moving coil galvanometer depends.

Ans. (*i*) Torsional constant of the suspension wire,
(*ii*) Area of the coil.

Q. 16. Can moving coil galvanometer be used to detect an ac in a circuit? Give reasons.

Ans. A moving coil galvanometer cannot be used to detect an ac in a circuit, since it measures the average value of current and the average value of an ac over a complete cycle is zero.

Q. 17. A charge 4 coulomb is moving with velocity $\vec{v} = (4\hat{i} + 3\hat{j})$ ms^{-1} in a magnetic field $\vec{B} = (\hat{i} + 3\hat{j})$ Wbm^{-2}. Find the force acting on the charge.

Ans. We have,

$$\vec{F} = q(\vec{v} \times \vec{B})$$
$$= 4[(4\hat{i} + 3\hat{j}) \times (\hat{i} + 3\hat{j})]$$
$$= 0 \qquad [\because \text{Cross product of two equal vector is zero}]$$

Q. 18. A long straight wire carries a current of 35A. What is the magnitude of the field $\vec{B}$ at a point 20 cm from the wire?

Ans. Here, $I = 35$ A, $r = 20$ cm $= 20 \times 10^{-2}$ m, $B = ?$

We have,
$$B = \frac{\mu_0 2I}{4\pi r} = 10^{-7} \times \frac{2 \times 35}{20 \times 10^{-2}} = 3.5 \times 10^{-5}\ T.$$

Q. 19. Classify the following into diamagnetic and paramagnetic substances: aluminium, copper, mercury, water, oxygen, hydrogen.

Ans. Diamagnetic substances – copper, water, mercury, hydrogen.
Paramagnetic substances – aluminium, oxygen.

Q. 20. What happens when a diamagnetic substance is placed in a varying magnetic field?

Ans. A diamagnetic substance tends to move from stronger parts of magnetic field to weaker parts.

Q. 21. A circular coil of wire of 50 turns, each of radius 0.08 m, carries a current of 0.8 A. Find the magnetic flux density at the centre of the coil.

Ans. Here, $N = 50$ turns,
$a = 0.08$ m $= 8 \times 10^{-2}$ m,
$I = 0.8$ A

Magnetic flux density is given by:

$$B = \frac{\mu_0}{4\pi}\frac{2\pi NI}{a}$$

$$= 10^{-7} \times 2 \times \frac{22}{7} \times \frac{50\times 0.8}{(8\times 10^{-2})}$$

$$= 3.1 \times 10^{-4} \text{ T.}$$

Q. 22. How will you convert a galvanometer into a voltmeter?

Ans. A galvanometer is converted into a voltmeter by adding a series resistor of high resistance with it.

Q. 23. State the principle of a moving coil galvanometer.

Ans. When a current carrying loop or coil is placed in the uniform magnetic field, it experiences a deflecting torque.

Q. 24. What is the direction of the force acting on a charged particle q, moving with a velocity $\vec{v}$ in a uniform magnetic field $\vec{B}$?

Ans. Direction of the force acting on a charged particle q, with uniform velocity $\vec{v}$ in a uniform magnetic field $\vec{B}$ is perpendicular to both $\vec{v}$ and $\vec{B}$ and is given by the direction of $(\vec{v} \times \vec{B})$.

Q. 25. Which materials have negative value of magnetic susceptibility?

Ans. Diamagnetic materials have negative susceptibility.

SHORT ANSWER TYPE QUESTIONS

(Carrying 3 marks)

Q. 1. Define SI unit of magnetic field. "A charge moving at right angle to a uniform magnetic field does not undergo change in kinetic energy." Why?

Ans. The SI unit of magnetic field ($\vec{B}$) is tesla (T). Magnetic field ($\vec{B}$) is said to be 1 tesla, if a charge (q) of 1C, while moving with a velocity ($\vec{v}$) of 1 ms^{-1} at right angle of the magnetic field ($\vec{B}$), experiences a force ($\vec{F}$) of 1 N.

When a charge is moving at right angle with a uniform magnetic field, no work is done on the charge by the magnetic field because force due to magnetic field acts in a direction perpendicular to motion and behaves as the centripetal force which changes the direction of motion only. Hence, in accordance with work-energy theorem, the KE of the charge remains unchanged.

Q. 2. Why do we not use galvanometer as an ammeter?

Ans. A galvanometer shows a full scale deflection with a very small current. Hence, a galvanometer can measure limited current. Therefore, a galvanometer cannot be used as an ammeter, which can measure the given current.

Q. 3. Write the mathematical form of tangent law in magnetism.

Ans. $F = H \tan\theta$, where F and H are strengths of two magnetic fields acting perpendicular to each other and θ is the angle which a freely suspended magnet makes with the direction of H.

Q. 4. A proton is moving vertically upward when it enters a magnetic field directed towards north. In which direction will the proton be deflected?

Ans. Magnetic Lorentz force on the moving protons is $\vec{F} = q(\vec{v} \times \vec{B})$, force acting on the proton is directed in the direction of $(\vec{v} \times \vec{B})$, *i.e.,* towards the west. So, the proton will be deflected westward.

Q. 5. What is the importance of the radial magnetic field in a moving coil galvanometer?

Ans. Radial magnetic field is always parallel to the plane of the coil. As deflection of the coil is directly proportional to the current flowing through the coil, hence, we can use a linear scale to note the deflection in current.

Q. 6. The coil of a galvanometer has a resistance of 100 Ω. It shows full scale deflection for a current of 5×10^{-4} A. How will you convert it into a voltmeter to read a maximum potential difference of 5 V?

Ans. Here, galvonometer resistance $G = 100\ \Omega$

Current $(I) = 5 \times 10^{-4}$ A, potential difference (V) = 5V.

By connecting a high resistance (R) given by:

$$R = \frac{V}{I_g} - G = \frac{5}{5\times10^{-4}} - 100 = 9900\ \Omega.$$

Q. 7. In what respect does a wire carrying current differ from a wire which carries no current?

Ans. In a wire carrying current, there is continuous flow of electrons through a cross section of wire in a particular direction. A magnetic field is setup around the wire carrying current. In a wire carrying no current, the electrons move at random and the net flow of electrons through a cross section of the wire is zero. No magnetic field is set up around such wire.

Q. 8. An iron bar magnet is heated to 1000°C and then cooled in a magnetic field free space. Will it retain its magnetism?

Ans. Curie temperature of iron is about 770°C. When heated to a very high temperature, magnetism of the iron is further lost. It will not retain its magnetism.

Q. 9. Why does a paramagnetic sample display greater magnification when cooled?

Ans. According to Curie's Law, magnetisation M or susceptibility χ_m of the paramagnetic sample is inversely proportional to its absolute temperature T, *i.e.* $\chi_m \propto \frac{1}{T}$. Thus, with decrease in temperature, the magnetisation of a paramagnetic sample is bound to increase.

Q. 10. A current carrying planar loop suspended in a vertical plane normal to the magnetic meridian is in stable equilibrium. The horizontal component of earth's magnetic field is 0.32 G. Another horizontal magnetic field of magnitude 0.48 G parallel to the plane of the loop is set up along magnetic west to east. Specify the stable equilibrium.

Ans. Here, $B = 0.45\text{G}$ and

$B_H = 0.32\ G$

As per tangent law, $B = B_H \tan\theta$

or $\tan\theta = \frac{B}{B_H} = \frac{0.45}{0.32} = 1.5$

or $\theta = 56.3°$ (north)

Q. 11. What are magnetic elements at a place? Define them.

Ans. They are magnetic declination, magnetic dip and horizontal component of earth's magnetic field. Magnetic declination (θ) at a place is defined as the angle between geographic and magnetic meridians at that place. Magnetic dip (δ) is the angle between direction of total intensity of magnetic field of earth and a horizontal line in the magnetic meridian. The component of total intensity of magnetic field of earth in the horizontal direction in magnetic meridian is called as horizontal component of earth's magnetic field (B_H).

Q. 12. The angle of dip of a location in Southern India is about 18°. Would you expect a greater or lesser dip angle in Britain?

Ans. A greater dip angle is expected in Britain as it is located close to North pole of the earth. Dip angle is about 4 times in Britain than in Southern India.

Q. 13. Three identical specimens of magnetic materials, nickel, antimony and aluminium are kept in a non-uniform magnetic field. Draw the modifications in the field lines in each case. Justify your answer.

Ans. The modifications in field lines are shown in Fig. 3.2. This is because nickel is ferromagnetic, Antimony is diamagnetic and aluminium is paramagnetic.

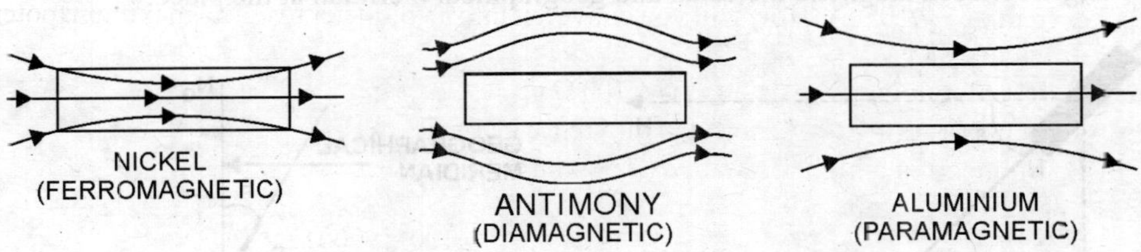

Fig. 3.2

Q. 14. What are the susceptibility and permeability of a perfectly diamagnetic substance?

Ans. For a perfectly diamagnetic substance,

$$B = \mu_0 (H + I) = 0$$

$$\Rightarrow \quad H + I = 0$$

$$\therefore \quad I = -H$$

Therefore,

$$\chi_m = \frac{1}{H} = -1$$

Also,

$$\mu_r = 1 + \chi_m = 1 - 1 = 0$$

$$\therefore \quad \mu = \mu_0 \mu_r = 0$$

Q. 15. Find the expression for the torque acting on a bar magnet, i.e., magnetic dipole placed in a uniform magnetic field.

Ans. Let us consider a bar magnet NS of magnetic charge q_m and length $2l$ is placed at angle θ from a uniform magnetic field ($\vec{B}$). The force on the North pole is $q_m . B$ in an opposite direction. Thus, the net force on the magnetic dipole is zero. But these two forces, being equally unlike and non-linear, constitute a couple, whose torque will be $\tau = (q_m . B)(AN) = (q_m . B)(2l \sin\theta) = mB \sin\theta$ and in vector form.

$$\vec{\tau} = \vec{m} \times \vec{B}.$$

Where $m = q_m \; 2l$ is the magnetic moment (dipole moment)

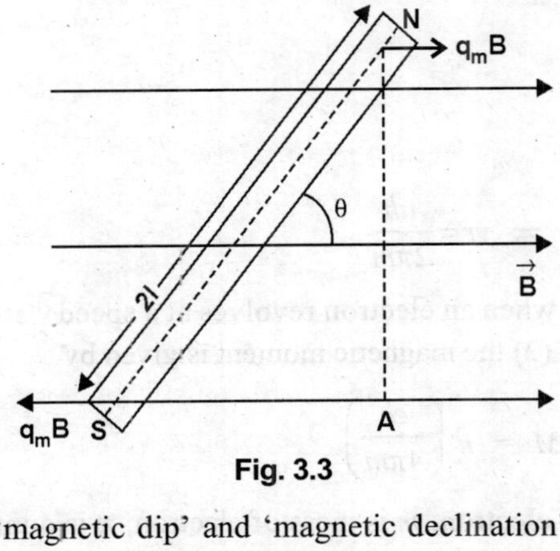

Fig. 3.3

Q. 16. Define the terms 'magnetic dip' and 'magnetic declination' with the help of relevant diagrams.

Ans. Magnetic Dip (δ): Magnetic dip (δ) at a place is defined as the angle which the direction of total strength of earth's magnetic field $\vec{B}_E$ makes with a horizontal line in magnetic meridian.

Magnetic Declination (θ): Magnetic declination (θ) at a place is defined as the smaller angle between magnetic meridian and geographical meridian at the place.

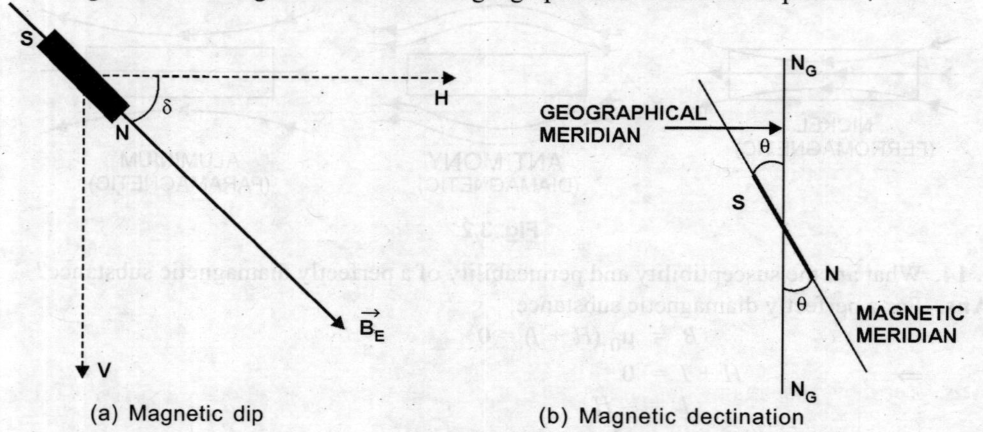

Fig. 3.4

Q. 17. Define the term magnetic dipole moment of a current loop. Write an expression for the magnetic moment when an electron revolves at a speed v around an orbit of radius *r* in hydrogen atom.

Ans. A current carrying loop behaves as a system of two equal and opposite magnetic poles separated by a distance. Hence, it behaves as a magnetic dipole. Magnetic dipole moment of current loop is the product of current *I* and area *A* enclosed by the loop of the current *i.e.,*

$$M = IA = \frac{e}{T}.\pi r^2$$

where $\quad T = \text{time period} = \frac{2\pi}{\omega} = \frac{2\pi r}{v}$

$$M = \frac{ev}{2\pi r}.\pi r^2$$

$$= \frac{evr}{2} \qquad \text{...(i)}$$

$$mvr = \frac{nh}{2\pi} \Rightarrow vr = \frac{nh}{2\pi m} \qquad \text{...(ii)}$$

In a hydrogen atom, when an electron revolves at a speed v around an orbit of radius *r*, we have from (i) and (2) the magnetic moment is given by

$$M = n\left(\frac{eh}{4\pi m}\right)$$

where *e* is charge on electron, *m* is mass of electron, *n* is number of orbit and *h* is the Planck's constant.

Q. 18. A steady current flows in the network shown in Fig. 3.5 made of uniform wire. What will be the magnetic field at the centre of the network?

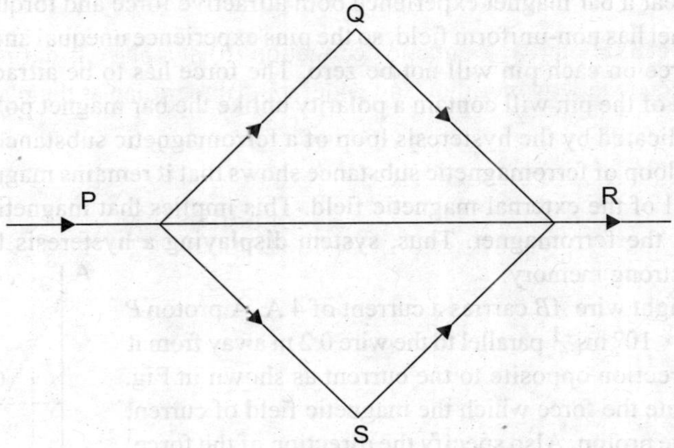

Fig. 3.5

Ans. Zero, because magnetic field at the centre of the network is equal and opposite due to the opposite arms of the network.

Q. 19. If a compass is taken to magnetic North Pole of earth, what will be the direction of the needle?

Ans. Earth's magnetic field at the poles is exactly vertical. A compass needle freely works in horizontal plane. The needle will not necessarily rest along North-South direction at the pole of earth. It may rest in any direction.

Q. 20. A loop of area 10^{-3} m^2 carries a clockwise current of 10A. What is the magnitude and direction of the magnetic moment of the current loop?

Ans. The relation between magnetic moment (m) of a current loop (I),

$$m = IA$$

Here, area (A) = 10^{-3} m^2, current (I) = 10A

$\therefore$ $m = 10 \times 10^{-3} = 10^{-2}$ Am^2

Applying RHS moment rule, the curl of fingers in the clockwise direction gives the magnetic moment in the direction of thumb *i.e.,* downward.

Thus, direction of $\vec{m}$ is away from the observer and perpendicular to plane of the loop.

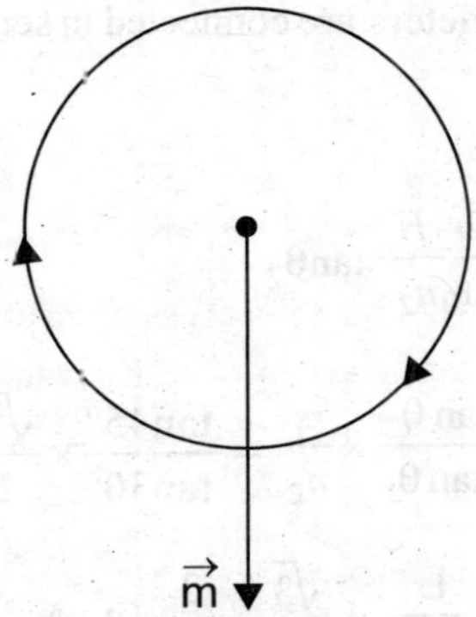

Fig. 3.6.

HIGHER ORDER THINKING SKILLS (HOTS)

Q. 1. Iron pins near a bar magnet experience both attractive force and torque. Why?

Ans. A bar magnet has non-uniform field, so the pins experience unequal and opposite forces. The net force on each pin will not be zero. The force has to be attractive because the nearest end of the pin will contain a polarity unlike the bar magnet pole.

Q. 2. What is indicated by the hysteresis loop of a ferromagnetic substance?

Ans. Hysteresis loop of ferromagnetic substance shows that it remains magnetised even after the removal of the external magnetic field. This implies that magnetism is stored as a memory in the ferromagnet. Thus, system displaying a hysteresis loop can act as a device for strong memory.

Q. 3. A long straight wire AB carries a current of 4 A. A proton P travels at 4×10^6 ms^{-1} parallel to the wire 0.2 m away from it and in a direction opposite to the current as shown in Fig. 3.7. Calculate the force which the magnetic field of current exerts on the proton. Also specify the direction of the force.

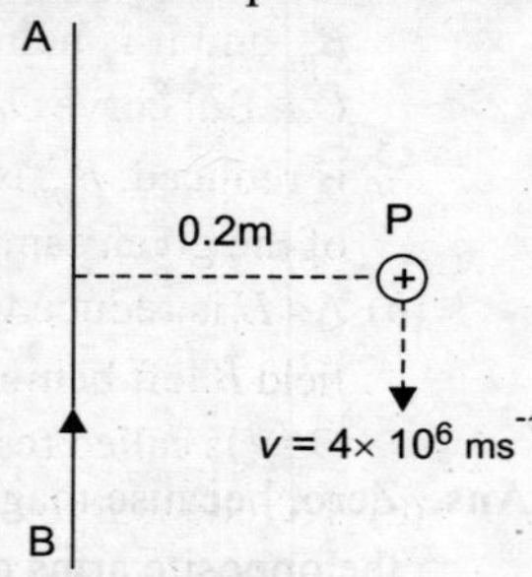

Fig. 3.7

Ans. Here, $I = 4$ A, $v = 4 \times 10^6$ ms^{-1} and $r = 0.2$ m.

Now, magnetic field induction at P is

$$B = \frac{\mu_0}{4\pi} \cdot \frac{2I}{r} = \frac{10^{-7} \times 2 \times 4}{0.2} = 4 \times 10^{-6} \text{ T}$$

The direction of $\vec{B}$, according to Right Hand Thumb Rule is perpendicular to the plane of paper directed inwards.

Since proton (p) is moving parallel to the current carrying straight wire, proton is moving perpendicular to the direction of magnetic field. The force (F) on moving proton of charge (q) due to magnetic field is $F = qvB \sin\theta = (1.6 \times 10^{-19}) \times (4 \times 10^6) \times 4 \times 10^{-6} \sin 90°$.

$= 2.56 \times 10^{-18}$ N

$\therefore$ The direction of force of proton, according to Flemming's Left Hand Rule acts in the plane of proton towards.

Q. 4. Two tangent galvanometers having number of turns in the ratio $\sqrt{3} : 2$ are connected in series to a *dc* source. If the mean deflections of the two tangent galvanometers are 30° and 45° respectively, calculate the ratio of radii of the coils of the tangent galvanometers.

Ans. Here $\frac{n_1}{n_2} = \frac{\sqrt{3}}{2}$, $\theta_1 = 30°$ and $\theta_2 = 45°$, $\frac{r_1}{r_2} = ?$

As the two tangent galvanometers are connected in series, current flowing through each is the same *i.e.,*

$$I_1 = I_2$$

or
$$\frac{2r_1H}{\mu_0 n_1} \tan\theta_1 = \frac{2r_2H}{\mu_0 n_2} \tan\theta_2$$

or
$$\frac{r_1}{r_2} = \frac{\tan\theta_2}{\tan\theta_1} \times \frac{n_1}{n_2} = \frac{\tan 45°}{\tan 30°} \times \frac{\sqrt{3}}{2}$$

$$= \frac{1}{1/\sqrt{3}} \times \frac{\sqrt{3}}{2} = \frac{3}{2} = 3:2.$$

Q. 5. Explain the phenomenon of hysteresis in magnetic materials.

Ans. A complete cycle of magnetisation (*i.e.*, graph between magnetisation of the sample B and magnetising intensity-H) for a given ferromagnetic material (say steel) is being shown in Fig. 3.8. With the help of the graph, we draw following conclusions:

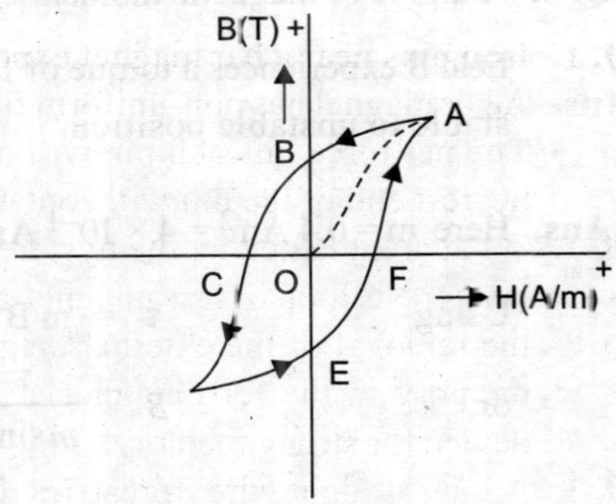

Fig. 3.8

(*a*) Initially, as H is raised from its zero (0) value, B also rises from zero (0) to a saturation value B_m and it is being represented by the curve OA. But curve OA does not retrace itself as H is reduced. B_m is called magnetic saturation of the given sample.

(*b*) As H is reduced, the curve goes along AB. Point B indicates the value of magnetic field B left behind even when H is reduced to zero. This value of field B_r (given by OB) is called residual magnetism or retentively.

(*c*) To reduce B to O, we have to increase value of H in the reverse direction. In Fig. 3.8, point C represents the state of $B = 0$. Value of H corresponding to point C *i.e.*, H_c is known as coercive force or coercivity.

(*d*) No segment OA, AB, BC, ..., etc. of the curve is linear. It means B is not directly proportional to H over any appreciable range.

(*e*) Lagging behind of B as compared to H is known as the hysteresis and the magnetisation cycle curve is known as hysteresis curve.

(*f*) The area within the B-H loop represents the energy dissipated per unit volume per cycle in the material.

Q. 6. A test charge having 1.6×10^{-19} C is moving with a velocity $\vec{v} = (2\hat{i} + 3\hat{j})\,ms^{-1}$ in a magnetic field $\vec{B} = (2\hat{i} + 3\hat{j})$ Wbm^{-2}. Determine the magnitude and direction of the force acting on the test charge.

Ans. Here, $q = 1.6 \times 10^{-19}$ C, $\vec{v} = (2\hat{i} + 3\hat{j})\,ms^{-1}$, $\vec{B} = (2\hat{i} + 3\hat{j})$ Wbm^{-2}

We have,
$$\vec{F} = q(\vec{v} \times \vec{B})$$
$$= 1.6 \times 10^{-19}\{(2\hat{i} + 3\hat{j}) \times (2\hat{i} + 3\hat{j})\}$$
$$= 1.6 \times 10^{-19}\{4(\hat{i} \times \hat{i}) + 6(\hat{i} \times \hat{j}) + 6(\hat{j} \times \hat{i}) + 9(\hat{j} \times \hat{j})\}$$

Since, $\hat{i} \times \hat{i} = \hat{j} \times \hat{j} = 0$, $\quad \hat{i} \times \hat{j} = \hat{k}$ and $\hat{j} \times \hat{i} = -\hat{k}$

$$\therefore \quad \vec{F} = 1.6 \times 10^{-19}(0 + 6\hat{k} - 6\hat{k} + 0) = 0$$

Q. 7. Earth's magnetic field does not affect the working of a moving coil galvanometer. Explain.

Ans. Since earth's magnetic field is very weak as compared to the radial magnetic field produced by the cylindrical pole pieces of the magnet, so earth's magnetic field does not affect the working of a moving coil galvanometer.

Q. 8. A dipole of magnetic moment 0.4 Am^2 is placed with its axis $\frac{\pi}{6}$ radian with an external field B experiences a torque of 1.6×10^{-2} Nm. Find $\vec{F}$ and work done in moving it from stable to unstable position.

Ans. Here $m = 0.4\ Am^2 = 4 \times 10^{-1}\ Am^2$, $\tau = 1.6 \times 10^{-2}$ Nm and $\theta = \frac{\pi}{6}$ radian

Using $\tau = m B \sin\theta$

or $B = \frac{\tau}{m \sin\theta}$

$$B = \frac{(1.6 \times 10^{-2})}{(4 \times 10^{-1})(\sin 30°)} = 0.08\ T$$

We have $W = -mB(\cos\theta_2 - \cos\theta_1)$, where $\theta_2 = 180°$ and $\theta_1 = 0$

$$W = -mB(-1-1) = 2\ mB$$
$$= 2 \times 0.4 \times 0.08 = 0.064\ J$$

❑❑❑

UNIT 4

ELECTROMAGNETIC INDUCTION AND ALTERNATING CURRENT

Important Points to Remember

1. Electromagnetic induction is the phenomenon of the production of *emf* (or current) in a circuit whenever the magnetic flux linked with the circuit changes. In other words, electromagnetic induction is the phenomenon in which electric current is generated in a circuit by varying magnetic field in that region.

2. The magnetic flux linked with a surface held in magnetic field is defined as the total number of magnetic field lines crossing the surface. Mathematically, magnetic flux linked with a surface $\phi_B = \vec{B}.\vec{s} = \int \vec{B}\hat{n}ds = \int B\cos\theta\, ds.$

3. Magnetic flux is a scalar quantity. SI unit of the magnetic flux is weber (*Wb*). Its dimensional formula is $ML^2\ T^{-2}\ A^{-1}$.

4. Faraday's laws of induction states that the magnitude of the induced e.m.f in a circuit is equal to the time rate of change of magnitude flux through the circuit.

$$\varepsilon = -\frac{d\Phi_B}{dt}$$

5. For a coil of *N*-times of same cross-sectional area, we have $\in = -N\frac{d\phi_B}{dt} = -\frac{d}{dt}(N\phi_E)$.

6. If an electrical circuit is complete, an induced current flows in the circuit on account of the induced *emf*. Magnitude of induced current is given by $I = \frac{\in}{R} = \frac{\phi_2 - \phi_1}{Rt} = \frac{N}{R}\cdot\frac{d\phi_B}{dt}$.

7. Lenz's law gives the direction of induced *emf*/current. According to Lenz's law, the polarity of the induced *emf* is such that it tends to produce a current which opposes the change in magnetic flux that produces it.

8. Lenz law obeys the principle of energy conservation.

9. The induced e.m.f can be produced by changing the (*i*) magnitude of *B* (*ii*) area *A* (*iii*) angle θ between the direction of *B* and normal to the surface area *A*.

10. When a metal rod of length *l* is placed normal to a uniform magnetic field *B* and moved with a velocity *v* perpendicular to the field, the induced e.m.f is called motional e.m.f produced across the ends of the rod which is given by $\varepsilon = Blv$.

11. Changing magnetic fields can setup current loops in nearby metal bodies (any conductor). Such currents are called eddy currents. They dissipate energy as heat which can be minimized by laminating the conductor.

12. Eddy currents cause electromagnetic damping which may be used in (*i*) electric brake system (*ii*) induction furnace (*iii*) speedometer (*iv*) electromagnetic shielding (*v*) moving coil galvonometer to make it dead beat (*iv*) *ac* induction motor, etc.

13. With the change in the magnetic flux, induced *emf* is a must, but induced current will appear only when the circuit is closed.

14. Inductance is the ratio of the flux linkage to current.

15. Self-induction is the phenomenon according to which an opposing *emf* is produced in a coil, as a result of change in current flowing through it. Self-induction is also referred to as the electrical inertia.

16. The coefficient of self-induction or self-inductance (L) of a coil is numerically equal to the magnetic flux linked with the coil, when a unit current flows through it.

17. The value of induced *emf* due to self-induction phenomenon is given by $\epsilon = -L\frac{dI}{dt}$.

18. The self-inductance of an air core long solenoid is given by $L = \frac{\mu_0 N^2 A}{l} = \mu_0 n^2 lA$ where $n = \frac{N}{l}$. For an iron core solenoid, $L = \mu_0\mu_r \frac{N^2 A}{l} = \mu_0\mu_r n^2 lA$.

19. A changing current in a coil can induce an e.m.f in a nearby coil. This relation, $\varepsilon = -M_{12}\frac{di_2}{dt}$, shows that Mutual inductance of coil 1 with respect to coil 2 (M_{12}) is due to change of current in coil 2. ($M_{12} = M_{21}$).

20. The mutual inductance of two co-axial coils is given by $M_{12} = M_{21} = \mu_0\, n_1 n_2 Al$ where n_1 and n_2 are the number of turns per unit length of coils 1 and 2. A is the area of cross-section and l is the length of the solenoids.

21. Energy stored in an inductor in the form of magnetic field is $U_n = \frac{1}{2}Li_{\max}{}^2$ and Magnetic energy density $U_B = \frac{B^2}{2\mu_0}$.

22. In a generator, mechanical energy of rotation of an armature coil is being transformed into electrical energy. It is, thus, only a converter rather than a generator.

23. A *dc* motor converts direct current energy from a battery into mechanical energy of rotation. It is based on the fact that when a coil carrying current is held in a magnetic field, it experiences a torque, which rotates the coil. The efficiency of *dc* motor is $\eta = \frac{E}{V} = \frac{\text{backemf}}{\text{emfofbattery}}$. The efficiency becomes maximum when $E = \frac{V}{2}$. A motor starter is variable resistance, which protects the motor from damage when it is switched on.

24. An alternating voltage $\varepsilon = \varepsilon_0 \sin \omega t$, applied to a resistor R drives a current $I = I_0 \sin \omega t$ in the resistor, $I_0 = \varepsilon_0 / R$ where ε_0 and I_0 are the peak values of voltage and current. (also represented by V_m and I_m)

25. The average value of *ac* over a complete cycle is zero.

26. The root mean square value of a.c. may be defined as that value of steady current which would generate the same amount of heat in a given resistance in a given time as is done by the a.c. when passed through the same resistance during the same time.

$$I_{rms} = I_0 / \sqrt{2} = 0.707 i_0$$

Similarly, $v_{rms} = v_0 / \sqrt{2} = 0.707\, v_0$

27. (i) For an a.c. $\varepsilon = \varepsilon_m \sin \omega t$ applied to a resistor, current and voltage are in phase.

(ii) In case of an a.c. circuit having pure inductance current lags behind e.m.f by a phase angle 90°. The resistance offered by inductance in the flow of a.c. is non-ohmic. Here, $X_L = \omega L$ and is called inductive reactance.

(iii) In case of an a.c. circuit having pure capacitance, current leads e.m.f by a phase angle of 90° and $X_C = 1/\omega C$ is called capacitive reactance.

28. Average power loss over a complete cycle in an LCR circuit is

$$P = \varepsilon_{rms} I_{rms} \cos\Phi$$

- $\cos\phi$ is called the power factor. Its value depends upon the nature of circuit
- In a purely resistive circuit $\Phi = 0$; $P = V_{rms} I_{rms}$
- In a purely inductive circuit $\Phi = \frac{\pi}{2}$; $P = 0$.
- In a purely capacitive circuit $\Phi = \frac{\pi}{2}$; $P = 0$

29. In an LCR circuit, the circuit admits maximum current if $X_C = X_L$, so that $Z = R$ and resonant frequency $\omega_r = \frac{1}{\sqrt{LC}}$ and $v_R = \frac{1}{2\pi\sqrt{LC}}$

30. Q factor of series resonant circuit is defined as the ratio of voltage developed across the inductance or capacitance at resonance to the applied voltage across 'R',

$$Q = \frac{\omega_r L}{R} \text{ or } \frac{1}{\omega_r CR} \text{ also } Q = \frac{w_r}{2\Delta\omega} \text{ where } 2\Delta\omega \text{ is bandwidth.}$$

31. A transformer is a device to increase or decrease the alternating voltage (or current)

32. When alternating current flows through the coil of a transformer, its core gets magnetised and demagnetised repeatedly. The energy spent in magnetising the core is not returned fully in demagnetisation. This energy left in the core appears in the form of heat

33. Electrical energy is transferred from primary coil to the secondary coil on account of mutual induction.

34. For a transformer, $\frac{E_s}{E_p} = \frac{N_s}{N_p} = \frac{i_p}{i_s} = K$

In an ideal transformer, $\varepsilon_p I_p = \varepsilon_s I_s$ i.e.

If $N_s > N_p$; $\varepsilon_s > \varepsilon_p$ and $I_s < I_p$ — step up, transformer

If $N_p > N_s$; $\varepsilon_p > \varepsilon_s$ and $I_p < I_s$ — step down, transformer

35. Primary coil in a step down transformer has larger number of turns.

36. The transformer core is laminated to minimise loss of energy due to eddy currents. By doing so, the magnitude to eddy currents is reduced considerably and, hence, the energy loss is minimised.

37. Iron loss is loss of energy in the form of heat in the iron core of a transformer.

VERY SHORT ANSWER TYPE QUESTIONS

(Carrying 1 mark)

Q. 1. Two concentric circular coils lie in perpendicular planes. If current is passed and increased in one coil, will this induce a current in the second coil?

Ans. No, the field due to current in the first coil will be parallel to the plane of second coil so that $\theta = 90°$ and flux will not change.

Q. 2. A vertical pole falls down through the plane of magnetic meridian, will any e.m.f. be induced between its ends?

Ans. No, the falling pole neither intercepts vertical component nor the horizontal component of Earth's magnetic field.

Q. 3. A wheel having N spokes is rotated in the plane of paper with certain angular velocity W. A uniform magnetic field exists in the region perpendicular to plane of paper. The emf induced between the axle and the rim of the wheel is ε. If the number of spokes is increased to $2N$, what will be the value of new induced emf.

Ans. It will remain ε. The number of spokes does not affect the emf.

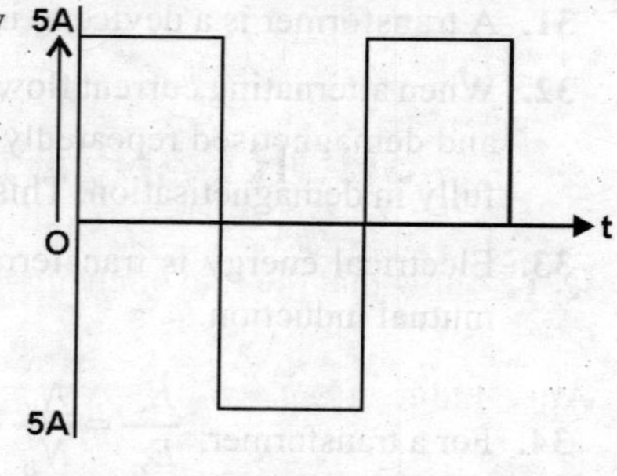

Q. 4. Find the RMS value of A.C. shown in the fig.

Ans. Peak value = $5A$

$$\text{RMS value} = \frac{I_0}{\sqrt{2}} = \frac{5}{\sqrt{2}} = 3.57A$$

Q. 5. An alternating current having a peak value of 1.4 A is used to heat a wire. What value of steady current will produce the same heating effect in the same time interval.

Ans. $$I_{rms}{}^2 Rt = I^2 R t$$

or $$I = I_{rms} = \frac{I_0}{\sqrt{2}} = \frac{1.4}{\sqrt{2}} = 1.0A$$

Q. 6. Induced current is not obtained even though induced emf is there, how?

Ans. Induced current is possible only when there is some portion of the closed path outside the field.

Q. 7. What type of current flows through a choke coil connected in a.c. circuit?

Ans. The ohmic resistance of choke coil is zero. Hence there will be no power loss. The current will be wattless.

Q. 8. The frequency of a *LCR* circuit is doubled. What will be the effect on the values of resistance (R), inductive reactance (X_L) and capacitive reactance (X_C).

Ans. R is independent of frequency, hence no effect.

$X_L = WL$, so X_L will be doubled

$X_C = \frac{1}{WC}$, So X_C will be halved

Q. 9. Can peak voltage across an inductor be greater than the peak value supplied.

Ans. It is possible. At the time of break of a circuit, a large back emf set up in the inductor.

Q. 10. What is the value of power factor in the condition of resonance in LCR circuit?

Ans. Power factor $\cos\phi = \frac{R}{\sqrt{R^2 + (X_L - X_C)^2}}$.

In the condition of resonance $X_L = X_C$, $\cos\phi = 1$

Q. 11. The turn ratio of an ideal transformer is 10. What is the output voltage if the input voltage is 5V.

Ans. $\frac{N_s}{N_p} = \frac{V_s}{V_p} \Rightarrow V_s = 5 \times 10 = 50V$

Q. 12. In the condition of resonance for series LCR circuit, which of the voltage across inductance (V_L) and voltage across capacitance (V_C) is greater than the applied voltage?

Ans. At resonance $X_L = X_C \Rightarrow iX_L = iX_C \Rightarrow V_L = V_C$

Also both V_L and V_C are greater than applied voltage.

SHORT ANSWER TYPE QUESTIONS (SA-I)

(Carrying 2 marks)

Q. 1. Show that the rate of change of magnetic flux has the same units as induced *emf.*

Ans. Induced *emf*, $e = V = \frac{work}{charge} = \frac{[ML^2T^{-2}]}{[AT]} = [ML^2T^{-3}A^{-1}]$

Rate of change of magnetic flux $= \frac{d\phi}{dt} = \frac{BA}{t}$ $\quad [\because F = Bqv]$

$$= \frac{FA}{qvt} = \frac{[MLT^{-2}][L^2]}{[AT][LT^{-1}][T]}$$

Both have the same units/dimensions = $[M^1L^2T^{-3}A^{-1}]$

Q. 2. State the condition under which the phenomenon of resonance occurs in a series *LCR* circuit. Plot a graph showing the variation of current with frequency of an *a.c.* source in a series of *LCR* circuit.

Ans. In a series *LCR* circuit, resonance occurs when $X_L = X_C$. Fig. 4.1 shows the variation of current with frequency of an *a.c.* source.

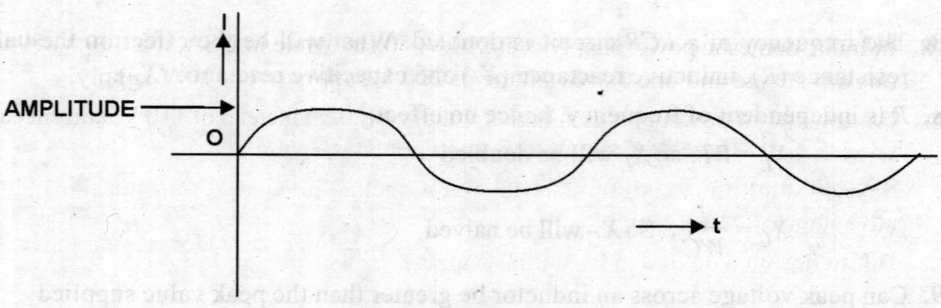

Fig. 4.1

Q. 3. What is the power dissipation in an *a.c.* circuit in which voltage and current are given by

$V = 300 \sin (wt + \frac{\pi}{2})$ and $I = 5 \sin wt$?

Ans. As the phase difference between voltage and current is $\frac{\pi}{2}$, therefore, power dissipation is zero.

Q. 4. A capacitor allows *a.c.* to pass through. Why?

Ans. The capacitative reactance is given by

$$X_c = \frac{1}{wC} = \frac{1}{2\pi \upsilon C}$$

For a.c., $\nu \neq 0 \quad \therefore \quad X_C \neq \infty$

Hence, a condenser does not block *a.c.*

Q. 5. A coil *B* is connected to low voltage bulb and placed near another coil *A* as shown in Fig. 4.2. Explain the following observations:

(*i*) The bulb lights; (*ii*) The bulb gets dimmer if the coil *B* is moved upwards.

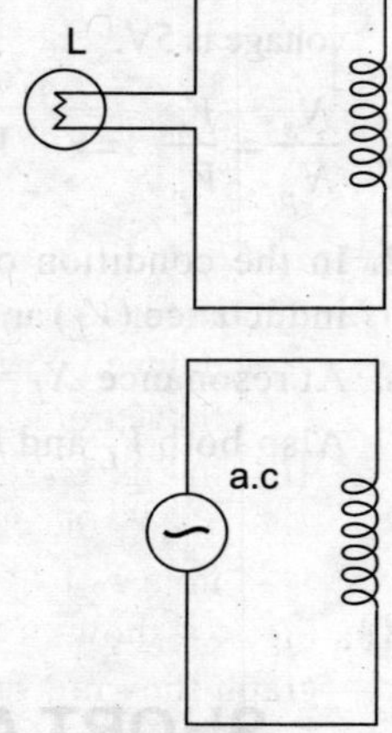

Fig. 4.2

Ans. (*i*) The bulb lights because of mutual induction.

(*ii*) When coil *B* is moved upwards, flux linking with it decreases. Hence, induced *emf* decreases the current and the bulb connected to it gets dimmer.

Q. 6. Find *emf* generated when a coil of 1000 turns to area 0.1 m² rotating with a speed of 1 revolution per 2 seconds in a uniform magnetic field of 1×10^{-2} T.

Ans. Here,

$$N = 1000, B = 1 \times 10^{-2} \text{ T}, A = 0.1 = 1 \times 10^{-2} \text{ m}^2$$

$$\nu = \frac{1}{2} \text{ Hz}$$

Using

$$\in = NBA\omega$$

$$\Rightarrow 1000 \times 10^{-2} \times 10^{-1} \left(2 \times \frac{22}{7} \times \frac{1}{2}\right) \quad (\because \omega = 2\pi\upsilon)$$

$$\therefore \quad \in = 3.14 \text{ V}$$

Q. 7. In an *a.c.* circuit, there is no power dissipation in an ideal inductor. Explain.

Ans. Average power/cycle in an *a.c.* circuit is

$$P = E_v I_v \cos \phi \text{ where } \phi = \text{power factor}$$

An ideal inductor, which has no ohmic resistance, phase angle $\phi = 90°$

$$\therefore \quad P = E_v I_v \cos 90°$$

$$P = 0$$

Q. 8. In India, domestic power supply is at 220 V, 50 Hz, while in USA, it is 110 V, 50 Hz. Give one advantage and one disadvantage of 220 V supply over 110 V supply.

Ans. For transfer of power ($V \times I$) at higher voltage (220 V) instead of 110 V, current carried by wires is half. Therefore, such series need not be very thick.

Saving lot of transmission material and reducing the cost of transmission. This is one advantage of 220 V supply.

But to design a device of particular wattage,

$$P = \frac{V^2}{R}, \text{ as } V^2 \text{ is 4 times, } R \text{ must be four times.}$$

Therefore, dissipation of power in the form of heat will be larger on 220 V supply. This is one disadvantage of 220 V supply.

Q. 9. Predict the direction of induced current in resistance R in Figs. 4.3 (*i*) and 4.3 (*ii*) given below. Give reason for answer.

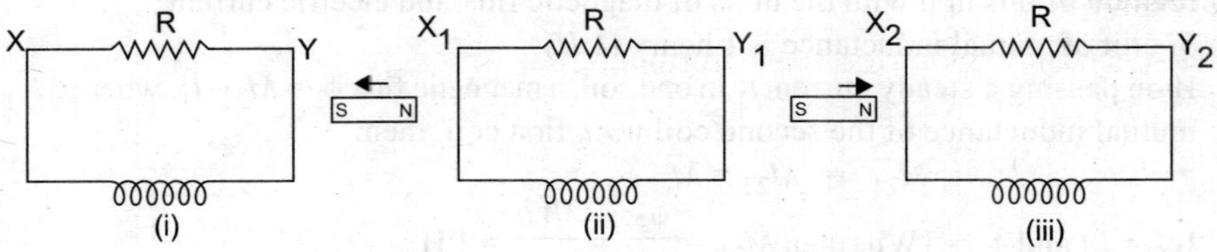

Fig. 4.3

Ans. (*i*) In Fig. 4.3 (*i*), in accordance with Lentz law, *S*-pole develops at *Y* and, hence, the induced current flows clockwise. Therefore, in resistance *R*, the induced current flows from *X* to *Y*.

(*ii*) In Fig. 4.3 (*ii*), *N*-pole develops both at Y_1 and at X_2. Consequently, in the first coil X_1, Y_1 the current flows from X_1 to Y_1 in the resistance *R* and in the second coil, from Y_2 to X_2 in the resistance *R*.

Q. 10. Fig. 4.4 shows a bar magnet *M* falling under gravity through an air cored coil *C*. Plot a graph showing variation of induced *emf* (*E*) with time (*t*). What does the area enclosed by the *E*-*t* curve depict?

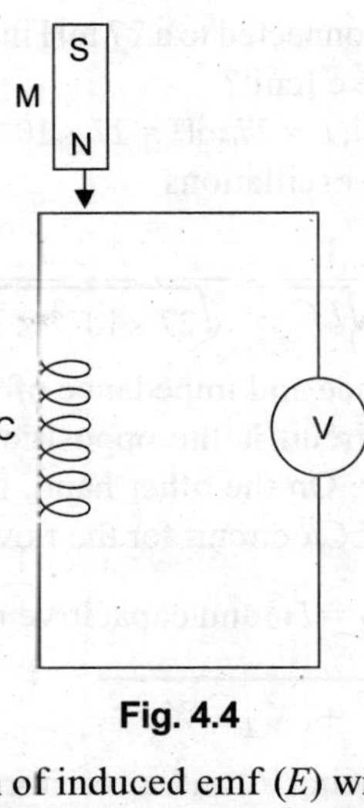

Fig. 4.4

Ans. The graph showing variation of induced emf (*E*) with time (*t*) is given in Fig. 4.5 below. The area enclosed by the *E*-*t* curve depicts the total change in magnetic flux linked with the coil during the time.

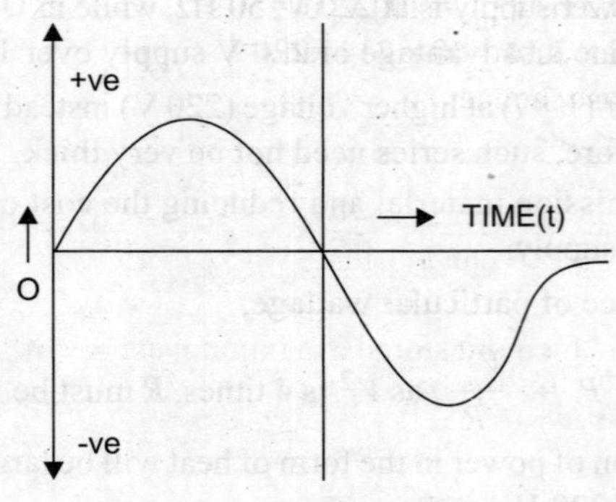

Fig. 4.5

Q. 11. Name and define the unit used for measuring coefficient of mutual inductance. State the relation of this unit with the units of magnetic flux and electric current.

Ans. *SI* unit of mutual inductance is 1 henry (1 *H*).

If on passing a steady current I_1 in one coil, a magnetic flux $\phi_2 = M_{21}.I_1$, where M_{21} is the mutual inductance of the second coil *w.r.t.* first coil, then:

$$M_{21} = M_{21} = M$$

If $I_1 = IA$ and $\phi_2 = 1\text{Wb}$, then $M_{21} = \dfrac{\phi_2}{I_1} = \dfrac{1Wb}{1A} = 1\text{ H}.$

Hence, mutual inductance of a given pair of coils is said to be 1 H, when on passing a steady current of 1 A in one coil, a magnetic flux of 1 Wb is linked with the other coil.

Q. 12. A coil has an inductance of 0.03 H. Determine the *emf* induced if the current in it charges at the rate of 150 As^{-1}.

Ans. Here, $L = 0.03$ H and $\dfrac{dI}{dt} = 150\ As^{-1}$

∴ Induced *emf*

$$|\epsilon| = L\frac{dI}{dt} = 0.03 \times 150 = 4.5\text{ V}..$$

Q. 13. A charge 30 µF capacitor is connected to a 27 mH inductor. What is the angular frequency of the free oscillations of the circuit?

Ans. Here, $C = 30\ \mu F = 30 \times 10^{-6}$ F, $L = 27$ mH $= 27 \times 10^{-3}$ H

∴ Angular frequency of free oscillations

$$\omega_0 = \frac{1}{\sqrt{LC}} = \frac{1}{\sqrt{27\times10^{-3}\times30\times10^{-6}}} = 1.11 \times 10^3\ s^{-1}$$

Q. 14. Distinguish between reactance and impedance of an *ac* circuit.

Ans. (*i*) Reactance in an *a.c.* circuit is the opposition offered to the flow of *a.c.* by an inductor or a capacitor. On the other hand, impedance of *a.c.* circuit is the total opposition offered by *LCR* circuit for the flow of *a.c.* through it.

(*ii*) Inductive reactance, $X_L = L\omega$ and capacitive reactance $X_C = \dfrac{1}{C\omega}$, but impedance,

$$Z = \sqrt{R^2 + (X_L - X_C)^2}$$

Q. 15. An inductor 200 mH, a capacitor *C* and a resistor 10Ω are connected in series with a 100 V, 50 s^{-1} *a.c.* source. If the current and voltage are in phase with each other, calculate the capacitance of the capacitor.

Ans. Here, $L = 200$ mH $= 0.2$ H, $V_{rms} = 100$ V, $\upsilon = 50\ s^{-1}$

We have $\omega = 2\pi\upsilon = 2 \times 3.14 \times 50 = 314$ rad s^{-1}

As V and I are in phase, hence

$$X_L = X_C$$

$$\Rightarrow \quad C = \frac{1}{L\omega^2} = \frac{1}{0.2 \times (314)^2} = 5.07 \times 10^{-5}\ F$$

$$= 50.7\ \mu F$$

Q. 16. A 1.5 mH inductor in LC circuit stored a maximum energy of 17 µJ. Find the peak current.

Ans. Here $L = 1.5$ mH $= 1.5 \times 10^{-3}$ H, $E_0 = 17\mu F = 17 \times 10^{-6}$ J and $I_0 = ?$

Using
$$E_0 = \frac{1}{2} L I_0^2$$

$$I_0 = \sqrt{\frac{2E_0}{L}} = \sqrt{\frac{2 \times 17 \times 10^{-6}}{1.5 \times 10^{-3}}}$$

$$= \sqrt{\frac{34}{15} \times 10^{-2}} = 0.15\ \mathbf{A}$$

Q. 17. Sketch a graph showing the variations of reactance of a capacitor with the frequency of applied voltage.

Ans.

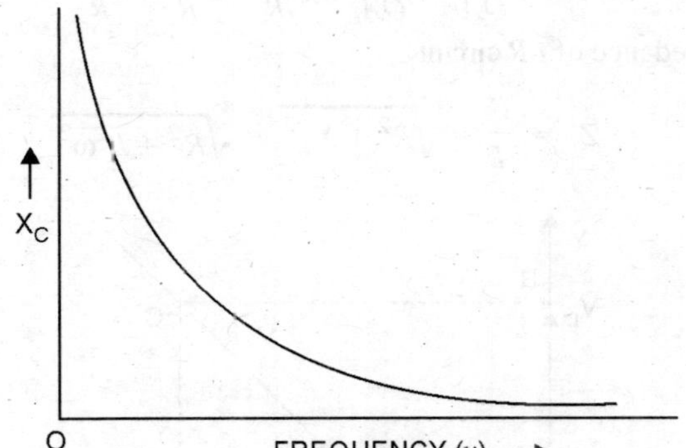

Fig. 4.6

Q. 18. Define copper loss in a transformer.

Ans. When current flows through the primary and secondary coils made of copper (Cu) of the transformer, power loss (I^2R) due to the resistance (R) of the copper wires takes place. This loss is known as copper loss.

Q. 19. Derive an expression for the impedance of an a.c. circuit consisting of an inductor and a resistor.

Ans. Let us consider a source of alternating *emf* applied across a series combination of an inductor of inductance L and a resistor of resistance R as shown in Fig. 4.7. As L and R are in series, same current I flows in them. Let V_L, V_R and V represent the magnitudes of instantaneous values of voltage across the inductance, resistance and the source. Then, from phaser diagram:

$V_R = IR$ in same phase as that of I and

$V_L = IX_L$ ahead in phase $\frac{\pi}{2}$ as compared to I.

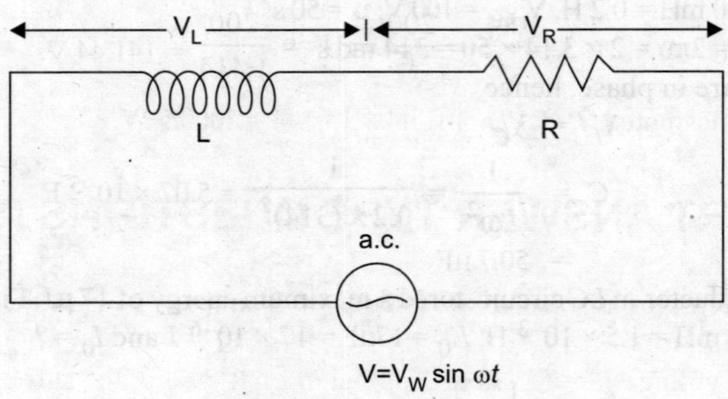

Fig. 4.7

In phase diagram, V_R and V_L are being represented by OA and OB respectively.

Then, $$V = OC = \sqrt{OA^2 + AC^2} = \sqrt{OA^2 + OB^2}$$

and source voltage $$= \sqrt{V_R{}^2 + V_L{}^2} = I\sqrt{\left(R^2 + X_L{}^2\right)}$$

V is in as phase as compared to circuit current I (or current I is langing the source voltage V) by a phase angle ϕ when

$$\tan\phi = \frac{AC}{OA} = \frac{OB}{OA} = \frac{IX_L}{IR} = \frac{X_L}{R} = \frac{L\omega}{R}$$

Moreover, impedance of LR circuit

$$Z = \frac{V}{I} = \sqrt{R^2 + X_L{}^2} = \sqrt{R^2 + L^2\omega^2}.$$

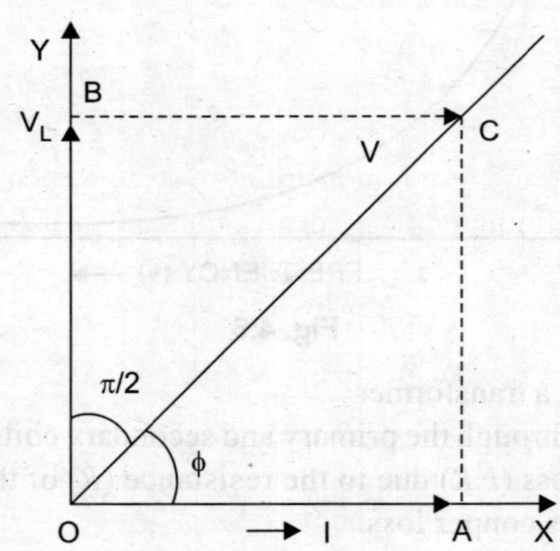

Fig. 4.8

Q. 20. The sinusoidal voltage $V = 200 \sin 314\, t$ is applied to a resistor of 10 Ω resistance. Calculate (*i*) rms value of voltage, (*ii*) rms value of current, and (*iii*) power dissipated as heat in watt.

Ans. Here $$V = 200 \sin 314\, t$$

Comparing it with standard equation

$$V = V \sin \omega t, \text{ we get}$$

$$V_m = 200 \text{ V}$$

(*i*) We have $V = \frac{V_0}{\sqrt{2}} = \frac{200}{\sqrt{2}} \Rightarrow V = \frac{200}{1.414} = 141.44$ V

(*ii*) Power dissipated, $P = VI = 141.44 \times 14.144 = 2000.5$ W.

SHORT ANSWER TYPE QUESTIONS (SA-II)

(Carrying 3 marks)

Q. 1. Explain the term for 'resonance' for a series LCR circuit. Calculate the resonant frequency.

Ans. We know that, for

Alternating voltage $V = V_m \sin \omega t$ applied in LCR circuit, the current (I) in the circuit is given by:

$$I = \frac{V_m}{\sqrt{R^2 + (X_L - X_L)^2}} . \sin(\omega t - \phi) = \frac{V_m}{Z} \sin(\omega t - \phi)$$

where impedance, $Z = \sqrt{R^2 + (X_L - X_C)^2}$

and phase angle, $\phi = \tan^{-1}\left(\frac{X_L - X_C}{R}\right)$

If it so happens that

$X_L = X_C$, then $Z = R$ minimum

and $\phi = \tan^{-1}(0) = 0°$,

i.e., the current will have a maximum value given by

$I = \frac{V}{R}$ and will be same phase as that of applied voltage,

then such a situation is called the phenomenon of electrical resonance. For electrical resonance, the necessary condition is:

$$X_L = X_C \text{ or } L\omega_0 = \frac{1}{C\omega_0}$$

Obviously, as L and C are fixed for a circuit, resonance occurs for a particular frequency known as "resonant frequency" ν_0 (or resonant angular frequency ω_0) given by:

$$L\omega_0 = \frac{1}{C\omega_0}, \text{ which leads as to } \omega_0 = \frac{1}{\sqrt{LC}}$$

$$\Rightarrow \quad \nu_0 = \frac{\omega_0}{2\pi} = \frac{1}{2\pi\sqrt{LC}}.$$

Q. 2. State the condition for resonance to occur in a series LCR a.c. circuit and devise an expression for the resonant frequency. Draw a plot showing the variation of the peak current i_m with frequency of the a.c. source used. Define the quality factor Q of the circuit.

Ans. In a series, *LCR* a.c. circuit, current L flowing in the circuit is given by:

$$i = \frac{\in}{2} = \frac{\in}{[R^2 + (X_L - X_C)^2]^{1/2}}$$

For resonance condition to occur, $X_L = X_C$, so that impedence of the LCR circuit is minimum possible and the circuit current is maximum.

$X_L = X_C$, hence, $L\omega_0 = \frac{1}{L\omega_0}$, where ω_0 is the angular frequency at resonance.

$$\Rightarrow \qquad \omega_0 = \frac{1}{\sqrt{LC}}$$

a resonant frequency, $\nu_0 = \dfrac{\omega_0}{2\pi} = \dfrac{1}{2\pi\sqrt{LC}}$

A plot showing the variation of peak current I_m with frequency ν of the a.c. is shown as in Fig. 4.9.

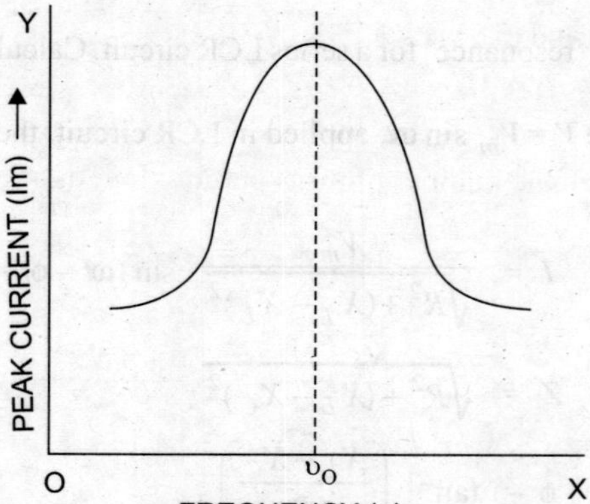

Fig. 4.9

The quality factor Q of a resonant circuit is defined as the ratio of inductive (or capacitive) reactance to the resistance of the circuit. Mathematically,

$$Q \text{ factor} = \frac{X_L}{R} = \frac{L\omega}{R} = \frac{1}{R}\sqrt{\frac{L}{C}}.$$

Q. 3. In series LCR circuit with $L = 5H$, $C = 80\ \mu F$ and $R = 40\ \Omega$ is connected to a variable frequency source of 230 V.

(*i*) Determine the resonance frequency of the circuit.

(*ii*) Obtain the impedence of the circuit and amplitude of the circuit at resonance.

Ans. Here, $L = 5$, $C = 80\ \mu F = 80 \times 10^{-6}$ F

$R = 40\ \Omega$, $E_{rms} = 230$ V

(*i*) Resonance frequency is given by

$$\nu_0 = \frac{1}{2\pi\sqrt{LC}} = \frac{1}{2\times3.14\sqrt{5\times80\times10^{-6}}}$$

$$= \frac{1}{6.28\times20\times10^{-3}} = 7.96 \text{ Hz}$$

(*ii*) Impedence of the circuit at resonance is given by

$$Z = R = 40\ \Omega$$

Amplitude of current, $I_0 = \dfrac{E_0}{2}$, But $E_0 = E_{rms}\sqrt{2}$

$$\therefore \qquad I_0 = \frac{E_{rms}\sqrt{2}}{Z} = \frac{230\times1.414}{40} = 8.13 \text{ A}$$

Q. 4. Derive an expression for the mutual inductance of a pair of coaxial solenoids having number of turns N_1 and N_2.

Ans. Let there be a solenoid of length l and having number of turns per unit length n_1. Another solenoid of same length and having n_2 number of turns per unit length wound around it.

On passing current I_1 through the first solenoid, magnetic field developed at its centre is

$$B = \mu_0 n_1 I_1 \quad ...(1)$$

If cross section area of second solenoid is A then magnetic flux linked with the second solenoid will be

$$\phi_2 = B A n_2 l = \mu_0 n_1 I_1 A n_2 l$$

$$\phi_2 = \mu_0 n_1 I_1 A n_2 l \quad ....(2)$$

As $\quad \phi_2 = M I_1 \quad ..(3)$

From equations (2) and (3), we get

$\therefore \quad \mu_0 A n_1 n_2 l I_1 = M I_1$

$\Rightarrow \quad M = \mu_0 A n_1 n_2 l \quad ...(4)$

Where n_1 and n_2 are the number of turns per unit length of two coils, i.e.,

$$n_1 = \frac{N_1}{l} \text{ and } n_2 = \frac{N_2}{l},$$

Thus, we have

$$M = \mu_0 A \frac{N_1}{l} \cdot \frac{N_2}{l} \cdot l = \frac{\mu_0 A N_1 N_2}{l} \quad ..(5)$$

If the core of inner solenoid is filled with a material of relative permeability μ_r, then the above relation is

$$M = \frac{\mu_0 \mu_r A N_1 N_2}{l}.$$

Q. 5. Calculate the current drawn by the primary coil of a transformer which steps down 200 V to 20 V to operate a device of resistance 20 Ω. Assume the efficiency of the transformer to be 80%.

Ans. Here, $I_P = ?$ $E_P = 200$ V, $E_S = 20$ V, $R_s = 20\ \Omega$

We know, $\quad I_s = \frac{E_S}{R_S} = \frac{20}{20} = 1A$

As $\quad \eta = \frac{E_S I_S}{E_P I_P}$

$\therefore \quad \frac{80}{100} = \frac{20 \times 1}{200 I_P}$, or $\quad I_P = \frac{1}{8} = 0.125$ A.

Q. 6. How much current is drawn by the primary coil of a transformer which steps down 220V to 22V to operate device with an impendence of 220 Ω.

Ans. Here, $\quad I_P = ?,\ E_P = 220$ V, $\ E_S = 22$ V

$R_S = 220\ \Omega$

We know, $\quad I_S = \frac{E_S}{R_S} = \frac{22}{220} = 0.1$ A.

In an ideal transformer,

$$\frac{I_P}{I_S} = \frac{E_S}{E_P}$$

$$\therefore \quad I_P = \frac{E_S}{E_P} \times I_S = \frac{22 \times 0.1}{220} = 10^{-2} \text{ A.}$$

Q. 7. Show diagrammatically two different arrangements used for winding the primary and secondary coils in a transformer.

Assuming the transformer to be an ideal one, write expressions for the ratio of its (*i*) output voltage to input voltage

(*ii*) output current to input current in terms of the number of turns in the primary and secondary coils.

Mention the two reasons for energy losses in an ideal transformer.

Ans. Two different arrangements used for winding of primary and secondary coils in a transformer are shown in Fig. 4.10.

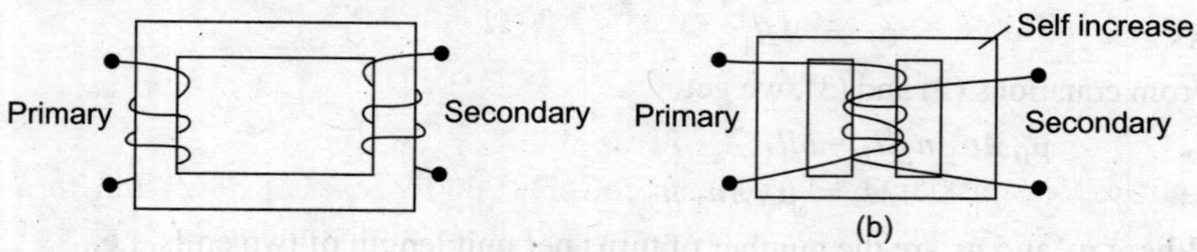

Fig. 4.10

For an ideal transformer:

$$(i)\ \frac{V_{output}}{V_{input}} = \frac{N_S}{N_P}, \qquad (ii)\ \frac{I_{output}}{I_{input}} = \frac{N_P}{N_S}$$

Two possible reasons for energy loss in an actual transformer are:

(*i*) Eddy currents; and (*ii*) Hysteresis.

Q. 8. Sketch a graph to show how the reactance of (*i*) capacitor, (*ii*) an inductor varies as a function of frequency?

Ans. The capacitative reactance of a capacitor is given by:

$$X_C = \frac{1}{\omega C} = \frac{1}{2\pi\nu C}$$

Clearly, $$X_C \propto \frac{1}{\nu}$$

As frequency (ν) increases, X_C decreases. This is shown in Fig. 4.11.

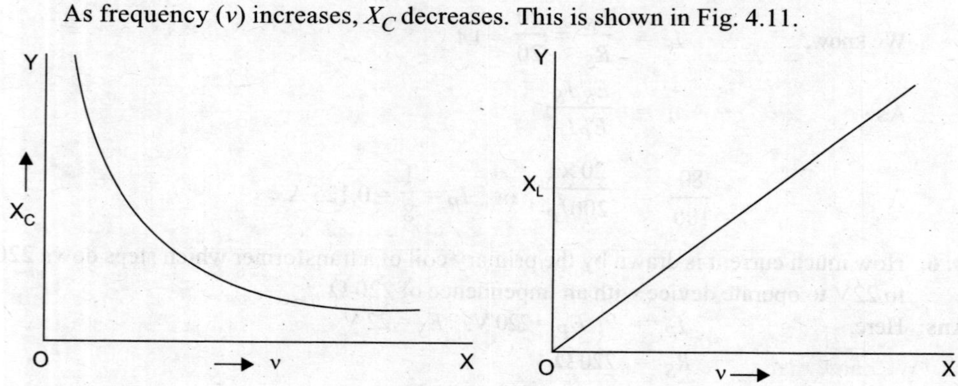

Fig. 4.11

The inductive reactance of an inductor is given by,

$$X_L = \omega L = 2\pi\nu L$$

Clearly, $$X_L \propto \nu$$

As ν increases, X_L increases.

Q. 9. An a.c. voltage of 100 V, 50 Hz is connected across a 20 Ω resistor and 2 mH inductor in series. Calculate (*i*) impedence of the circuit, (*ii*) rms current in the circuit.

Ans. Here, $E_V = 100\text{ V},\ \nu = 50\text{ Hz}$

$R = 20\,\Omega,\ L = 2\text{ mH}$

$Z = ?,\ I_v = ?$

We know, $X_L = \omega L = 2\pi\nu L$

$$= 2 \times \frac{22}{7} \times 50 \times 2 \times 10^{-3} = 0.63\ \Omega$$

As $Z = \sqrt{R^2 + X_L^2}$

$$= \sqrt{20^2 + 0.63^2} = 20\ \Omega$$

So $I_v = \frac{E_V}{z} = \frac{100}{20} = 5\text{A}.$

Q. 10. **A power transmission line feeds input power at 2300 V to a step down transformer. with its primary windings having 4000 turns. What should be the number of turns in the secondary windings in order to get output power at 230 V?**

Ans. Here, $E_P = 2300\text{ V}, \; n_P = 4000, \; n_s = ?$

$$E_s = 230\text{ V}$$

As, $\frac{E_S}{E_P} = \frac{n_S}{n_P}$

$\therefore$ $\frac{230}{2300} = \frac{n_s}{4000}$

$$n_s = \frac{230 \times 4000}{2300} = 400.$$

Q. 11. **In the circuit shown in Fig. 4.12, *R* represents resistance of an electric bulb. If the frequency *v* of the supply is doubled, how should the values of *C* and *L* be changed so that glow in the bulb remains uncharged?**

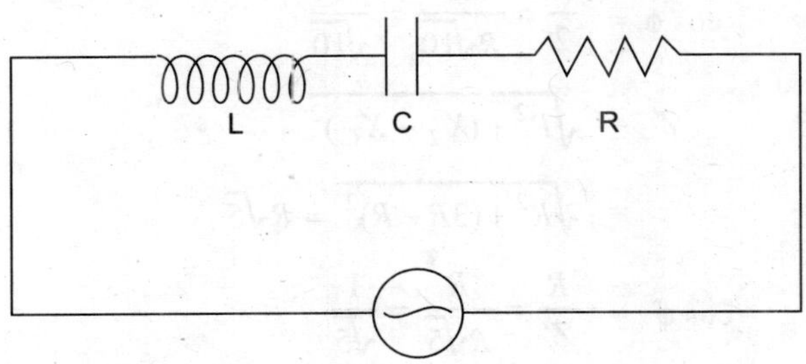

Fig. 4.12

Ans. We know that $X_L = \omega L = 2\pi\nu L$

$$X_C = \frac{1}{\omega C} = \frac{1}{2\pi\nu C}$$

Glow in the bulb will remain uncharged, if X_L, X_C remain unchanged.
Hence, when v is doubled L should becomes half and C should also become half.

HIGHER ORDER THINKING SKILLS (HOTS)

Q. 1. A light bulb is rated at 100 W for a 220 V supply. Find out:

(*i*) the resistance of the bulb
(*ii*) the peak voltage of the source
(*iii*) the rms current through the bulb

Ans. Here, $P = 100$ W, $E_V = 220$ V, $R = ?$ $E = ?$

From
$$P = \frac{E_V^2}{R}$$

$$R = \frac{E_V^2}{P} = \frac{220\times 220}{100} = 484\ \Omega$$

$$E_0 = \sqrt{2}\ E_V = 1.414 \times 220 = 311\text{ V}$$

$$I_V = \frac{P}{E_V} = \frac{100}{220} = 0.45\text{ A}$$

Q. 2. Given below are two electrical circuits A and B as shown in Fig. 4.13. Calculate the ratio of power factor of circuit B to power factor of circuit A.

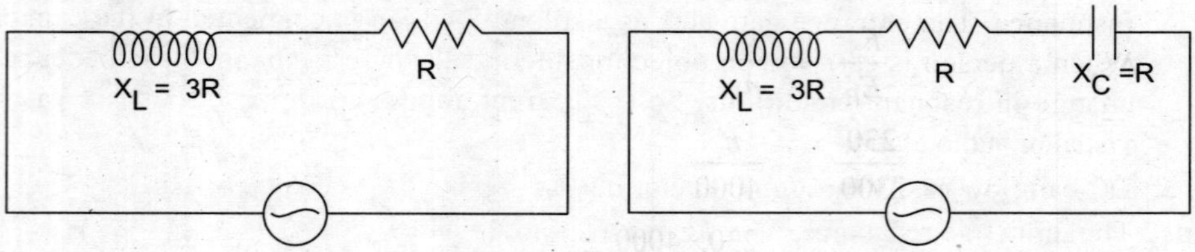

Fig. 4.13

Ans. For circuit A,
$$Z = \sqrt{X_L^2 + R^2} = \sqrt{(3R)^2 + R^2} = R\sqrt{10}$$

$$\cos\phi = \frac{R}{2} = \frac{R}{R\sqrt{10}} = \frac{1}{\sqrt{10}}$$

For circuit B,
$$Z' = \sqrt{R^2 + (X_L - X_C)^2}$$

$$= \sqrt{R^2 + (3R - R)^2} = R\sqrt{5}$$

$$\cos\phi' = \frac{R}{Z'} = \frac{R}{R\sqrt{5}} = \frac{1}{\sqrt{5}}$$

$$\frac{\cos\phi'}{\cos\phi} = \frac{\sqrt{10}}{\sqrt{5}} = \frac{\sqrt{2}}{1} = \sqrt{2}:1$$

Q. 3. Sketch a graph showing the variation of impedance of LCR circuit with the frequency of applied voltage.

Ans. The impedence of LCR circuit is
$$Z = \sqrt{R^2 + (X_L - X_C)^2}$$

$$= \sqrt{R^2 + \left(2\pi\nu L - \frac{1}{2\pi\nu C}\right)^2}$$

The variation of Z with ν is shown in Fig. 4.14. At $\nu = \nu_r$, $X_L = X_C$
$$Z = R = \text{minimum.}$$

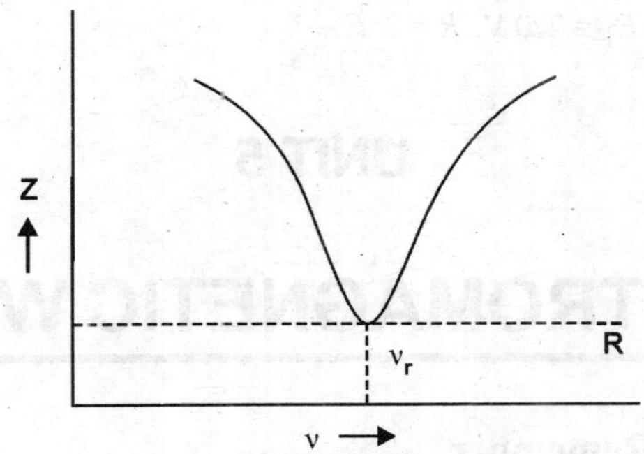

Fig. 4.14

Q. 4. A railway station metal detector is used at the entrance gate to check gun, etc. How does it operate?

Ans. It operates on the principle of resonance. A parallel *LC* circuit draws no current at resonance. The entrance gate acts as a solenoid which is connected to the capacitor. When a person is carrying an objectionable metal, there is change in impedence and change in resonant conditions. So the current appearing in the circuit activates the visual or audio alarm.

Q. 5. DC can flow easily through inductor but a.c. cannot pass easily. Explain.

Ans. The inductive reactance, $X_L = L\omega = 2\pi\nu L$ for dc = $\nu = 0$, $\therefore X_L = 0$

Since inductor offers no resistance to the flow of d.c., so it cannot flow easily through the inductor.

Q. 6. How does low power factor account for larger power loss in lines?

Ans. The average power loss in ac is given by

$$P = E_{rms} I_{rms} \cos \phi$$

If the power factor $\cos \phi$ is low, then large value of rms current (I_{rms}) flows in the transmission line for a given value of E_{rms}.

$\therefore$ Large power loss ($I^2_{rms} R$) occurs in the line.

Q. 7. The core of transformer is laminated. Explain why?

Ans. The core of a transformer is laminated to reduce the energy loss due to eddy currents. Laminations break the path of eddy currents. The energy loss due to eddy current also results in unnecessary heating of the transformer which may be harmful for the winding of the transformer.

Q. 8. Why can't transformer be used to step up and down a d.c. voltage?

Ans. A transformer works on the principle of mutual inductance for which a.c. is best suited. Steady voltage cannot induce emf in the secondary of a transformer.

Q. 9. Why is the core of transformer made of a magnetic material of high permeability?

Ans. When the core of the transformer is made of a magnetic material of high permeability, almost whole of the magnetic flux will be linked with the core. This implies that the magnetic flux linked with the primary coil is equal to magnetic flux linked with the secondary coil. Thus, the energy loss due to magnetic flux leakage is reduced considerably.

Q. 10. Iron pins near a bar magnet experience both attractive force and torque. Why?

Ans. A bar magnet has non-uniform field, so iron pins experience unequal and opposite forces. The net force on each pin will not be zero and the torque will also be not zero. The force has to be attractive because the nearest end of the pin is induced with a polarity unlike the bar magnet pole.

❑❑❑

UNIT 5

ELECTROMAGNETIC WAVES

Important Points to Remember

1. Electromagnetic waves are produced by accelerated charges.
2. The frequency of the electromagnetic wave is the same as the frequency of oscillation of the charge (electric field $\vec{E}$) or the frequency of oscillating magnetic field ($\vec{B}$).
3. Light being electromagnetic wave does not require any material medium for its propagation. Hence, light can travel in the vacuum. On the other hand, sound is a mechanical wave. It requires a material medium for its propagation. Hence, sound cannot travel in vacuum.
4. In the absence of any dielectric or magnetic material, the four Maxwell's equations are given below:

   (i) $\oint_s \overrightarrow{E}\overrightarrow{ds} = \frac{q}{\epsilon_0}$. Gauss's law in electrostatics.

   (ii) $\oint_s \overrightarrow{B}\overrightarrow{ds} = 0$. Gauss's law in magnetostatics.

   (iii) $\oint \vec{E}.\vec{dl} = -\frac{d}{dt}\int_S \overrightarrow{B}\overrightarrow{ds}$. Faraday's law of electromagnetic induction.

   (iv) $\oint \overrightarrow{B}\overrightarrow{dl} = \mu_0 I + \mu_0 \epsilon_0 \frac{d}{dt}\int \overrightarrow{E}\overrightarrow{ds}$. Ampere's law as modified by Maxwell.

   The expression $\vec{F} = q\left(\vec{E} + \vec{v}\times\vec{B}\right)$ for Lorentz force has also been included by Maxwell.
5. Electromagnetic waves do not require any material medium for their propagation. In free space, the speed is given by $c = \frac{1}{\sqrt{\mu_0 \epsilon_0}} = 3\times 10^8 \text{ ms}^{-1}$

   In a medium of absolute permittivity ϵ and permeability μ, the speed of electromagnetic wave is given by $v = \frac{1}{\sqrt{\mu \epsilon}} = \frac{c}{\sqrt{K\mu_r}}$. Where K = dielectric constant of the medium.
6. Average energy density of electric field is given by $U_E = \frac{1}{2}\epsilon_0 E^2$.

   Average energy density of magnetic field, $U_B = \frac{1}{2\mu_0}B^2$.
7. The electromagnetic waves cantain wide range of radiation but all these radiations have the following common properties:
   1. They are transverse in nature.
   2. They do not require any material medium for propagation.
   3. They travel with same speed of $3 \times 10^8 \text{ ms}^{-1}$ in vacuum.
   4. They consist of mutually transverse varying electric and magnetic fields.

8. To make the Ampere circuital law logically correct, Maxwell introduced the concept of displacement current. The expression for displacement current is

$$I_D = \epsilon_0 \cdot \frac{d\phi_E}{dt}$$

where ϕ_E = electric flux.

9. Conduction current is due to the flow of electrons in the circuit. It exists even if the flow of electrons is at uniform rate.

   Displacement current is due to time varying electric field. It does not exist under steady condition.

10. Conduction current and displacement current are individually discontinuous in a circuit containing capacitor. However their sum is continuous.

11. Conduction current and displacement current are always equal *i e.,*

$$I_C = I_D \Rightarrow \frac{dq}{dt} = \epsilon_0 \frac{d\phi_E}{dt}$$

12. When fastly moving electrons are stopped suddenly on a metal target of higher atomic number, then *X*-rays are produced. The electromagnetic waves are also be produced when an electron jumps from higher orbits to a vacancy on the inner complete orbits in an atom of the element.

13. Radiowaves are produced by accelerated motion of charges in conducting wires and are used in radio and TV communication. They are in the frequency range of 500 KHz to about 1000 MHz (1 GHz). They are further subdivided as medium band, short band, HF band and UHF band.

14. Ozone layer present in the atmosphere at an altitude of about 40-50 km absorbs most of the ultraviolet rays coming from sun and, thus, form a protective ring around the earth.

15. *X*-rays cover the wavelengths from 1 nm to 10^{-3} nm.

16. Gamma rays (γ-rays) are hardest electromagnetic waves having wavelengths even less than 10^{-3} nm (or 10^{-12} m). These are produced in nuclear reactions and are also emitted during radioactive decays of the nuclei. These are used for destroying cancer cells.

❑❑❑

VERY SHORT ANSWER TYPE QUESTIONS

(Carrying 1 mark)

Q. 1. Give the ratio of velocities of light rays of wavelengths 4000Å and 8000Å in vacuum.

Ans. The velocity of all light waves in vacuum is same (3×10^8 ms^{-1}). Thus, the ratio of velocities of light of wavelength 4000Å and 8000Å is 1 : 1.

Q. 2. What is the approximate wavelength of *X*-rays?

Ans. 0.1Å to 100Å.

Q. 3. Write down the Maxwell's equations for steady electric field.

Ans. (*i*) $\oint_s \vec{E}.\vec{ds} = \frac{q}{\epsilon_0}$ (*ii*) $\oint \vec{E}.\vec{dl} = 0$

Q. 4. What is the name given to that part of electromagnetic spectrum which is used in Radar?

Ans. Microwave.

Q. 5. Write an expression for speed of electromagnetic waves in free space.

Ans. The speed of em waves in free space

$$v = \frac{1}{\sqrt{\mu_0 \epsilon_0}}$$

where μ_0 is absolute permeability and ϵ_0 is the absolute permittivity of the free space.

Q. 6. Microwaves are used in Radar. Why?

Ans. As microwaves are of smaller wavelengths, hence, they can be transmitted as a beam signal in a particular direction much better than radio waves because microwaves do not bend around the corners of any obstacle coming in their path.

Q. 7. Identify the part of electromagnetic spectrum to which the following wavelengths belong:

(*i*) 10^{-1} m   (*ii*) 10^{-12} m

Ans. (*i*) Microwaves   (*ii*) Gamma rays

Q. 8. Which physical quantity, if any, has the same value for waves belonging to the different parts of the electromagnetic spectrum?

Ans. The electromagnetic waves of different wavelengths travel with the same speed (3×10^8 ms^{-1}) in vacuum.

Q. 9. Name the electromagnetic radiation to which the following wavelengths belong:

(*i*) 10^{-2} m   (*ii*) 1Å

Ans. (*i*) Microwaves   (*ii*) *X*-rays.

Q. 10. State the condition under which a microwave oven heats up food item containing water molecules most efficiently.

Ans. Frequency of the microwaves should match the resonant frequency of water molecules.

Q. 11. Write the frequency limit of visible range of electromagnetic spectrum in kHz.

Ans. 4×10^{11} kHz to 8×10^{11} kHz.

Q. 12. Arrange the following radiations in the descending order of wavelength.
γ-rays, infrared rays, red light, yellow light, radio waves.

Ans. Radio waves, infrared rays, red light, yellow light and γ-rays.

Q. 13. Name the part of the electromagnetic spectrum which is used in greenhouse to keep the plants warm.

Ans. Infrared rays.

Q. 14. Which of the following has the shortest wavelength microwaves, ultraviolet rays or *X*-rays?

Ans. *X*-rays.

Q. 15. What evidence is there that sound waves are not electromagnetic in nature?

Ans. Sound waves cannot travel through free space.

Q. 16. What oscillates in electromagnetic waves? Are these waves transverse or longitudinal?

Ans. In electromagnetic waves, electric and magnetic fields oscillate in mutually perpendicular directions. These waves are transverse waves.

Q. 17. State two properties of electromagnetic waves.

Ans. (*i*) Velocity of electromagnetic waves in free space is 3×10^8 ms^{-1}.
(*ii*) They are transverse in nature.

Q. 18. What is the phase difference between the electric and magnetic fields of an em wave?

Ans. Electric and magnetic fields either oscillate in the same phase or with a constant phase difference.

Q. 19. Long distance radio broadcast uses short wave bands. Why?

Ans. This is because ionosphere reflects the waves lying in the frequency range of short wave band.

Q. 20. What is the name given to that part of electromagnetic spectrum which is used for taking photographs of earth under foggy conditions from great heights?

Ans. Infrared rays.

Q. 21. The charging current for a capacitor is 0.2 A. What is the displacement current?

Ans. Displacement current = charging current = 0.2 A.

Q. 22. State two applications of ultraviolet radiations.

Ans. Ultraviolet radiations are used: (*i*) to preserve the food stuff, (*ii*) for sterilizing the surgical instruments.

Q. 23. Which waves are used in mobile phones?

Ans. Radio waves of extremely short wavelengths (or of ultra high frequency) are used in mobile phones to transmit voice communication.

Q. 24. The wavelength of electromagnetic radiation is doubled. What will happen to the energy of photons?

Ans. The energy is halved because

$$E = h\nu = \frac{hc}{\lambda}$$

and

$$E' = \frac{hc}{2\lambda} = \frac{1}{2}E$$

Q. 25. State two applications of infrared radiations.

Ans. Infrared radiations are used: (*i*) to treat muscular strain, (*ii*) for taking photographs during the conditions of fog, smoke, etc.

Q. 26. What is the time period of the light for which the eye is most sensitive?

Ans. We know that time period,

$$T = \frac{1}{\nu} = \frac{\lambda}{C} = \frac{5600 \times 10^{-11}}{3 \times 10^{8}} \text{ s} = 1.88 \times 10^{-15} \text{ s.}$$

Q. 27. How are *X*-rays produced?

Ans. If fast moving electrons are stopped suddenly on the metal target of higher atomic number, then *X*-rays are produced. The *X*-rays will also be produced when an electron jumps higher orbits to a vacancy of an inner complete orbits in an atom of the element.

Q. 28. For which frequency of light, the eye is most sensitive?

Ans. The eye is most sensitive to the light of wavelength,

$$\lambda = 5600 \text{Å} = 5600 \times 10^{-10} \text{ m}$$

$\therefore$ Its frequency, $$\nu = \frac{c}{\lambda} = \frac{3 \times 10^{8}}{5600 \times 10^{-10}} = 5.36 \times 10^{14} \text{ Hz.}$$

SHORT ANSWER TYPE QUESTIONS

(Carrying 2 marks)

Q. 1. Find the wavelength of electromagnetic wave with frequency 4×10^9 Hz in free space. Give its two applications.

Ans. Here, $c = 3 \times 10^8 \text{ ms}^{-1}$

and $\nu = 4 \times 10^9$ Hz

We know that $c = \nu\lambda$

or $$\lambda = \frac{c}{\nu} = \frac{3 \times 10^{8}}{4 \times 10^{9}} = 0.075 \text{ m}$$

This wavelength belongs to microwave region. The microwaves are used (*i*) in microwave ovens, (*ii*) in radar system for the navigation of aircraft.

Q. 2. What is greenhouse effect for the atmosphere of the earth? Write its importance.

Ans. During a day the earth receives heat and light from the sun and is heated up. After sunset, the earth emits radiation, which is in the infrared region only. These infrared radiations are trapped by CO_2 and water vapour present in the earth's atmosphere. Consequently, the earth remains warm enough. It is known as greenhouse effect for the atmosphere of the earth. Greenhouse effect is very useful for the human beings. If greenhouse effect had not been present, then during the night, the temperature of the earth would have fallen much, causing extreme cold on the earth, which may cause much discomfort for human beings.

Q. 3. When can a charge act as a source of electromagnetic waves? How are the directions of the electric and magnetic field vectors, in an electromagnetic wave, related to each other and to the direction of propagation of the em waves.

Ans. Only an accelerated charge can act as a source of em waves. The directions of electric and magnetic field vectors are perpendicular to each other as well as perpendicular to the direction of propagation of the electromagnetic waves.

Q. 4. State any four properties of electromagnetic waves. Write an expression for the velocity of electromagnetic waves in terms of permittivity and magnetic permeability of free space.

Ans. (*i*) They are transverse in nature.

(*ii*) They travel with the same speed of $3 \times 10^8 \text{ ms}^{-1}$ in vacuum.

(*iii*) They consist of mutually transverse varying electric and magnetic fields.

(*iv*) They do not require any material medium for their propagation

$$c = \frac{1}{\sqrt{\epsilon_0 \mu_0}}.$$

Q. 5. Which waves are used in Radar system? Give their frequency range and mention the source of their production.

Ans. The electromagnetic waves, which are used in Radar system, are microwaves. Their frequency range is 1 GHz to 300 GHz. They are produced by special vacuum tubes, namely klystrons, magnetrons, etc.

Q. 6. Name the following constituent radiations of electromagnetic spectrum which:

(*i*) produce intense heating effect

(*ii*) are absorbed by the ozone layer

(*iii*) are used for studying crystal structure

Ans. (*i*) Infrared rays

(*ii*) Ultraviolet rays (UV rays)

(*iii*) *X*-rays.

Q. 7. In an electromagnetic wave, the electric field oscillates with frequency of $2 \times 10^{10}\ s^{-1}$ and an amplitude of 40 Vm^{-1}.

(*i*) What is the wavelength of the wave?

(*ii*) What is the energy density due to electric field?

Ans. Here $\nu = 2 \times 10^{10}\ s^{-1}$ and $E_0 = 40\ Vm^{-1}$

(*i*) The wavelength, $\lambda = \frac{c}{\nu} = \frac{3\times10^8}{2\times10^{10}} = 1.5 \times 10^{-2}$ m

(*ii*) Energy density due to electric field,

$$U_E = \frac{1}{2}\epsilon_0 E_{rms}^2 = \frac{1}{4}\epsilon_0 E_0^2 = \frac{1}{4} \times (8.85 \times 10^{-12}) \times (40)^2$$

$$= 3.54 \times 10^{-9}\ Jm^{-3}.$$

Q. 8. The amplitude of oscillating magnetic field in an electromagnetic wave is 2×10^{-6} T. What will be the amplitude of the oscillating electric field?

Ans. Here $B_0 = 2 \times 10^{-6}\ T,$

$$c = 3 \times 10^8\ ms^{-1}$$

We know $E_0 = c\,B_0$

$\therefore$ $E_0 = 3 \times 10^8 \times 2 \times 10^{-6} = 600\ Vm^{-1}$

Q. 9. The electric field of an electriomagnetic wave is given by

$$E = 20 \sin \omega \left(t - \frac{x}{c}\right)\ Vm^{-1}$$

(*i*) Find the intensity of the wave and

(*ii*) rms value of electric field.

Ans. Here, $E = 20 \sin \omega \left(t - \frac{x}{c}\right)\ Vm^{-1}$

Compare it with the standard equation

$$E = E_0 \sin \omega \left(t - \frac{x}{c}\right)\ Vm^{-1}$$

$\therefore$ $E_0 = 20\ Vm^{-1}$

(*i*) Now, $I = \frac{1}{2} \in_0 c\, E_0^2$

$$= \frac{1}{2} \times 8.85 \times 10^{-12} \times 3 \times 10^8 \times (20)^2 \text{ Wm}^{-2}$$

$$= 8.85 \times 10^{-12} \times 1.5 \times 10^8 \times 400 \text{ Wm}^{-2} = 0.53 \text{ Wm}^{-2}$$

(*ii*) $E_{rms} = \frac{E_0}{\sqrt{2}} = \frac{20}{1.414} = 14.14 \text{ Vm}^{-1}$

Q. 10. What is displacement current? Explain its cause.

Ans. Displacement current is that current which is produced in a region, whenever the electric field and, hence, the electric flux is changing with time. The displacement current is given by

$$I_D = \in_0 \cdot \frac{d\phi_E}{dt}$$

Where $\in_0$ = absolute permittivity of space and $\frac{d\phi_E}{dt}$ = rate of change of electric flux.

Q. 11. Give one use of each of the following:

(*i*) Infrared rays (*ii*) Gamma rays (*iii*) Microwaves (*iv*) Ultraviolet rays

Ans. (*i*) Infrared rays are used in physical therapy, *i.e.*, to treat muscular problems.

(*ii*) Gamma rays are used in the treatment of cancer and tumors.

(*iii*) Microwaves are used in Radar system for aircraft navigation.

(*iv*) Ultraviolet rays are used to destroy the bacteria and sterilizing the surgical instruments.

Q. 12. A plane electromagnetic wave of frequency 25 MHz travels in free space along the *x*-direction. At a particular point in space and time, the electric vector is $\vec{E} = 6.3 \text{ Vm}^{-1}\, \hat{j}$. Calculate $\vec{B}$ at this point.

Ans. As plane electromagnetic wave is travelling in free space along the *x*-direction and at a particular point in space and time, the electric vector is $\vec{E} = 6.3 \text{ Vm}^{-1}\, \hat{j}$, hence, magnetic vector $\vec{B}$ must be the along the *z*-axis with

$$B_0 = \frac{E_0}{C} = \frac{6.3}{3 \times 10^8} = 2.1 \times 10^{-8} \text{ T}$$

$$\therefore \quad \vec{B} = 2.1 \times 10^{-8} \text{ T}\, \hat{k}$$

Q. 13. Write two applications each of (*i*) radio waves, (*ii*) microwaves and (*iii*) infrared rays.

Ans. (*i*) **Applications of Radio Waves**

(*a*) Radio waves are used in radio and television communication systems.

(*b*) Mobile phones use radio waves to transmit voice communication.

(*ii*) **Applications of Microwaves**

(*a*) Due to their short wavelengths, these waves are used in Radar system in aircraft navigation.

(*b*) Microwaves are used in microwave ovens.

(*iii*) **Applications of Infrared Rays**

(*a*) Infrared detectors are used in earth satellites, both for scientific survey and millitary purposes.

(*b*) Infrared camps are used at airports clear fog and mist.

(*c*) Electronic devices like LED emit infrared, which are used in electronic devices on remote switch.

Q. 14. Find the energy of photon in watt-hour for electromagnetic waves of wavelength 3000Å. Given $h = 6.6 \times 10^{-34}$ Js.

Ans. Here $\lambda = 3000$ Å $= 3000 \times 10^{-10}$ m $= 3 \times 10^{-7}$ m

Now,
$$E = \frac{hc}{\lambda} = \frac{6.6\times10^{-34}\times3\times10^{8}}{3\times10^{-7}}$$
$$= 6.6 \times 10^{-19} \text{ J (or Ws)}$$
$$= \frac{6.6\times10^{-19}}{60\times60} \text{ Wh} = 1.83 \times 10^{-22} \text{ Wh.}$$

HIGHER ORDER THINKING SKILLS (HOTS)

Q. 1. If the earth did not have an atmosphere, would its average surface temperature be higher or lower than what it is now?

Ans. Due to greenhouse effect, the temperature of the earth's surface is raised. In the absence of the atmosphere, the heat received by the earth during day time will be completely lost during night. So, the average surface temperature will be lower than that of the present temperature.

Q. 2. What is the role of ozone layer in the atmosphere?

Ans. Ozone layer absorbs the ultraviolet rays emitted by the sun. These ultraviolet rays are very harmful to the living tissues. Since ozone layer prevents these harmful ultraviolet rays from reaching the earth's surface, hence, the damage to the living tissue is not done.

Q. 3. Long distance radio broadcast uses short wave bands. Why?

Ans. This is because ionosphere reflects the waves lying in the frequency range of short wave bands.

Q. 4. Find the wavelength of electromagnetic waves of frequency 6×10^{12} Hz in free space. Give its two applications.

Ans. We have
$$\lambda = \frac{c}{\nu} = \frac{3\times10^{8}}{6\times10^{12}} = 5 \times 10^{-5} \text{ m.}$$

These waves belong to infrared rays, which are used:

(*i*) in greenhouses to keep the plants green.

(*ii*) in revealing the secret writings on the ancient walls.

Q. 5. What features of electromagnetic waves led Maxwell to conclude that light itself is an electromagnetic wave?

Ans. Light and electromagnetic waves are transverse in nature and they travel with the same velocity in vacuum This led Maxwell to conclude that light itself is an electromagnetic wave.

Q. 6. The radio transmitter operates at a frequency of 880 kHz and a power of 10 kW. Find the number of photons per second emitted.

Ans. Number of photons

$$n = \frac{P}{h\nu} = \frac{10\times10^{3}}{6.6\times10^{-34}\times880\times10^{3}} = 1.171 \times 10^{31}.$$

Q. 7. What is the angle made by direction of travel of an electromagnetic wave with y-axis when the wavefront travelling in free space is given by $\vec{a} = \hat{k} + \hat{j} + \hat{i}$?

Ans. Let a be the desired angle. Then

$$\vec{a}.\hat{j} = a\cos\theta$$

i.e., $$\cos\theta = \frac{\vec{a}.\hat{j}}{a} = \frac{(\hat{k}+\hat{j}+\hat{i}).\hat{j}}{\sqrt{1+1+1}} = \frac{1}{\sqrt{3}}$$

i.e., $$\theta = \cos^{-1}\frac{1}{\sqrt{3}}$$

Q. 8. Electromagnetic waves in a cavity with conduction walls can exist only in certain modes (*i.e.*, they cannot exist, for example, with any arbitrary wavelength). Suggest a simple reason why this should be so?

Ans. The waves must satisfy a boundary condition. The electric field should be zero on the walls of the conductor. This restricts the modes possible. (It is something like the restricted modes of a strong wave fixed at two ends.)

Q. 9. Electromagnetic waves travel in a medium at a speed of 2.0×10^8 ms^{-1}. The relative permeability of the medium is 1.0. Find the relative permittivity.

Ans. Here $$v = 2\times10^8 \text{ ms}^{-1}, \mu_r = 1$$

$$c = 3\times10^8 \text{ ms}^{-1}$$

Speed of electromagnetic wave in a medium is given by

$$v = \frac{1}{\sqrt{\mu\in}} = \frac{1}{\sqrt{\mu_0\mu_r(\in_0\in_r)}} = \frac{1}{\sqrt{\mu_0\in_r}}\times\frac{1}{\sqrt{\mu_r\in_r}}$$

or $$\in_r = \frac{c^2}{v^2\mu_r} = \frac{(3\times10^8)^2}{(2\times10^8)^2\times1} = 2.25.$$

□□□

UNIT 6

OPTICS

(A) RAY OPTICS

Important Points to Remember

A.1. Reflection of light by spherical mirrors

(*i*) Focal length of the spherical mirror is half of the radius of curvature *i.e.*, $f = \frac{R}{2}$.

(*ii*) The mirror formula is $\frac{1}{f} = \frac{1}{v} + \frac{1}{u}$

Where u = object distance, v = image distance and

f = focal length of the mirror

(*iii*) By a convex mirror, the image formed is virtual, erect and small in size compared to the object for all positions of the object. The field of view of this mirror is thus large.

(*iv*) In case of a concave mirror, the image formed for the object lying beyond the focus is real and inverted. But for the position of object between the focus and the pole, the image formed is virtual and erect.

(*v*) The magnification $m = -\frac{v}{u} = \frac{f - v}{f} = \frac{f}{f - u}$

m is positive for virtual images and negative for real images.

A.2. Refraction of light at plane surfaces

(*i*) There are two laws of refraction, which are as follows:

(*a*) The incident ray, the refracted ray and normal to the interface at the point of incidence, all lie in the same plane.

(*b*) The ratio of the sine of the angle of incidence in 1st medium to sine of angle of refraction in 2nd medium is a constant, known as the refractive index of 2nd medium w.r.t. 1st medium. Mathematically, $\frac{\sin i}{\sin r} = \mu$. It is known as Snell's law.

(*ii*) When a ray of light enters from an optically rarer medium to an optically denser medium, the light ray bends towards the normal. However, if a light ray travels from a denser to rarer medium, it bends away from the normal.

(*iii*) Absolute refractive index of a medium is the ratio of velocity of light in vacuum (c) to the velocity of light in the medium (v), i.e.

$$\mu = \frac{c}{v}$$

(*iv*) As a consequence of refraction—

(*a*) Sun can be seen before actual sunrise and after actual sunset due to atmospheric refraction.

Light from the rising sun reaches the earth's surface obliquely through different parts of the earth's atmosphere, suffering unequal refractions. The vertical diameter appears shorter and the horizontal diameter appears bigger. Therefore, the rising sun appears oval.

(*b*) An object under water appears to be raised when observed from air

$$\mu = \frac{Real depth}{Apparent\ depth}$$

and apparent shift in the position of object

$$x = t\left(1 - \frac{1}{\mu}\right)$$

where t is the actual depth of the object.

A.3. Total Internal reflection :

(*i*) Total internal reflection is the phenomenon of complete reflection of light back into the denser medium, when a light ray coming from a denser medium is incident on the surface of a rarer medium at angle of incidence greater than critical angle.

(*ii*) If μ_R is the refractive index of rare medium and μ_D is that of denser medium, then critical angle *C* (in the denser medium) is given by

$$\sin C = \frac{\mu_R}{\mu_D}$$ (Imp. for proof)

(iii) Consequences of total internal reflection are

(*a*) Brilliance of diamond : Diamond has a high refractive index resulting in the low value of critical angle (24.4°). This promotes a multiple total internal reflection causing the brilliance and luster.

(*b*) Formation of mirage in hot and cold regions.

(*c*) Working of optical fibre.

(*d*) Formation of rainbows.

A.4. Refraction at Spherical Surfaces

(*i*) When light falls on a convex or concave surface, having refractive index μ_2 and placed in a medium of refractive index μ_1, then relation between object distance (*u*), image distance (*v*) and radius of curvature (*R*) of curved surface is given by

$$\frac{\mu_2}{v} - \frac{\mu_1}{u} = \frac{\mu_2 - \mu_1}{R}$$ (Imp. for proof)

(*ii*) The lens maker's formula is

$$\frac{1}{f} = \left(\frac{\mu_2}{\mu_1} - 1\right)\left(\frac{1}{R_1} - \frac{1}{R_2}\right)$$

(*iii*) A lens may behave as converging or diverging depending upon the values of μ_1 and μ_2. When a lens is taken from air to a medium, the focal length of the lens increases.

(*a*) When $\mu_1 < \mu_2$, the nature of lens does not change.

(*b*) When $\mu_1 > \mu_2$, the nature of the lens becomes opposite.

(*c*) When $\mu_1 = \mu_2$, the focal length becomes infinite.

(*iv*) The lens formula is

$$\frac{1}{v}-\frac{1}{u}=\frac{1}{f}$$

All the relations are true for convex as well as concave surface lenses and for real as well as virtual images.

(*v*) Power of the lens is equal to the reciprocal of focal length

$$P=\frac{1}{f}$$

when f is in m, P is in dioptre. For convex lens, P is positive and for concave lens, P is negative.

(*vi*) When two lenses of focal lengths f_1 and f_2 are placed in contact, the focal length of equivalent lens is given by

$$\frac{1}{F}=\frac{1}{f_1}+\frac{1}{f_2}$$

and the power $P = P_1 + P_2$.

The values are put with proper sign.

A.5. Refraction through Prism and dispersion

(*i*) The prism formula is

$$\mu=\frac{\sin(A+\delta_m)/2}{\sin A/2},$$

where $\mu \rightarrow$ refractive index

$\delta_m \rightarrow$ angle of minimum deviation.

(*ii*) For the prism of small refracting angle, the angle of deviation is $\delta = (\mu - 1)A$.

(*iii*) The phenomenon of splitting of white light into colours on passing through a prism is called dispersion of light.

(*iv*) Angular dispersion produced by a prism for white light is the difference in the angles of deviation of two extreme colours *i.e.,* violet and red colours.

Mathematically, angular dispersion, $(\delta_v - \delta_r) = (\mu_v - \mu_r)A$.

(*v*) The dispersive power of a prism is the ratio of angular dispersion to the mean deviation produced by the prism, *i.e.,* dispersive power $(\omega) = \dfrac{\mu_v - \mu_r}{\mu - 1}$.

(*vi*) Rainbow is formed due to combined effect of dispersion, refraction and total internal reflection of sunlight by spherical waterdroplets of rain.

(*vii*) The sunlight travels through the earth's atmosphere. It gets scattered by the large number of molecules present in the atmosphere. Scattering represents basically change in the direction of light. The intensity of scattered light (I_s) varies directly as square of amplitude of scattered light (a^2). Therefore,

$$I_s \propto \frac{1}{\lambda^4}$$

A.6. Optical Instruments :

(*i*) For normal eye, value of least distance of distinct vision, $d = 25$ cm.

(*ii*) Defects of human eye are

(a) **Myopia :** image is formed in front of retina. Corrected using concave lens.

(b) **Hypermetropia :** image is formed behind the retina. Corrected using convex lens.

(c) **Presbiopia :** power of accomodation becomes low. Corrected using bifocal lens.

(d) **Astigmatism :** cornea has different curvature in different directions. Corrected using cylindrical lenses.

(iii) Astigmatism can occur along with myopia or hypermetropia.

(iv) A microscope is used for observing magnified images of nearby tiny objects. A simple microscope is a convex lens of small focal length held near the object such that $U \leq f$.

(v) In a simple microscope, if image is formed at near point, the magnification of image is

$$m = \left(1 + \frac{D}{f}\right)$$

However, if image is formed at ∞, then magnification

$$m = \frac{D}{f}$$

(vi) Magnifying power of a compound microscope is

(a) If final image is formed at near point of eye, then

$$m = m_0 \times m_e = -\frac{v_0}{u_0}\left(1 + \frac{D}{f_e}\right) = -\frac{L}{f_0}\left(1 + \frac{D}{f_e}\right)$$

(b) If final image in a microscope is formed at ∞, then

$$m = -\frac{L}{f_0} \cdot \frac{D}{f_e}$$

(vii) The magnifying power of the astronomical telescope is defined as the ratio of the angle subtended at the eye by the final image to the angle subtended at the eye by the object directly. It is found that in normal adjustment

$$m = -\frac{f_0}{f_e}$$

(viii) Newtonian Telescope and Cassergrain telescope are reflecting type. In these the final image formed is more intense.

(ix) Resolving power of an optical instrument is the reciprocal of limit of resolution [i.e., the minimum distance between two objects so that they can be resolved by the instrument].

(x) Resolving power of compound microscope

$$= \frac{2\mu \sin\theta}{\lambda}$$

where μ is the refractive index of the medium between the object and the objective, λ is the wavelength of light illuminating the object and θ is the half angle of the cone of light from one of the objects.

(xi) Resolving power of a telescope is

$$= \frac{d}{1.22\lambda}$$

and depends upon (a) wavelength λ of light illuminating the object (beyond control) (b) diameter d of objective.

(B) WAVE OPTICS

Important Points to Remember

B.1. Huygen's Principle

(*i*) Huygen's principle provides a geometrical description of wave propagation. It is based on the following postulates:

(*a*) Every point on a given wavefront acts as a fresh source of secondary wavelets, which travel in all directions with the velocity of light in the medium.

(*b*) The common envelope of these secondary wavelets in the forward direction gives the new wavefront at that instant.

(*ii*) Light rays always move perpendicular to the wavefront and the time taken by the light to travel from one wavefront to another is the same along any ray.

(*iii*) The shape of the wave front depends upon the nature of light source. It may be spherical, cylindrical or plane, the shape may change on reflection or refraction.

(*iv*) Reflection and refraction of light are explained on the basis of Huygen's principle using concept of secondary wavelets (Imp. for proof).

(*v*) When light travels from one medium to another medium, frequency does not change while both velocity and wavelength change depending upon the refractive index of the medium

$$\frac{v_1}{v_2}=\frac{\lambda_1}{\lambda_2}=\frac{\mu_2}{\mu_1}$$

Also, the refractive index depends upon wavelength in accordance with Cauchy's formula

$$\mu = A+\frac{B}{\lambda^2}+\frac{C}{\lambda^4}+....$$

Where $A, B, C, ...$ are constants.

B.2. Interference

(*i*) In Young's double slit experiment, the path difference between waves reaching P from S_1 and S_2 (coherent sources) is

$$S_2P-S_1P=\frac{xd}{D}$$

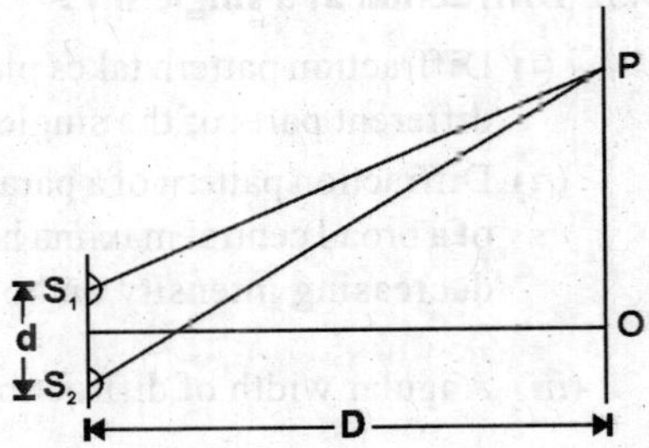

(*a*) For nth bright fringe

$$S_2P-S_1P=2n.\frac{\lambda}{2}=n\lambda$$

(*b*) For nth dark fringe

$$S_2P-S_1P=(2n-1)\frac{\lambda}{2}$$

(*c*) Fringe width, the distance between two consecutive maxima (bright fringes) or two consecutive minima (dark fringes) is

$$\beta=\frac{D\lambda}{d}$$

Angular fringe width $\theta=\frac{\beta}{D}=\frac{\lambda}{d}$.

(*d*) The ratio of intensities of maxima and minima

$$\frac{I_{max}}{I_{min}} = \frac{(a_1 + a_2)^2}{(a_1 - a_2)^2}$$

Where a_1 and a_2 are the amplitudes of interfering waves.

(*e*) The relation between intensity, amplitude of wave and width (w) of the slit is

$$\frac{I_1}{I_2} = \frac{(a_1)^2}{(a_2)^2} = \frac{w_1}{w_2}$$

(*ii*) In the interference experiment, if the light is monochromatic, bright and dark fringes will be formed at the point. However, if light is white, the fringes seen will be coloured. However, the yellow colour and its neighbouring colour shall be absent. The central fringe will be white.

(*iii*) Two independent sources of light can never be coherent sources. To obtain coherent sources, these sources of light must be originated from a single pattern source as in Young's double slit experiment.

(*iv*) Interference phenomenon is strictly in accordance with the conservation of law of energy.

(*v*) The colours of a soap bubble are seen due to interference of light. In the prism, colours appear due to dispersion of light.

(*vi*) The conditions to obtain sustained interference are

(*a*) The two sources producing interfering waves must be coherent.

(*b*) The two interfering wave trains must have the same plane of polarisation.

(*c*) The two waves must have same amplitude for better contrast.

(*d*) The two sources must be close to each other (d small) and D should be large to have sufficient fringe width.

(*vii*) If the Young's double slit experiment arrangement is immersed in water, λ will decrease so that fringe width will decrease

B.3. Diffraction at a single slit :

(*i*) Diffraction pattern takes place due to superposition of secondary wavelets emitted by different parts of the single slit.

(*ii*) Diffraction pattern of a parallel beam of light incident normally on a single slit consists of a broad central maxima having alternate dark and weak bright bands of successively decreasing intensity on both sides.

(*iii*) Angular width of diffraction band $= \frac{\lambda}{a}$

Where a = width of the slit. Linear width $= \frac{D\lambda}{a}$

(*iv*) Width of central maximum $= \frac{2D\lambda}{a}$

(*v*) When the slit is wide (*i.e.*, $a >> \lambda$), bending of light becomes so small that it cannot be detected upto a certain distance of screen from the slit. Hence, no diffraction occurs.

(*vi*) The intensity of the interference fringes in a double slit experiment is modified by the diffraction pattern of each slit.

(*vii*) The intensity of bands in diffraction pattern go on decreasing as the order of band increases. Central maximum is brightest.

(*viii*) Fresnel's distance, i.e. the distance after which appreciable bending occurs is given by

$$d_f = \frac{a^2}{\lambda}$$

(*ix*) We can read newspaper because the light is scattered by the paper into our eyes. This is called diffuse reflection. Newspaper has a rough surface. It cannot produce regular reflection.

(*x*) The coloured spectrum is due to diffraction of white light passing through fine slits made by fine threads in the muslin cloth.

B.4. Polarisation

(*i*) Light waves are transverse and therefore produce the phenomenon of polarisation.

(*ii*) Polarisation of light is the phenomenon of restricting the vibrations of light (electric vector) in a particular direction perpendicular to the direction of propagation of light wave. Such light is called plane polarised light.

(*iii*) **Brewster's Law :** When unpolarised light falls on a medium at polarising angle (p), then $\mu = \tan p$

This gives that $r + p = 90°$. i.e. reflected and refracted rays are perpendicular to each other.

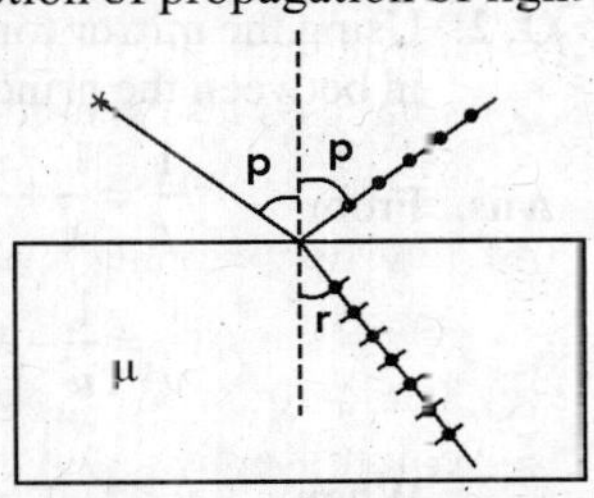

(*iv*) Polarised light may also be obtained by scattering phenomenon.

(*v*) **Law of Malus :** When a beam of plane polarised light (intensity I_0) is passed through a polaroid (used as analyser) then the intensity of transmitted light is

$$I = I_0 \cos^2 \theta$$

Where θ is the angle between the polarization axes of the analyser and the polariser

(*vi*) When unpolarised light falls on a polaroid (polariser) then intensity of transmitted light (which is polarised)

$$= \frac{I_{unpolarised}}{2}$$

(*vii*) The phenomena of interference, diffraction and polarisation are essentially the wave phenomena. The existence of these phenomena can be explained only when we assume that light is a wave motion.

(A) RAY OPTICS

VERY SHORT ANSWER TYPE QUESTIONS

(Carrying 1 mark)

Q. 1. Mirrors in search lights are parabolic and not spherical, why?

Ans. Parabolic mirrors produce intense parallel beam free from spherical aberation.

Q. 2. Using the mirror formula show that a virtual image is obtained when an object is placed in between the principal focus and pole of the concave mirror.

Ans. From $\frac{1}{f}=\frac{1}{v}+\frac{1}{u}$ we have

$$\frac{1}{v}=\frac{1}{u}-\frac{1}{f}$$

When $u<f, \frac{1}{u}>\frac{1}{f}$ so that v is positive. Thus the image is virtual.

Q. 3. Plot a graph between $\frac{1}{v}$ and $\frac{1}{u}$ for a concave mirror. What does the slope of the graph yield.

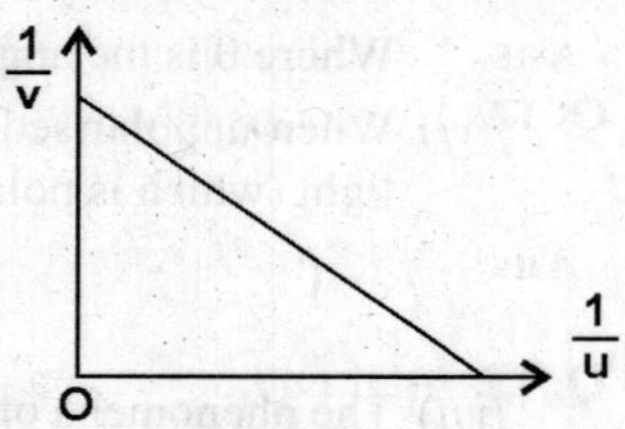

Ans. For $\frac{1}{v}+\frac{1}{u}=\frac{1}{f}=\text{constant}$

The graph is shown. It is a straight line. The slope gives

$$\frac{\frac{1}{v}}{\frac{1}{u}}=\frac{u}{v}=\frac{1}{m}$$

Where m is the magnification.

Q. 4. When light undergoes refraction at the surface of separation of two media, what happens to its wavelength?

Ans. Wavelength changes. If light enters into an optically denser medium, the wavelength decreases. On entering into a rarer medium, wavelength increases.

Q. 5. Rainbow is never observed on the surface of the moon. Why?

Ans. It is because there is no atmosphere on the surface of the moon.

Q. 6. Sun glasses are made up of curved surfaces, but the power of the sunglasses is zero why?

Ans. The sunglasses are the convex concave combination of same powers. The resultant power $P' = P - P = 0$.

Q. 7. A glass slab is placed over a page in which letters are printed in different colours. Will the image of all the letters lie in the same plane?

Ans. The refractive index (μ) of glass is different for different colours, therefore, images of different coloured letters will not be raised equally and, hence, they will not lie in the same plane.

Q. 8. The refractive index of glass is 1.5 for light waves of $\lambda = 6000$Å. Calculate their wavelength in glass.

Ans.
$$\mu = \frac{c}{v} = \frac{v\lambda_v}{v\lambda_g}$$

or
$$\lambda_g = \frac{\lambda_v}{\mu} = \frac{6000}{1.5} = 4000\text{Å}.$$

Q. 9. An object is held at the principal focus of a concave lens of focal length *f*. Where is the image formed?

Ans. As $u = -f$ and for concave lens *f* is also –ve.

We have
$$\frac{1}{v} = \frac{1}{u} + \frac{1}{f}$$
$$= \frac{1}{(-f)} + \frac{1}{(-f)} = \frac{-2}{f}$$

or
$$v = -\frac{f}{2}.$$

Thus, the virtual image is formed on the same side of lens at a distance $f/2$ from the lens.

Q. 10. A diverging lens of focal length '*f*' is cut into identical parts each forming a plano concave lens. What is the focal length of each part?

Ans. Focal length of each part, which behaves as plano-concave lens, will be double the focal length of original lens. Thus, each part has a focal length 2*f*.

Q. 11. If the wavelength of incident light of convex lens is increased, how will its focal length change?

Ans. Focal length of a convex lens increases if the wavelength of the incident light is increased.

Q. 12. How does focal length of a lens change when red light is replaced by blue light?

Ans. $\frac{1}{f} = (\mu - 1)\left(\frac{1}{R_1} - \frac{1}{R_2}\right)$. As $\mu_b > \mu_r$ $\therefore$ $f_b < f_r$ *i.e.,* focal length of lens decreases.

Q. 13. A glass lens of refractive index 1.5 is placed in a liquid. What must be the refractive index of the liquid in order to make the lens disappear?

Ans. Refractive index of the liquid should be 1.5 *i.e.,* same as that of glass so that the lens disappears when immersed in the liquid.

Q. 14. A lens of focal length *f* is split into two parts as shown in Fig. 6.1. What is the focal length of either part?

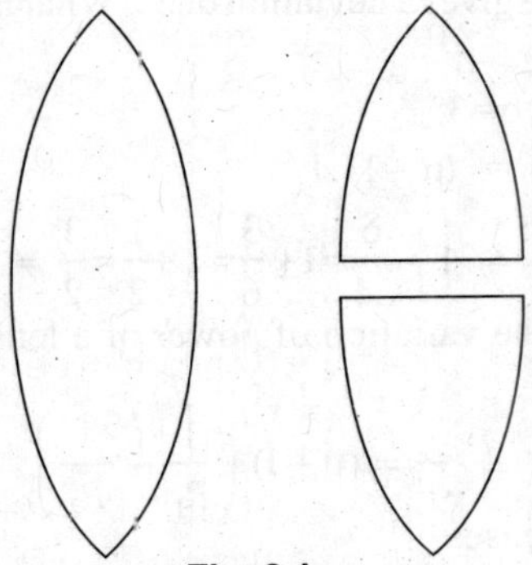

Fig. 6.1

Ans. Focal length of each part is the same as that of the original lens.

Q. 15. What are the advantages of totally reflected prisms over a plane mirror?

Ans. The advantage is that the reflection is 100%, therefore, bright image is formed and multiple images are not formed and no silvering required.

Q. 16. Refractive indices of glass for lights of yellow, green and red colours are μ_y, μ_g and μ_r respectively. Rearrange these symbols in an increasing order of values.

Ans. The increasing order is : $\mu_r < \mu_y < \mu_g$.

Q. 17. Draw a ray diagram for the pattern followed by the ray of light passing through a glass prism immersed in a liquid with refractive index greater than glass.

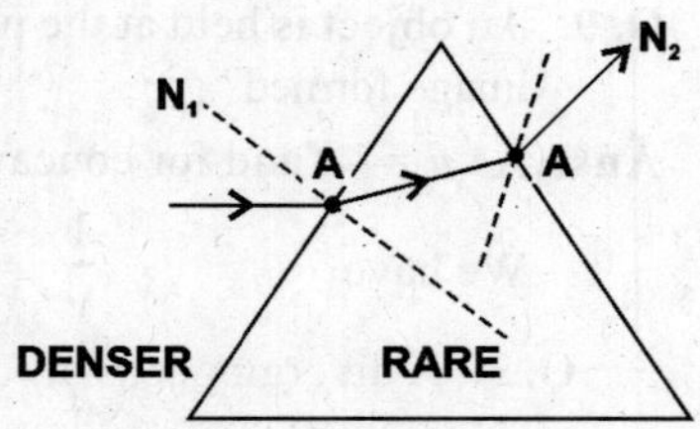

Ans. At A the ray is travelling from denser to rare medium, hence moves away from the normal. At B, the ray travels from rare to denser medium and bends towards the normal at B.

Q. 18. Show that a concave lens always produces a virtual image irrespective of the position of the object.

Ans. For a lens, $\frac{1}{f} = \frac{1}{v} - \frac{1}{u} \Rightarrow v = \frac{f.u}{f+u}$

For concave lens, f is negative and u is also negative.

So that $v = -$ve i.e. the image is always virtual.

Q. 19. How does resolving power of a microscope change on decreasing diameter of objective lens?

Ans. On decreasing diameter of an objective lens, resolving power of microscope decreases.

Q. 20. What is the magnifying power of telescope whose objective and eye-piece focal length are 180 cm and 3 cm respectively?

Ans. We have magnifying power

$$m = \frac{f_0}{f_e} = \frac{180}{3} = 60.$$

SHORT ANSWER TYPE QUESTIONS (SA–I)

(Carrying 2 marks)

Q. 1. A thin prism of 6° angle gives a deviation of 3°. What is the refractive index of material of prism?

Ans. Here $A = 6°$ and $\delta = 3°$

For a thin prism, $\delta = (\mu - 1) A$

or $\mu = 1 + \frac{\delta}{A} = 1 + \frac{3}{6} = 1 + \frac{1}{2} = \frac{3}{2} = 1.5.$

Q. 2. Draw a plot showing the variation of power of a lens with the wavelength of incident light.

Ans. We know $P = \frac{1}{f} = (\mu - 1)\left(\frac{1}{R_1} - \frac{1}{R_2}\right)$

As λ increases, μ decreases

$\therefore$ Power P decreases.

The variation of P with λ is shown in Fig. 6.2.

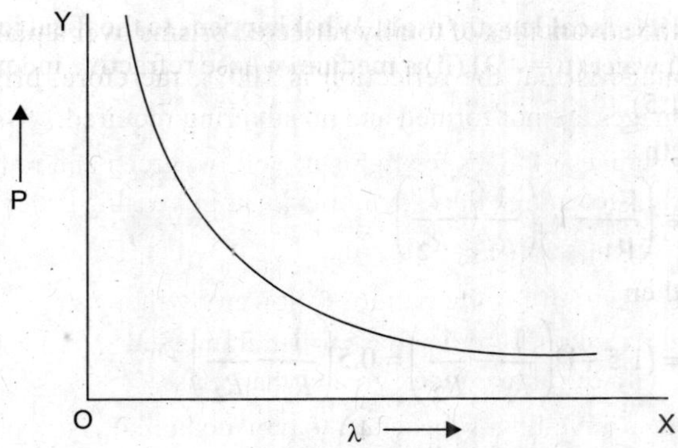

Fig. 6.2

Q. 3. A diverging lens of focal length F is cut into two parts, each forming a plano concave lens. What is the focal length of each part?

Ans. For a single diverging lens,

$$\frac{1}{F} = (\mu - 1)\left(\frac{1}{R_1} - \frac{1}{R_2}\right)$$

Let $R_1 = -R, R_2 = R$

$$\therefore \quad \frac{1}{F} = (\mu - 1)\left(\frac{1}{-R} - \frac{1}{R}\right) = \frac{-2(\mu - 1)}{R}$$

For each half (which is plano concave) as shown in Fig. 6.5,

$R_1 = -R$ and $R_2 = \infty$

$$\therefore \quad \frac{1}{F_1} = \frac{1}{F_2} = (\mu - 1)\left(\frac{1}{-R} - \frac{1}{\infty}\right) = \frac{-(\mu - 1)}{R} = \frac{1}{2F}$$

$$\therefore \quad F_1 = F_2 = 2F.$$

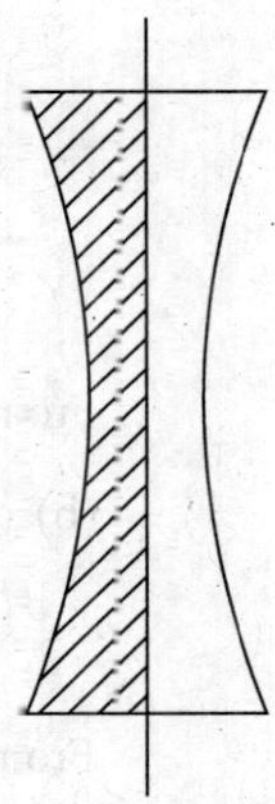

Fig. 6.3

Q. 4. A ray of light falls normally on one face of a right angled prism. If critical angle for material of the prism is 45°, trace the course of rays. Calculate μ.

Ans. The incident ray PQ falling normally on face AB of prism goes straight striking face AC at 45° as shown in Fig. 6.4. As $C = 45°$, therefore, the refracted ray QR suffers total internal reflection and goes along RD.

Further $\quad \mu = \frac{1}{\sin C} = \frac{1}{\sin 45°} = \sqrt{2}$

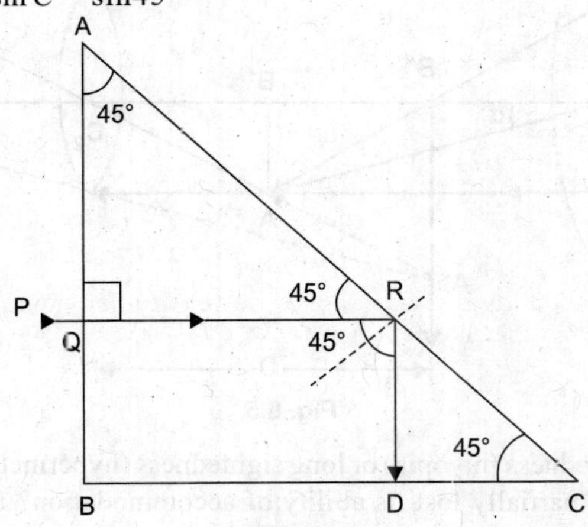

Fig. 6.4

Q. 5. A convex lens has focal length f in air. What happens to the focal length of the lens when immersed in (i) water ($\mu = 4/3$) (ii) a medium whose refractive index is twice that of glass (μ for glass = 1.5)

Ans. The focal length

$$\frac{1}{f} = \left(\frac{\mu_2}{\mu_1} - 1\right)\left(\frac{1}{R_1} - \frac{1}{R_2}\right) \quad ...(i)$$

In air, $\mu_1 = 1$, then

$$\frac{1}{f} = (1.5 - 1)\left(\frac{1}{R_1} - \frac{1}{R_2}\right) = 0.5\left(\frac{1}{R_1} - \frac{1}{R_2}\right) \quad ...(ii)$$

(a) When immersed in water $\left(\mu_1 = \frac{4}{3}\right)$

$$\frac{1}{f_\omega} = \left(\frac{3 \times 1.5}{4} - 1\right)\left(\frac{1}{R_1} - \frac{1}{R_2}\right)$$

$$= \frac{1}{8}\left(\frac{1}{R_1} - \frac{1}{R_2}\right) \quad ...(iii)$$

From (ii) and (iii) $\frac{f_\omega}{f} = 0.5 \times 8 = 4 \Rightarrow f_\omega = 4f$

(b) When $\mu_1 = 2\mu_2$ in (i)

$$\frac{1}{f'} = \left(\frac{1}{2} - 1\right)\left(\frac{1}{R_1} - \frac{1}{R_2}\right) = -\frac{1}{2}\left(\frac{1}{R_1} - \frac{1}{R_2}\right) \quad ...(iv)$$

From (ii) and (iv)

$$f' = -f$$

Q. 6. Draw a ray diagram showing how the final image of a distant object is formed using an astronomical telescope in the near point position.

Ans. The ray diagram showing image formation by an astronomical telescope in near point position is shown in Fig. 6.5.

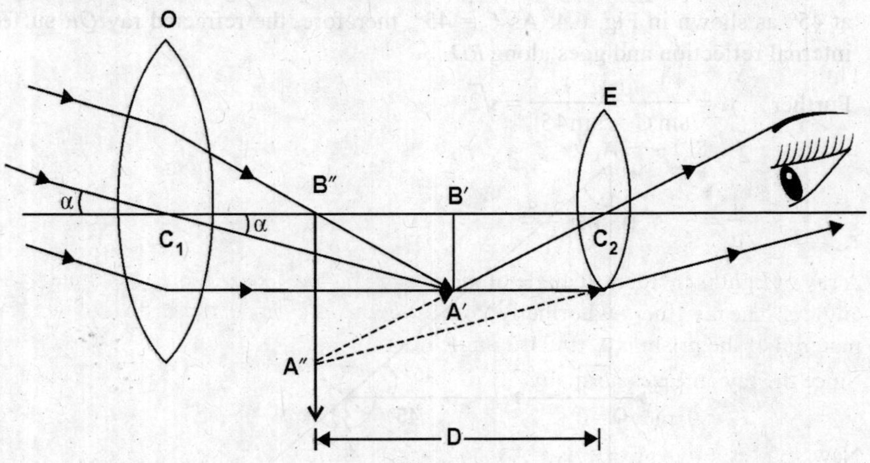

Fig. 6.5

Q. 7. Does short sightedness (myopia) or long sightedness (hypermetropia) imply necessarily that the eye has partially lost its ability of accommodation? If not, what might cause these defects of vision?

Ans. No, a person may have normal ability of accommodation and yet he may be myopic or hypermetropic. Infact, myopia arises when length of eye ball (from front to back) get elongated and hypermetropia arises when length of eye ball gets shortened. However, when eye ball has normal length, but the eye lens loses partially its power of accommodation, the defect is called presbiopia.

Q. 8. Three rays of light, red (R), blue (B) and green (G) are incident on face AB of a right angled isosceles prism (fig.). The refractive index for the material of the prism for red, blue and green light are 1.39, 1.47 and 1.43 respectively. Which of these rays will emerge out of the face AC of the prism.

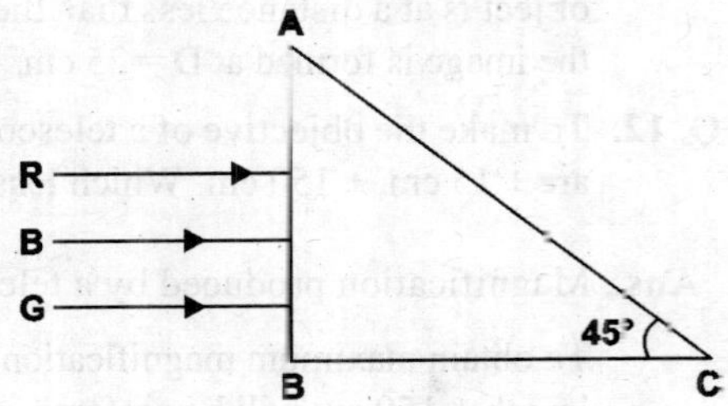

Ans. For each ray, the angle of incidence on face AC will be 45°.

Critical angle for red ray $C_R = Sin^{-1}\left(\frac{1}{1.39}\right) = 46.5°$

Critical angle for blue ray $C_B = Sin^{-1}\left(\frac{1}{1.47}\right) = 43.5°$

Critical angle for green ray $C_G = Sin^{-1}\left(\frac{1}{1.43}\right) = 44°$

Since C_B and C_G are less than the angle of incidence, hence these rays will undergo total internal reflection on face AC of the prism while the red ray for which the angle of incidence (45°) is less than C_R will come out of the prism through face AC.

Q. 9. A mark on the bottom of a beaker is focussed by a vertical microscope. When water is poured in the beaker up to a height of 8 cm, the microscope has to be raised through a distance of 2 cm in order to bring the mark in focus again. Calculate the refractive index of water.

Ans. Real depth of mark in water = 8 cm.

Shift in the position of mark = distance raised
= 2 cm

Thus $\Delta x = t\left(1 - \frac{1}{\mu}\right)$

$$2 = 8\left(1 - \frac{1}{\mu}\right)$$

$$\frac{1}{\mu} = \frac{3}{4} \text{ so that } \mu = \frac{4}{3}$$

Q. 10. A ray of light is incident at angle of incidence *i* on one face of a prism of small refracting angle *A*. The ray emerges normally from the opposite surface. If the refractive index of the material of the prism is μ, find the angle of incidence.

Ans. Since the ray emerges normally

$i_2 = 0$ and $r_2 = 0$

Now, $r_1 + r_2 = A \Rightarrow r_1 = A$

For the first face $\mu = \frac{\sin i_1}{\sin r_1} = \frac{i_1}{r_1}$ (Since prism is thin)

Thus $i_1 = \mu r = \mu A$

Q. 11. The angle subtended at the eye by an object is equal to the angle subtended at the eye by the virtual image produced by a magnifying glass. In what sense then does a magnifying glass provide angular magnification?

Ans. The image size formed by a magnifying glass is bigger than the object, the angular size of the image is equal to the angular size of the object. In case of magnifying glass, the object is at a distance less than the least distance of distinct vision (D = 25 cm) whereas the image is formed at D = 25 cm.

Q. 12. To make the objective of a telescope, there are four lenses available. Their focal lengths are ± 15 cm, ± 150 cm. Which lens you will prefer and why?

Ans. Magnification produced by a telescope $= \frac{f_0}{f_e}$

To obtain maximum magnification, f_0 must be large and positive. Therefore lens of focal length + 150 cm will be prefered.

SHORT ANSWER TYPE QUESTIONS (SA-II)

(Carrying 3 marks)

Q. 1. Prove that vertical image produced by a convex mirror is always smaller in size and is located between the focus and the pole.

Ans. We know from mirror formula,

$$\frac{1}{f} = \frac{1}{v} + \frac{1}{u} \quad \text{or} \quad \frac{1}{v} = \frac{1}{f} - \frac{1}{u}$$

For a convex mirror, $f > 0$ (being positive) and $u < 0$ (being negative)

$$\therefore \quad \frac{1}{v} > \frac{1}{f} \quad \text{or} \quad v < f$$

Hence, the image is located between the pole and the focus. It must be at the back of the mirror and, hence, virtual, independent of location of the object.

As $v < u$, therefore, $m = \frac{v}{u} = 1$. $\therefore$ Image is always diminished.

Q. 2. A convex lens made of a material of refractive index μ_1 is kept in a medium of refractive index μ_2. A parallel beam of light is incident on the lens. Complete the path of rays of light emerging from the convex lens if *(i)* $\mu_1 > \mu_2$, *(ii)* $\mu_1 = \mu_2$ and *(iii)* $\mu_1 < \mu_2$.

Ans. The path of the rays of light emerging from the convex lens in different cases is shown in given Fig. 6.6.

(i) $\mu_1 > \mu_2$ *(ii)* $\mu_1 = \mu_2$ *(iii)* $\mu_1 < \mu_2$

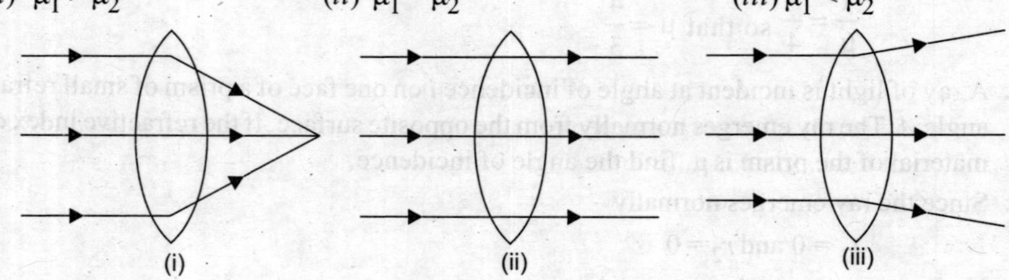

Fig. 6.6

Q. 3. Find the position of an object, when placed in front of a concave mirror of focal length 20 cm, and produces a real image, twice the size of an object.

Ans. Here, focal length of a concave length $(f) = -20$ cm.
Since the real image is formed,

so, $$m = \frac{-v}{u} = -2$$

or $$\frac{v}{u} = 2 \Rightarrow v = 24$$

By mirror formula, $\frac{1}{f} = \frac{1}{u} + \frac{1}{v}$, we get

$$\frac{1}{u} + \frac{1}{2u} = -\frac{1}{20}$$

$$\Rightarrow \quad \frac{2+1}{2u} = -\frac{1}{20}$$

$$\Rightarrow \quad \frac{3}{2u} = -\frac{1}{20} \quad \text{or} \quad 2u = -60 \quad \text{or} \quad u = -30 \text{ cm.}$$

Position of an object is 30 cm.

Q. 4. A person can see clearly only upto 3 m. Prescribe a lens for his spectacles so that he can clearly see upto 12 m.

Ans. Here $u = -12$ m, $v = -3$m and $f = ?$

As $$\frac{1}{f} = -\frac{1}{u} + \frac{1}{v}$$

$$= \frac{1}{12} - \frac{1}{3} = \frac{1-4}{12} = -\frac{3}{12} = -\frac{1}{4}$$

$\therefore$ $$f = -4\text{m} = -400 \text{ cm}$$

Also, $$P = \frac{100}{f} = \frac{100}{-400} = -0.25 \text{ dioptre.}$$

Q. 5. An astronomical telescope has a magnifying power of 10. In normal adjustment, distance between the objective and eye piece is 22 cm. Calculate the focal length of objective lens.

Ans. Here $m = -10$, $L = 22$ cm, $f_0 = ?$

As $$m = -\frac{f_0}{f_e}$$

$\therefore$ $$-10 = -\frac{f_0}{f_e} \quad \text{or} \quad f_0 = 10 f_e$$

As $$L = f_0 + f_e$$

$\therefore$ $$22 = 10 f_e + f_e = 11 f_e$$

or $$f_e = \frac{22}{11} = 2 \text{ cm}$$

$\therefore$ $$f_0 = 10 f_e = 10 \times 2 = 20 \text{ cm.}$$

Q. 6. A glass of prism is immersed in water. If the angle of prism is 70°, calculate the angle of minimum deviation for a ray of light while passing through the prism in water. Given $_a\mu_g = 1.62$ and $_a\mu_w = 1.33$

Ans. Here $A = 70°$, $_a\mu_g = 1.62$, $_a\mu_w = 1.33$

We have $$_w\mu_g = \frac{_a\mu_g}{_a\mu_w} = \frac{1.62}{1.33} = 1.2180$$

$$_w\mu_g = \frac{\sin(A + \delta_m)/2}{\sin A/2}$$

$$\sin\left(\frac{A+\delta_m}{2}\right) = {}_w\mu_g \times \sin\frac{A}{2}$$

$$= 1.2180 \times \sin\frac{70}{2} = 1.2180 \times \sin 35°$$

$$= 1.2180 \times 0.5736 = 0.6986$$

Then, $\frac{A+\delta_m}{2} = \sin^{-1}(0.6986) = 44.32°$

$$\delta_m = 2 \times 44.32° - 70 = 18.64°.$$

Q. 7. **A point source of light is placed 4m below the surface of a transparent liquid of refractive index $\frac{5}{3}$. Find the minimum diameter of a disc whch should be placed over the source, on the surface of liquid so that the source is not seen when viewed from above.**

Ans. The rays falling on disc between A and B will not emerge out. Radius of disc $OA = OB = r$

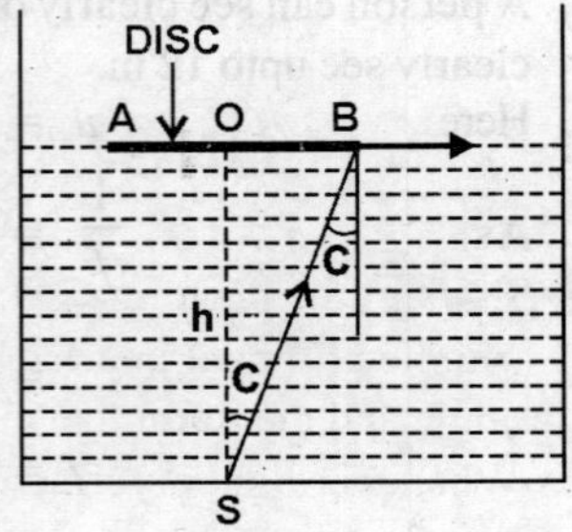

Then $SinC = \frac{r}{\sqrt{h^2+r^2}}$

or $\frac{1}{\mu} = \frac{r}{\sqrt{h^2+r^2}}$

or $r^2 = \frac{h^2}{\mu^2-1} = \frac{16}{\frac{25}{9}-1} = 9$

$\Rightarrow$ $r = 3$ m and diameter = 6 m

Q. 8. **Derive the formula for refractive index of the material of prism in terms of prism angle and angle of minimum deviation.**

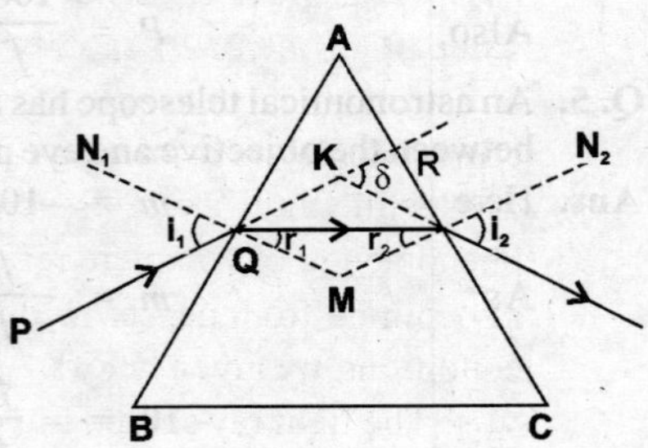

Ans. In the fig. monochromatic light ray PQ falls on face AB of the prism at angle of incidence i_1. The corresponding angle of refraction is r_1. The emergent ray is RS and i_2 is the angle of mergence. The angle of deviation is δ.

By geometry $\angle A + \angle M = 180°$

and $r_1 + r_2 + \angle M = 180°$

So that $r_1 + r_2 = A$ ...(i)

Also $\delta = i_1 - r_1 + i_2 - r_2$

$i_1 + i_2 - (r_1 + r_2)$

$i_1 + i2 - A$ ...(ii)

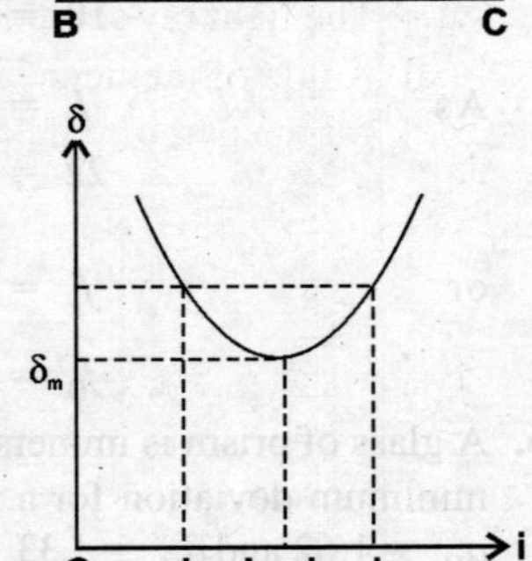

The variation of δ with i is shown in the fig. In the position of min. deviation $\delta = \delta_m$, $i_1 = i_2 = i$ (say) and then $r_1 = r_2 = r$ (say)

From (i) and (ii)

$$\delta_m = 2i - A \Rightarrow i = \frac{A+\delta_m}{2}$$

and $$2r = A \Rightarrow r = \frac{A}{2}.$$

For refraction $\mu = \dfrac{Sin\, i_1}{Sin\, r_1} = \dfrac{Sin\, i}{Sin\, r} = \dfrac{Sin\dfrac{A+\delta_m}{2}}{Sin\dfrac{A}{2}}$

Q. 9. There is a small air bubble inside a glass sphere ($\mu = 1.5$) of radius 10 cm. The bubble is 4.0 cm below the surface and is viewed normally from the out side. Find the apparent position of the bubble.

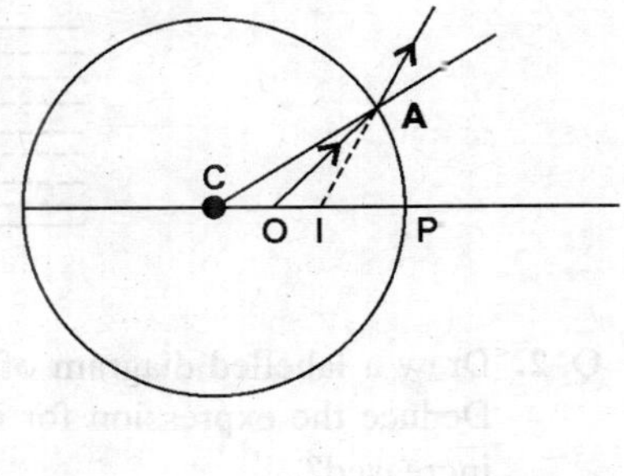

Ans. As given, $u = -4$ cm, $R = -10$ cm

In the fig. bubble is at O.

The image is seen at I

$\mu_1 = 1.5 \quad \mu_2 = 1.0$

Applying

$$\frac{\mu_2}{v} - \frac{\mu_1}{u} = \frac{\mu_2 - \mu_1}{R} \Rightarrow \frac{1}{v} - \frac{1.5}{-4} = \frac{1-1.5}{-10} \Rightarrow v = -3\text{cm}$$

LONG ANSWER TYPE QUESTIONS

(Carrying 5 marks)

Q. 1. Explain the phenomenon of total internal reflection. State two conditions that must be satisfied for total internal reflection to take place. Derive the relation between the critical angle and the refractive index of the medium.

Ans. Whenever light is refracted from a denser to a rarer medium, the angle of refraction $\angle r$ has a value greater than the angle of incidence $\angle i$. As value of $\angle i$ is gradually increased, value of $\angle r$ increases rapidly and for a certain value of incidence angle (known as the critical angle i_c) the angle of refraction is 90°. For an angle of incidence greater than the critical angle, no refraction takes place and whole light is totally internally reflected in denser medium itself as shown in given Fig. 6.7. Total internal reflection is the phenomenon of complete reflection of light back into the denser medium, when a light ray coming from denser medium is incident on the surface of a rarer medium. The two conditions are given below.

(*i*) The light ray should travel in a denser medium towards a rarer medium

(*ii*) Angle of incidence in the denser medium should be greater than the critical angle for the pair of media in contact.

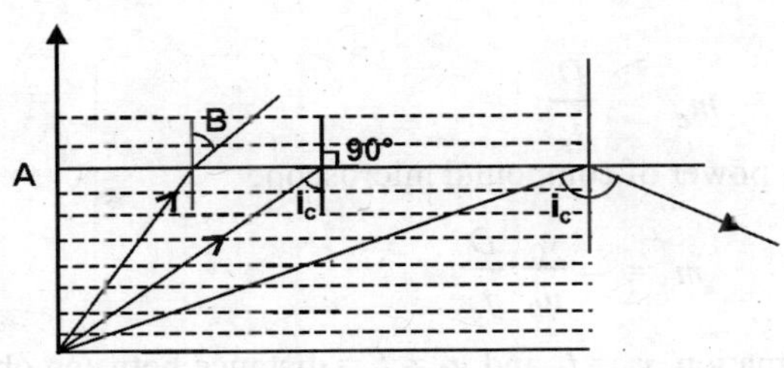

Fig. 6.7

In Fig. 6.7, let i_c be the initial angle in an optically denser medium number 2 for which angle of refraction in rarer medium number, 1 is 90°. Then from Snell's law, we have

$$\frac{\sin i}{\sin 90°} = n_{12}$$

But $\sin 90° = 1, i = i_c$ hence $\sin i_c = \dfrac{1}{n_{21}}$

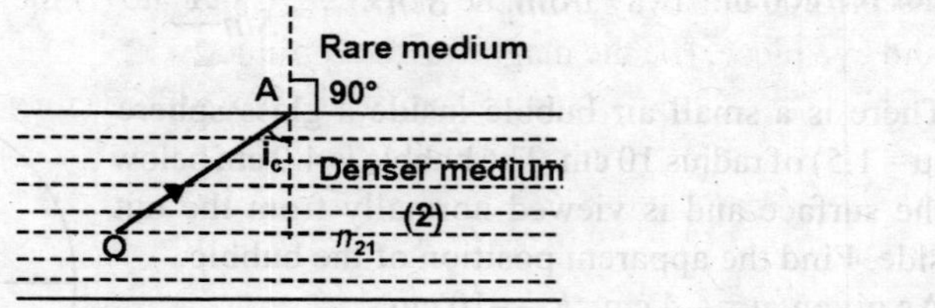

Fig. 6.8

Q. 2. Draw a labelled diagram of a compound microscope when the image is formed at ∞. Deduce the expression for its magnifying power. How can the magnifying power be increased?

Ans. A labelled ray diagram of a compound microscope, when the final image is formed at infinity, has been shown in given Fig. 6.15.

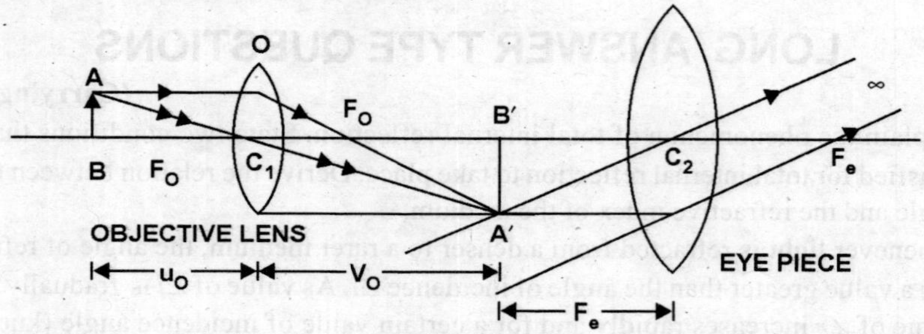

Fig. 6.9

If m_0 and m_e be the magnifications produced by an objective lens and eye lens respectively, the total magnifying power of microscope

$$m = m_0 \times m_e \qquad ...(i)$$

If u_0 be the distance of object AB from the objective lens and v_0 be the distance of image $A'B'$ formed by objective from itself, then

$$m_0 = -\frac{v_0}{u_0} \qquad ...(ii)$$

The magnifying power of eye piece, where the final image is formed at infinity (*i.e.*, $u_e = f_e$) is

$$m_e = \frac{D}{f_e} \qquad ...(iii)$$

∴ Magnifying power of compound microscope

$$m = -\frac{v_0}{u_0} \cdot \frac{D}{f_e} \qquad ...(iv)$$

As first approximation, $v_0 = f_0$ and $v_0 = L$ = distance between objective and eye piece, then

$$m = -\frac{L}{f_0} \cdot \frac{D}{f_e}$$

To increase the magnifying power of compound microscope, focal length of an objective lens as well as eye piece should be small enough.

Q. 3. A telescope has an objective of focal length 50 cm and eye piece of focal length 5 cm. The least distance of distinct vision is 25 cm. The telescope is focussed for distinct vision on a scale 200 cm away from the objective. Calculate (*i*) the separation between objective and eye piece, (*ii*) the magnification product.

$$f_0 = 50 \text{ cm}, f_e = 5 \text{ cm}, d = 25 \text{ cm}, u_0 = -200 \text{ cm}, m = ? L = ?$$

Ans. As $$\frac{1}{v_0} - \frac{1}{u_0} = \frac{1}{f_0}$$

$$\therefore \quad \frac{1}{v_0} = \frac{1}{f_0} + \frac{1}{u_0} = \frac{1}{50} - \frac{1}{200} = \frac{4-1}{200} = \frac{3}{200} \Rightarrow v_0 = \frac{200}{3} \text{ cm}$$

Linear magnification produced by objective lens

$$m_0 = \frac{v_0}{u_e} = -\frac{200/3}{200} = -\frac{1}{3}$$

Now, $$v_e = d = -25 \text{ cm}$$

From $$\frac{1}{v_e} - \frac{1}{u_e} = \frac{1}{f_e} \Rightarrow -\frac{1}{u_e} = \frac{1}{f_e} - \frac{1}{v_e} = \frac{1}{5} + \frac{1}{25} = \frac{5+1}{25}$$

$$\Rightarrow \quad v_e = -\frac{25}{6} \text{ cm}$$

Linear magnification produced by eye piece

$$m_e = \frac{v_e}{u_e} = \frac{-25}{-25/6} = 6$$

Net magnification produced,

$$m = m_0 \times m_e = -\frac{1}{3} \times 6 = -2 \text{ Ans.} \qquad \text{...(ii)}$$

Distance between objective and eye piece

$$L = |v_0| + |u_e|$$

$$= \frac{200}{3} + \frac{25}{6} = \frac{400+25}{6} = \frac{425}{6}$$

$$\therefore \quad L = 70.8 \text{ cm. Ans.} \qquad \text{...(i)}$$

Q. 4. Draw and describe an astronomical telescope. Derive an expression for its magnifying power when final image is (*i*) at infinity, (*ii*) at the least distance of distant vision.

Ans. An astronomical telescope is an opitcal instrument which is used for observing distinct images of heavenly bodies like stars, planets, etc.

(*i*) We have, in normal adjustment of telescope, the final image at infinity. As the object lies at very huge distance, therefore, angle subtended by the object at C_2 (when eye is held) is almost the same at the angle subtended by the object at C_1 (because C_1 is very close to C_2). Let it be α *i.e.*, $\angle A'C_1B' = \alpha$, rays coming from the final image.

(*ii*) The course of rays in astronomical telescope, when the final image is formed, is at the least distance vision (*d*) from the eye.

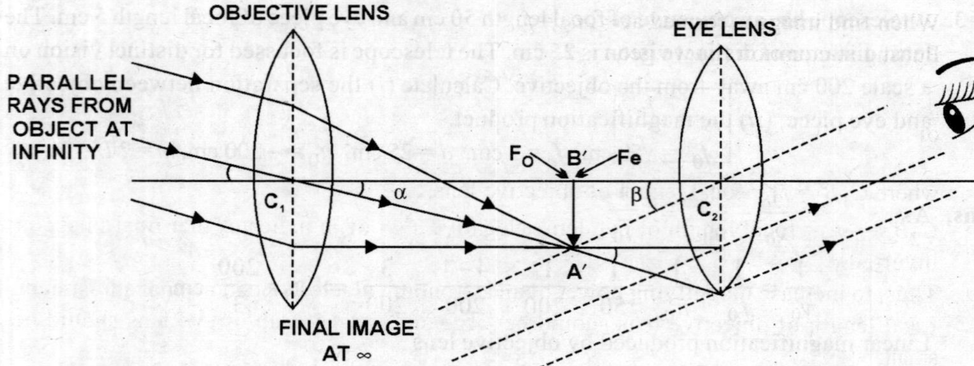

Fig. 6.10

As the object is very far off, angle subtended by the object on the eye is almost the same as the angle subtended by it at C_1. Let it be α,

$\therefore \quad \angle A'C_1B' = \alpha$

Further, Let $\angle A'' C_2 B'' = \beta$,

where $\quad C_2 B'' = d$

∴ By definition, magnifying power,

$$m = \frac{\beta}{\alpha} \quad \ldots(i)$$

As angles α and β are small, therefore, $\beta \simeq \tan \beta$ and $\alpha \simeq \tan \alpha$.

From (*iv*), $\quad m = \dfrac{\tan \beta}{\tan \alpha}$

In $\Delta A'B'C_2$, $\tan \beta = \dfrac{A'B'}{C_2B'}$

In $\Delta A'B'C_1$, $\tan \alpha = \dfrac{A'B'}{C_1B'}$

Putting in (*v*), we get

$$m = \frac{A'B'}{C_2B'} \times \frac{C_1B'}{A'B'}$$

$$m = \frac{C_1B'}{C_2B'} = \frac{f_0}{-u_e} \quad \ldots(ii)$$

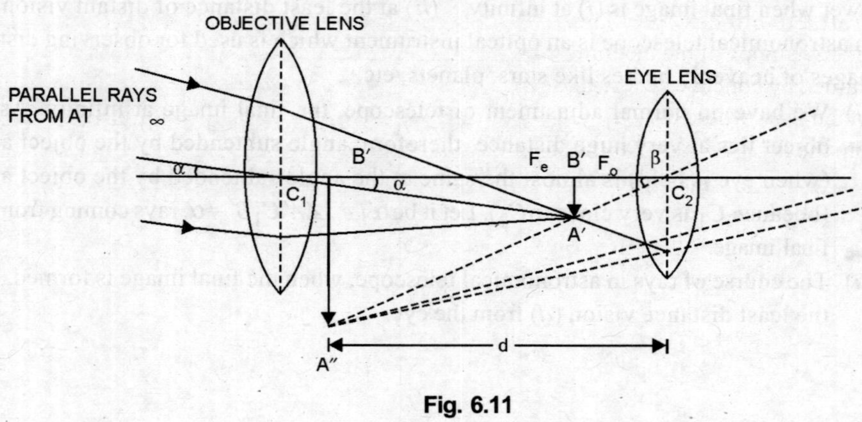

Fig. 6.11

When find image is formed at ∞ . $u_e = f_e$
Putting in equation (ii) we get,

or
$$\boxed{m = \frac{f_0}{-f_e}}$$

where $C_1B' = f_0$ = focal length of objective lens.
$C_2B' = -f_e$ = focal length of eye lens. Negative sign of m indicates that final image is inverted.
Thus, to increase magnifying power of an astronomical telescope in normal acjustment, focal length of objective lens should be large and focal length of eye lens should be small.

Note: (*i*) In normal adjustment, distance between the objective lens and eye lens $= (f_0 + f_e)$.

(*ii*) Angular magnification produced by the telescope $= \frac{\beta}{\alpha}$. Clearly, visual angle β is much larger as compared to α.
where $C_1B' = f_0$ = focal length of objective lens.
$C_2B' = -u_e$, distance of $A'B'$ acting as the object for eye lens.
Now, for eye lens, $\frac{1}{v} = \frac{1}{u} - \frac{1}{f}$
Taking $v_e = -d$, $u = -u_e$ and $f = +f_e$, we get $\frac{1}{-d} - \frac{1}{-u_e} = \frac{1}{f_e}$

$$\frac{1}{u_e} = \frac{1}{f_e} + \frac{1}{d} = \frac{1}{f_e}\left(1 + \frac{f_e}{d}\right)$$

Putting in (*ii*), we get

$$\boxed{m = -\frac{f_0}{f_e}\left(1 + \frac{f_e}{d}\right)}$$

Q. 5. Derive the formula for refraction at spherical surface and hence obtain the lens maker's formula.

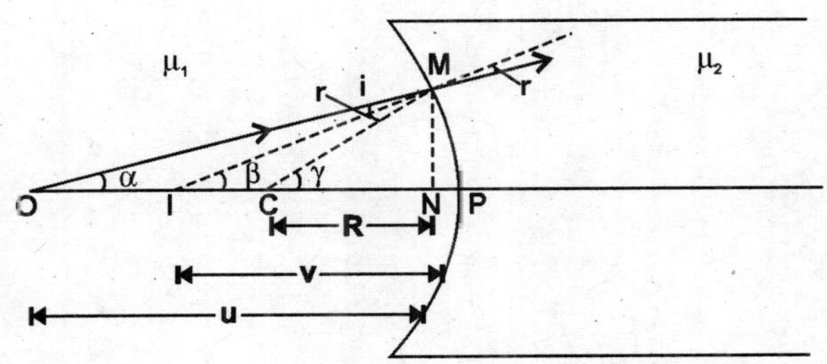

Fig. 6.12

Ans. Object O is placed in medium of refractive index μ_1. The refractive index of the medium bounded by concave spherical surface is μ_2 where $\mu_2 > \mu_1$.
From the fig $\quad i + \alpha = \gamma$ so that $i = \gamma - \alpha$
and $\quad r + \beta = \gamma$ so that $r = \gamma - \beta$
By Snell's Law

$$\mu_1 \text{ Sin } i = \mu_2 \text{ . Sin } r$$

Taking i and r small

$$\mu_1 \,.\, i = \mu_2 \,.\, r$$

or $\quad \mu_1(\gamma - \alpha) = \mu_2 \,.\, (\gamma - \beta)$

or $\quad \mu_2 \,.\, \beta - \mu_1 \,.\, \alpha = (\mu_2 - \mu_1)\gamma \quad$ ...(i)

We can take $\quad \alpha \approx \tan\alpha = \dfrac{MN}{ON} = \dfrac{MN}{OP} = \dfrac{MN}{-u}$

$$\beta \approx \tan\beta = \frac{MN}{IN} = \frac{MN}{IP} = \frac{MN}{-v}$$

$$\gamma \approx \tan\gamma = \frac{MN}{CN} = \frac{MN}{CP} = \frac{MN}{-R}$$

Putting these values in (i)

$$\frac{\mu_2}{-v} - \frac{\mu_1}{-u} = \frac{\mu_2 - \mu_1}{-R}$$

or $\quad \dfrac{\mu_2}{v} - \dfrac{\mu_1}{u} = \dfrac{\mu_2 - \mu_1}{R}$ ...(ii)

Lens maker's formula

For refraction at surface *I* of lens,

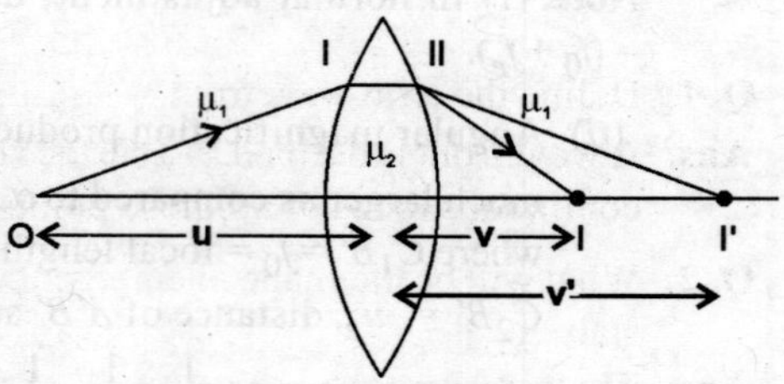

$$\frac{\mu_2}{v'} - \frac{\mu_1}{u} = \frac{\mu_2 - \mu_1}{R_1} \quad ...(iii)$$

For refraction at surface (ii)

$$\frac{\mu_1}{v} - \frac{\mu_2}{v'} = \frac{\mu_1 - \mu_2}{R_2} \quad ...(iv)$$

Adding (iii) and (iv)

$$\mu_1\left(\frac{1}{v} - \frac{1}{u}\right) = (\mu_2 - \mu_1)\left(\frac{1}{R_1} - \frac{1}{R_2}\right)$$

or $\quad \dfrac{1}{v} - \dfrac{1}{u} = \left(\dfrac{\mu_2}{\mu_1} - 1\right)\left(\dfrac{1}{R_1} - \dfrac{1}{R_2}\right)$

When $\quad u = \infty, v = f$

Thus $\quad \dfrac{1}{f} = \left(\dfrac{\mu_2}{\mu_1} - 1\right)\left(\dfrac{1}{R_1} - \dfrac{1}{R_2}\right)$

❑❑❑

(B) WAVE OPTICS

VERY SHORT ANSWER TYPE QUESTIONS

(Carrying 1 mark)

Q. 1. Define the term wavefront.

Ans. A wavefront is defined as a surface of constant phase. In other words, a wavefront is the continuous locus of all those points which are in same phase at any instant of time.

Q. 2. What will be the shape of emergent wavefront when a spherical wave front falls on glass slab.

Ans. The emergent wave front will be spherical due to the reason that the glass slab has uniform thickness.

Q. 3. What are coherent sources of light?

Ans. Light sources which emit light waves of same wavelength (or frequency) having either zero or a constant originating phase difference.

Q. 4. Why does a soap bubble show beautiful colours when illuminated by white light?

Ans. In case of soap bubble, the light is reflected from the outer and inner surfaces of the soap bubble. The interference of the reflected light waves produces beautiful colours.

Q. 5. If the path difference produced in the light waves coming out of two slits for yellow colour of light at a point on the screen is $\frac{3\lambda}{2}$, what will be the colour of the fringe at that point?

Ans. Since the path difference for yellow light is odd multiple of $\frac{\lambda}{2}$, hence there will be minimum for yellow light i.e., yellow colour will be absent.

Q. 6. How the angular separation of interference fringes in young's double slit experiment will change if (i) The distnace between the slits is increased (ii) distance of screen from the slits is increased?

Ans. Angular fringe width $\beta = \frac{\lambda}{d}$. Thus

(*i*) When d is increased, β will decrease

(*ii*) No effect of D (The distance of screen from slits).

Q. 7. Interference fringe of which colour (violet or red) will be close to the central white fringe when white light is used in YDSE?

Ans. Distance of nth bright fringe from the central fringe

$$= \frac{nD\lambda}{d}$$

Since $\lambda_r > \lambda_v$, hence bright fringe of violet colour will be closer.

Q. 8. Why is the diffraction in sound wave very common but not so common in light waves?

Ans. Because wavelength of sound waves is much greater as compared to the wavelength of visible light.

Q. 9. How does the intensity of central maxima change, if the width of the slit is halved in a single slit diffraction experiment?

Ans. The width of central maxima is doubled out and the intensity is reduced to $\frac{1}{4}$th of its original value.

Q. 10. Why are danger signals red in colour?

Ans. As λ_r is largest in the visible region, therefore, red colour is least scattered. Hence, it can be seen from large distances. That is why danger signals are red.

Q. 11. In a single slit diffraction experiment, the width of the slit is halved. How does it affect the size and intensity of the central maxima?

Ans. As size of central max. $\propto \frac{\lambda}{a}$

$\therefore$ Size becomes double.

Hence, intensity reduces to ¼th.

Q. 12. What evidence is there to show that sound is not electromagnetic in nature?

Ans. Sound waves are not electromagnetic in nature. This is evident from the fact that sound waves do not exhibit the phenomenon of polarisation.

Q. 13. In what way is diffraction from each slit related to the interference pattern in a double slit experiment?

Ans. The interference pattern in a double slit experiment is modulated by diffraction from each slit. The pattern is the result of interference of the diffracted wave fronts from the two slits.

Q. 14. At what angle of incidence should a light beam strike a glass slab of refractive index $\sqrt{3}$ such that the reflected and refracted rays are perpendicular to each other?

Ans. By Brewster's Law

$$\mu = \tan p \Rightarrow \quad p = 60°$$

Q. 15. What does red shift in the spectra of galaxies indicate?

Ans. The universe is expanding.

SHORT ANSWER TYPE QUESTIONS (SA-I)

(Carrying 2 mark)

Q. 1. Widths of two slits in Young's experiment are in the ratio 4 : 1. What is the ratio of the amplitudes of light waves from them?

Ans. Here $\frac{w_1}{w_2} = \frac{I_1}{I_2} = \frac{a^2}{b^2} = \frac{4}{1}$

or $\frac{a}{b} = \frac{2}{1} \quad \Rightarrow \quad a : b = 2 : 1.$

Q. 2. Two slits in Young's double slit experiment are illuminated by two different sodium lamps emitting light of same wavelength. Do you observe any interference pattern on the screen?

Ans. No, interference pattern is not obtained. This is because phase difference between the light waves emitted from two lamps will change continuously.

Q. 3. What are coherent sources of light? Why no interference pattern is observed when two coherent sources are (*i*) too close, (*ii*) very far apart?

Ans. The sources of light which emit light waves of same wavelength, same frequency and in same phase or having a constant phase difference, are called coherent sources.

(*i*) When these sources are too close, distance (d) between them tends to be zero.

Fringe width $\beta = \dfrac{\lambda D}{d}$ tends to be ∞. Hence, no interference pattern will be observed.

(*ii*) When distance (d) between them becomes too large, fringe width β becomes too small and may no longer be in the visible region. Hence, no interference pattern will be observed.

Q. 4. Consider interference between waves from two sources of intensities I and $4I$. Find intensities at points where phase difference is (*i*) $\pi/2$ (*ii*) π.

Ans. We know $R^2 = a^2 + b^2 + 2ab\cos\phi$

$$\therefore \quad I_R = I_1 + I_2 + 2\sqrt{I_1 \times I_2}\cos\phi$$

In case (*i*), $\phi = \dfrac{\pi}{2} = 90°$

$$\therefore \quad I_R = I + 4I + 2\sqrt{I \times 4I}\cos\frac{\pi}{2}$$

$$I_R = 5I$$

In case (*ii*), $\phi = \pi$, $I_R = I + 4I + 2\sqrt{I \times 4I}\cos\pi = I.$

Q. 5. How does diffraction limit the resolving power of an optical instrument?

Ans. The problem in identification of nearby points arises on account of diffraction of light *i.e.,* bending of light around the corners. When two point objects are close by, their diffraction patterns may overlap. Therefore, their images can no longer be identified separately. Hence, their resolution becomes difficult. Thus, the resolving power of the optical instrument is limited.

Q. 6. In a single slit diffraction, the slit width is equal to the wavelength of light used. What will be the nature of an image on the screen?

Ans. We know that $d\sin\theta = n\lambda$

Here, $n = 1$, the first minima occurs, if $d\sin\theta = \lambda \sin\theta = \pm\lambda$, and $\theta = \pm 90°$. Thus, the whole screen will be illuminated. However, the intensity at the centre will be maximum and goes on decreasing with distance.

Q. 7. Determine the angular separation between central maxima and first order maxima of the diffraction pattern due to a single slit of width 0.25 mm, when light of wavelength 5890Å is incident normally.

Ans. Here $\lambda = 5890\text{Å} = 5890 \times 10^{-10}$ and $a = 0.25$ mm $= 2.5 \times 10^{-4}$ m. As condition of 1st order maxima is $a \sin\theta = \frac{3}{2}\lambda$

$$\therefore \qquad \theta = \sin\theta = \frac{3\lambda}{2a} = \frac{3\times 5890\times 10^{-10}}{2\times 2.5\times 10^{-4}} = 3.534 \times 10^{-3} \text{ radian.}$$

Q. 8. **Why a coloured spectrum is seen, when we look through a muslin cloth and not in other clothes?**

Ans. **Muslin cloth is made of very fine threads and as such fine slits are formed. White light passing through these slits gets diffracted giving rise to coloured spectrum. The central maximum is white while the secondary maxima are coloured. In a coarse cloth, the slits formed between the threads are wider and diffraction is not so pronounced.**

Q. 9. **Why does the light from a clear blue portion of the sky show a rise and fall of intensity when viewed through a polaroid which is rotated?**

Ans. **The light from the clean blue sky is partially plane polarised. When it is passed through a rotating polaroid then according to law of Malus, the intensity of emerging light is**

$$I = I_0 \cos^2\theta$$

For partially plane polarised light, this is written as

$$I = I_0 + \frac{I_0}{2}\cos^2\theta$$

The variation of *I* with *q* is shown in the fig.

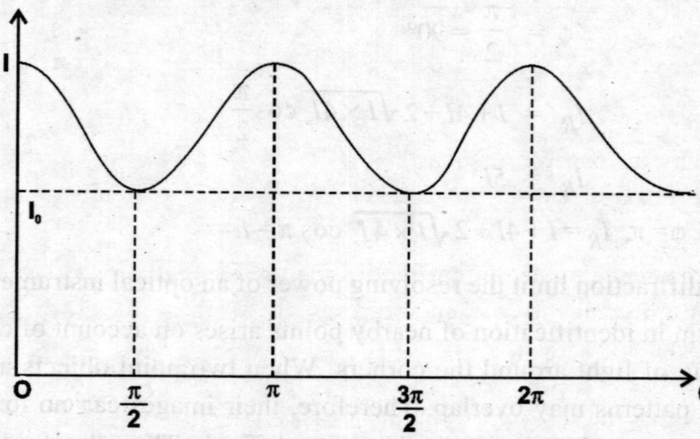

Q. 10. A parallel beam of light of wavelength 600 nm is incident on a slit of width '*a*'. If the distance between the slit and the screen is 0.8 m and the distance of second order maximum from the centre of the screen is 1.5 mm, calculate '*a*'.

Ans. We have $a.\frac{x}{D} = n\lambda$

or $\qquad a = \frac{Dn\lambda}{x}$

Given $\lambda = 600$ nm $= 6 \times 10^{-7}$ m, $n = 2$, $x = 1.5$ mm $= 15 \times 10^{-3}$ m and $D = 0.8$ m. Then

$$a = \frac{2\times 0.8\times 6\times 10^{-7}}{1.5\times 10^{-13}} = 6.4\times 10^{-4}\ mm$$

SHORT ANSWER TYPE QUESTIONS (SA-II)

(Carrying 3 mark)

Q. 1. State Huygen's principle. Prove the laws of refraction on the basis of wave theory

Ans. Huygen's Principle:

(*i*) Energy point on the given wavefront (called primary wavefront) acts as a fresh source of new disturbance and emits waves which are called secondary wavelets. Secondary wavelets travel in all directions with the velocity of light in the medium.

(*ii*) A surface touching these secondary wavelets, tangentially in the forward direction at any instant gives the position of the wavefront at that instant.

In Fig. 6.13, *XY* is a plane surface that reparates two media. If c_1 is velocity of light in rarer medium and c_2 is velocity of light in denser medium, then by the definition

$$\mu = \frac{c_1}{c_2} \quad \text{...(1)}$$

AB is the plane wavefront incident on *XY* at $\angle BAA' = \angle i$, 1, 2, 3 are corresponding incident rays normal to *AB*.

According to Huygen's principle, every point on *AB* is a source of secondary wavelets. Let the secondary wavelets from *B* strike *XY* at *A'* in *t* seconds.

$$\therefore \quad BA' = c_1 \times t \quad \text{...(2)}$$

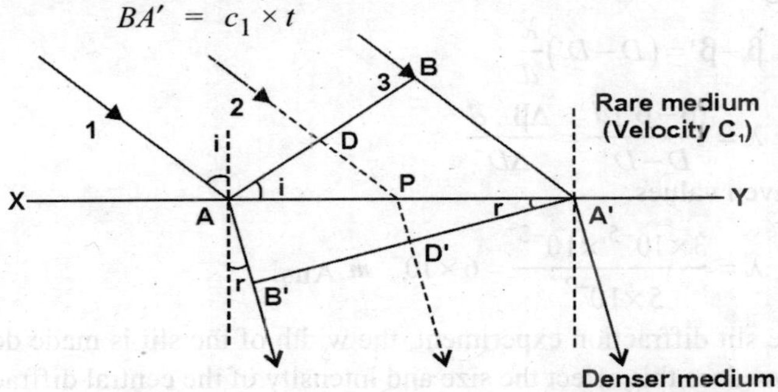

Fig. 6.13

The secondary wavelets from *A* travel in the denser medium with the velocity c_2 and would cover a distance ($c_2 \times t$) in *t* seconds. So, with *A* as centre and radius equal to ($c_2 \times t$), draw an arc,

then $AB' = c_2 t$ ...(3)

We can show that the secondary wavelets striking from any other point *D* on the incident wavefront *AB*, after refraction at *P*, must reach the point *D'* on *A'B'* in the same time in which the secondary wavelets from *B* reach *A'*.

Therefore, *A'B'* is the true refracted wavefront. Let *r* be the angle of refraction.

Then, $\angle AA'B' = r$, angle of refraction

In $\Delta\, AA'B$, $\sin i = \dfrac{BA'}{AA'} = \dfrac{c_1 \times t}{AA'}$

In $\Delta AA'B'$, $\sin r = \dfrac{AB'}{AA'} = \dfrac{c_2 \times t}{AA'}$

$$\therefore \quad \frac{\sin i}{\sin r} = \frac{c_1}{c_2} = \mu$$

Thus, $\mu = \dfrac{\sin i}{\sin r}$, which proves Snell's law of refraction.

Q. 2. **Light waves from two coherent sources of intensity ratio 81:1 produce interference. Calculate the ratio of the maxima and minima in the interference pattern.**

Ans. Here, $\frac{I_1}{I_2} = \frac{a^2}{b^2} = \frac{81}{1}$

$\therefore \quad \frac{a}{b} = \frac{9}{1}$ or $a : b = 9 : 1$

In the interference pattern,

$$\frac{I_{max}}{I_{min}} = \frac{(a+b)^2}{(a-b)^2} = \frac{(9b+b)^2}{(9b-b)^2} = \frac{100b^2}{64b^2} = \frac{25}{16} = 25:16$$

Q. 3. **In a double slit experiment with monochromatic light, fringes are obtained on a screen at distance D from the slits. If the screen moved 5×10^{-2} m towards the slits, the change in fringe width is 3×10^{-5} m. The distance between the slits is 10^{-3} m, calculate the wavelength of light used.**

Ans. The fringe widths in two cases are

$$\beta = \frac{D\lambda}{d} \text{ and } \beta' = \frac{D'\lambda}{d}$$

The change

$$\beta - \beta' = (D - D')\frac{\lambda}{d}$$

or $$\lambda = \frac{(\beta - \beta')d}{D - D'} = \frac{\Delta\beta \cdot d}{\Delta D}$$

Putting given values,

$$\lambda = \frac{3 \times 10^{-5} \times 10^{-3}}{5 \times 10^{-2}} = 6 \times 10^{-7}\, m \text{ Ans.}$$

Q. 4. **In a single slit diffraction experiment, the width of the slit is made double the original width. How does this affect the size and intensity of the central diffraction band? Draw a plot of the intensity distribution.**

Ans. The width of central maxima in single slit diffraction experiment is $2x = \frac{2D\lambda}{a} = \frac{2f\lambda}{a}$.

If the width of slit (=*a*) is doubled, the size of the central diffraction band will become half. Area of central diffraction band will become ¼th and, hence, its intensity would become 4 times. The plot of intensity distribution is shown in Fig. 6.14. The dotted line curve is when width of slit is halved.

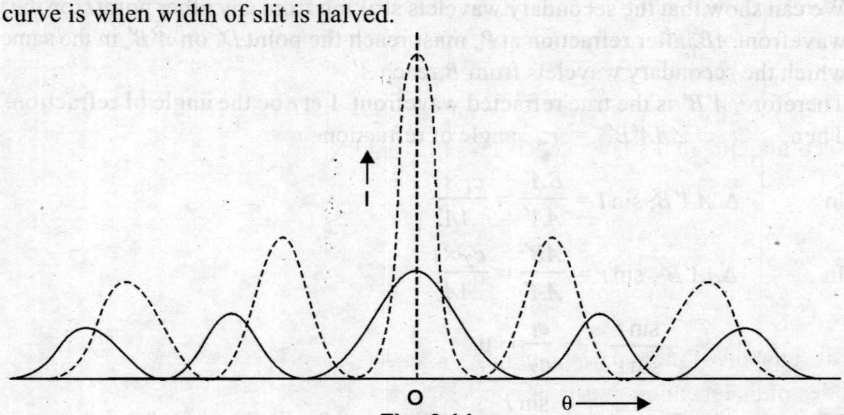

Fig. 6.14

Q. 5. The light of wavelength 600 nm is incident normally on a slit of width 3 mm. Calculate the linear width of central maxima on a screen kept 3 m away from the slit.

Ans. Here $\lambda = 600 \text{ nm} = 600 \times 10^{-9} \text{ m} = 6 \times 10^{-7} \text{ m}$

$a = 3 \text{ mm} = 3 \times 10^{-3} \text{ m}, D = 3 \text{ m}.$

We have width of central maxima

$$2x = \frac{2D\lambda}{a} = \frac{2 \times 3 \times 6 \times 10^{-7}}{3 \times 10^{-3}} = 12 \times 10^{-4} \text{ m} = 1.2 \text{ mm.}$$

Q. 6. Define polarising angle. Derive the relation connecting polarising angle and the refractive index of a medium.

Ans. Polarising angle: Polarising angle for a given transparent refracting medium is that angle of incidence of unpolarised light for which the reflected light is completely plane polarized.

From Fig. 6.15, it has been observed experimentally that when ordinary light is incident at the polarising angle i_P, the reflected component along OB and refracted component along OC are mutually perpendicular to each other.

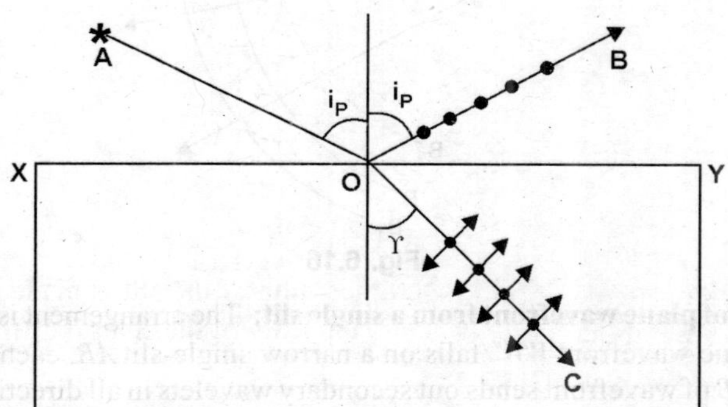

Fig. 6.15

Therefore, $\angle BOY + \angle YOC = 90°$

ro $(90° - i_P) + (90° - r) = 90°$, where r is angle of refraction

ro $(90° - i_P) = r$

According to Snell's law, we have $\mu = \dfrac{\sin i}{\sin r}$

If $i = i_P$, then, $r = (90° - i_P)$

$$\therefore \quad \mu = \frac{\sin i_P}{\sin(90° - i_P)} = \frac{\sin i_P}{\cos i_P} = \tan i_P$$

This tangent of the polarising angle for a transparent medium is equal to the refractive index of that medium. It is commonly known as Brewster's law.

LONG ANSWER TYPE QUESTIONS

(Carrying 5 mark)

Q. 1. Using Huygen's principle, draw a diagram to show propagation of a wavefront originating from a monochromatic point source. Describe diffraction of light due to a single slit. Explain the formation of a pattern of fringes obtained on the screen and plot showing variation of intensity with angle θ in a single slit diffraction.

Ans. Huygen gave a hypothesis for geometrical construction of the position of common wavefront at any instant. A diagram showing propagation of wavefront originating from a monochromatic point source is given in Fig. 6.16.

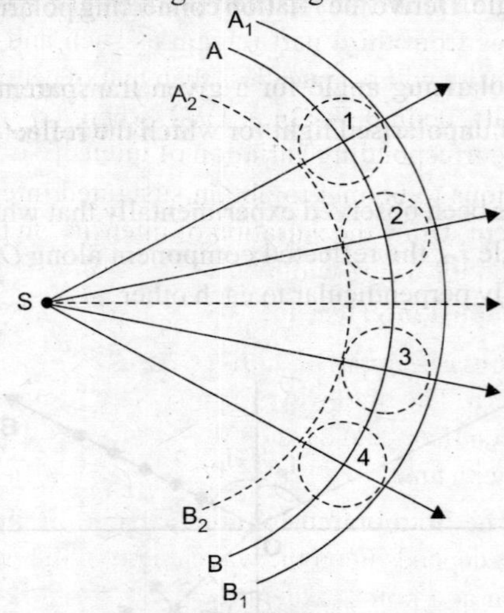

Fig. 6.16

Diffraction of plane wavefront from a single slit: The arrangement is shown in Fig. 6.17. When a plane wavefront *WW′* falls on a narrow single-slit *AB*, each point on unlocked portion *ADB* of wavefront sends out secondary wavelets in all directions. For secondary wavelet meeting at symmetrical central point *O* on the screen, the path difference between waves is zero and, hence, the secondary waves reinforce each other giving rise to central max. at point *O*.

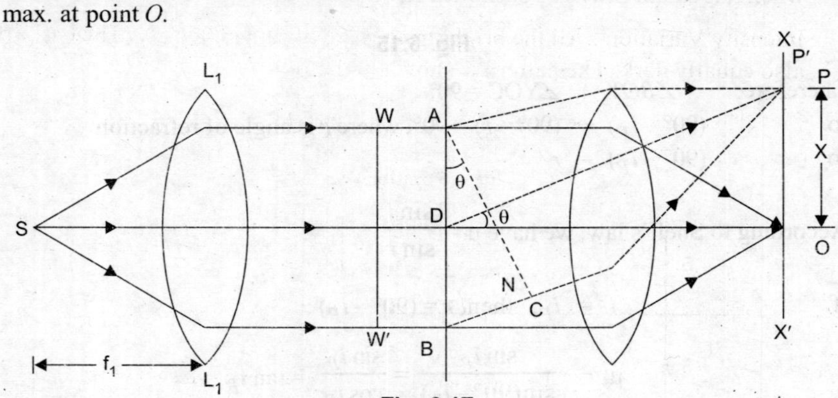

Fig. 6.17

Let us consider secondary waves travelling in a direction making an angle θ with *DO* and reaching the screen at point *P*. Obviously, path diff. between extreme secondary waves reaching *P* from *A* and *B*:

$$\Delta = BC = AB \sin\theta = a \sin\theta$$

If this path diff. $a \sin \theta = \lambda$, then point P will have maximum intensity. In this situation, wavefront may be supposed to consist of two equal halves AD and DB and for every point on AD there will be corresponding point on DB having path difference $d/2$. Consequently, they nullify effect of each other and point P behaves on first secondary minima.

In general, if path diff. $a \sin \theta_n = n\lambda$, when $n = 1, 2, 3$ .... then we have nth secondary minima corresponding to that angle of diffraction θ_n.

However, if for some point P_1 on the screen secondary waves BP_1 and AP_1 differ in path by $3\lambda/2$, then point P_1 will be the position of first secondary maxima. Because in this situation, wavefront AB may be divided into three equal parts such that path difference between corresponding points on first and second parts will be $\lambda/2$ and they will nullify. But secondary waves from third part remain as such and give rise to first secondary maxima, whose intensity will be much less than that of central maxima.

In general, if path diff. $a \sin \theta_n = (2n + 1)\lambda/2$, where $n = 1, 2, 3$ ..... this we have nth secondary maxima corresponding variation of intensity is not given to these angles.

Q. 2. Mention the conditions to be met to obtain sustained interference pattern in young's double slit experiment. Draw the variation of intensity on the screen.
Obtain the expression for fringe width?

Ans. Conditions for sustained interference

(*i*) **The two light sources must be coherent :** This is essential to have stationary interference pattern. The light waves from coherent sources will have constant phase difference between them and as such the brightness of various points on the screen will remain fixed with time.

(*ii*) **The slits should be illuminated by monochromatic light :** In this case the phase difference (which depends upon the wavelength) will remain fixed at a point. If white light is used, then at a point (except the central point) the phase difference will be different for different colours and coloured fringes overlapping each other will be obtained.

(*iii*) **The slits must be narrow :** The fringe widh

$$\beta = \frac{D\lambda}{d}$$

when d is small, β will be sufficient to be resolved.

Intensity Variation : All the bright fringes are of same intensity. The dark fringes are also equally dark. The pattern is shown in the fig.

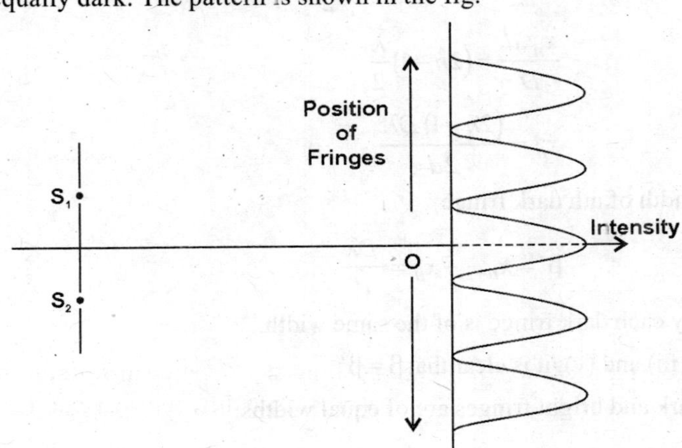

Expression for fringe width : In the fig., $S_1 S_2 = d$ and distance of screen from sits $= D$.

Wavelength of monochromatic light $= \lambda$

From the $\Delta PS_1 M$

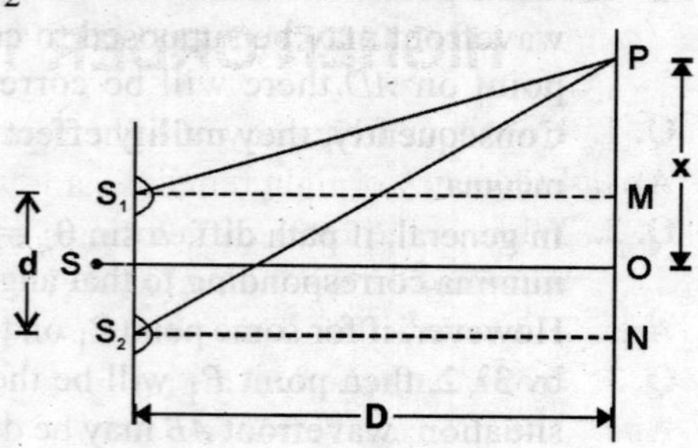

$$S_1P^2 = D^2 + \left(x - \frac{d}{2}\right)^2$$

and from ΔPS_2N, $S_2P^2 = D^2 + \left(x + \frac{d}{2}\right)^2$

Subtracting, $S_2P^2 - S_1P^2 = \left(x + \frac{d}{2}\right)^2 - \left(x - \frac{d}{2}\right)^2$

or $(S_2P + S_1P)(S_2P - S_1P) = 2x \, . \, d$

Since x is small and $D >> d$, we can take $S_2P + S_1P = 2D$

Thus

$$2D \, . (S_2P - S_1P) = 2x \, . \, d$$

or $$S_2P - S_1P = \frac{x \, . \, d}{D} \qquad ...(i)$$

Let nth bright fringe fall at P, then

$$S_2P - S_1P = 2n \, . \frac{\lambda}{2} \text{ where } n = 1, 2, 3, ...$$

or $$\frac{x_n \, . d}{D} = n_1 \lambda \Rightarrow x_n = \frac{Dn\lambda}{d} \qquad ...(ii)$$

The width of nth bright fringe

$$\beta = x_n - x_{n-1} = \frac{D\lambda}{d} \qquad ...(iii)$$

This is independent of n, hence each bright fringe is of same width.

Now for nth dark fringe at P,

$$S_2P - S_1P = (2n - 1)\frac{\lambda}{2} \text{ where } n = 1, 2, 3, ...$$

or $$\frac{x_n \, . d}{D} = (2n - 1)\frac{\lambda}{2}$$

or $$x_n = \frac{(2n - 1) \, D\lambda}{2d} \qquad ...(iv)$$

The width of nth dark fringe

$$\beta' = x_{n+1} - x_n = \frac{D\lambda}{d} \qquad ...(v)$$

Clearly each dark fringe is of the same width.

From (iii) and (v), it is clear that $\beta = \beta'$

i.e., dark and bright fringes are of equal widths.

HIGHER ORDER THINKING SKILLS (HOTS)

Q. 1. How does frequency of light change when it goes from air into water?

Ans. Frequency of light remains same.

Q. 2. What is the ratio of velocities of two light waves travelling in vacuum and having wavelengths 4000Å and 8000Å.

Ans. The ratio is 1:1. This is because in vacuum, all colours travel with the same velocity.

Q. 3. Prove that spherical mirror formula is applicable equally to a plane mirror.

Ans. The spherical mirror formula is

$$\frac{1}{f} = \frac{1}{u} + \frac{1}{u} \qquad ...(1)$$

For the plane mirror, $R = \infty$

$$f = \frac{R}{2} = \infty$$

From (1), $$\frac{1}{u} + \frac{1}{v} = \frac{1}{\infty} = 0 \text{ or } \frac{1}{v} = -\frac{1}{u} \text{ or } v = -u$$

As u is negative, v becomes + 1.

Hence, image is formed behind the mirror at the same distance as the object is in front of it. This is what happens in a plane mirror.

Q. 4. A convex lens of focal length 1 m and a concave lens of focal length 0.25 m are kept 0.75 m apart. A parallel beam of light first passes through convex lens and then through the concave lens. Where does it come to focus?

Ans. Here

$$C_1F_1 = 1 \text{ m}$$
$$C_2F_2 = 0.25 \text{ m}$$
$$C_1C_2 = 0.75 \text{ m}$$

A parallel beam of light falling on convex lens tends to converge of F_1. It is intercepted by concave lens.

As $$C_2F_1 = C_1F_1 - C_1C_2 = 1 - 0.75 = 0.25 \text{ m}$$

and $$C_2F_2 = 0.25 \text{ m}$$

F_1 and F_2 coincide

Hence, the ray emerges from concave lens in a direction parallel to the principal as show in Fig. 6.18.

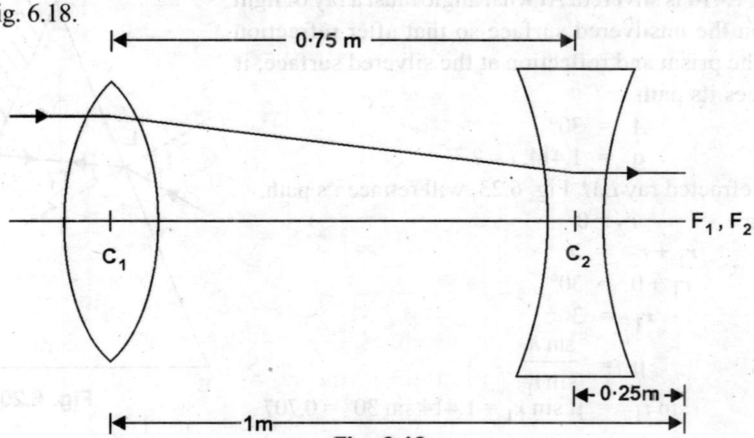

Fig. 6.18

Q. 5. A ray of light falls on transparent glass slab of refractive index 1.5. If the reflected and refracted rays are mutually perpendicular, calculate the angle of incidence.

Given $\sin^{-1}\left(\frac{2}{3}\right) = 42°$ and $\tan^{-1}\left(\frac{3}{2}\right) = 56°$.

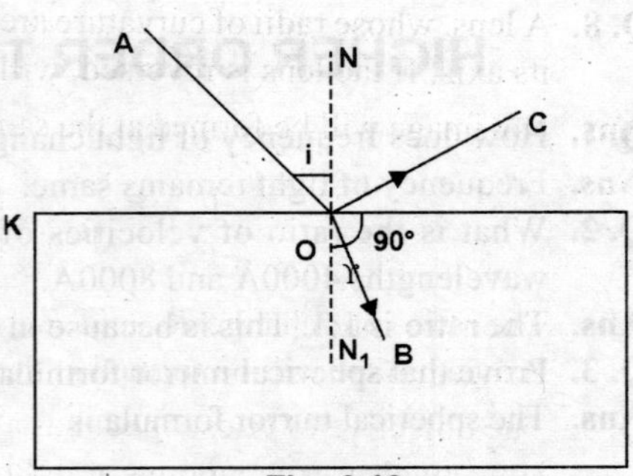

Fig. 6.19

Ans. As it is clear from Fig. 6.22

$$\angle BOC = 90°$$
$$\angle BOL + \angle LOC = 90°$$
$$(90° - r) + (90° - i) = 90°$$
$$\therefore \quad r = (90° - i)$$

According to Snell's law,

$$\mu = \frac{\sin i}{\sin r} = \frac{\sin i}{\sin(90° - i)} = \frac{\sin i}{\cos i} = \tan i$$

$$\therefore \quad \tan i = \mu = 1.5 = \frac{3}{2}$$

$$i = \tan^{-1}\left(\frac{3}{2}\right) = 56°.$$

Q. 6. The least distance of distinct vision of a long sighted man is 50 cm. He reduces this distance to 10 cm by wearing spectacles. What is the power and type of lenses used by him?

Ans. For such a person, $u = -10$ cm and $v = -50$ cm

From,
$$\frac{1}{f} = \frac{1}{v} - \frac{1}{u}$$
$$= -\frac{1}{50} + \frac{1}{10} = +\frac{4}{50}$$
$$f = +\frac{50}{4} = +12.4 \text{ cm}$$
$$P = \frac{100}{f} = \frac{100}{12.5} = 8 \text{ D}$$

$\therefore$ The type of lenses used are convex.

Q. 7. One face of a prism of refracting angle 30° and refractive index 1.414 is silvered. At what angle must a ray of light fall on the unsilvered surface so that after refraction into the prism and reflection at the silvered surface, it retraces its path.

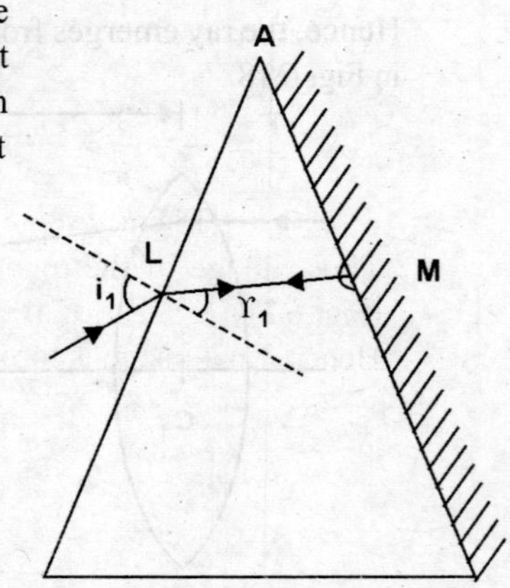

Fig. 6.20

Ans. Here
$$A = 30°$$
$$\mu = 1.414, i = ?$$

The refracted ray *LM*, Fig. 6.23, will retrace its path.

When $r_2 = 0$

As
$$r_1 + r_2 = A$$
$$\therefore \quad r_1 + 0 = 30°$$
$$\text{or} \quad r_1 = 30°$$

From
$$\mu = \frac{\sin i_1}{\sin r_1}$$
$$\sin i_1 = \mu \sin r_1 = 1.414 \sin 30° = 0.707$$
$$\therefore \quad i_1 = 45°$$

Q. 8. A lens, whose radii of curvature are different, is forming the image of an object placed on its axis. If the lens is reversed, will the position of the image change?

Ans. No, image will be formed at the same position. This follows from lens maker's formula

$$\frac{1}{f} = (\mu - 1)\left(\frac{1}{R_1} - \frac{1}{R_2}\right)$$

when we interchange R_1 and R_2, the value of f does not change except for the sign. Hence, image will be formed at the same position.

Q. 9. The objective of telescope A has a diameter 3 times that of the objective of telescope B. How much greater amount of light can be gathered by A compared to B? Show that range of A is three times the range of B.

Ans. As diameter of objective of A is 3 times that of B, its area of cross section is 9 times that of B. Therefore, light gathering capacity of A is 9 times that of B. Now, range tells us how far away a star of some standard brightness can be spotted by the telescope.

As intensity $\propto \frac{1}{(\text{distance})^2}$, therefore, when distance of star is 3 times, the intensity would reduce to 1/9th. As light gathering capacity of A is 9 times that of B, the star whose distance is 3 times, can just be seen by A.

Q. 10. A convex and concave mirror each of radius 10 cm are placed facing each other and 15 cm apart, as shown in Fig. 6.21. A point object is placed midway between then. Find the position of the final image if the reflection takes place first at the concave mirror and then at the convex mirror.

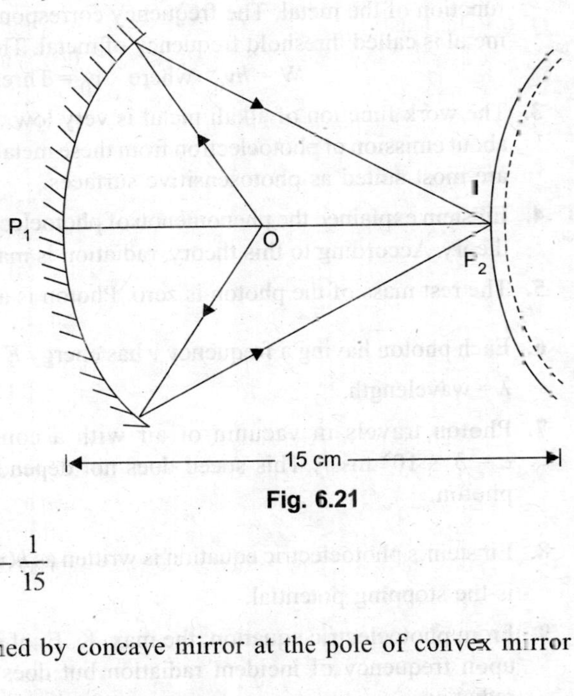

Fig. 6.21

Ans. For a concave mirror,

$$f = -\frac{10}{2} = -5 \text{ cm}$$

$$u = PO = -7.5 \text{ cm}$$

As, $\frac{1}{v} + \frac{1}{u} = \frac{1}{f}$

$$\therefore \frac{1}{v} = \frac{1}{f} - \frac{1}{u} = \frac{1}{-5} + \frac{1}{7.5} = -\frac{1}{15}$$

$$v = -15 \text{ cm}$$

Thus, image of the oject is formed by concave mirror at the pole of convex mirror (Fig. 6.21).

Hence, final image is formed at the pole of convex mirror.

❑❑❑

UNIT 7

DUAL NATURE OF MATTER AND RADIATION

Important Points to Remember

1. Photoelectric effect is the phenomenon of emission of electrons from the surface of metals when radiations of suitable frequency are incident on them. The emitted electrons are called photoelectrons and the current so obtained is called the photoelectric current.
2. The minimum energy required to remove an electron from the metal surface is called work function of the metal. The frequency corresponding to energy equal to work function of metal is called threshold frequency of metal. Thus

$$W = h\nu_0 \quad \text{where} \quad \nu_0 = \text{Threshold frequency}$$

3. The work function of alkali metal is very low. Even the ordinary visible light can bring about emission of photoelectron from these metals. Due to this reason, alkali metal surfaces are most suited as photosensitive surfaces.
4. Einstein explained the phenomenon of photoelectric effect on the basis of Plank's quantum theory. According to this theory, radiation is made of very tiny particles, called photons.
5. The rest mass of the photon is zero. Photon is a bundle of energy.
6. Each photon having a frequency ν has energy $E = h\nu$ and momentum $p = \frac{h\nu}{c} = \frac{h}{\lambda}$, where λ = wavelength.
7. Photon travels in vacuum or air with a constant speed c, the speed of light *i.e.*, $c = 3 \times 10^8$ ms^{-1}. This speed does not depend on frequency or energy/momentum of photon.
8. Einstein's photoelectric equation is written as $h(\nu - \nu_0) = K_{max} = \frac{1}{2}mv_{max}^2 = eV_0$, where V_0 is the stopping potential.
9. From photoelectric equation, the max. K. E. of ejected photo electrons linearly depends upon frequency of incident radiation but does not depend upon intensity of incident radiation.
10. For a given metal and frequency ν (provided that $\nu > \nu_0$), the number of photoelectrons ejected per second is directly proportional to the intensity of incident radiation.
11. The stopping potential is the negative anode potential to make the photo-electric current zero. It is related to max. K.E. of emitted photo electrons as $eV_0 = K_{max}$.
12. The stopping potential is independent of the intensity of the incident light but depends on the frequency of the incident light, hence, the stopping potential will remain unchanged.

13. A photoelectric cell converts changes in intensity illumination into changes in electric current. The applications of photoelectric cells are:
   (*i*) in burglar alarm
   (*ii*) in fire alarm
   (*iii*) in the reproduction of sound from films in a cinema hall.
14. Photo electric effect could not be explained by wave theory.
15. It was established that radiation possesses dual nature i.e. both particle nature and wave nature.
16. de-Broglie introduced the dual nature for matter.
17. The wavelength of wave associated with a photon is given by $\lambda = \frac{h}{mc} = \frac{h}{p}$ where p is the momentum of photon and h is the Plank's constant.

    The de-Broglie wavelength for a material particle is

$$\lambda = \frac{h}{mv} = \frac{h}{p}$$

where p = momentum of particle

m = mass of particle

(*i*) for an electron moving with kinetic energy K, de-Broglie wavelength is given by

$$\lambda = \frac{h}{\sqrt{2mK}}$$

(*ii*) for an electron accelerated by potential difference V, de-Broglie wavelength is

$$\lambda = \frac{h}{\sqrt{2meV}}$$

18. Wave nature of electrons was first experimentally verified by Davisson and Germer, who observed diffraction effects with the electron beams scattered by the crystals.

❑❑❑

VERY SHORT ANSWER TYPE QUESTIONS

(Carrying 1 mark)

Q. 1. What is photoelectric effect?

Ans. It is the phenomenon of emission of electrons from metal surface, when radiations of suitable frequency fall on them.

Q. 2. Define work function of a metal.

Ans. It is defined as the minimum energy required to liberate an electron from the surface of metal.

Q. 3. What is the momentum of photon of frequency ν?

Ans. Momentum of a photon of frequency ν is given by, $p = h\nu/c$, where h = Plank's constant and c = velocity of light.

Q. 4. Light from the bulb falls on the wooden table, but no photoelectrons are emitted. Why?

Ans. The wave function of the wood is much higher than the energy of photon of visible light coming from the bulb.

Q. 5. The work function for Al is 4.2 eV. Find the threshold wavelength for the photoelectric emission.

Ans. We have
$$\lambda_0 = \frac{hc}{\phi_0} = \frac{6.62\times10^{-34}\times3\times10^{8}}{4.2\times1.6\times10^{-19}}$$
$$= 2.955\times10^{-7}\text{ m} = 2955\text{ Å}.$$

Q. 6. Calculate the energy of a photon of frequency 6×10^{14} Hz in electron volt. Given that $h = 6.62\times10^{-34}$ J-s.

Ans. $$E = h\nu = \frac{6.63\times10^{-34}\times6\times10^{14}}{1.6\times10^{-19}} = 2.49\ eV.$$

Q. 7. Does the stoping potential of photoelectric emission depend upon the frequency of the incident radiation.

Ans. Yes, the stopping depend upon frequency of the incident radiation.

Q. 8. How will the photoelectric current change on decreasing the wavelength of incident radiation for a given photo-sensitive material?

Ans. Photoelectric current is not affected by decreasing the wavelength of incident radiation.

Q. 9. Two metals A and B have work function 2 eV and 5 eV respectively. Which metal has lower threshold wavelength?

Ans. $$\phi_0 = \frac{hc}{\lambda_0} \text{ or } \lambda_0 = \frac{hc}{\phi_0} \text{ or } \lambda_0 \propto \frac{1}{\phi_0}.$$

So, metal B with greater work function has lower threshold wavelength of radiation.

Q. 10. For a photosensitive surface, threshold wavelength is λ_0. Does photoelectric emission occur if the wavelength (λ) of the incident radiation is (*i*) more than λ_0(*ii*) less than λ_0? Justify your answer.

Ans. (i) When $\lambda > \lambda_0$, $v < v_0$ *i.e.*, frequency of incident radiation is less than the threshold frequency, and hence no photoelectric emission occurs.

(*ii*) When $\lambda < \lambda_0$, $v > v_0$. So that photoelectric emission will ocur.

Q. 11. If the intensity of the incident radiation in a photocell is increased, how does the stopping potential vary.

Ans. As $eV_0 = h(v - v_0)$, so stopping potential V_0 remains unchanged on increasing intensity of the incident radiation

Q. 12. How does the stopping potential applied to a photo cell change, if the distance between the light source and cathode of the cell is doubled.

Ans. When the distance between the light source and the cathode of cell is doubled, the intensity of light falling on the cathode of cell becomes one-fourth $\left(I \propto \frac{1}{r^2}\right)$. But the value of stopping potential remains unchanged.

Q. 13. How many electron volts make up 1 joule.

Ans.
$$1 \text{ joule} = \frac{1}{1.6 \times 10^{-19}} = 6.25 \times 10^{18}\, eV.$$

Q. 14. What is the expression for wavelength of an electron moving under a potential difference of V volt.

Ans.
$$\lambda = \frac{12.27}{\sqrt{V}}\ A°.$$

Q. 15. What is the rest mass of photon?

Ans. The rest mass of photon is zero.

Q. 16. Calculate the threshold frequency of photon for photo-electric emission from a metal of work function 0.1 eV. Given $h = 6.6 \times 10^{-34}$ Js.

Ans. Here
$$\phi_0 = .1 \text{ eV} = 0.1 \times 1.6 \times 10^{-19}$$
$$\phi_0 = hv_0$$
$$v_0 = \frac{\phi_0}{h} = \frac{.1 \times 1.6 \times 10^{-19}}{6.6 \times 10^{-34}} = 2.4 \times 10^{13}\text{Hz}.$$

Q. 17. Show graphically how the stopping potential for a given photosensitive surface varies with the frequency of the incident radiation.

Ans.

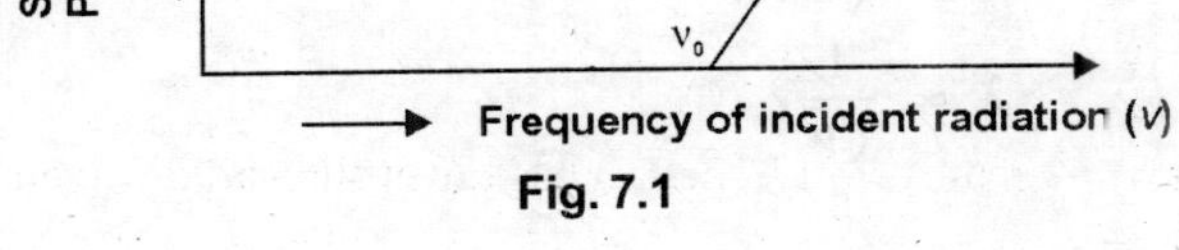

Fig. 7.1

Q. 18. Write down the relation between the energy and momentum of a photon.

Ans. $p = \frac{E}{c}$, where c is the speed of light.

Q. 19. What is the main aim of Davisson Germer experiment.

Ans. To verify the wave nature of electron.

Q. 20. What is the momentum of an electron beam of wavelength 4Å?

Ans. We have $p = \frac{h}{\lambda} = \frac{6.62\times10^{-34}}{4\times10^{-10}} = 1.65 \times 10^{-24}$ kg ms^{-1}.

Q. 21. An electron, an α-particle and a photon have the same KE. Which one of these particles have the largest de-Broglie wavelength?

Ans. As $\lambda = \frac{1}{\sqrt{2mE}}$ and KE is constant, hence $\lambda \propto \frac{1}{\sqrt{m}}$, *i.e.*, electron being lightest will have the largest de-Broglie wavelength.

Q. 22. What will be the wavelength of a photon of momentum 6.6×10^{-24} kg ms^{-1}?

Ans. We have, $\lambda = \frac{h}{p} = \frac{6.62\times10^{-34}}{6.6\times10^{-24}} = 10^{-10}$ m = 1Å

Q. 23. A photon and electron have got same de-Broglie wavelength (= 10^{-10} m). Which has a greater kinetic energy?

Ans. For electron, let λ be the de-Broglie wavelength of electron

$$\text{K.E. of electron } E = \frac{1}{2}mv^2$$

$$mv^2 = 2E_1$$

$$m^2v^2 = 2\,mE_1$$

$$mv = \sqrt{2mE}$$

$$\lambda = \frac{h}{mv}\quad \lambda_1 = \frac{h}{\sqrt{2mE_1}}$$

For photon,
$$E_2 = \frac{hc}{\lambda}$$

$$\frac{E_2}{E_1} = \frac{2c\lambda m}{h}$$

$$= \frac{2\times3\times10^{-8}\times10^{-10}\times9\times10^{-31}}{6.6\times10^{-34}}$$

$$= \frac{9.0}{1.1} > 1$$

$$E_2 > E_1.$$

Q. 24. de-Broglie wavelength associated with an electron accelerated through a potential difference 1 V is λ. What will be its wavelength when the accelerating potential is increased to 4 V?

Ans.
$$\lambda = \frac{h}{\sqrt{2meV}}$$

$$\lambda \propto \frac{1}{\sqrt{V}}$$

$$\frac{\lambda'}{\lambda} = \sqrt{\frac{V}{4V}} = \frac{1}{2}$$

$$\lambda' = \frac{\lambda}{2}.$$

Q. 25. What is the nature of trajectory of the scattered α-particle?

Ans. A hyperbola.

SHORT ANSWER TYPE QUESTIONS

(Carrying 2 or 3 marks)

Q. 1. If we go on increasing the wavelength of light incident on a metal surface, what changes in the number of electrons take place?

Ans. If we increase the wavelength of incident light, then the energy of incident photon, $E = \frac{hc}{\lambda}$ will decrease due to which the energy of photoelectron emitted decreases but the number of electrons emitted will not change. When the wavelength of the incident light becomes greater than threshold wavelength, then no photoelectron will be emitted.

Q. 2. Define the term (*i*) Work function, (*ii*) Threshold frequency, (*iii*) Stopping potential.

Ans. (i) Work function—Work function of a metal is the minimum energy required by an electron to just escape from the metal surface by overcoming the restraining force at the surface.

(ii) Threshold frequency—Threshold frequency is the minimum frequency of the incident radiation by which the photoelectrons are just emitted from the metal surface without any kinetic energy.

(iii) Stopping potential—Stopping potential or cut-off potential is that minimum (–ve) potential given to anode in a photo cell for which the photoelectric current becomes zero.

Q. 3. An electron and a proton are moving in the same direction and possess the same kinetic energy. Find the ratio of de-Broglie wavelength associated with these particles

Ans.

$$\text{K.E.} = \frac{1}{2} m^2v^2$$

$$mE = \frac{1}{2} m^2v^2$$

$$mv = \sqrt{2mE}$$

$$\lambda = \frac{h}{mv} = \frac{h}{\sqrt{2mE}}$$

$$\lambda \propto \frac{1}{\sqrt{m}}$$

$$\frac{\lambda_e}{\lambda_p} = \sqrt{\frac{m_p}{m_e}}.$$

Q. 4. Is photoelectric emission possible at all frequencies? Give reason for your answer.

Ans. The photoelectric emission is possible if the energy of incident photon is more than work function of the metal *i.e.*, the energy required to just liberate an electron from the metal surface. If the energy of incident photon is less than the work function of a metal, no emission of photoelectron will take place from metal surface.

Q. 5. How does (*i*) photoelectric current (*ii*) kinetic energy of the photoelectron emitted in a photocell vary if the intensity of the incident radiation is doubled.

Ans. (*i*) Photoelectric current is directly proportional to the intensity of incident radiation, so the photo electric current becomes double when intensity of incident radiation is doubled.

(*ii*) Kinetic energy of the emitted photoelectron is independent of the intensity of the incident light, hence, K.E. of emitted photoelectron remains unchanged if the intensity of incident radiation is doubled.

Q. 6. The threshold frequency of a metal is ν_0. When the light of frequency $2\nu_0$ is incident on the metal plate, the maximum velocity of electron emitted is ν_1. When the frequency of the incident radiation is increased to $5\nu_0$, the maximum velocity of electron emitted is ν_2. Find the ratio of ν_1 and ν_2.

Ans. As f_0 is the threshold frequency

$$\phi_0 = h\nu_0$$

Using Einstein's photoelectric equation

$$\frac{1}{2}mv_1^2 = h \times 2\nu_0 - \phi_0$$

$$\frac{1}{2}mv_1^2 = h \times 2\nu_0 - h\nu_0 = h\nu_0$$

$$\frac{1}{2}mv_2^2 = h \times 5\nu_0 - \phi_0$$

$$= 5h\nu_0 - h\nu_0 = 4h\nu_0$$

$$\frac{v_1^2}{v_2^2} = \frac{1}{4}$$

$$\frac{v_1}{v_2} = \frac{1}{2}.$$

$$\Rightarrow \quad v_1 : v_2 = 1:2.$$

Q. 7. Green light ejects photoelectrons from a given photosensitive surface while yellow light does not. What will happen in case of violet and red light? Give reason for your answer.

Ans. The photoelectron can be emitted from a metal surface if the frequency of incident radiation is more than threshold frequency *i.e.*, more than that of green light for the given surface. As the frequency of violet light is more than that of green light, hence, violet light will eject photoelectron. But the frequency of red light is less than that of green light, hence, red light cannot eject photoelectrons from the given surface.

Q. 8. An X-Ray tube operates at 10 kV. Find the ratio of X-ray wavelength to that of de-Broglie wavelength, of electron.

Ans. $V = 10\text{ kV} = 10 \times 10^3\text{V} = 10^4$ volts.

For X-ray
$$eV = \frac{hc}{\lambda}$$

$$\lambda = \frac{hc}{eV}$$

$$eV = \frac{1}{2}mv^2$$

$$2meV = m^2v^2$$

$$mv = \sqrt{2meV}$$

$$\lambda' = \frac{h}{mv} = \frac{h}{\sqrt{2meV}}$$

$$\lambda = \frac{hc}{eV}$$

$$\frac{\lambda}{\lambda'} = c\sqrt{\frac{2m}{eV}}$$

$$= 3 \times 10^8 \sqrt{\frac{2 \times 9 \times 10^{-31}}{1.6 \times 10^{-19} \times 10^4}}$$

$$= \mathbf{10.062}$$

Q. 9. A 100-watt light bulb is placed at the centre of a spherical chamber of radius 10 m. Assume that 66% of the energy supplied to the bulb is converted into light and that the surface of chamber is perfectly absorbing. Calculate the pressure exerted on the surface.

Ans. $E = \frac{66}{100} \times 100 = 66$ watt.

Momentum, $p = \frac{E}{c}$.

As the light is completely absorbed, the momentum per second of the reflected light is zero. The force exerted by light on the surface is equal to change in momentum.

$$\frac{E}{c} - 0 = \frac{E}{c}$$

Pressure on the surface $= \frac{\text{Force}}{\text{Area}} = \frac{E/c}{4\pi R^2}$

$$= \frac{\frac{66}{3 \times 10^8}}{4 \times \frac{22}{7} \times .01} = 1.75 \times 10^{-6} \text{ Pa.}$$

Q. 10. Find the de-Broglie wavelength of neutron at 127°C. Given Boltzman's constant $k = 1.38 \times 10^{-23}$ J/mol K.

Ans. $T = 127 + 273 = 400$ K

Energy of neutron at 127°C.

$$E = \frac{3}{2} kT$$

$$= \frac{3}{2} \times 1.38 \times 10^{-23} \times 400$$

$$= 8.28 \times 10^{-21} \text{ joule}$$

$$\lambda = \frac{h}{\sqrt{2mE}} = \frac{6.63 \times 10^{-34}}{\sqrt{2 \times 1.66 \times 10^{-27} \times 8.28 \times 10^{-21}}}$$

$$= 1.264 \times 10^{-10} \text{ m}$$

$$= \mathbf{1.264\ \text{Å}.}$$

Q. 11. Show that de-Broglie wavelength λ of electron accelarated through a potential difference of V volts can be expressed as:

$$\lambda = \frac{h}{\sqrt{2meV}} = \frac{12.3}{\sqrt{V}} = \text{Å}.$$

Ans. Consider an electron of mass m and charges. Let v be the velocity acquired by it when it is accelerated from rest through a potential difference of V volt. Then, K.E. gained by the electron $= \frac{1}{2}mv^2$.

Work done on electron $= eV$

$$\frac{1}{2}mv^2 = eV$$

$$v = \sqrt{\frac{2eV}{m}}$$

Hence, de-Broglie wavelength of electron

$$\lambda = \frac{h}{mv} = \frac{h}{m\sqrt{\frac{2eV}{m}}} = \frac{h}{\sqrt{2meV}}$$

$$\lambda = \frac{6.63\times10^{-34}}{\sqrt{2\times9.1\times10^{-31}\times1.6\times10^{-19}\times V}}$$

$$= \frac{12.3}{\sqrt{V}}\ \text{Å}.$$

Q. 12. State the laws of photoelectric emission.

Ans. On the basis of the experimental result on photoelectric effect, following laws were given

1. For a given photosensitive material, there exists a certain minimum cut-off frequency, below which no photoelectrons are emitted. This frequency is called threshold frequency.
2. Above the threshold frequency, the stopping potential or the maximum kinetic energy of the photoelectron increases linearly with the frequency of incident radiation.
3. For a given photosensitive material and frequency of incident radiation, the photo-electric current is directly proportional to the intensity of light.
4. The photoelectric emission is an instantaneous process. The time lag between the incidence of light radiation and emission of photoelectron is very small.

Q. 13. Draw a graph showing the variation of stopping potential with the frequency of incident radiation in relation to photoelectric effect.

(*a*) What does the slope of this graph represent?

(*b*) How can the value of Plank's constant be determined from this graph?

Ans. According to Einstein's photoelectron equation, the maximum K.E. of photoelectron

$$K_{max} = hv - W_0$$

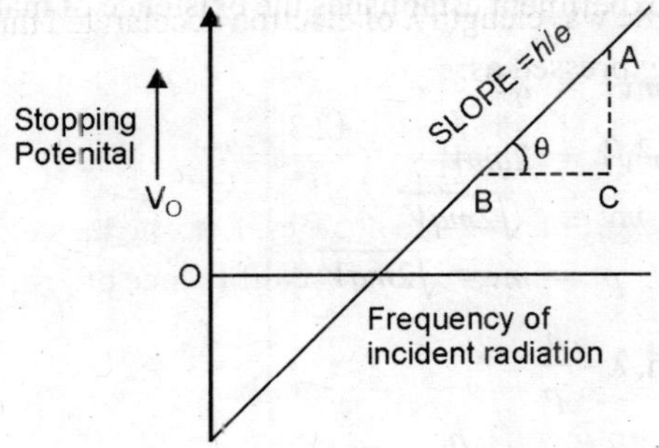

Fig. 7.3

If V_0 is the stopping potential

$$K_{max} = eV_0$$

$$eV_0 = hV - w_0$$

$$V_0 = \left(\frac{h}{e}\right)v - \frac{W_0}{e}$$

It follows from the above equation that V_0 versus v graph is a straight line

(*a*) Slope of $V_0 - v$ graph $= \frac{h}{e}$.

(*b*) To determine the slope, take two points A and B on the straight line graph. This gives

$$m = \tan\theta = \frac{AC}{BC} = \frac{h}{e}.$$

Q. 14. What is the de-Broglie wavelength associated with (*i*) an electron moving with a speed of 5.4×10^6 m/s, (*ii*) A ball of mass 1.50 gm travelling at 30 m/s.

Ans. (*i*) $\lambda_e = \frac{h}{m_e v_e} = \frac{6.63\times10^{-34}}{9.1\times10^{-31}\times5.4\times10^{-6}} = 0.135 \times 10^{-9} = 0.135$ nm.

(*ii*) $\lambda_b = \frac{h}{m_b v_b} = \frac{6.63\times10^{-34}}{1.5\times10^{-3}} = 1.47 \times 10^{-32}$ m.

Q. 15. An electron and a proton are moving in the same direction and possess same kinetic energy. Find the ratio of de-Broglie wavelength associated with these particles.

Ans. KE of a particle of mass *m*, moving with velocity *v*, is given by $K = \frac{1}{2} mv^2 = \sqrt{2mK}$ de-Broglie wavelength $\lambda = \frac{h}{mv} = \frac{h}{\sqrt{2mK}}$

$$\lambda \propto \frac{1}{\sqrt{m}}$$

$$\frac{\lambda_e}{\sqrt{\lambda_p}} = \sqrt{\frac{m_p}{m_e}}$$

Q. 16. Mention the significance of Davisson-Germer experiment. An α-particle and a proton are accelerated from rest through the same potential difference V. Calculate the ratio of their de-Broglic wavelength.

Ans. Davisson-Germer experiment establishes the existence of matter wave of electron

$$\frac{1}{2}mv^2 = qV$$

$$m^2v^2 = 2qmV$$

$$mv = \sqrt{2mqV}$$

$$p = mv = \sqrt{2mqV}$$

de-Broglie wavelength, $\lambda = \frac{h}{p}$

$$= \frac{h}{\sqrt{2mqV}}$$

$$\frac{\lambda_{\alpha-\text{particle}}}{\lambda_{(\text{proton})}} = \sqrt{\frac{m_p q_p}{m_\alpha q_\alpha}} = \sqrt{\frac{m_p e}{4m_p 2e}} = \frac{1}{2\sqrt{2}}.$$

Q. 17. Obtain the relationship between stopping potential and frequency of incident radiations for photoelectric emission.

Ans. Energy of incident photon = Maximum K.E. of emitted photoelectron + work function

$$hv = \frac{1}{2}mv_{\max}^2 + W_0$$

If V_0 is the stopping potential

$$\frac{1}{2}mv_{\max}^2 = eV_0$$

$$hv = eV_0 + W_0.$$

$$\boxed{eV_0 = hv - W_0}$$

Q. 18. An electromagnetic wave of wavelength λ is incident on a photosensitive surface of negligible work function. Prove that $\lambda = \left(\frac{2mc}{h}\right).\lambda_1^2$.

Ans.

$$\frac{1}{2}mv^2 = hv$$

$$\frac{m^2v^2}{2m} = hv$$

$$\frac{P^2}{2m} = \frac{hc}{\lambda}$$

$$P = \sqrt{\frac{2mhc}{\lambda}}$$

$$\lambda_1 = \frac{h}{P} = \frac{h}{\sqrt{\frac{2mhc}{\lambda}}}$$

$$\lambda_1 = \sqrt{\frac{h\lambda}{2mc}}$$

$$\lambda_1^2 = \frac{h\lambda}{2mc} \Rightarrow \boxed{\lambda = \left(\frac{2mc}{h}\right)\lambda_1^2}$$

HIGHER ORDER THINKING SKILLS (HOTS)

Q. 1. A small metal plate of work function ϕ is kept at a distance r from a singly ionised fixed ion. A monochromatic light beam is incident on the metal plate and photoelectrons are emitted. Find maximum wavelength of the light beam so that some of the electrons may go round the ion along a circle.

Ans. If the electron is to move around the ion in circular path of radius r

$$\frac{mv^2}{r} = \frac{1}{4\pi \epsilon_0} \cdot \frac{e \times e}{r^2}$$

$$mv^2 = \frac{1}{4\pi \epsilon_0} \cdot \frac{e^2}{r}$$

$$\text{K.E. of electron } \frac{1}{2} mv^2 = \frac{e^2}{8\pi \epsilon_0 r}$$

As
$$\frac{1}{2} mv^2_{max} = \frac{hc}{\lambda} - \phi$$

$$\frac{e^2}{8\pi\epsilon_0 r} = \frac{hc}{\lambda} - \phi_1$$

$$\frac{hc}{\lambda} = \frac{e^2}{8\pi\epsilon_0 r} + \phi_1$$

$$\lambda = \frac{8\pi\epsilon_0 r hc}{e^2 + 8\pi\epsilon_0 r\phi}.$$

Q. 2. Work function of Na is 2.3 eV. Does sodium (Na) show photoelectric emission for orange light (λ = 6800 Å)?

Ans. Here, Work function of Na = 2.3 eV, wavelength of orange light λ = 6800Å = 6800×10^{-10} m. The energy of the photon of orange light is given as

$$E = \frac{hc}{\lambda} = \frac{6.63\times10^{-34} \times 3\times10^{8}}{6800\times10^{-10}} \text{J} = \frac{6.63\times 3}{68} \times \frac{10^{-18}}{1.6\times10^{-19}} \text{eV} = 1.83 \text{ eV which is less than } \phi_0.$$

$\therefore$ Photoelectric emission cannot take place.

Q. 3. Light of wavelength 3500 Å is incident on two metals A and B. Which metals yield photo-electron if their work function are 4.2 eV and 1.9 eV respectively.

Ans. The metal, whose work function is less than energy of the incident light, will emit photo-electron

$$E = \frac{hc}{\lambda} = \frac{6.62\times10^{-34} \times3\times10^{8}}{35\times10^{-8} \times1.6\times10^{-19}} = 3.5 \text{ eV}.$$

Since the work function of metal A (= 4.2 eV) is greater than energy of light, so it will not emit photoelectrons.

Q. 4. The threshold frequency of a certain metal is 3.3×10^{14} Hz. If light of frequency 8.2×10^{14} Hz is incident on the metal, predict the cut off voltage for photoelectric emission. Given plants contant $h = 6.62 \times 10^{34}$ Js.

Ans. We have $eV_0 = h(v - v_0)$

or
$$V_0 = h\frac{(v - v_0)}{e}$$

$$= \frac{6.62\times10^{-34}}{1.6\times10^{-19}}\left(8.2\times10^{14}-3.3\times10^{14}\right) = \mathbf{202.74\ V.}$$

Q. 5. In the photoelectric effects, there is a cut-off frequency. How does the photon picture explain this fact?

Ans. According to photon picture, the photoelectric effect is due to the interaction between a photon and free electron in the metal. The free electron will be emitted only if it has sufficient energy equal to the work function of the metal. This energy is supplied by photon. The work function = $h\nu_0$ determines the minimum energy required for photo electric emission. If the frequency of photon is less than ν_0 no photo electric emission will take place.

Q. 6. Why rest of the mass of a photon is zero?

Ans. According to the theory of relativity, the mass m of a particle moving with velocity v, comparable with the velocity of light c, is given by

$$m = \frac{m_0}{\sqrt{1-v^2/c^2}} \text{ or } m_0 = m\sqrt{1-v^2/c^2}$$

where m_0 is the rest mass of particle. As a photon moves with speed of light i.e., $v = c$.

$$m_0 = m\sqrt{1-\frac{c^2}{c^2}} \quad (\because v = c),$$

$$= \sqrt{1-1} = 0$$

Hence, rest mass of photon is zero.

Q. 7. Red light, however bright, cannot produce the emission of electron from a clean zinc surface. But even weak ultraviolet radiation can do so. Why?

Ans. The frequency of red light is less than threshold frequency of zinc surface, hence, it cannot cause photoelectric emission from zinc surface, whatever may be its intensity. The frequency of ultraviolet radiation is greater than threshold frequency of zinc surface, which leads to emission of photo electrons.

Q. 8. Describe Davisson and Germer experiment to establish the wave nature of electron. Draw a labelled diagram of the apparatus used.

Ans.

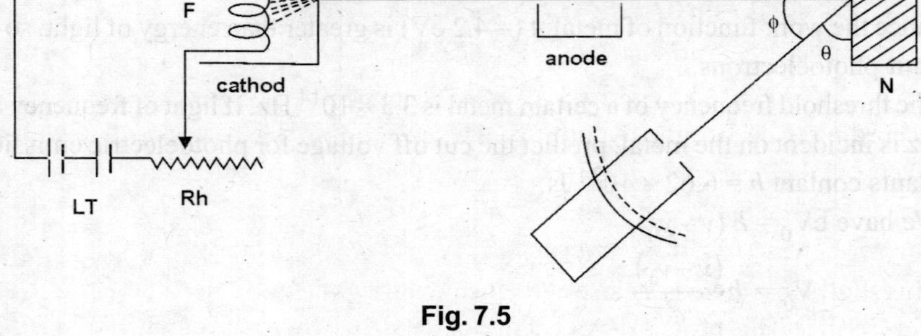

Fig. 7.5

Wave nature of slow moving electron has been established experimentally by Davisson and Germer in 1927. The apparatus, is shown in Fig. 7.5. It consists of a filament *F* of tungsten coated with barium oxide, which, on heating with current from low tension battery, emits large number of electrons. *C* is a hollow metallic cylinder with a hole along the axis. It surrounds the filaments and is kept at (–ve) potential so that electron emitted from the filament may form a convergent beam of electrons. The cathode and anode form an electron gun by which a fine beam of electrons can be obtained under different accelerative potentials applied between cathode and anode. *N* is a nickel crystal cut along cubical diagonal. *D* is an electron detector. It can be rotated on a circular scale and is connected to a sensitive galvanometer, which records the current.

Working—A fine beam of accelerated electron obtained from electron gun is made to fall normally on the surface of nickel crystal. The incident electrons are scattered in different directions by the atoms of the crystal. The intensity of the electron beam, scattered in a given direction is found by the use of detector. It can be calculated by rotating the electron detector on a circular scale at different positions. The intensity of the scattered beam is measured for the different value of scattering angle ϕ, the angle between the incident and scattered electron beam.

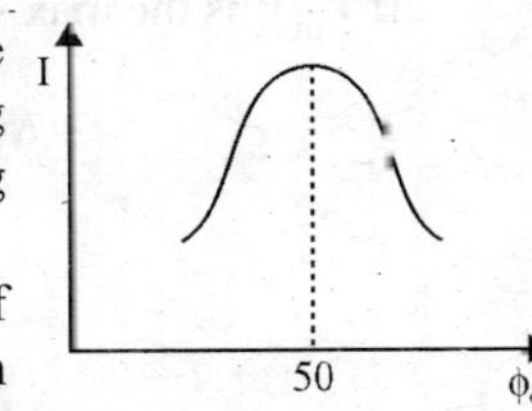

The experiment was performed by varying the accelerative voltage from 44 to 68 volts. It was noticed that at accelerating voltage 54 V, there is variation of intensity *I* and scattering angle ϕ.

We note that for the scattering angle ϕ = 50°, the angle of glancing (angle between the scattered beam of electron with plane of atom of crystal) (θ) for the electron beam will be given by

$$\theta + \phi + \theta = 180^\circ$$

$$2\theta = 180^\circ - \phi$$

$$\theta = \frac{1}{2}(180^\circ - \phi) = \frac{1}{2}$$

$$\theta = \frac{1}{2}(180^\circ - 50^\circ) = \mathbf{65^\circ}.$$

$$\theta = 65^\circ$$

Now for the Nickel crystal, the interatomic separation

$$d = 0.91\ \text{Å}.$$

According to Bragg's law for first order diffraction maximum ($n = 1$), we have

$$2d \sin\theta = n\lambda$$

$$n = 1$$

$$2d \sin\theta = 1 \times \lambda$$

$$\lambda = 2 \times 0.91 \times \sin 65^\circ$$

$$= \mathbf{1.65\ Å.}$$

According to de-Broglie hypothesis, the wavelength of wave assciated with electron is given by

$$\lambda = \frac{12.27}{\sqrt{V}} = \frac{12.27}{\sqrt{54}} = \mathbf{1.66\ Å.}$$

This shows that there is a close agreement with estimated value of de-Broglie wavelength and Germer. This proves the existence of de-Broglie wave for slow moving electron.

Q. 9. Establish Einstein photoelectric relation. Explain the law of photoelectric emission on the basis of this relation.

Ans. Laws of photo-electric emission

Einstein's photoelectric equation—According to Plank's quantum theory, light radiations consist of tiny packets of energy called quanta. One quantum of light radiation is called a photon, which travels with the speed of light.

$$E = h\nu$$

where h is Plank's constant and ν is frequency.

Einstein assumed that one photoelectron is ejected from a metal surface if one photon of suitable light radiation falls on it.

Consider a photon of light of frequency ν, incident on a photosensitive metal surface. The energy of the photon $h\nu$ is spent in two ways.

(*i*) A part of the energy of photon is used in liberating the electron from metal surface which is equal to work function ϕ_0 of the metal.

(*ii*) The rest of the energy of the photon is used in imparting the maximum kinetic energy k_{max} to the emitted photoelectron.

If V_{max} is the max velocity of the emitted photoelectron, max K.E. of photoelectron

$$K_{max} = \frac{1}{2}mv^2$$

$$h\nu = \phi_0 + \frac{1}{2}mv_{max}^2$$

$$\text{K.E.} = \frac{1}{2}mv^2 = h\nu - \phi_0.$$

This equation is called Einstein's photoelectric equation. If the incident photon is of threshold frequency ν_0, then the incident photon of energy $h\nu_0$ is just sufficient to eject the electron from the metal surface without imparting in any KE, hence, $h\nu_0$ must be equal to the work function ϕ_0 of the metal, i.e.,

$$h\nu_0 = \phi_0$$

$$\frac{1}{2}mv^2 = h\nu - h\nu_0$$

$$\boxed{K_{max} = h(\nu - \nu_0)}$$

Explanation of Laws

(*i*) When $\nu < \nu_0$, K_{max} is –ve which is not possible, hence photo emission will not take place.

(*ii*) From (*i*), K_{max} linearly depends upon ν, the frequency of incident radiation.

(*iii*) Increase in intensity of incident radiation will increase the number of incident photons and hence the number of photo electrons in the same ratio.

(*iv*) The energy transfer from photon to free electron is perfectly elastic collision in which no time is elapsed.

Q. 10. Find the number of photons emitted per second by a 25 W surface of monochromatic source of light of wavelength 6600Å. What is the photoelectric current assuming 3% efficiency for photoelectric effect? Plank's constant = 6.6×10^{-34} Js.

Ans. No. of photons emitted per second by 25 watt-source will be

$$n = \frac{E}{hc/A} = \frac{E\lambda}{hc} = \frac{25 \times 6600 \times 10^{-10}}{6.6 \times 10^{-34} \times 3 \times 10^{8}}$$

$$= \frac{25}{3 \times 10^{-19}} = 8.33 \times 10^{19}\ s^{-1}$$

Current I = 3% of no. of photoelectrons emitted per second × charge on electron

$$= \frac{3}{100} \times ne$$

$$= \frac{3}{100} \times \frac{25}{3 \times 10^{-19}} \times 1.5 \times 10^{-19} = 0.4\ \text{Å}$$

Q.11. In a photoelectric effect experiment, the following graphs were obtained between the photoelectric current (I) and the applied voltage (V) on anode. Name the characteristics of the incident radiation that was kept constant in this experiment.

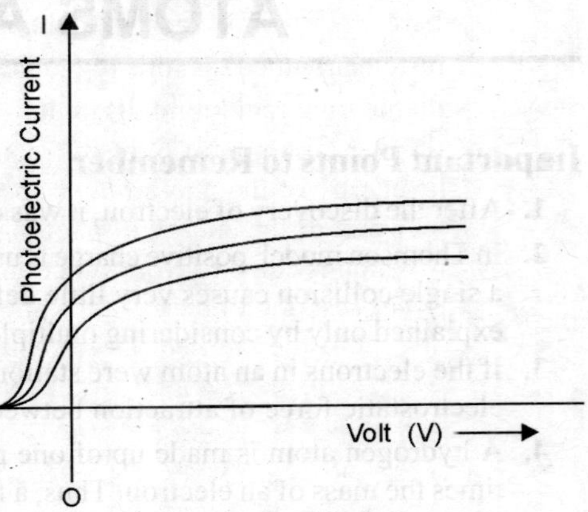

Fig. 7.6

Ans. As the value of stopping potential is the same for all the curves, so the frequency of the incident radiations must be constant but their intensity is different.

Q.12. The mercury line of wavelengths 2536Å is used to eject photoelectrons from silver (Ag) metal. The difference in potential required to bring all the ejected electrons to rest is 0.11 V. Calculate the energy in electron volt necessary to remove an electron from Ag metal. Given hc = 1.2500 eVÅ.

Ans. Here λ = 2536Å = 2536 × 10^{-10} m, V_0 = 0.11 V. Energy required to remove an electron from Ag metal is equal to work function of Ag (= ϕ_0)

Using the relation,

$$eV_0 = \frac{1}{2} mv_{max}^2 = \frac{hc}{\lambda} - \phi_0$$

or

$$\phi_0 = \frac{hc}{\lambda} - eV_0$$

$$= \frac{12400\, eV\text{Å}}{2536\text{Å}} - e \times 0.11\ \text{V}$$

$$= 4.88\ \text{eV} - 0.11\ \text{eV} = 4.77\ \text{eV}.$$

□□□

UNIT 8

ATOMS AND NUCLEI

Important Points to Remember

1. After the discovery of electron, it was concluded that each atom has a structure of its own.
2. In Thomson model, positive charge is uniformly distributed in the spherical atom. Therefore, a single collision causes very little deflection. However, average scattering angle can be explained only by considering multiple scattering.
3. If the electrons in an atom were stationary, they would fall into the nucleus on account of electrostatic force of attraction between electrons and the nucleus.
4. A hydrogen atom is made up of one proton and one electron. Mass of a proton is 1836 times the mass of an electron. Thus, a fraction 1836/1837 of the atomic mass is carried by the positive charge.
5. The implication is that an electron revolving in any stationary orbit is bound to the nucleus and cannot leave the nucleus on its own.
6. The radius of the atom is of the order of 10^{-10} m.
7. Distance of the closest approach of α-particle from a nucleus in α-scattering experiment is given by the formula:

$$r_0 = \frac{1}{4\pi\varepsilon_0} \cdot \frac{2Ze^2}{\left(\frac{1}{2}mv^2\right)} = \frac{1}{4\pi\varepsilon_0}\frac{2Ze^2}{K}$$

where $K = \frac{1}{2}mv^2$ initial value of KE of α-particle.

8. Impact parameter of the α-particle is defined as the perpendicular distance of the velocity vector of α-particle from the central line of the nucleus when it is far away from the atom. Impact parameter,

$$b = \frac{1}{4\pi\varepsilon_0} \cdot \frac{Ze^2 \cot\theta/2}{1/2\,mv^2} = \frac{1}{4\pi\varepsilon_0} \cdot \frac{Ze^2 \cot\theta/2}{K},$$

when θ is the angle of scattering of α-particle.

9. According to Bohr, an electron can revolve only in certain discrete non-radiating orbits, called stationary orbits, for which total angular momentum of the revolving electron is an integral multiple of $h/2\pi$, where h is Plank's constant.
10. Orbit radius of the electron around the nucleus

$$r_n = \frac{\epsilon_0 n^2 h^2}{\pi m e^2} \quad \text{where } n = 1, 2, 3, \ldots$$

and velocity of electron in nth orbit

$$v_n = \frac{e^2}{2\epsilon_0 nh}$$

11. Energy of the electron in the nth orbit of hydrogen atom

$$E_n = -\frac{me^4}{8 \epsilon_0^2 n^2 h^2} = -\frac{13.6}{n^2} eV$$

$$= -\frac{2.18 \times 10^{-18}}{n^2} . J$$

12. **Angular momentum of electron in any orbit is integral multiple of $h/2\pi$**

$$L = mvr = nh/2\pi, n = 1, 2, 3, ...$$

13. (*i*) **Lyman series** in UV region of hydrogen spectrum

$$\bar{v} = R\left[\frac{1}{1^2} - \frac{1}{n^2}\right] \text{ where } n = 2, 3, 4, ...$$

(*ii*) **Balmer series** in visible region $\bar{v} = R\left(\frac{1}{2^2} - \frac{1}{n^2}\right)$ where $n = 3, 4, 5.$

(*iii*) The empirical formula for Paschen series lines of *H*-spectrum is $\bar{v} = R\left[\frac{1}{3^2} - \frac{1}{n^2}\right]$, where $n = 4, 5, 6,$ ....

The series lies in infrared region of e.m. spectrum.

(*iv*) **Brackett series** in infrared, $\bar{v} = R\left[\frac{1}{4^2} - \frac{1}{n^2}\right]$, where n is an integer more than 4

(*v*) ***P* fund series** in far infrared region $\bar{v} = R\left(\frac{1}{5^2} - \frac{1}{n^2}\right)$, where $n > 5$.

14. Nuclear density $P = 3m / 4\pi r_0^{\ 3}$

15. **Isotopes**

Same *Z* and different *A* *Ex*, $^1H_2$, $^1H_3$, $^1h_1$ and C^{12}, C^{14}, C^{16}

16. **Isobars**

Same A and different Z $[_{18}Ar^{40}, _{20}Co^{40}]$ and $(_1H^3, _2H^3)$

17. **Isotones**

Same no. of neutrons $[_1H^3, _2He^4]$

18. **Mass defect of the nucleus is defined as the difference in the sum of the masses of the neutrons and protons forming a nucleus and the mass of the nucleus formed. If *m* is the mass of nucleus X^A, then mass defect**

$$\Delta m = [Z m_p + (A - Z) m_n - m]$$

19. **The amu is defined as 1/12th of the mass of an atom of $_6C^{12}$ isotope. 1 amu = 1.66 × 10^{-27} kg. In terms of the energy, 1 amu = 931 MeV.**

20. **Binding energy E_b**

$E_b = \Delta m \times c^2$ (Δm = mass of reactants – mass of products)

21. **Binding energy per nucleon is the average energy required to remove a nucleon from the nucleus of an atom.**

22. **A nucleus is more stable when value of binding energy per nucleon is larger.**

23. **The three types of radiations emitted in radioactive disintegration are — alpha, beta and gamma.**

24. **An α-particle is a helium nucleus and a β-particle is a fast moving electron.**

25. **γ-rays are photons of short wavelength. They travel with the speed of electromagnetic waves and exhibit those phenomena which are being exhibited by electromagnetic waves. Hence, γ-rays are called electromagnetic waves.**

26. α, β and γ-rays when arranged. In order of increasing ionising power, are γ-rays, β-particle and α-particle.
27. The ionising power is directly proportional to KE, which varies directly as mass of particle and square to its velocity. That is why, ionising power of α-particle is more than that of β-particle.
28. Penetrating power varies inversely to its mass of the particle (for the given KE). As $m_\alpha >> m_\beta$, therefore, the penetrating power of α-particle is less than that of β-particle.
29. (*i*) With the emission of α-particle, the mass number (A) decreases by 4 and the atomic number (Z) or the charge number decreases by 2.
(*ii*) With the emission of β-particle, the mass number (A) does not change while the atomic number (Z) increases by 1.
(*iii*) No effect on A and Z due to emission of *r*-rays.
30. With the emission of α-particle ($_2He^4$) and a β-particle ($_{-1}e^0$), mass number = $(m-4)$ and charge number = $(n-1)$.
31. Radioactive decay law

$$\frac{dN}{dt} = -\lambda N$$

$$\frac{-dN}{dt} = R = \text{Activity (unit Bq.)}$$

32. No: of nuclei remaining un-decayed at any instant of time

$$N = N_0 e^{-\lambda t} \text{ or } N = N_0\left(\frac{1}{2}\right)^n, n = \frac{t}{t_{1/2}}$$

33. Half life $\quad t_{1/2} = \dfrac{0.693}{\lambda}$
34. Electron and proton have almost infinite lifetime.
35. Emission of an α-particle involves the emission of 2 protons and 2 neutrons. As number of neutrons ≥ no. of protons, the ratio of neutrons to protons must increase.
36. Energy distribution of β-rays is continuous because β-emission occurs along with the emission of another particle called antineutrino. The energy of the pair of particles emitted is constant. But on account of interaction between the two particles, their energy is shared. Hence, β-rays have continuous energy.
37. Nuclear forces act amongst the nucleons in a nucleus.
38. Nuclear forces do not depend upon the charge in the nucleons. This follows from the fact that magnitude of *p-p* forces, *p-n* forces and *n-n* forces inside an atomic nucleus is the same.
39. Nuclear forces are saturated in character. They properly make BE/nucleons constant for most of the nuclei.
40. (*i*) Nuclear fission is the process in which a heavier nucleus breaks into lighter ones.
(*ii*) Nuclear fusion is the process in which higher nuclei is fused into a heavier one.
41. Mass of (π^+) is 273 times the mass of an electron.
42. In a nuclear reactor, the role of moderator is to slow down neutrons, the thermal neutrons so produced cause farther fission of $_{92}U^{235}$ nuclei.
43. An uncontrolled nuclear chain reaction can occur only when the lump of uranium (target) is greater than a certain minimum size. This is called critical size.

❑❑❑

VERY SHORT ANSWER TYPE QUESTIONS

(Carrying 1 mark)

Q. 1. Name the series of hydrogen spectrum lying in the infrared region.

Ans. Paschen series, Brackett series and Pfund series.

Q. 2. Name the series of hydrogen spectrum which lies in the visible region of electromagnetic spectrum?

Ans. Balmer series lies in visible region.

Q. 3. What is impact parameter for scattering of α-particle by 180°?

Ans. Zero. This follows from the relation

$$b = \frac{Ze^2 \cot\frac{\theta}{2}}{4\pi \epsilon_0 \left(\frac{1}{2} mv^2\right)}$$

Q. 4. Show that Bohr's second postulate "The electron revolves around the nucleus only in certain fixed orbits without radiating energy" can be explained on the basis of de-Broglie hypothesis of wave nature of electron.

Ans. When an electron of mass m is confined to move on a line of length $2l$ with velocity v, the de-Broglie wavelength λ associated with electron is:

$$\lambda = \frac{h}{mv} = \frac{h}{p}$$

$$P = \frac{h}{\lambda} = \frac{h}{\frac{2l}{n}} = \frac{nh}{2l}$$

When electron revolves in a circular orbit of radius r, then $2l = 2\pi r$

$$p = \frac{nh}{2\pi r}$$

or $$p \times r = \frac{nh}{2\pi}$$

i.e., angular momentum ($p \times r$) of electron is integral multiple of $\frac{h}{2\pi}$. This is the Bohr's quantisation condition of angular momentum.

Q. 5. What is pair production?

Ans. Pair production is the phenomenon of production of a pair of particle (particle + anti particle), when a gamma-ray photon strikes a heavy nucleus. Thus, energy is converted into matter by this phenomenon.

Q. 6. How is half-life of a radioactive substance related to its average life.

Ans. $\tau = 1.44\, T$.

Q. 7. Arrange radioactive radiation in the order of increasing penetrating power.

Ans. α, β and γ rays.

Q. 8. Name two elementary particles which have almost infinite lifetime.

Ans. Electrons and protons have almost infinite lifetime.

Q. 9. Define Decay constant?

Ans. Decay constant of a radioactive element is the reciprocal of the time during which the number of atoms left in the sample reduces to $\frac{1}{e}$ times the original number of atoms in the sample.

Q. 10. Name two radioactive elements which are not found in observable quantities.

Ans. Tritium and plutonium.

Q. 11. Compare the radii of two nuclei with mass number 1 and 27.

Ans. $\frac{R_1}{R_2} = \left(\frac{A_1}{A_2}\right)^{\frac{1}{3}} = \left(\frac{1}{27}\right)^{\frac{1}{3}} = \frac{1}{3}.$

Q. 12. A radioactive isotope decays in the following sequence $A \xrightarrow{{}_0n^1} A_1 \xrightarrow{\alpha} A_2$. If the mass number and atomic number of A_2 are 176 and 71 respectively, find the mass number and atomic number of A_1 and A. Which of the three elements are isobars?

Ans. As $\alpha = {}_2He^4$, therefore, mass number $A_1 = 176 + 4 = 180$ and charge number of $A_1 = 71 + 2 = 73$. Clearly mass number of $A = 180 + 1 = 181$ and change number of $A = 73 + 0 = 73$. Elements A_1 and A_2 are isobars.

Q. 13. Which one of ${}_3X^7$ and ${}_3Y^4$ is likely to be more stable? Give reason.

Ans. ${}_3X^7$ is likely to be more stable as it contains larger number of neutrons $(7 - 3 = 4)$ as compared to $3Y^4$, which contains only 1 neutron $(4 - 3)$.

Q. 14. Define nuclear binding energy.

Ans. Binding energy of a nucleus is the energy with which nucleons are bound in the nucleus. It is measured by work done to separate the nucleons infinite distance apart from the nucleus, so that they may not interact with one another.

Q. 15. Define atomic mass unit. Write its energy equivalent.

Ans. 1 a.m.u. is defined as $\frac{1}{12}th$ of the mass of an atom of ${}_6C^{12}$ isotope

1 a.m.u. = 1.66×10^{-27} kg. In terms of energy, 1 a.m.u. = 931 MeV.

Q. 16. What is meant by mass defect of a nucleus?

Ans. Mass defect of a nucleus is defined as the difference in the sum of the masses of the neutrons and protons forming a nucleus and mass of the nucleus formed. If m is the mass of a nucleus ${}_ZX^A$, then mass defect

$$\Delta m = [Z m_p + (A - Z) m_n - m].$$

Q. 17. Draw the graph showing the distribution of kinetic energy of electron emitted during beta-decay.

Ans. The distribution of K.E. of electron emitted during beta decay.

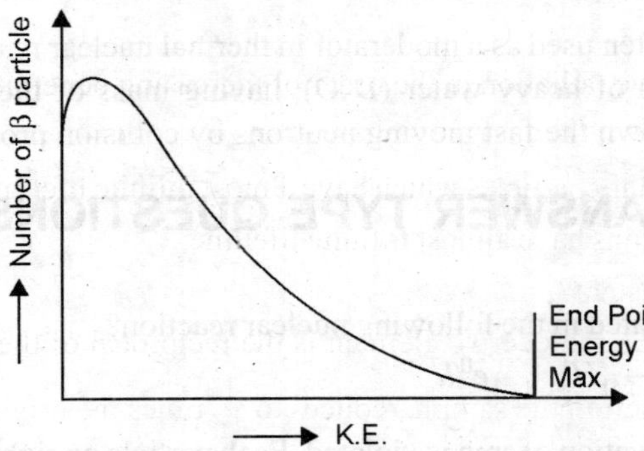

Fig. 8.1

Q. 18. Proton and neutron exist together in an extreme space within the nucleus. How is this possible when protons repel each other?

Ans. Due to strong attractive nuclear force.

Q. 19. Is a free neutron a stable particle?

Ans. No, a free neutron is not a stable particle. It decays spontaneously into a proton, an electron and antineutrino.

$$_0n^1 \longrightarrow {}_1H^1 + {}_{-1}e^0 + \bar{v}.$$

Q. 20. Complete the equation

$$_{92}U^{235} + {}_0n^1 = \longrightarrow$$

Ans. $_{92}U^{235} + {}_0n^1 \rightarrow {}_{56}Ba^{147} + {}_{36}Kr^{56} + 3\ {}_0n^1 + 200\text{ MeV}$

Q. 21. What fraction of tritium will remain after 25 years? Given its half-life is 12.5 years.

Ans. $\dfrac{N}{N_0} = \left(\dfrac{1}{2}\right)^{t/T} = \left(\dfrac{1}{2}\right)^{25.5/12.5} = \dfrac{1}{4}$

Hence, the fraction of initial sample of $_1H^3$ that would remain undecayed after 25 years would be ¼th.

Q. 22. The total energy of an electron in the first excited state of the hydrogen atom is about –3.4 eV. What is the potential energy of the electron in this state?

Ans. P.E. of an electron = 2 × total energy = 2 × (–3.4 eV) = – 6.8 eV.

Q. 23. What is the energy equivalent to 10 mg mass?

Ans. As $m = 10\text{ mg} = 10 \times 10^{-6}\text{ kg} = 10^{-5}\text{ kg}$

Hence, equivalence energy, $E = mc^2 = 10^{-5} \times (3 \times 10^8)^2 = 10^{-5} \times 9 \times 10^{16}\text{ J} = 9 \times 10^{11}\text{ J}$.

Q. 24. Write the nuclear decay process for β-decay of $_{15}P^{32}$.

Ans. Here $_{15}P^{32} \rightarrow {}_{16}S^{32} + {}_{-1}e^0 + \bar{v} + Q$.

Q. 25. What would happen if the electrons in an atom were stationary?

Ans. If the electrons in an atom were stationary, they would fall into the neuleus on account of electrostatic force of attraction between electrons and the nucleus.

Q. 26. Assuming Bohr's atomic model void, what is the ground state energy of an electron in case of $_3Li^7$?

Ans. Here $Z = 3,\ n = 2$

$$E_n = \frac{-13.6Z^2}{n^2} eV = \frac{-13.6(3)^2}{2^2} = -30.4\text{ eV}.$$

Q. 27. Write the SI unit for the activity of a radioactive nuclide.

Ans. Becqueral (1 Bq).

Q. 28. Heavy water is often used as a moderator in thermal nuclear reactors. Give reason.

Ans. Because deutrons of heavy water (D_2O), having mass of the same order as that of neutrons, slow down the fast moving neutrons by collision process effectively.

SHORT ANSWER TYPE QUESTIONS (SA-I)

(Carrying 2 marks)

Q. 1. Which law is violated in the following nuclear reaction?

$${}_0n^1 \longrightarrow {}_1H^1 + {}_{-1}e^0?$$

Ans. The law of conservation of spin is violated. Each particle on right side has a spin $\frac{h}{2\pi}$. So that resultant spin on the right side is 0 or $1\left(\frac{h}{2\pi}\right)$ and on the left side, spin is $\frac{1}{2}\left(\frac{h}{2\pi}\right)$.

Q. 2. The sequence of decay of radioactive nucleus is

$$D \xrightarrow{-\alpha} D_1 \xrightarrow{-\beta} D_2 \xrightarrow{\alpha} D_3 \xrightarrow{-\alpha} D_4.$$

If the nucleons number and atomic number of D_2 are 176 and 71 respectively, what are their value for D and D_4?

Ans. As mass number of each α particle is 4 units and the chrnge number is 2 units, therefore, for D_4

$$A = 176 - 8 = 168$$
$$Z = 71 - 4 = 67.$$

Now, the charge number of β is –1 and its mass number is zero, therefore, for D

$$A = 176 + 0 + 4 = 180$$
$$Z = 71 - 1 + 2 = 72.$$

Q. 3. What are thermal neutrons? Why are neutrons considered as ideal particles for nuclear fission?

Ans. Thermal neutrons are low energy neutrons = $\frac{1}{40}$ eV. Neutrons are considered as ideal particles for nuclear fission because they are neutral particles on which neither any force of attraction nor any force of repulsion can act.

This is because a neutron carries no charge. It can hit the nucleus directly without being repelled or attracted by the protons in the nucleus or electrons.

Q. 4. What is the effect on neutron to proton ratio in a nucleus when (*i*) an electron, (*ii*) a positron is emitted?

Ans. In emission of an electron, a neutron is converted into a proton. Therefore, number of neutrons decreases and the number of protons increases. The neutron to proton ratio is decreased. In the emission of a positron, a proton is converted into a neutron. Hence, the ratio increases.

Q. 5. How many electrons, protons and neutrons are there in a nucleus of atomic number 11 and mass number 24?

Ans. No. of electrons in the nucleus = 0, No. of protons = atomic no. = 11

No. of (protons + neutrons) = mass no. = 24

No. of neutrons = 24 – 11 = 13.

Q. 6. Calculate the energy equivalent of 1 a.m.u. in MeV.

Ans. $E = mc^2$

When $m = 1$ amu $= 1.66 \times 10^{-27}$ kg

$$E = (1.66 \times 10^{-27})(3 \times 10^8)^2 \text{ joule}$$

$$= \frac{1.66 \times 9 \times 10^{-11}}{1.6 \times 10^{-13}} = 933.75 \text{ MeV.}$$

Q. 7. What is meant by critical mass in a nuclear chain reaction?

Ans. Critical mass in a nuclear chain reaction is the minimum mass of fissionable material that would sustain the nuclear chain reaction at a steady rate. The neutron reproduction factor *K*, in this case, becomes equal to one *i.e.*, rate of production of neutrons is just equal to the rate of loss of neutrons.

Q. 8. What do you mean by the charge independent nature of nuclear force?

Ans. Nuclear force does not depend upon charge on the nucleons. This follows from the fact that magnitude of a *p–p* force, *p–n* force and *n–n* force inside an atomic nucleus is the same.

Q. 9. Explain the function of a moderator in a nuclear reactor.

Ans. The function of moderator in nuclear reactor is to slow down fast neutron to the desired extra. Generally, paraffin, deuterium and heavy water are used as moderator. On colliding against the hydrogen nucleus or protons of roughly equal to mass, their velocity gets interchanged.

Q. 10. Calculate binding energy of an α-particle from the following data:

mass of free proton = 1.007825 a.m.u.
mass of free neutron = 1.008665 a.m.u.
mass of helium nucleus = 4.002800 a.m.u.
1 a.m.u. = 931.5 MeV

Ans. An α-particle is helium nucleus containing 2 protons and 2 neutrons

$$\text{Mass Defect } \Delta m = 2 \times 1.007825 + 2 \times 1.008665 - 4.002800$$
$$= 103018 \text{ a.m.u.}$$
$$\text{Binding Energy} = \Delta m \times 931.5 \text{ MeV} = 0.03018 \times 931.5 = 28.1 \text{ MeV.}$$

Q. 11. Calculate the binding energy per neucleon of ${}_{20}Ca^{40}$ nucleus. Given

$$m({}_{20}Ca^{40}) = 39.962589\, u$$
$$m_n = 1.008665\, u$$
$$m_p = 1.007825\, u.$$

Ans. In a nucleus of ${}_{20}Ca^{40}$

number of protons = 20
number of neutrons = 40 – 20 = 20.

Total mass of 20 protons and 20 neutrons

$$= 20\, m_p + 20\, m_n = 20\,(m_p + m_n)$$
$$= 20\,(1.007825 + 1.008665)$$
$$= 40.3298\, u$$
$$\text{Mass defect } \Delta m = 40.3298 - 39.963589 = 0.36711$$
$$\text{Binding energy} = 0.367211 \times 931 \text{ MeV}$$
$$= 341.873441 \text{ MeV}$$

$$\text{B.E./neucleon} = \frac{341.873441}{40} = 8.547 \text{ MeV/N.}$$

Q. 12. What is Fast Breeder Reactor?

Ans. When fast neutron strikes uranium fuel in a reactor, $_{92}U^{238}$ absorbs a neutron and becomes $_{92}U^{239}$. This is radioactive and undergoes β-decay twice to produce $_{94}Pu^{239}$, as represented

$$_{92}U^{238} + {_0n^1} \rightarrow {_{92}U^{239}} \xrightarrow{-\beta} {_{93}P^{239}}$$

$$_{92}U^{235} \xleftarrow{-\alpha} {_{94}Pu^{239}} - \beta$$

Now $_{94}Pu^{239}$ is fissionable and undergoes α-decay to produce $_{92}U^{235}$.

Q. 13. Find the energy equivalent of one atomic mass unit, first in joule and then in MeV. Using this, express the mass defect of $_8O^{16}$ in MeV/C^2.

Ans. Given mass of proton $= 1.60727\,u$

mass of neutron $= 1.00866\,u$

mass of $_8O^{16}$ nucleus $= 15.99053\,u$

1 a.m.u. $= 1.66 \times 10^{-27}$ kg

$$E = mc^2$$

$$E = (1.66 \times 10^{-27})(3 \times 10^8)^2$$

$$= 1.494 \times 10^{-10}\text{ J}$$

$$E = \frac{1.494 \times 10^{-10}}{1.6 \times 10^{-13}}\text{ MeV} = 933.75\text{ MeV.}$$

For oxygen $_8O^{16}$, mass defect

$$\Delta m = 8\,m_p + 8\,m_n - M_{oxygen}$$

$$= 8 \times 1.00727 + 8 \times 1.00866 - 15.99053$$

$$= 0.13691\text{ amu}$$

$$= 0.13691 \times 933.75\text{ MeV}/c^2$$

$$= 127.8\text{ MeV}/c^2$$

Q. 14. The half-life of $_{92}U^{238}$ against α-decay is 4.5×10^9 years. What is the activity of 1 gm sample of $_{92}U^{238}$?

Ans.

$$T = 4.5 \times 10^9\text{ years}$$

$$= 4.5 \times 10^9 \times 365 \times 24 \times 60 \times 60$$

$$= 1.42 \times 10^{17}\text{ sec}$$

As number of atoms in 238 gm

= Avogadro's no.

$= 6.023 \times 10^{23}$

∴ Number of atoms in 1 gm of sample

$$N = \frac{6.023 \times 10^{23}}{238}$$

$$R = -\frac{dN}{dt} = \lambda N = \frac{0.693}{T} N$$

$$= \frac{0.693 \times 6.023 \times 10^{23}}{1.42 \times 10^{17} \times 238}$$

$$= 1.235 \times 10^3\text{ Bq.}$$

SHORT ANSWER TYPE QUESTIONS (SA-II)

(Carrying 3 marks)

Q. 1. What do you understand by atomic number and mass number?

Ans. **Atomic Number:**—Total number of protons present in the nucleus is called atomic number. It is represented by Z.

Mass Number:—Total number of protons and neutrons present in the nucleus is called mass number. It is represented by A.

Q. 2. How is the size of a nucleus estimated? Write the relation between the radius of a nucleus and its mass number.

Ans. Like an atom, a nucleus is not a solid object. Its surface is not a well defined boundary. Still we can assign a size to the nucleus.

By performing scattering experiments using energy probes, such as fast moving protons, neutrons or electrons, nucleus sizes of different elements have been accurately measured. Assuming nuclei to be spherical, their volumes can be estimated.

If R is the radius of a nucleus having mass number A, then

$$\frac{4}{3}\pi R^3 \propto A.$$

$$R \propto A^{1/3}.$$

Thus, the radius R of a nucleus is proportional to cube root of its mass number

$$R = R_0 A^{1/3}.$$

Here R_0 is a constant.

Q. 3. State and deduce radioactive decay law. Hence, define disintegration at that instant constant.

Ans. The number of nuclei disintegrating per second of a radioactive sample at any instant is directly proportional to the number of undecayed nuclei present.

Let N_0, the number of radioactive nuclei present initially at time $t = 0$, is a sample of radioactive substance.

$N \rightarrow$ the number of radioactive nuclei present in the sample at any instant t, and

$dN \rightarrow$ the number of radioactive nuclei which disintegrate in the small time interval dt. According to radioactive law, the rate of decay at any instant is proportional to the number of undecayed nuclei

$$-\frac{dN}{dt} \propto N$$

$$-\frac{dN}{dt} = \lambda N$$

Where λ is proportionally constant called the decay or disintegration constant

$$\frac{dN}{N} = -\lambda\, dt$$

Integrating $$\int \frac{dN}{N} = -\lambda \int dt$$

$$\log N = -\lambda t + C$$

where C is a constant of integration.

At $$t = 0; N = N_0$$

$$\log N_0 = C$$

$$\log_e N = -\lambda t + \log_e N_0$$

$$\log_e N - \log_e N_0 = \lambda t$$

$$\frac{N}{N_0} = e^{-\lambda t}$$

$$N = N_0 e^{-\lambda t}.$$

This equation represents the radioactive decay law.

Q. 4. Define half-life of a radioactive substance. Deduce its relation with disintegration constant.

Ans. The time interval in which one half of radioactive nuclei is present in radioactive sample disintegration is called half-life of the radioactive substance.

Relation between half-life and decay constant:—

Let N_0 = Number of radioactive nuclei present in the radioactive sample initially (at $t = 0$).

$N \rightarrow$ Number of radioactive nuclei left at any instant.

at $t = T_{1/2}$; $N = \frac{N_0}{2}$

$$N = N_0 e^{-\lambda t}$$

$$\frac{N_0}{2} = N_0 e^{-\lambda T_{1/2}}$$

$$\frac{1}{2} = e^{-\lambda T_{1/2}}$$

$$e^{\lambda T_{1/2}} = 2$$

$$\lambda T_{1/2} = \log_e 2$$

$$T_{1/2} = \frac{\log_e 2}{\lambda}$$

$$= \frac{2.303 \log_{10}^2}{\lambda}$$

$$= \frac{2.303 \times .3010}{\lambda}$$

$$\boxed{T_{1/2} = \frac{0.693}{\lambda}}$$

Thus, the half-life of a radioactive substance is inversely proportional to its decay constant and is independent of the number N_0, the number of radioactive nuclei present initially in the sample.

Q. 5. Define Mean or Average life of a radioactive substance. Deduce its relation with decay constant and half-life.

Ans. Average life-time of a radioactive element can be obtained by calculating the total life-time of all atoms of the element and dividing it by the total number of atoms present initially in the sample of the element.

Let us consider a radioactive element containing N_0 atoms to start with at $t = 0$. Let the number of atoms left at time t be N. Suppose, a small number of atoms = dN disintegrate further in a small time dt.

Therefore, the life-time of these dN atoms = $t \, . \, dN$ is smaller.

Total life-time of all the atoms in sample of the element

$$= \int_0^{N_0} t \, dN.$$

By the definition, average life-time of the radioactive element.

$$\tau = \frac{\int_0^{N_0} t\, dN.}{N_0}$$

$$dN = -\lambda N\, dt$$

$$dN = -\lambda (N_0 e^{-\lambda t})\, dt$$

Since, $\quad N = N_0 . e^{-\lambda t}$

When $N = 0$, $t = \infty$ and when $N = N_0$, $t = 0$

Thus
$$\tau = \frac{\int_\infty^0 -\lambda N_0 e^{-\lambda t}\, dt \times t}{N_0}$$

$$\tau = \int_0^\infty t - e^{-\lambda t}\, dt.$$

Integrating by parts

$$\tau = \lambda \left[\left\{ \frac{t - e^{-\lambda t}}{-\lambda} \right\}_0^\infty - \int_0^\infty \frac{e^{-\lambda t}}{-\lambda} dt \right]$$

$$= \lambda \left[0 + \frac{1}{\lambda} \int_0^\infty e^{-\lambda t}\, dt \right]$$

$$= \int_0^\infty e^{-\lambda t}\, dt$$

$$= \left[\frac{e^{-\lambda t}}{-\lambda} \right] = 0 - \frac{1}{-\lambda}$$

$$\boxed{\tau = \frac{1}{\lambda}}$$

Further $\quad \lambda = \dfrac{0.693}{T}$

So that $\quad \tau = \dfrac{T}{0.693} = 1.44T$

Q. 6. **What is nuclear energy? With the help of the binding energy curve, explain how nuclear energy can be released.**

Ans. The energy released during a nuclear reaction is called nuclear energy. As the curve of binding energy per nucleon has long flat region in the mass number range from 30 to 170. Here the binding energy per nucleon is almost constant, around 8.5 MeV. However, for $A < 30$ and $A > 170$, B.E./nucleon is less than this plateau value. This indicates that there the nuclei are less stable than the nuclei with mass number between 30 and 170. Hence, whenever an element with a smaller binding energy is transmitted into an element with a larger binding energy, tremendous amount of energy is released. This is due to the conversion of some mass Δm into energy in accordance with Einstein's mass energy relation

$$E = -\Delta mc^2$$

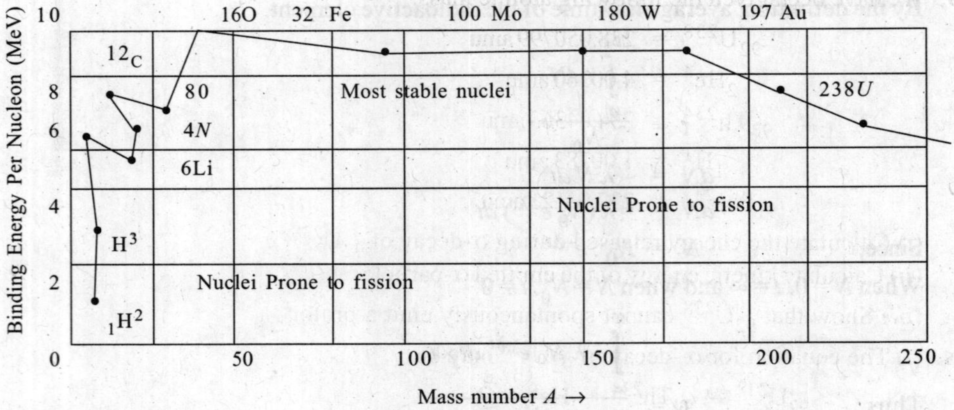

Fig. 8.2

Q. 7. What is a moderator? Explain the action in slowing down the neutrons.

Ans. Any substance which is used to slow down fast moving neutrons to thermal energies is called a moderator. The commonly used moderators are water, heavy water (D_2O), graphite and beryllium.

Action of moderator:—Fast neutrons are passed through a moderator like paraffin, deutrium or water, which contains large number of hydrogen nucleus protons. Neutrons and protons have nearly same mass. When fast moving neutrons are passed through paraffin, they make elastic collision with protons which have comparatively much smaller velocity. As a result, the neutrons are slowed down.

Q. 8. The half-life of $_6C^{14}$ is 5,700 years. What does it mean? Two radioactive nuclei x and y initially contain an equal number of atoms. Their half-life is 1 hour and 2 hours respectively. Calculate the ratio of their rate of disintegration after two hours.

Ans. The half-life of $_6C^{14}$ is 5,700 years. This means that one-half of the original number of radioactive nuclei will remain undecayed after 5,700 years. Let both the samples x and y have initially N radioactive nuclei each. Then, by definition of half-life:

No. of nuclei x left undecayed after $1h$.

$$= \frac{N}{2}$$

No. of nuclei x left undecayed after 2 h.

$$= \frac{1}{2} \times \frac{N}{2} = \frac{N}{4}.$$

No. of nuclei y left undecayed after 2 h.

$$= \frac{N}{2}.$$

Let R_1 and R_2 be the rate of disintegration after $2h$. If λ_1 and λ_2 are the decay constants of the two samples, then

$$\frac{R_1}{R_2} = \frac{\lambda_1 N_1}{\lambda_2 N_2} = \frac{T_2 N_1}{T_1 N_2}$$

$$= \frac{2 \times \frac{N}{4}}{1 \times \frac{N}{2}} = 1:1.$$

Q. 9. We have been given the following atomic mass:

$$_{92}U^{238} = 238.050799 \text{ amu}$$
$$_{2}He^{4} = 4.00260 \text{ amu}$$
$$_{90}Th^{234} = 234.04363 \text{ amu}$$
$$_{1}H^{1} = 1.00783 \text{ amu}$$
$$_{91}Po^{\,237} = 237.03121 \text{ amu}$$

(*i*) Calculate the energy released during α-decay of $_{92}U^{238}$.
(*ii*) Calculate kinetic energy of the emitted α-particle.
(*iii*) Show that $_{92}U^{238}$ cannot spontaneously emit a proton.

Ans. (*i*) The equation for α–decay of $_{92}U^{238}$ may be

$$_{92}U^{238} \rightarrow {}_{90}Th^{234} + {}_{2}He^{4} + Q$$

where Q (called Q–value) represents kinetic energy released during the process. Using Einstein's mass energy equivalence:

$$Q = [m_N({}_{92}U^{238}) - m_N({}_{90}Th^{234}) - m_N({}_{2}He^{4})] \times c^2.$$

By adding and subtracting 92 m_e in the bracket:

$$Q = [\{m_N({}_{92}U^{238}) + 92\, m_e\} - \{m_N({}_{90}Th^{234}) + 90\, m_e\}$$
$$- \{m_N({}_{2}He^{4}) + 2\, m_e\}]\, c^2$$
$$= [238.05079 - (234.04363 + 4.00260)] \times 931.5 \text{ MeV}$$
$$= .00456 \times 931.5 \text{ MeV}$$
$$= 4.25 \text{ MeV}.$$

(*ii*) The kinetic energy of the α-particle

$$E_\alpha = \left(\frac{A-4}{4}\right) Q = \frac{238-4}{238} \times 425 = 4.18 \text{ MeV}.$$

(*iii*) If $_{92}U^{238}$ spontaneously emits a proton, the decay process:

$$_{92}U^{238} \rightarrow {}_{91}Pa^{237} + {}_{1}H^{1}$$

For this process to happen:

$$Q = [m({}_{92}U^{238}) - m({}_{91}Po^{237}) - m({}_{1}H^{1})]\, c^2$$
$$= [238.05079 - 237.05121 - 1.00783] \text{ amu} \times c^2$$
$$= (-0.00825) \text{ amu} \times \frac{931.5 \text{ MeV}}{9 \text{ amu}}$$
$$= -7.68 \text{ MeV}.$$

As the Q value of the process is negative, it cannot occur spontaneously.

Q. 10. A radioactive isotope has a half-life of 5 years. How long will it take the activity to reduce to 3.125%?

Ans. Since the activity is proportional to the number of radioactive atoms, therefore,

$$\frac{R}{R_0} = \frac{N}{N_0} = \left(\frac{1}{2}\right)^n$$

$$\frac{R}{R_0} = 3.125 = \frac{3.125}{100} = \frac{1}{32} = \left(\frac{1}{2}\right)^5$$

$$\left(\frac{1}{2}\right)^5 = \frac{N}{N_0} = \left(\frac{1}{2}\right)^n$$

$$n = 5$$

Reduced time $t = nT_{1/2} = 5 \times 5 = 25$ years.

Q. 11. The half-life of radium is 1,500 years. After how many years will one gram of the pure radium

(*i*) reduce to 1 centigram

(*ii*) lose one milligram.

Ans. Half-life $T_{1/2} = 1{,}500$ years

Decay constant $\lambda = \frac{0.693}{T_{1/2}} = \frac{0.693}{1500}$

(*i*) Initial amount, $N_0 = 1$ gm

Remaining $N = 1$ centigram $= 0.01$ gm

Required time $t = \frac{2.303}{\lambda} \log \frac{N_0}{N} = \frac{2.303 \times 1500}{.693} \log \frac{1}{.01}$

$$= \frac{2.303 \times 1500 \times 2}{.693} = 9.972 \times 10^3 \text{ years.}$$

(*ii*) Initial amount $N_0 = 1$ gm

Remaining amount $N = 1 - 10^{-3} = 0.999$ gm

Required time $t = \frac{2.303}{\lambda} \log \frac{N_0}{N} = \frac{2.303 \times 1500}{0.693} \log \frac{1}{0.999}$

$$= \frac{2.303 \times 1500 \times .0004}{0.693}$$

$$= 1.995 \text{ years.}$$

Q. 12. Obtain the maximum kinetic energy of β particles and the radiation frequencies corresponding to γ-decay in the decay scheme shown in Fig. 8.3. You have been given that

$$m\,({}_{79}\text{Au}^{198}) = 197.968233 \text{ amu}$$

$$m\,({}_{80}\text{Hg}^{198}) = 197.966760 \text{ amu}$$

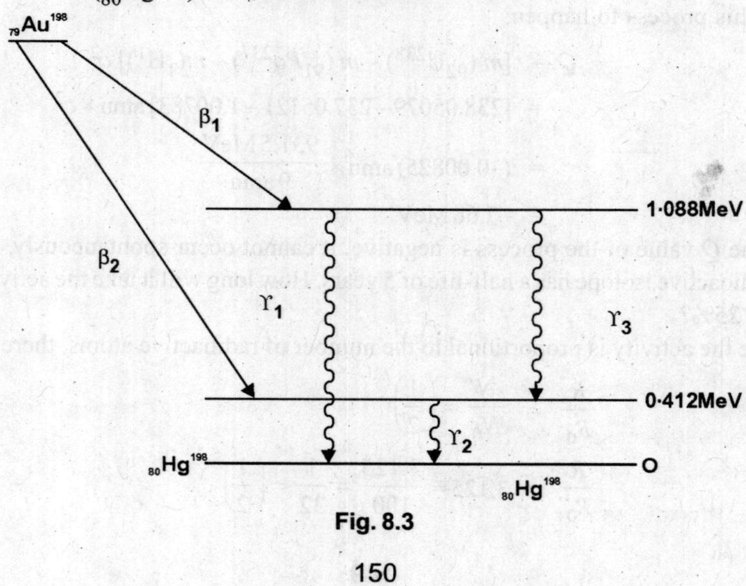

Fig. 8.3

Ans. The energy corresponding to γ_1

$E_1 = 1.088 - 0 = 1.088\ \text{MeV} = 1.088 \times 1.6 \times 10^{-13}\ \text{joule}$

$$\nu(\gamma_1) = \frac{E_1}{h} = \frac{1.088 \times 1.6 \times 10^{-13}}{6.6 \times 10^{-34}} = 2.63 \times 10^{20}\ \text{Hz}$$

Similarly, $$\nu(\gamma_2) = \frac{E_2}{h} = \frac{0.412 \times 1.6 \times 10^{-13}}{6.6 \times 10^{-34}} = 9.8 \times 10^{19}\ \text{Hz}$$

and $$\nu(\gamma_3) = \frac{E_3}{h} = \frac{(1.088 - 0.412) \times 1.6 \times 10^{-13}}{6.6 \times 10^{-34}} = 1.64 \times 10^{19}\ \text{Hz}$$

Maximum kinetic energy of β_1^- particle is

$$K_{max}(\beta_1^-) =$$

$$\left[m\left({}_{79}\text{Au}^{198} \right) - \text{mass of second excited state of } {}_{80}\text{Hg}^{198} \right] \times 931\text{MeV}$$

$$K_{max}(\beta_1^-) = \left[m\left({}_{79}\text{Au}^{198} \right) - \left\{ m\left({}_{80}\text{Hg}^{198} - \frac{1.088}{931} \right) \right\} \times 931\ \text{MeV} \right]$$

$$= 931\,(197.968233 - 197.966760) - 1.088\ \text{MeV}$$

$$= 1.371 - 1.088$$

$$= 0.283\ \text{MeV}$$

Similarly, $K_{max}(\beta_2^-) = 0.957\ \text{MeV}$

HIGHER ORDER THINKING SKILLS (HOTS)

Q. 1. Show that the instantaneous rate of change of activity of a radioactive substance is inversely proportional to the square of its half-life.

Ans. The instantaneous activity of a radioactive sample is given by $A = A_0 e^{-\lambda t}$. Differentiating both sides w.r.t. to

$$\frac{dA}{dt} = A_0 e^{-\lambda t}(-\lambda)$$

$$\frac{dA}{dt} = -\lambda A_0 e^{-\lambda t}$$

$$= -\lambda A$$

$$\frac{dA}{dt} = -\lambda(\lambda N) = -\lambda^2 N$$

Using $$\lambda = \frac{0.693}{T}$$

$$\frac{dA}{dt} = -\left(\frac{0.693}{T} \right)^2 N$$

$$\frac{dA}{dt} \propto \frac{1}{T^2}$$

Q. 2. Calculate the mass of one curie of U^{234}.

Ans. 1 curie $= 3.7 \times 10^{10}$ disintegration/sec.

No. of atoms in 1 curie $= 3.7 \times 10^{10}$

Mass of 6.023×10^{23} atoms of $U^{234} = 234$ gm

Mass of 3.7×10^{10} atoms of U^{234}

$$\frac{234 \times 3.7 \times 10^{10}}{6.023 \times 10^{23}} = 1.437 \times 10^{-11} \text{ gm.}$$

Q. 3. The radioactive decay rate of a radioactive element is found to be 10^3 disintegration/sec at a certain time. If half-life of the element is one second, what would be the decay rate after 1 sec. and after 3 sec.?

Ans. It is known that radioactive rate is directly proportional to the number of nuclei left. No. corresponding to 10^3 (disintegration/sec.):

(*i*) No. of half-life in 1 sec. $n = 1$

$$N = N_0 \left(\frac{1}{2}\right)$$

$$N = 1000 \left(\frac{1}{2}\right)^2 = 500$$

$\therefore$ No. of disintegrations/sec. = 500.

(*ii*) No. of half-life $n = \frac{3}{1} = 3$

$$N = N_0 \left(\frac{1}{2}\right)^n$$

$$N = 1000 \left(\frac{1}{2}\right)^3 = \frac{1000}{8} = 125$$

No. of disintegrations/sec. after three seconds = 125

Q. 4. The disintegration rate of a certain radioactive sample at any instant in 4,750 disintegrations per minute, after 5 minutes, the rate becomes 2,700 disintegrations per minute. Calculate

(*i*) Decay constant (*ii*) Half-life of sample.

($\log_{10} 1.76 = .2455$)

Ans. As rate of disintegration is proportional to the number of atoms present

$$\frac{N_0}{N} = \frac{4750}{2700} = 1.76$$

$$N = N_0 \, e^{-\lambda t}$$

$$\frac{N_0}{N} = e^{\lambda t}$$

$$\log \frac{N_0}{N} = \lambda t$$

$$\lambda = \frac{\log_e \left(\frac{N_0}{N}\right)}{t} = \frac{2.3026 \log_{10}(1.76)}{t}$$

$$= \frac{2.3026 \times .2455}{5} = .1131 \text{ min}^{-1}.$$

Further, half life

$$T_{½} = \frac{0.693}{\lambda} = \frac{0.693}{0.1131} = 6.1 \text{ min}$$

Q. 5. **The isotopes of U^{238} and U^{235} occur in nature in the ratio 140.1. Assuming that at the time of earth's formation, they were present in equal ratio, make an estimate of the age of earth. The half lives of U^{238} and U^{235} are 4.5×10^9 years and 7.13×10^8 years. Given $\log_{10} 140 = 2.1461, \log_{10} 2 = 0.3010$.**

Ans.

$$N_1 = N_0\, e^{-\lambda_1 t}$$

$$N_2 = N_0\, e^{-\lambda_2 t}$$

$$\frac{N_1}{N_2} = e^{(\lambda_2 - \lambda_1)t}$$

$$t = \frac{\log_e \left(\frac{N_1}{N_2}\right)}{\lambda_2 - \lambda_1} = \frac{\log_e \frac{140}{1}}{\log_e 2\left(\frac{1}{\tau_2} - \frac{1}{\tau_1}\right)}$$

$$t = \frac{\log_{10} 140}{\log_{10} 2}\left(\frac{\tau_2\, \tau_1}{\tau_1 - \tau_2}\right)$$

On putting the value $t = 6 \times 10^9$ years.

Q. 6. **State and explain the laws of radioactive disintegration. Hence, define disintegration constant and half-life period.**

Ans. **Laws of Radioactive Disintegration:**—Soddy and Rutherford, from their experimental study regarding the radioactive disintegration, formulated the following laws:

1. Radioactivity is a spontaneous process, which does not depend upon external factors like temperature, pressure, etc. i.e., radioactive element is in a state of disintegration, which depends upon law of chance. It means it is impossible to predict which particular atom of radioactive element will disintegrate in a given time interval.
2. During disintegration of an atom, either an α-particle or β-particle is emitted. Both of these particles are never emitted simultaneously. Also at a time, an atom will not emit more than one α-particle or more than one β-particle.
3. The emission of α-particle from an atom will change it into a new atom whose charge number is reduced by two and mass number is reduced by four.
4. The emission of a β-particle from an atom will change it into a new atom whose charge number is raised by one, without any change in its mass number.
5. The number of atoms disintegrated per second (rate of disintegration of radioactive atoms) at any instant is directly proportional to the number of radioactive atoms actually present in the sample at that instant.

Let N_0 = total number of atoms present originally in a sample at time = 0.

N = Total number of atoms left undecayed in the sample at time t.

dN = a small number of atoms that disintegrate in a small interval of time dt

Rate of disintegration of the element

$$R = -\frac{dN}{dt}.$$

According to radioactive decay law,

$$-\frac{dN}{dt} \propto N$$

$$R = -\frac{dN}{dt} = \lambda N.$$

Where λ is a constant of proportionality and is called disintegration constant

$$\frac{dN}{N} = -\lambda dt.$$

Integrating both sides

$$\int \frac{dN}{N} = -\lambda \int dt$$

$$\log_e N = -\lambda t + c$$

where c is a constant of integration at $t = 0$; $N = N_0$

$$\log_e N_0 = \lambda \times 0 + c$$

$$c = \log_e N_0$$

$$\log_e N = -\lambda t + \log_e N_0$$

$$\log_e N - \log_e N_0 = -\lambda t$$

$$\log_e \frac{N}{N_0} = -\lambda t$$

$$\frac{N}{N_0} = e^{-\lambda t}$$

$$N = N_0 e^{-\lambda t}.$$

Disintegration Constant

Substituting $t = \frac{1}{\lambda}$

$$N = N_0 e^{-\lambda . \frac{1}{\lambda}}$$

$$N = N_0 e^{-1} = \frac{N_0}{e}.$$

Thus, the disintegration constant of a radioactive element is the reciprocal of time, at the end of which the number of atoms left undecayed in a radioactive sample reduce to $\left(\frac{1}{e}\right)$ time the original number of atoms (N_0) in the sample.

Half-life of Radioactive element. Half-life of radioactive element is defined as the time during which half the number of atoms present initially in the sample of the element decayed or it is the time during which the number of atoms left undecayed in the sample is half the total number of atoms present initially in the sample.

When $t = T, N = \frac{N_0}{2}$

$$\frac{N_0}{2} = N_0 e^{-\lambda T}$$

$$\frac{1}{2} = e^{-\lambda T}$$

$$2 = e^{\lambda T}$$

$$\lambda T = \log_e 2$$

$$\lambda T = 2.303 \log_{10} 2$$

$$T = \frac{2.303 \times .3010}{\lambda}$$

$$T = \frac{0.6931}{\lambda}$$

$$\boxed{T = \frac{0.6931}{\lambda}}$$

Q. 7. Explain:

(*a*) Impact parameter

(*b*) Postulates of Bohr's Theory

(*c*) Total Energy of an electron in the nth orbit of *H*-atom.

Ans. (*a*) Impact Parameter:—Perpendicular distance of the velocity vector of α-particle from the central line of the nucleus, when the particle is far away from the nucleus of the atom is called impact parameter.

(*b*) Postulates of Bohr's Theory:

(*i*) An electron in an atom could revolve in certain stable orbits without the emission of radiant energy.

(*ii*) Electrons revolve around the nucleus only in those orbits for which angular momentum is sum of integral & multiple of $\frac{h}{2\pi}$, where *h* is Plank's constant

$$L = \frac{nh}{2\pi}$$

$$h = 6.6 \times 10^{-34} \text{ Js}$$

(*iii*) An electron might make a transition from one of its specified non-radiating orbits to another of lower energy.

(*c*) Total energy of an electron in the nth orbit of H-atom:—For hydrogen atom $Z = 1$, Electrostat force of attraction provides centripetal force to the electron to revolve in its orbit

$$F_e = F_c$$

$$\frac{1}{4\pi\epsilon_0}\frac{e^2}{r^2} = \frac{mv^2}{r}$$

$$r = \frac{e^2}{4\pi\epsilon_0 mv^2} \quad \text{...(1)}$$

According to Bohr's quantisation condition

$$L = mvr = \frac{nh}{2\pi}$$

$$r = \frac{nh}{2\pi mv} \quad \text{...(2)}$$

From equations (1) and (2)

$$v = \frac{e^2}{2\epsilon_0 nh} \quad \text{...(3)}$$

On substituting equation (3) in equation (2)

$$r = \frac{n^2h^2}{4\pi^2 kme^2} \text{ where } K = \frac{1}{4\pi\epsilon_0} \quad \text{...(4)}$$

As $r \propto n^2$, the radii of the permitted orbits increase in ratio 1 : 4 : 9 : 16.

$$r_0 = \frac{h^2}{4\pi^2 Kme^2}$$

$$= \frac{(6.6\times10^{-34})^2}{4\pi^2\times(9.1\times10^{-31})(9\times10^9)(1.6\times10^{-19})^2}$$

$$r_0 = 5.29 \times 10^{-11} \text{ m}$$

$$r_0 = 0.53 \text{ Å}.$$

Kinetic energy of electron in *n*th orbit

$$K.E. = \frac{1}{2}mv^2 = \frac{Ke^2}{2r}$$

P.E. of electron in *n*th orbit

$$U = \frac{-Ke^2}{r}$$

Total energy of electron in *n*th orbit

$$E_n = \text{K.E.} + \text{P.E.}$$

$$E_n = \frac{Ke^2}{2r} - \frac{Ke^2}{r} = -\frac{Ke^2}{2r}$$

On substituting value of *r* from equation (4), we get

$$E_n = \frac{-2\pi^2 mK^2 e^4}{n^2 h^2}$$

Hence (–ve) value of total energy indicates that electron is bound to nucleus.

Q. 8. Explain:

(*i*) Energy levels of hydrogen atom.

(*ii*) Line spectra of the hydrogen atom.

Ans. (*i*) Total energy of an electron in *n*th orbit is

$$E_n = -\frac{2\pi^2 mK^2 e^4}{n^2 h^2}$$

For 1st orbit $n = 1$

$$E_1 = -\frac{2\pi^2 mK^2 e^4}{h^2}$$

$$= -\frac{2\pi^2 (9.1\times 8^{31})(9\times 10^9)^2 \times (1.6\times 10^{-19})^2}{(6.6\times 10^{-34})^2}$$

$$E_1 = -21.76 \times 10^{-19} \text{ Joul}$$

$$E_1 = -\frac{21.76\times 10^{-19}}{1.6\times 10^{-19}}$$

$$E_1 = -13.6 \text{ ev}$$

$$E_n = \frac{E_1}{n^2} = \frac{-13.6}{n^2} \text{ eV}$$

Putting $n = 2, 3, 4, \ldots\ldots\ldots\ldots$ etc.

(*ii*) **Line spectra of the hydrogen atom:**—According to Bohr's third postulate, when an atom jumps from higher energy state with quantum number *ni* to lower energy state with quantum number $(n_1 > n_2)$, the difference of energy appears in the form of photon of frequency v_{if}, such that

$$hv_{if} = E_2 - E_1$$

$$hv_{if} = \frac{-2\pi^2 mK^2 e^4}{n_2^2 h^2} + \frac{2\pi^2 mK^2 e^4}{n_1^2 h^2}$$

$$\frac{hc}{\lambda} = \frac{2\pi^2 mK^2 e^4}{h^3}\left[\frac{1}{n_1^2} - \frac{1}{n_2^2}\right]$$

$$\frac{hc}{\lambda_{if}} = \frac{2\pi^2 mK^2 e^4 Z^2}{h^2}\left[\frac{1}{n_1^2}-\frac{1}{n_2^2}\right]$$

$$\frac{1}{\lambda} = \frac{2\pi^2 mK^2 e^4 Z^2}{ch^3}\left(\frac{1}{n_1^2}-\frac{1}{n_2^2}\right)$$

$$\bar{v} = R\left[\frac{1}{n_1^2}-\frac{1}{n_2^2}\right].$$

Now, $\frac{1}{\lambda} = \bar{v}$ is the wave number of radiation emitted, i.e., number of complete waves in unit length.

$$R = \frac{2\pi^2 mK^2 e^4}{ch^3}$$

where R is called Rydberg constant for hydrogen and Z = 1.

(i) *Lyman Series*:—When an electron jumps from any higher energy level to first level

$$\bar{v} = R\left[\frac{1}{1^2}-\frac{1}{n_i^2}\right]$$

$$n_i = 2, 3, 4, ...$$

This series is called ultraviolet region.

(ii) *Balmer Series*

$$\bar{v} = R\left[\frac{1}{2^2}-\frac{1}{n_i^2}\right]$$

$$n_i = 3, 4, 5, ...$$

This series lies in the visible region.

(iii) *Paschan Series*

$$\bar{v} = R\left[\frac{1}{3^2}-\frac{1}{n_i^2}\right]$$

$$n_i = 4, 5, 6, ...$$

This series lies in the infra-red region.

(iv) *Brackett Series*

$$\bar{v} = R\left[\frac{1}{4^2}-\frac{1}{n_i^2}\right]$$

$$n_i = 5, 6, 7, ...$$

This series lies in the infra-red region.

(v) *Pfund Series*

$$\bar{v} = R\left[\frac{1}{5^2}-\frac{1}{n_i^2}\right]$$

$$n_i = 6, 7, 8, ...$$

This series lies in the far infra-red region.

❑❑❑

UNIT 9

SEMICONDUCTOR DEVICES

Important Points to Remember

1. (*i*) The valence band is a lower band belonging to valence electrons. This band may be partially or completely filled with electrons.

   (*ii*) The conduction band is an upper band in which the electrons are not present at 0K. At room temperature, this band is either empty or partially filled with electrons.

2. Forbidden energy gap (E_g) is the energy difference between valence band and conduction band.

3. In metals, the conduction band and valence band partly overlap each other and there is no forbidden energy gap.

4. In insulators, the conduction band is empty and valence band is completely filled and forbidden gap is quite large = 6 eV. No electron from valence band can cross over to conduction band at room temperature, even if electric field is applied. Hence there is no conductivity of the insulators.

5. In semiconductors, the conduction band is empty and valence band is totaly filled. But the forbidden gap between conduction band and valence band is quite small.

6. The conductivity of a semiconductor increases with rise of temperature because more covalent bonds in a semiconductor get broken with rise of temperature, providing more number of electrons and holes as current carriers.

7. Electron has higher mobility than hole in a semiconductor.

8. Hole is a seat of positive charge, which is produced when an electron breaks away from a covalent bond in a semiconductor.

9. In a semiconductor, Ohm's law is obeyed for low electric field (less than 10^6 Vm^{-1}). Above this field, the current becomes almost independent of the applied field.

10. The electrical conductivity of a metal depends upon the number of free electrons and their drift velocity through the metal on applying the field.

11. In an energy band, the highest energy level occupied by free electrons at 0K is called fermi level and its energy is called fermi energy.

12. Dopping is a process of deliberate addition of desirable impurity in a pure semiconductor to mobilise its properties in controlled manner.

13. (*i*) In *n*-type semiconductor, electrons (having negative charge) are majority charge carriers which are responsible for the conduction.

    (*ii*) In *p*-type semiconductor, holes (having positive charge) are majority charge carriers which are responsible for the conduction.

14. Two important processes occur during the formation of *p-n* junction, diffusion and drift.

15. In junction diode, the direction of the diffusion current is from *p*-region to *n*-region.

16. Depletion region is a region created around the *p-n* junction which is devoid of free charge carriers and has immobile ions.

17. In equilibrium state, there is no current across *p-n* junction and potential barrier across *p-n* junction has maximum value.

18. *p-n* junction is FB when *p*-type connected to the positive of battery and *n*-type connected to negative of battery. Potential barrier height is reduced and width of depletion layer decreases.

19. *p-n* junction in RB *p*-type connected to the negative of battery and *n*-type connected to positive. Resistance of *p-n* junction is high to the flow of current.

20. A small increase in forward voltage across *p-n* junction shows large increase in forward current. Hence, the resistance (= voltage/current) of *p-n* junction is low when forward biased.
A large increase in reverse voltage across *p-n* junction shows small increase in reverse current. Hence, the resistance of the *p-n* junction is high when reverse biased.

21. (*i*) In a half-wave rectifier, the output voltage is uni-junction intermittent and varying voltage.
(*ii*) In a full-wave rectifier, the output voltage is unidirectional varying voltage.

22. Zener breakdown is due to production of electron-hole pair on account of thermal excitation.

23. Zener diode is used to regulate the output of an unregulated dc supply.

24. Solar cell is a *p-n* junction device which converts solar energy into electrical energy.

25. In a light emitting diode (*LED*) and diode laser electron excitation by a bias voltage results in the generation of light

26. Transistor is a three layer of semiconductor device (*npn* or *pnp*). Its two extreme layers are of the same type (*n* in case of *npn* and *p* in case of *pnp* transistor). For rectification, the two extreme layers must be of different types.

27. The emitter is always forward biased to enable the majority carriers to cross the emitter-base junction, so that current flows through the transistor.

28. For a junction transistor, we know $I_e = I_b + I_c$.

29. Applications of transistor
(*i*) Transistor as a switch
(*ii*) Transistor as an amplifier
(*iii*) Transistor as an oscillator

30. Transistor-Amplifier : An amplifier is a device which is used for increasing the amplitude of variation of alternating voltage or current or power, thus it produces an enlarged version of the input signal.

31. Current amplification factor (β) in common emitter mode of transistor is defined as the ratio of change in collector current (ΔI_c) to the change in base current (ΔI_b) corresponding to input signal voltage, when collector voltage is kept constant
i.e.,
$$\beta = \Delta I_c / \Delta I_b$$

32. A transistor can also be used as an oscillator. Electromagnetic oscillations are produced by an LC circuit and energy to sustain the oscillation is provided by transistor amplifier on the principle of positive feedback.

33. Digital Electronics :

(*i*) A continuous time varying current or voltage signal is called analogue signal.

(*ii*) The signal which has two levels of voltage only (represented by 0 and 1) is called digital signal.

(*iii*) A digital circuit which either allows a signal to pass through or stops it, when some logical conditions are satisfied, is called logic gate.

34. The three basic logic gates are :

(*i*) OR gate OUTPUT $Y = A + B$

(*ii*) AND gate OUTPUT $Y = A . B$

(*iii*) NOT gate OUTPUT $Y = Y'$

35. Combination of gates

(*i*) NOR gate OUTPUT $Y = \overline{A + B}$

(*ii*) NAND gate OUTPUT $Y = \overline{A . B}$

36. Integrated circuit (IC) is that circuit in which the circuit components such as resistors, capacitors, diodes and transistors, etc. are automatically the parts of a small semiconductor chip.

❑❑❑

VERY SHORT ANSWER TYPE QUESTIONS

(Carrying 1 mark)

Q. 1. Energy gap of a conductor, semi conductor and insulator are E_1, E_2 and E_3 respectively. Arrange them in increasing order.

Ans. $E_1 < E_2 < E_3$

Q. 2. The ratio of number of free electrons to holes (n_e/n_h) for two different materials A and B are 1 and < 1 respectively. Name the type of semiconductor to which A and B belong.

Ans. For $\frac{n_e}{n_h} = 1$, the material *A* is intrensic semi conductor.

For $\frac{n_e}{n_h} < 1$, then material *B* is *p*-type semi conductor.

Q. 3. Name three factors on which the resistivity of a semiconductor depend.

Ans. These are :

(*i*) number density of electrons and holes

(*ii*) mobilities of electrons and holes

(*iii*) Temperature

Q. 4. Can we measure the potential barrier of a p-n junction by putting a sensitive voltmeter across its terminals?

Ans. We cannot measure the potential barrier of a p-n junction by connecting a sensitive voltmeter across its terminals because in the depletion region, there are no free electrons and holes and in the absence of forward biasing, p-n junction offers infinite resistance.

Q. 5. Draw the graph indicating temperature dependence of resistivity of a semi conductor.

Ans. Variation is shown

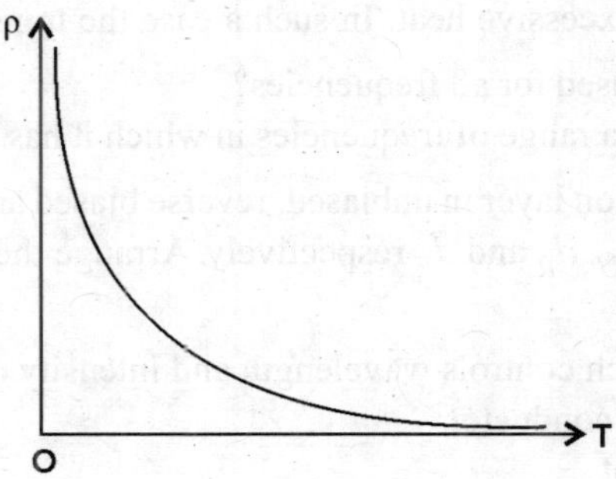

Q. 6. In which of the three regions– emitter, base, collector of a transistor maximum current flows?

Ans. Maximum current flows in the emitter region ($I_e = I_b + I_c$).

Q. 7. What is the minimum potential difference between the base and the emitter required to switch a silicon transistor 'ON'?

Ans. It is approximately 1 volt.

Q. 8. What is the value of electric field in the middle of the depletion layer under reverse biased condition of *p-n* junction?

Ans. Electric field is zero (note - potential is not zero).

Q. 9. A full wave rectifier circuit operates at 50 Hz mains frequency. What is the frequency of the output wave form?

Ans. 100 Hz (note : in half wave rectifier it is 50 Hz).

Q. 10. Indicate the heights of potential barrier under unbiased, reversed biased, low forward biased and high forward biased conditions in the same fig.

Ans. The situations are shown in fig.

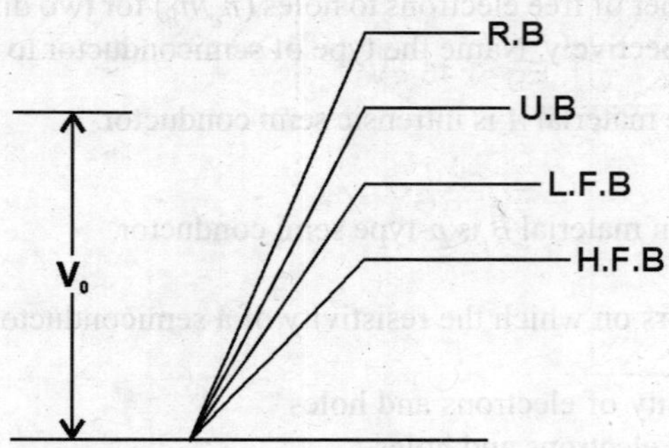

U.B → Unbiased

R. B → Reverse Biased

L.F.B → Low Forward Biased

H.F.B → High Forward Biased

Q. 11. Why in a transistor, the forward bias voltage is always smaller than the reverse bias voltage?

Ans. The forward bias voltage controls the velocities of charge carriers moving from emitter to the collector through the base. If it is kept high, the velocities of charge carriers will increase producing excessive heat. In such a case the transistor may get damaged.

Q. 12. Can an amplifier be used for all frequencies?

Ans. No, an amplifier has a range of frequencies in which it has better performance.

Q. 13. The widths of depletion layer in unbiased, reverse biased and forward biased conditions of *p-n* junction are d_U, d_R and d_F respectively. Arrange these in increasing order.

Ans. $d_F < d_U < d_R$

Q. 14. State the factors which controls wavelength and intensity of light emitted by LED

Ans. (*i*) Nature of semi conductor

(*ii*) Forward current

Q. 15. Modern technology use poly silicon instead of metal to form the gate why?

Ans. Poly silicon has high conductivity compared to metal.

❑❑❑

SHORT ANSWER TYPE QUESTIONS (SA-I)

(Carrying 2 marks)

Q. 1. Draw energy band diagram of (*i*) *n*-type semiconductor; and (*ii*) *p*-type semiconductor.

Ans. We have

(*i*) *n*-type semiconductor (*ii*) *p*-type semiconductor

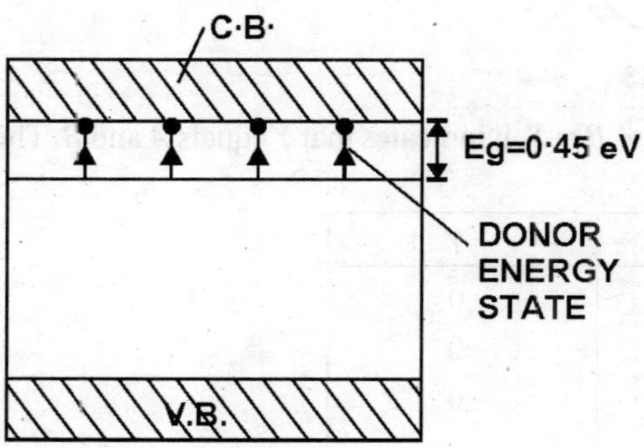

Fig. 9.1

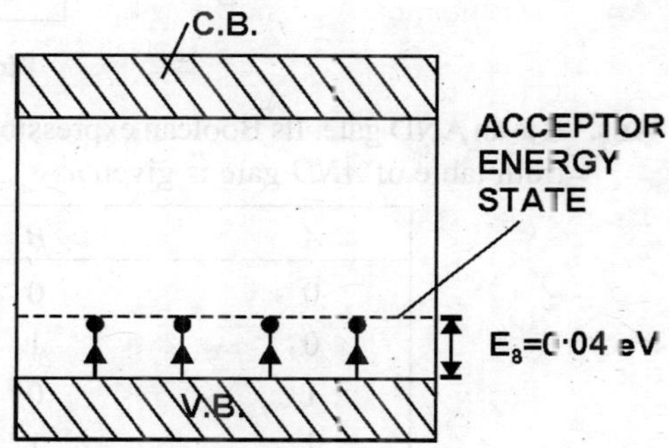

Fig. 9.2

Q. 2. What is depletion region in a *p-n* junction?

Ans. A thin layer between *p*- and *n*-sections of the *p-n* junction, devoid of free electrons and holes (or having immobile electrons and holes only), is called depletion region.

Q. 3. What is an intrinsic semiconductor? How can you convert an intrinsic semiconductor into n-type extrinsic semiconductor?

Ans. An intrinsic semiconductor is a pure semiconductor without any doping. An intrinsic semiconductor *e.g.,* silicon (Si) or germanium (Ge) can be converted into an n-type extrinsic semiconductor by doping it with a pentavalent impurity element *e.g.,* phosphorus (P), antimony (At) or arsenic (As).

Q. 4. Name the purpose for which common base transistor amplifier is preferred over common emitter transistor amplifier.

Ans. Common base transitor amplifier is preferred over common emitter transistor amplifier, if we do not want the phase shift in our output signal and we want better voltage gain.

Q. 5. In the working of a transistor, emitter base (EB) junction is forward biased while collector base (CB) junction is reverse biased. Why?

Ans. The emitter will send the majority carriers (electrons or holes) towards base only, when it is forward biased. The collector will collect the majority carriers only when it is reverse biased.

Q. 6. Give any two differences between a half-wave rectifier and a full-wave rectifier.

Ans.

S. No.	Half-wave rectifier	Full-wave rectifier
1.	The output voltage is unidirectional intermittent and varying voltage.	1. The output voltage is unidirectional varying voltage.
2.	The frequency of output signal is same as that of input signal.	2. The frequency of output signal is double than that of input signal.

Q. 7. Name the logic gate shown in Fig. 9.3; and give its truth table.

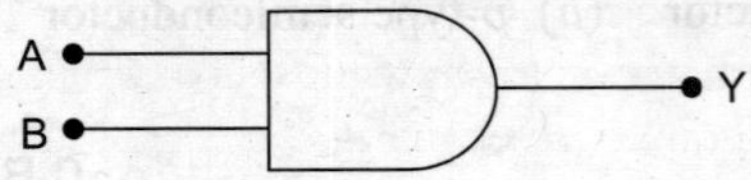

Fig. 9.3

Ans. It is an AND gate. Its Boolean expression is $A.B = Y$, it indicates that Y equals A and B. The truth table of *AND* gate is given as

A	*B*	*Y*
0	0	0
0	1	0
1	0	0
1	1	1

Q. 8. Identify the logic gates marked *X, Y* in Fig. 9.4. Write down the output at *Y*, when $A = 1$, $B = 1$ and $A = 0$ and $B = 0$.

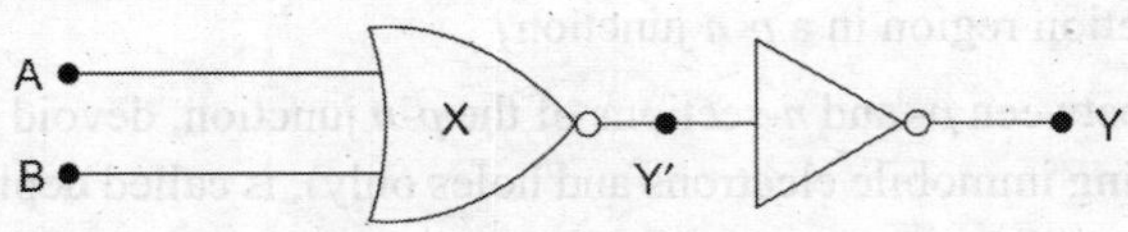

Fig. 9.4

Ans. Here, the logic gate marked *X* is NOR gate and the gate marked as *Y* is NOT gate. The Boolean expression for this combination of gates is

$$Y = \overline{Y'} = \overline{\overline{A+B}} = A + B$$

Therefore, the output at Y will be as given below:

A	*B*	$Y = \overline{A+B}$	$Y = \overline{Y'}$
1	1	0	1
0	0	1	0

Q. 9. A p-type semiconductor has acceptor level 57 meV above the valence bond. What is the maximum wavelength of light required to create a hole? $h = 6.62 \times 10^{-34}$ Js.

Ans. Here,

$$E = 57 \text{ meV}$$

$$= 57 \times 10^{-3} \times 1.6 \times 10^{-19} \text{ V},$$

$$c = 3 \times 10^{8} \text{ ms}^{-1} \text{ and } h = 6.62 \times 10^{-34} \text{ Js.}$$

We have wavelength, $\lambda = \dfrac{hc}{E} = \dfrac{6.62 \times 10^{-34} \times (3 \times 10^{8})}{57 \times 10^{-3} \times 1.6 \times 10^{-19}} = 217100 \text{ Å}.$

Q. 10. Why is the semiconductor damaged by a strong current?

Ans. When a strong current is passed through a semiconductor, it heats up the semiconductor, due to which a large number of covalent bonds break up in semiconductor, resulting in a large number of charge carriers, as a result of which, the material starts behaving as a conductor. At this stage, the semiconductor loses the property of low conduction, hence, it is said to be damaged.

Q. 11. Name the *p-n* junction diode which emits spontaneous radiation when forward biased. How do we choose the semiconductor to be used in those diodes if the emitted radiations are to be in the visible region?

Ans. Light emitting diode (LED) emits spontaneous radiation when forward biased. For visible region LED's phosphorus doped GaAs and GaP are the suitable semiconductors.

Q. 12. Draw a labelled circuit diagram to show the use of zener diode as a voltage regulator.

Ans. The labelled circuit diagram is given in Fig. 9.5.

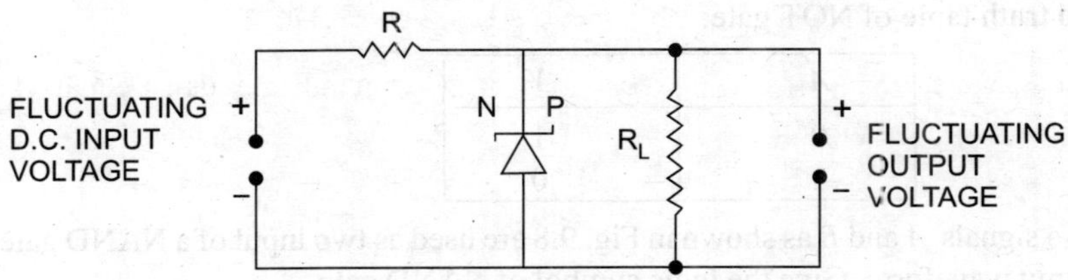

Fig. 9.5

Q. 13. In a transistor connected in a Common Emitter (CE) mode, R_c = 4 kΩ, R_i = 1kΩ, I_c = 1 mA, and I_b = 20 μA. Find the voltage gain.

Ans. We have, $\beta = I_c/I_b = 10^{-3}/(20 \times 10^{-6}) = 50$;

Voltage gain, $$A_v = \beta \frac{R_c}{R_i} = 50 \times \frac{4000}{1000} = 200$$

Q. 14. The current gain of a transtor in common emitter configuration is 70. What is the base current if the emitter current is 8.8mA?

Ans. We have $$\beta = \frac{I_c}{I_B} \text{ or } I_c = \beta I_b = 70\, I_b,$$

Now, $$I_e = I_b + I_c = I_b + 70\, I_b = 71\, I_b$$

So, $$I_b = \frac{I_e}{71} = \frac{8.8}{71} = 0.124 \text{ mA}$$

Q. 15. Draw and explain the output waveform across the load resistor R, if the input waveform is as shown in Fig. 9.6.

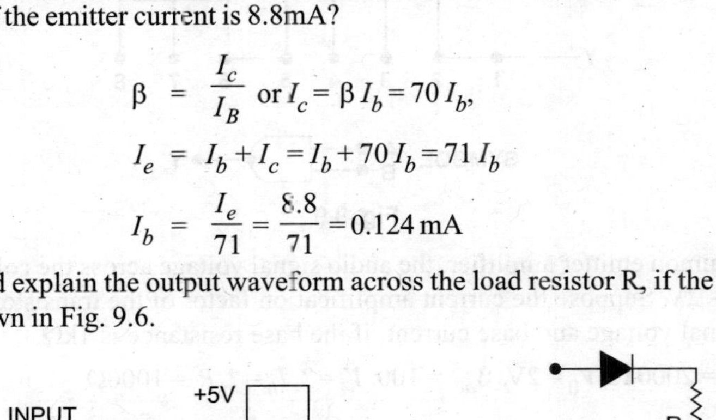

Fig. 9.6

Ans. When the input voltage is +5V, the p-n junction diode is forward biased. The output across R is +5V. When the input voltage is –5V, the p-n junction diode gets reverse biased. Therefore, the output across R is zero. The output waveform is as shown in Fig. 9.6a.

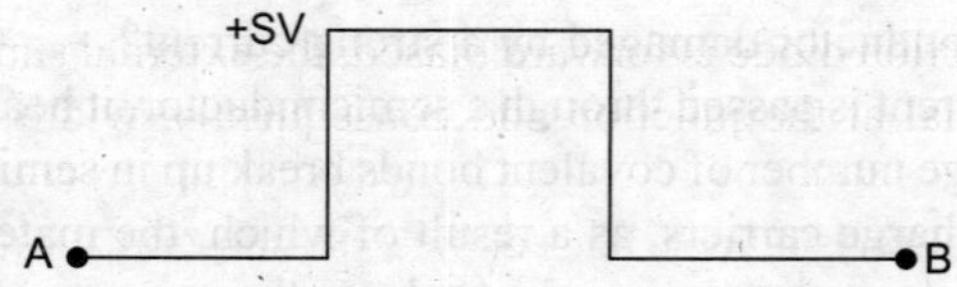

Fig. 9.6a

Q. 16. Give the logic symbol and truth table for NOT gate.

Ans. The logic symbol of NOT gate is

Fig. 9.7

and truth table of NOT gate:

A	*Y*
0	1
1	0

Q. 17. Two signals *A* and *B* as shown in Fig. 9.8 are used as two input of a NAND gate. Draw its output waveform. Give the logic symbol of NAND gate.

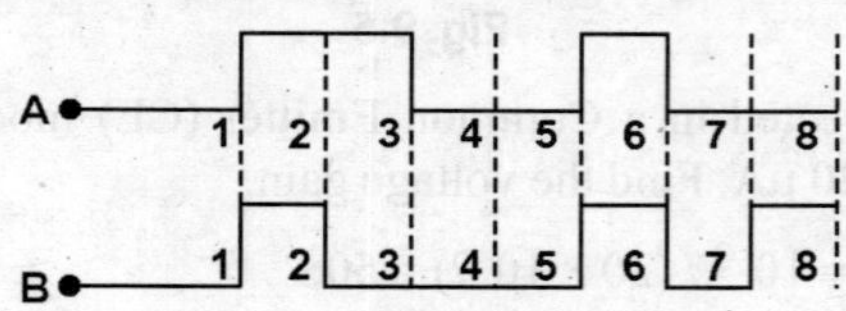

Fig. 9.8

Ans. The output waveform

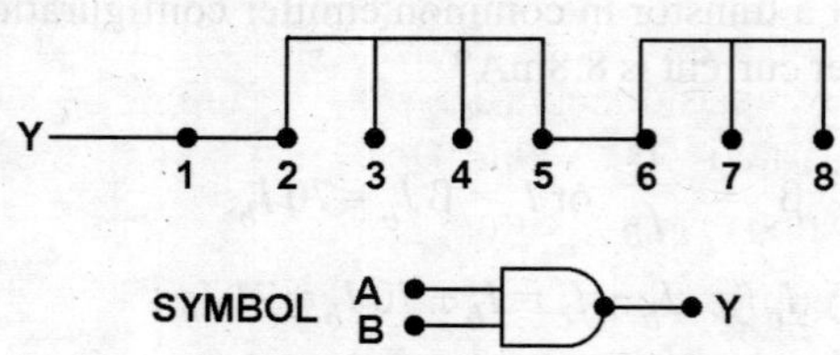

Fig. 9.9

Q. 18. For a common emitter amplifier, the audio signal voltage across the collector resistance of 2kΩ is 2V. Suppose the current amplification factor of the transistor is 100, find the input signal voltage and base current, if the base resistance is 1kΩ.

Ans. Here, $R_0 = 2000\ \Omega$, $V_0 = 2\text{V}$, $\beta_{ac} = 100$, $V_i = ?$, $I_b = ?$, $R_i = 1000\Omega$

$$\text{As, } A_v = \frac{V_0}{V_i} = \beta_{ac}\frac{R_o}{R_I} \quad \text{or } V_i = \frac{V_0}{\beta_{ac}(R_0/R_i)} = \frac{2}{100(2000/1000)} = 0.01\text{V}$$

$$I_b = \frac{V_i}{R_i} = \frac{0.01V}{1000\Omega} = 10\mu\text{A}.$$

Q. 19. Show that the thickness (width) of depletion region will change when the p-n junction diode is (*i*) forward biased (*ii*) reverse biased.

Ans. (*i*) When p-n junction diode is forward biased, the external supply voltage opposes the barrier potential at the junction and consequently, width of the depletion region shrinks.

(*ii*) When p-n junction is reverse biased, the external supply voltage further fortifies the potential barrier and, consequently, thickness of depletion region increases.

Q. 20. In Fig. 9.10, circuit symbol of a logic gate and input waveform is shown.

(*i*) Name the logic gate

(*ii*) Write its truth table, and

(*iii*) Give the output waveform.

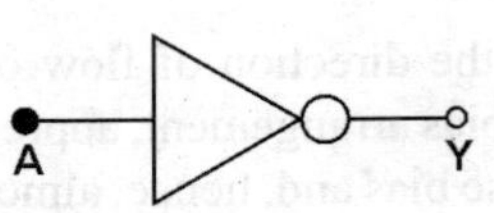

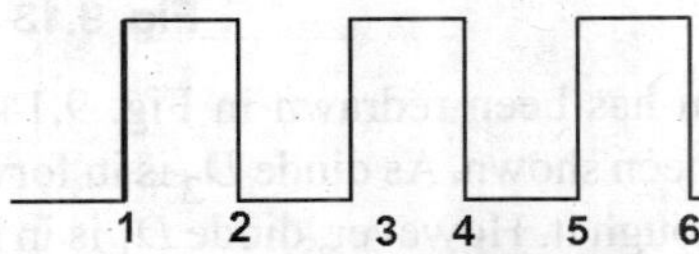

Fig. 9.10

Ans. (*i*) The given logic gate is a NOT gate. (*ii*) Truth table is

A	*Y*
0	1
1	0

(*iii*) The output waveform is being shown in Fig. 9.11.

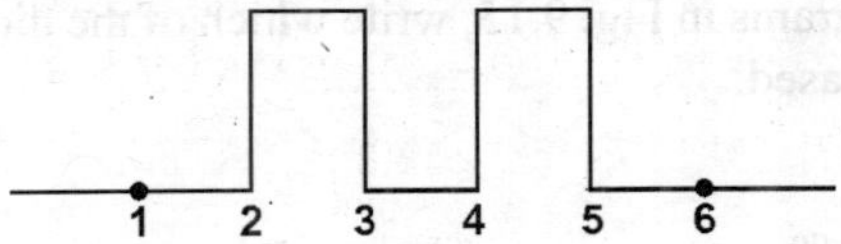

Fig. 9.11

Q. 21. In a common emitter transistor amplifier, $\beta = 62$; output resistance = 5000Ω and internal resistance of the transistor is 500Ω. Find the voltage amplification and power amplification.

Ans. Here, $\beta = 62$, $R_0 = 5000\ \Omega$ and $R_i = 500\Omega$

We have, voltage amplification,

$$A_v = \frac{\beta R_o}{R_i} = \frac{62 \times 5000}{500} = 620$$

$$\text{Power amplification} = \beta^2 \frac{R_o}{R_i} = 62^2 \times \frac{5000}{500} = 38440.$$

Q. 22. Fig. 9.12 shows a piece of pure semiconductor S in series with a variable resistor R, and a source of constant voltage V. Would you increase or decrease the value of R to keep the reading of ammeter (A) constant, when semiconductor S is heated? Give reason.

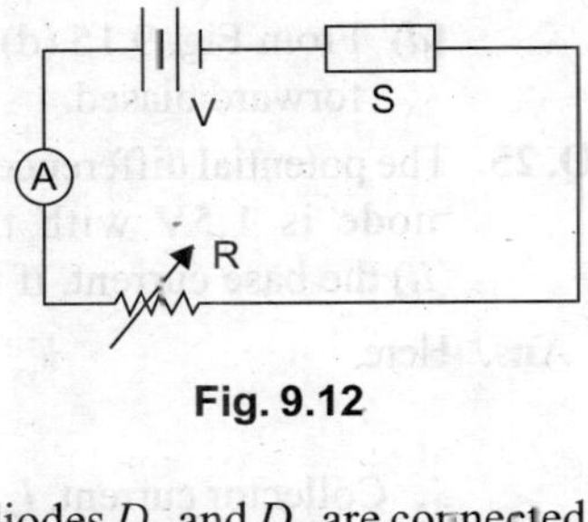

Fig. 9.12

Ans. When the pure semiconductor S is heated, its resistance decreases, due to which the current in the circuit increases. To keep the reading of an ammeter (A) constant, the value of R has to be increased.

Q. 23. In the given circuit diagram (Fig. 9.13) two p-n junction diodes D_1 and D_2 are connected with a resistance *R* and a d.c. battery. Redraw the diagram and indicate the direction of flow of appreciable current in the circuit. Justify your answer.

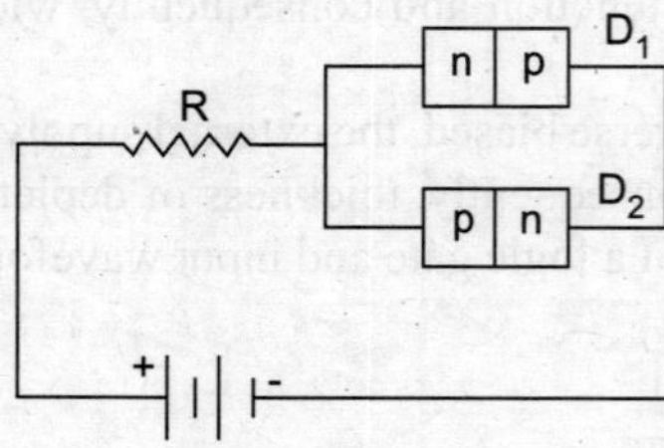

Fig. 9.13

Ans. The diagram has been redrawn in Fig. 9.14 and the direction of flow of appreciable current has been shown. As diode D_2 is in forward bias arrangement, appreciable current will pass through it. However, diode D_1 is in reverse bias and, hence, almost nill current will pass through it.

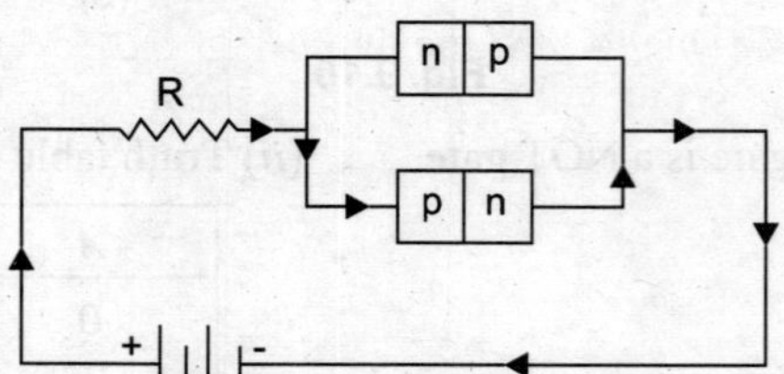

Fig. 9.14

Q. 24. In the following diagrams in Fig. 9.15, write which of the diodes are forward biased and which are reverse biased.

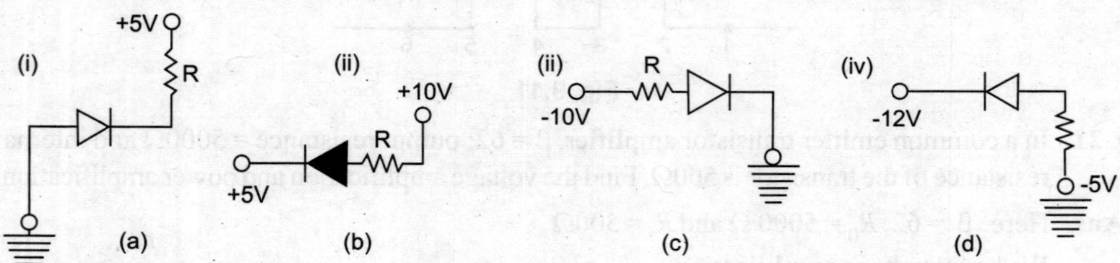

Fig. 9.15

Ans. (*a*) From Fig. 9.15 (a), as $V_p - V_n = 0 – 5V = –5V$, thus, diode is reverse biased.

(*b*) From Fig. 9.15 (b), as $V_p - V_n = 10V – 5V = +5V$, hence, diode is forward biased.

(*c*) From Fig. 9.15 (c), as $V_p - V_n = –10V – 0 = –10V$, hence, diode is reverse biased.

(*d*) From Fig. 9.15 (d), as $V_p - V_n = –5V – (–12V) = –5V + 12V = +7V$, hence, diode is forward biased.

Q. 25. The potential difference (p.d.) across the collector of a transistor used in common emitter mode is 1.5V with the collector resistance of 3kΩ. Find (*i*) the emitter and (*ii*) the base current, if the dc gain of the transistor is 50.

Ans. Here, $V_c = 1.5V, R_c = 3k\Omega = 3 \times 10^3 \Omega$ and $\beta_{ac} = 50$

$$\therefore \text{ Collector current, } I_c = \frac{V_c}{R_c} = \frac{1.5}{3 \times 10^3} = 0.5 \times 10^{-3} \text{A}$$

$\therefore$ Base current, $I_B = \dfrac{I_c}{\beta_{dc}} = \dfrac{0.5 \times 10^{-3}}{50} = 0.01 \times 10^{-3}$A

$\therefore$ Emitter current, $I_E = I_C + I_B = 0.51 \times 10^{-3}$A.

SHORT ANSWER TYPE QUESTIONS (SA-II)

(Carrying 3 marks)

Q. 1. *C, Si* and *Ge* have same lattice structure. Why is *C* an insulator while *Si* and *Ge* are intrinsic semiconductors?

Ans. We know that *C, Si* and *Ge* are four valence atoms. Their four valence electrons are present in the second, third and fourth orbits of the respective atoms. The energy gap (E_g) of *Ge* is 0.72 eV, of *Si* is 1.1eV and of *C* is 5.54eV. The energy required to take out an electron from these atoms (*i.e.*, isolation energy E_g) will be the least for *Ge*, more for *Si* and maximum for *C*. Due to this, the number of free electrons for conduction will be significant in *Ge* and *Si* but will be negligibly small for *C*. That is why, *C* is an insulator while *Si* and *Ge* are intrinsic semiconductors.

Q. 2. Derive a relation between current gain of common base amplifier and current gain of common emitter amplifier.

Ans. For a junction transistor, we know $I_e = I_b + I_c$ ...(*i*)

Current gain for common base amplifier, $\alpha = I_c / I_e$ ...(*ii*)

Current gain for common emitter amplifier, $\beta = I_c / I_b$ ...(*iii*)

From (i), we get $\dfrac{I_e}{I_c} = \dfrac{I_b}{I_c} + 1$ or $\dfrac{1}{\alpha} = \dfrac{1}{\beta} + 1$

or $\dfrac{1}{\beta} = \dfrac{1}{\alpha} - 1 = \dfrac{1-\alpha}{\alpha}$ or $\beta = \dfrac{\alpha}{\alpha - 1}$

Q. 3. Two signals *A, B* as given below are applied to (*i*) AND, (*ii*) NOR and (*iii*) NAND gates. Draw the output waveform in each case.

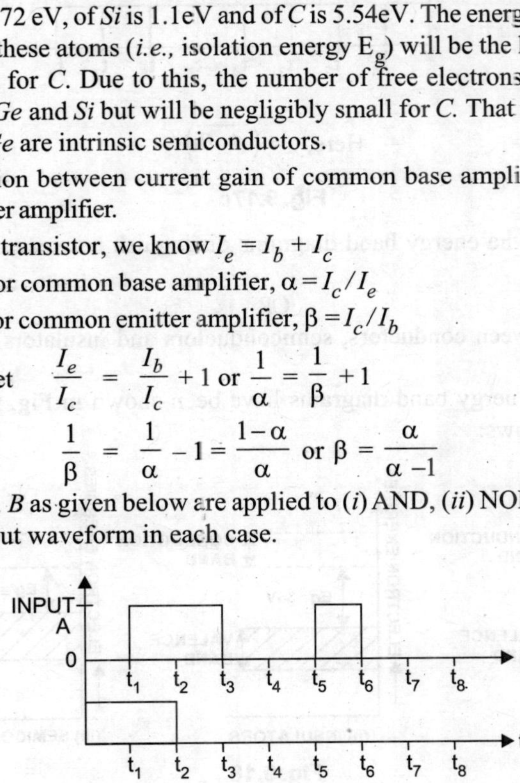

Fig. 9.16

Ans.

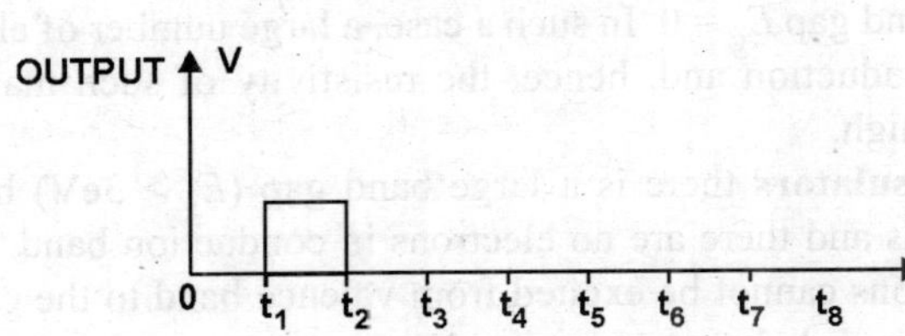

Here, $Y = (A \,.\, B)$

Fig. 9.17a

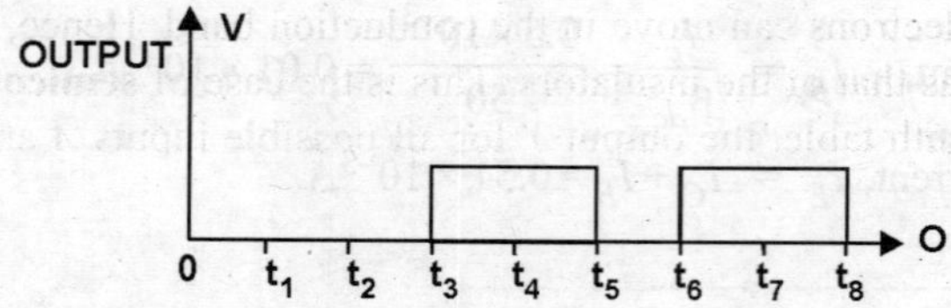

Here, $y = A + B$

Fig. 9.17b

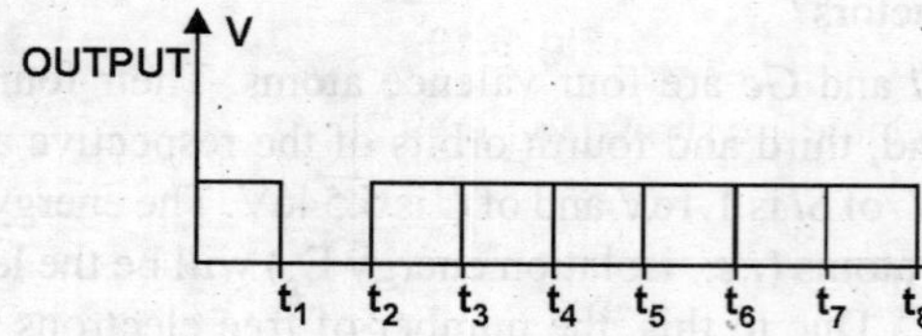

Here, $y = (\overline{A \cdot B})$

Fig. 9.17c

Q. 4. On the basis of the energy band diagrams distinguish between metals, insulators and semiconductors.

OR

Distinguish between conductors, semiconductors and insulators on the basis of band theory of solids.

Ans. Three types of energy band diagrams have been shown in Fig. 9.18. From these, we conclude as follows:

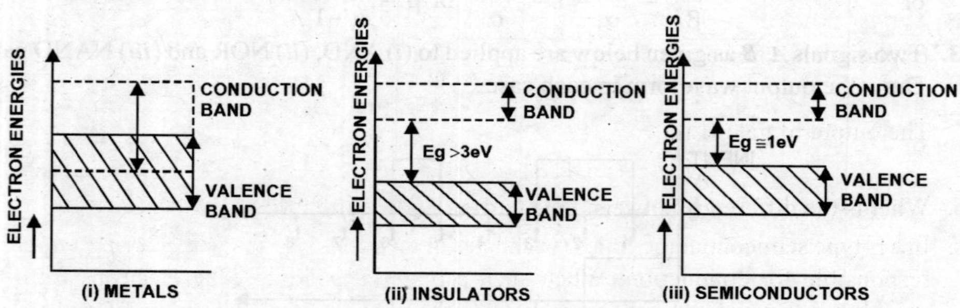

Fig. 9.18

Case I: Here conduction and valence bands are overlapping. It is the case of a **metal** where energy band gap $E_g = 0$. In such a case, a large number of electrons are available for electrical conduction and, hence, the resistivity of such materials is low or the conductivity is high.

Case II: For **insulators** there is a large band gap ($E_g > 3$eV) between valence and conduction bands and there are no electrons in conduction band. On account of large band gap, electrons cannot be excited from valence band to the conduction band and, hence, the substance behaves as an insulator.

Case III: Here, energy band gap E_g is small ($E_g < 3$eV) and of the order 1eV. Because of the small band gap, some electrons can be thermally excited to the conduction band and these excited electrons can move in the conduction band. Hence, the resistance would not be as high as that of the insulators. This is the case of **semiconductors.**

Q. 5. Express by a truth table, the output Y for all possible inputs A and B in the following circuit Fig. 9.19.

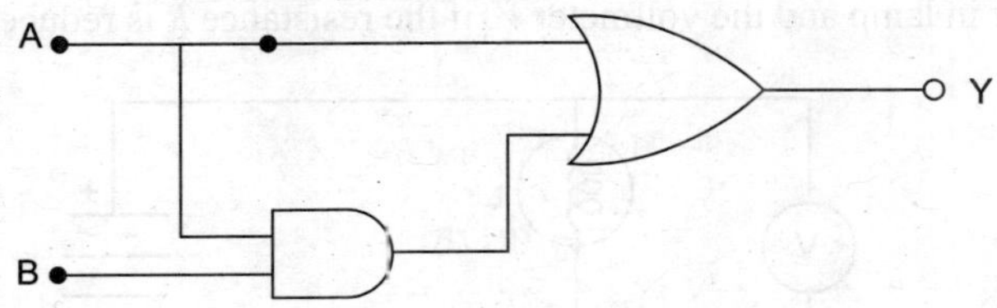

Fig. 9.19

Ans. The circuit and truth table are shown in Fig. 9.20.

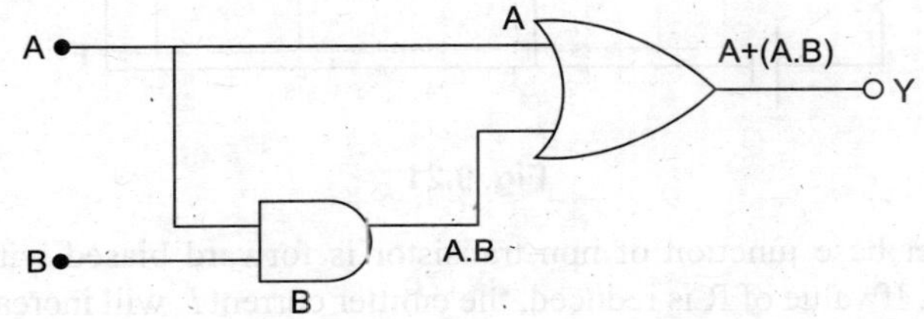

Fig. 9.20

Truth table.

A B	$Y' = (A.B)$	$Y = A + (A.B)$
0 0	0	0
1 0	0	1
0 1	0	0
1 1	1	1

Explanation: The output of gate I is

$$Y' = A.B$$

The output of gate II is

$$Y = A+(A.B)$$

Q. 6. What is the difference between hole current and electron flow?

Ans. In a p-type semiconductor, holes (vacancies of electrons) are majority carriers which are responsible for conduction. When such a material conducts, the electrons from the neighbouring covalent bond jumps into a vacancy of electrons in order to fill it. This will result in shifting of hole to the covalent bond from which electrons has jumped. The movement of the holes constitutes the hole current.

In an n-type semiconductor, electrons are majority carriers which are responsible for conduction. The movement of electrons constitutes the electrons current.

In fact, during conduction in a semiconductor, the direction of hole current is opposite to that of electrons current.

Q. 7. Why are Si and $GaAs$ are preferred materials for solar cells?

Ans. The energy for the maximum intensity of the solar radiation is nearly 1.5eV. In order to have photoexcitation, the energy of radiation (hv) must be greater than energy band gap (E_g). Therefore, the semiconductor with energy band gap about 1.5eV or lower and with higher absorption coefficient, is likely to give better solar convection efficiency. The energy band gap for *Si* is about 1.1 eV, while for *GaAs*, it is about 1.53eV. The *GaAs* is bitter inspite of its higher band gap than *Si* because it absorbs relatively more energy from the incident solar radiations and of relatively higher absorption coefficient.

Q. 8. In the circuit shown in Fig. 9.21, a voltmeter is connected across lamp *L*. What changes would occur in lamp and the voltmeter *V*, if the resistance *R* is reduced in value?

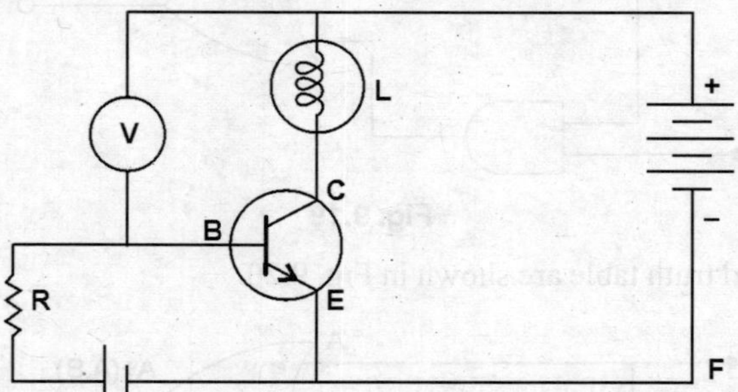

Fig. 9.21

Ans. Here, emitter base junction of npn transistor is forward biased with the battery and resistance *R*. If value of R is reduced, the emitter current I_e will increase.

Therefore, the collector current $I_c = I_e - I_b$ will also increase, due to which the bulb will glow more brilliantly. potential difference across *L* increases, hence, the reading of voltmeter V will increase.

Q. 9. Explain (*i*) forward biasing (*ii*) reverse biasing of a p-n junction diode with the help of circuit diagram. Explain the use of this device as a half-wave rectifier.

Ans. (*a*) In the forward biasing of a *p-n* junction diode, as shown in Fig. 9.22, p-side of diode is joined to positive terminal of battery and side to the negative terminal of the battery. Thus, depletion region is reduced in width, the potential barrier is overcome and drift of free electrons and holes takes place easily.

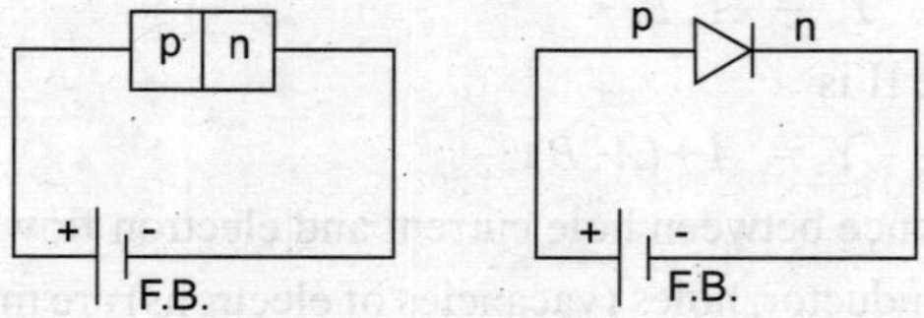

Fig. 9.22

(*b*) In a reverse biasing as shown in Fig. 9.23, p-side of diode is joined to the negative terminal of battery and n-side of diode to the positive terminal of battery. Thus, depletion region expands in width, the potential barrier is fortified and no drift of electrons or holes takes place.

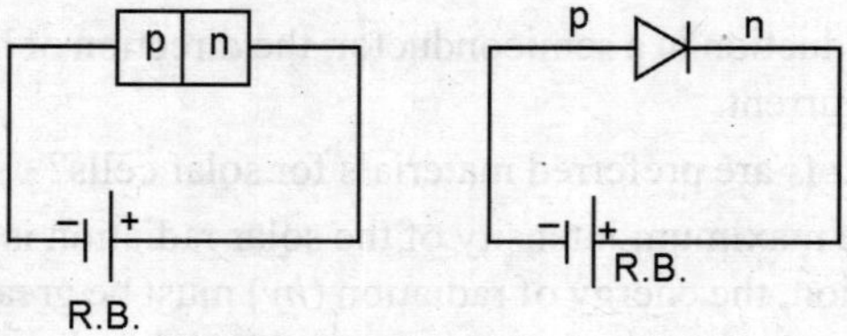

Fig. 9.23

Q. 10. In a silicon transitor, a change of 7.89 mA in the emitter current produces a charge of 7.8 mA in the collection current. What change in the base current is necessary to produce an equivalent change in the collector current?

Ans. Here $\Delta I_e = 7.89$ mA, $\Delta I_c = 7.8$ mA, $\Delta I_b = ?$

As $$\alpha_{ac} = \frac{\Delta I_c}{\Delta I_e} = \frac{7.8}{7.89} = 0.9886$$

Now $$\beta_{ac} = \frac{\alpha}{1-\alpha} = \frac{0.9886}{1-0.9886} = 86.72.$$

As $$\beta_{ac} = \Delta I_c / I_b$$

$$\therefore \quad \Delta I_b = \frac{\Delta I_c}{\beta_{ac}} = \frac{7.8}{86.72} = 89.94 \times 10^{-3} \text{ mA.}$$

Q. 11. For a common emitter transistor amplifier, the audio signal voltage across the collector resistance of 2kΩ is 2V. If the current amplification factor of the transistor is 100, calculate (*i*) input signal voltage, (*ii*) base current and (*iii*) power gain. Given that the value of the base resistance is 1kΩ.

Ans. Here, $r_0 = R_c = 2\text{k}\Omega = 2 \times 10^3 = 2000\Omega$, $V_0 = 2\text{V}$, $\beta = 100$ and $r_i = R_0 = 1\text{k}\Omega = 1000\Omega$

(*i*) We have, as voltage gain,

$$A_v = \frac{V_0}{V_i} = \beta \times \frac{r_0}{r_i} = 100 \times \frac{2000}{1000} = 200$$

$$\therefore \quad V_i = \frac{V_0}{200} = \frac{2}{200} V = 0.01 V$$

(*ii*) The base current $$I_B = \frac{V_i}{r_i} = \frac{0.01V}{1000\Omega} = 10^{-5} \text{ A} = 10 \times 10^{-6} \text{ A}$$

$$= 10\mu\text{A}$$

(*iii*) Power gain $= A_v \times \beta = 200 \times 100 = 2 \times 10^4$.

Q. 12. Draw a circuit diagram of a full-wave rectifier. Explain its working principle. Draw the input/output waveforms indicating clearly the functions of the two diodes used.

Ans. The circuit arrangement of a full-wave rectifier has been shown in Fig. 9.24(a).

In it we use a centre tap transformer having its secondary wound into two equal parts such that voltages at any instant at *A* (input of diode D_1) and *B* (input of diode D_2) are out of phase with each other. Let initially input voltage at *A* is positive, then it will be negative voltage at *B* at that instant. Therefore, diode D_1, being in forward bias, conducts but D_2 being in reverse bias, does not conduct. We get output across load resistance R_L joined between *X* and *Y* due to diode D_1. After half cycle of a.c. input, the voltage at *A* becomes negative and that at *B*, positive. Now diode D_1 does not conduct but D_2 conducts and output voltage is again obtained across R_L in the same direction. Thus, output is obtained throughout the input wave cycle.

Input and output waveforms indicating the functions of the two diodes have been shown in the Fig. 9.24 (b) and (c).

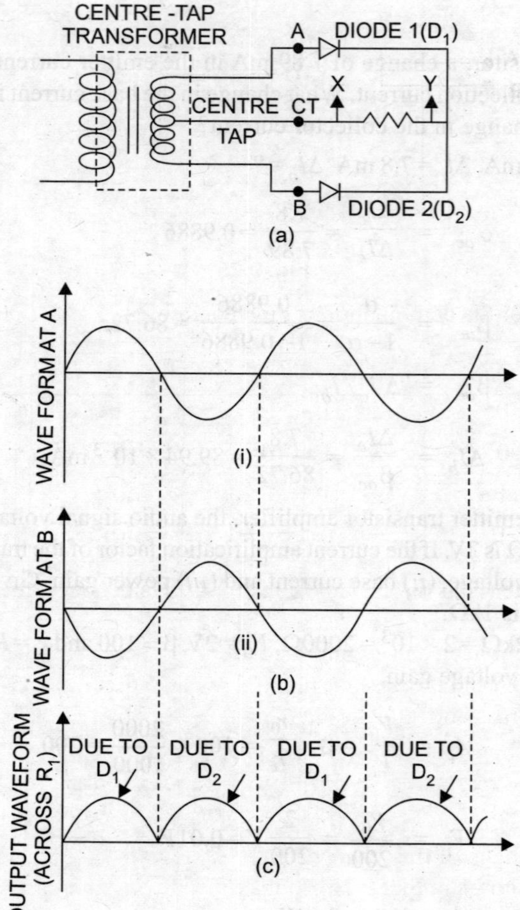

Fig. 9.24

HIGHER ORDER THINKING SKILLS (HOTS)

Q. 1. What will happen if emitter as well as collector in a transistor are forward biased?

Ans. In this situation, the majority charge carriers will flow in the emitter base circuit and those of the collector will flow in the collector base circuit. In this case, the working of transistor will be equivalent to two p-n junction diodes with a common base. It means the purpose of transitor will be defeated.

Q. 2. A light emitting diode (LED) has a voltage drop of $2V$ across it and passes a current of 10 mA. What should be the value of limiting resistance R to make it operate with a $6V$ battery?

Ans. Current in the circuit $I = 10\text{ mA} = 10 \times 10^{-3}\text{ A}$

Voltage $= 6 - 2 = 4V$

Then $V = IR$ gives $R = \dfrac{V}{I} = \dfrac{4}{10 \times 10^{-3}} = 400\,\Omega$

Q. 3. Produce the truth table of combination of gates shown in Fig. 9.25. Also name the gate so obtained.

Ans. Output of gate I is $Y_1 = \overline{A.B}$

Output of gate II is $Y_2 = \overline{A+B}$

Output of gate III is $Y = \overline{y_1 \cdot y_2}$

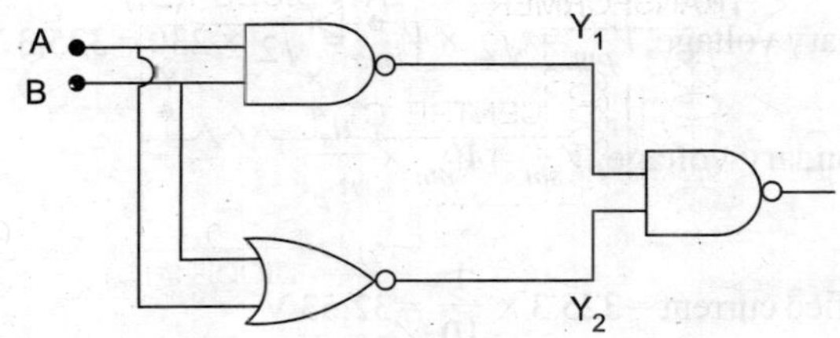

Fig. 9.25

The truth table of the combination is given below:

A	B	$Y_1 = \overline{A.B}$	$Y_2 = \overline{A+B}$	$Y = \overline{y_1 . y_2}$
0	0	1	1	0
1	0	1	0	1
0	1	1	0	1
1	1	0	0	1

As the truth table (read for A, B and Y) is for OR gate, hence, the arrangement works as OR gate.

Q. 4. For a transistor connected in common-emitter mode, the voltage drop across the collector is $2\,V$ and β is 50. Find the base current if R_c is $2\text{k}\Omega$.

Ans. Voltage drop across collector $= I_c R_c$, thus

$$2 = I_c \times (2 \times 10^3) \text{ or } I_c = 10^{-3} A;$$
$$I_b = I_c/\beta = 10^{-3}/50$$
$$= 20 \times 10^{-6} A.$$

Q. 5. A sinusoidal voltage of rms value of $200V$ is connected to the diode and capacitor C in the circuit. (as shown in Fig. 9.26) so that half wave rectification occurs. Find the final potential difference across C.

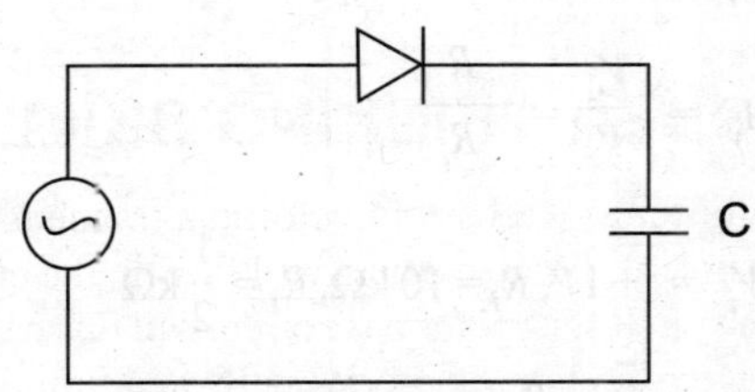

Fig. 9.26

Ans. In half-wave rectifier, the output voltage is the rms voltage stored in capacitor

$$= \frac{V_0}{2} = \frac{200\sqrt{2}}{2}$$
$$= 100\sqrt{2}$$
$$= 141.4\text{V}.$$

Q. 6. An a.c. supply of 230V is applied to a half-wave rectifier circuit through a transformer of turn ratio 10:1. Find the output d.c. voltage. Assume the diode to be ideal.

Ans. Here, $\frac{n_p}{n_s} = 10$; rms primary voltage, $V_{rms} = 230\,V$

Maximum primary voltage, $V_{pm} = \sqrt{2} \times V_{rms} = \sqrt{2} \times 230 = 325.3$ V

Maximum secondary voltage, $V_{sm} = V_{pm} \times \dfrac{n_s}{n_p}$

Half wave rectified current $= 325.3 \times \dfrac{1}{10} = 32.53$ V

$$I_{dc} = \frac{I_o}{\pi}$$

$\therefore$ Output d.c. voltage $= I_{dc} \times R_L$

$$= \frac{I_o}{\pi} \times R_L = \frac{V_{sm}}{\pi} = \frac{32.53}{22/7} = 10.36 \text{ V}$$

Q. 7. In the circuit shown in Fig. 9.26, an input of 1V is fed into the inverting input an ideal operational amplifier *A*. What is the output signal voltage V_{out} ?

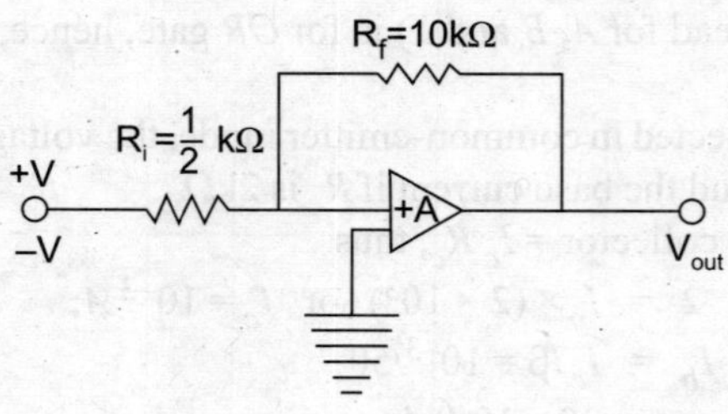

Fig. 9.27

Ans. It is an operational inverting amplifier.
Therefore, voltage amplification is

$$A_v = \frac{V_0}{V_i} = \frac{-R_f}{R_i}$$

Given, $\quad V_i = +1V, R_f = 10 \text{ k}\Omega, R_i = \frac{1}{2} \text{ k}\Omega$

$$\therefore \quad V_0 = -V_i \frac{R_f}{R_i} = -1 \times \frac{10}{1/2} = -20 \text{ V.}$$

Q. 8. How does the reverse current suddenly increase at the breakdown voltage in case of zener diode?

Ans. We know that the reverse current through the junction diode is due to the flow of minority carriers (*i.e.*, flow of electrons from *p* to *n* side and holes from *n* to *p*-side of *p*-*n* junction diode). As the reverse bias voltage across the junction is increased, the electric field at junction becomes significant. When the reverse bias voltage becomes equal to zener voltage (*i.e.*, $V = V_1$) then the electric field strength across the junction becomes quite high. This electric field across the junction is sufficient to pull valence electrons from the host atoms in the p-side and accelerate them towards n-side. The movement of these electrons across the junction account for high current which is observed at the break-down reverse voltage.

Q. 9. Explain why the energy of a hole farther from the top of a valence band is high.

Ans. To understand it, consider an electron is removed from the filled valence band to the bottom of the empty conduction band. This creates a hole in the valence band. After this, more energy is required to remove another electron which is farther from the top of the valence band. Therefore, a hole in the valence state farther from the top of the valence band has higher energy, just as a conduction electron farther from the bottom of the conduction band has higher energy.

Q. 10. A *p*-type semiconductor has large number of holes but still it is electrically neutral Explain.

Ans. A *p*-type semiconductor is formed by doping pure *Ge* or *Si* crystal with suitable impurity atoms of valence three. As the impurity atoms take the positions of *Ge* atoms in *Ge* crystal, its three electrons form covalent bond by sharing of electrons with the neighbouring three atoms of *Ge,* whereas the fourth covalent bond is left incomplete for want of one electron. This creates a hole. Since the atom in the whole is electrically neutral, the *p*-type semiconductor is also neutral.

❑❑❑

UNIT 10
COMMUNICATION SYSTEMS

Important Points to Remember

1. (*i*) An analog communication system makes use of an analog signal, which varies continuously with time.

   (*ii*) A digital communication system makes use of a digital signal, which has only two values of voltage, either high or low.
2. Modulation index determines the strength and quality of the transmitted signal. Higher modulation index ensures better quality and better strength.
3. The audio frequency ranges from 20 Hz to 20 kHz.
4. The equation of the carrier wave may be expressed as $e = E \sin(\omega t + \phi)$, where $e \rightarrow$ instantaneous voltage at time t, $\omega \rightarrow$ angular frequency and ϕ is the phase.
5. A communication system is the set up used for communication of information from one place to another.
6. In modern communication systems, the information is generally in the form of electrical voltage or current signals.
7. Any device that converts one form of energy into another is termed as a transducer.
8. Fax is the electric reproduction of a document at a distance.
9. A modem is a device that connects one computer to another across ordinary telephone lines.
10. The frequency range in which a transmitting system makes transmission is called band-width of transmission.
11. Data interval is recovering the original data from modulated wave.
12. Transmitter processes the incoming message signal and makes it suitable for transmission through a transmission channel. On the other hand, a receiver extracts the desired message signal from the receiver signals at the channel output.
13. A carrier wave is an electromagnetic wave of high frequency and of constant amplitude, which is employed to carry the audio signal from one location to another on the surface of the earth.
14. As $d = \sqrt{2hR}$, so by increasing height of tower h, the distance d, upto which TV coverage can be done, will increase. That is why, to have greater TV coverage, transmission has to be made using tall antenna.
15. Remote control is an electronic device which helps the observer to operate the television from a distance without leaving his/her seat.
16. In radar, a beam signal is needed in particular direction, which is possible if wavelength of signal wave is very small. Since the wavelength of microwaves is a few millimetres, hence they are used in radar.
17. TV signals are those signals which have frequency range 50 MHz to 200 MHz. Since these waves neither follow the curvature of the earth nor get reflected by ionosphere, their reception is possible either by using communication geostationary satellite, which reflects

the TV signals back to earth by using tall antennas, which may directly intercept the signals.

18. When an aircraft flies at small height from the surface of the earth and passes over the antenna, it intercepts the TV waves reaching the antenna of our TV. This causes a slight shaking of picture of our TV set.

19. The Line of Sight (LoS) in communication system is the distance between transmitting antenna and receiving antenna at which they can see each other.

20. A communication satellite is that satellite which can provide a communication line between two stations on the earth at large distance apart. Geostationary satellite having electronic equipment by which the signals may be received, amplified and transmitted back to the earth, can act as a communication satellite.

21. The detector is basically a rectifier followed by an envelope detector. The detector signal is amplified and then converted into an appropriate form, so that the user can use it.

22. In amplitude modulation, the amplitude of the carrier signals wave change in accordance with the modulating signal. Amplitude modulation technique is the simplest and is commonly used for radio transmission. However, noise content is more and transmission efficiency is less in AM wave.

23. **INTERNET:** The global interconnected network of worldwide computers is known as INTERNET.

24. Networking of computers at small scale (e.g. within an office, a building or a school) is called Local Area Network **(LAN)**. Every LAN has one or more main computers known as Servers.

25. A network of many interconnected LANS through telephone lines or satellites is known as Wide Area Network **(WAN)**.

26. For exchange of information and communication through Internet nowadays, standard sets of protocols called Transmission Control protocol/Internet Protocol **(TCP/IP)** are used.

27. The transmission of information/messages (electronic signals) on internet is very fast at the speed of light as communication is through electromagnetic waves.

28. A website is a set of inter connected web pages which contain information in text, images and audio/visual format. One can navigate from one page/website to another through a system called interlinked hypertext documents. This way of accessing information on internet is known as **www** or **World Wide Web**.

29. One can connect its computer to the internet through Internet Service Providers **(ISP)**.

30. **Internet Uses:** searching and viewing information; emailing; e-banking; e-shopping/commerce; e-ticketing; social networking etc.

31. **Mobile Telephony:** A low power device (transmitter) which can wirelessly send and receive radio frequency signals thereby providing possibility to make and receive phone calls while moving; store contact information, send or receive email, use the built in calculator, get information from internet, play games, listen radio/music and watch TV, take photos and videos, keep track of appointments etc.

32. Works through cellular radio network technology in which multiple interconnected (like internet) radio antennae are installed in a particular area/zone to receive and send radio signals to and from mobile phones. All incoming and outgoing calls are managed by a central control room called mobile telephone switching office **(MTSO)**.

33. **Mobile network generations: 1G** were based on analogue signals; **2G** were narrow band digital signal based network with good quality of calls; **3G** increased the data transfer speed; **4G** are going to provide high-speed internet facility in mobile phones.

34. For identity purposes a small IC chip called SIM card is inserted in every mobile phone to give the phone a unique identity.

35. **Global Positioning System:** It is method of identifying location or position of any point or a person on earth using a system of 24 satellites orbiting and mapping the earth surface continuously. For using the **GPS**, a person needs a GPS device fitted with a transmitter/receiver for sending /receiving signals to link up with GPS satellites in real time. Since all 24 satellites orbit in precise predefined orbits, it is easy to calculate longitudinal co-ordinates of a GPS user precisely with the help of known precise locations of 3-4 satellites (3 - 4 longitudinal co-ordinates). **Uses:** Navigation on water, air and land; Map designing; Measurement of speed of a moving object; Mountain heights; Glaciers position, Birds and animals movement; Road traffic control etc.

❑❑❑

VERY SHORT ANSWER TYPE QUESTIONS (I)

(Carrying 1 mark)

Q. 1. Explain why TV transmission towers are usually made high?

Ans. As $d = \sqrt{2hR}$, so by increasing height of tower h, the distance d upto which TV coverage can be done will increase. That is why, to have greater TV coverage, transmission has to be made using tall antennas.

Q. 2. It is necessary to use satellites for long distance TV transmission. Why?

Ans. Yes, TV signals being of high frequency are not reflected by the ionosphere. Therefore, to reflect them, satellites are needed. That is why, salellites are used for long distance TV transmission.

Q. 3. What is a transducer? Give two examples.

Ans. A tranducer is a device which converts one form of energy into another. A microphone at the transmitting station and a loudspeaker at the receiving station are the two examples of transducers.

Q. 4. What should be the length of the dipole antenna for a carrier wave of frequency 3×10^8 Hz?

Ans. Here, frequency $v = 3 \times 10^8$ Hz

We have length of the dipole antenna

$$= \frac{\lambda}{2} = \frac{c}{2v} = \frac{3 \times 10^8}{2 \times 3 \times 10^8} = 0.5 \text{ m}$$

Q. 5. Why is an FM signal less susceptible to noise than an AM signal?

Ans. The noise is related to the amplitude variation of the signal emitted by a source. As the amplitude remains constant in FM signal, it is less susceptible to noise than AM signal.

Q. 6. Why are the sky waves not used in the transmission of TV signals?

Ans. If the sky waves are of frequency more than 40 MHz, the ionosphere is unable to reflect them back to earth . TV signals have a frequency range of 80 MHz to 200 MHz, therefore, the transmission of TV signals via sky waves is not possible.

Q. 7. A TV tower has a height of 400 m at a given place. Calculate its coverage range, if the radius of earth is 6400 km.

Ans. Here, $h = 400$ m, radius of earth,

$$R = 6400 \text{ km} = 6.4 \times 10^6 \text{ m}$$

$$\therefore \text{Coverage range, } d_m = \sqrt{2Rh} = \sqrt{2 \times 6.4 \times 10^6 \times 400}$$

$$d_m = 7.155 \times 10^4 \text{ m or } 71.55 \text{ km.}$$

Q. 8. State two factors by which the range of TV signals can be increased.

Ans. The range of TV transmission can be increased by:

(*i*) increasing the height of transmission tower of TV station.

(*ii*) by using the satellite communication method.

Q. 9. What mode of communication is employed for the transmission of TV signals?

Ans. The TV signals have the frequency range upto 200 MHz. These waves neither follow the curvature of the earth nor get reflected by ionosphere. Therefore, their communication as a surface wave or sky wave is not possible.

Q. 10. What should be the height of transmitting antenna, if the TV telecast is to cover the radius 128 km? $R_e = 6.4 \times 10^6$ m. If the average population density around the tower is 1000/km^3, how much population is covered?

Ans. We have height of transmitting antenna

$$h = \frac{d^2}{2R} = \frac{(128\times10^3)^2}{2\times6.4\times10^6} = 1280\text{ m}$$

Total population covered

$$= \pi d^2 \times \text{population density}$$
$$= 3.14\times(128)^2\times1000$$
$$= 5.14\times10^7$$

Q. 11. A message signal of frequency 5 kHz and peak voltage of 2V is used to modulate a carrier wave of frequency 2 MHz and peak voltage of 10V. Determine (*i*) modulation index, (*ii*) the side bands produced.

Ans. (*i*) Here $A_m = 2V$ and $A_c = 10$V

$$\therefore \text{Modulation index } (\mu) = \frac{A_m}{A_c} = \frac{2V}{10V} = 0.2$$

(*ii*) The side bands are 2 MHz + 5 kHz = 2005 kHz (or 2.005 MHz) and 2 MHz – 5 kHz = 1995 kHz (or 1.995 MHz)

Q. 12. What is transmission medium? What are the various transmission media used in communication system?

Ans. A transmission medium or communication channel is a link through which information or message signal may propagate from the source to the destination without any noise or distortion. It is a sort of elecrtronic roadways along which signals travel. Broadly, transmission media have been divided into two types:

(*i*) Guided transmission media, such as in line communication.

(*ii*) Unguided transimssion media, such as in space communication.

Q. 13. What do you mean by point-to-point communication and broadcast. Give example.

Ans. In point-to-point communication mode, the communication takes place over a link between a single transmitter and single receiver. Telephony is an example of point-to-point communication. In broadcast mode, there are a number of receivers corresponding to a single transmitter. Radio and television are examples of broadcast mode of communication.

Q. 14. Breifly describe the three basic parts of a communication system.

Ans. The communication system consists of following three parts:

(*i*) **Transmitter**, which transmits the information (message) after it is modified to suitable form for transmission. Generally, before transmission, the information is transformed into an electrical signal by the use of a transducer and AF signal. This is modulated with a high frequency carrier wave.

(*ii*) **Communication channel**, which can either be a line communication or communication through space.

(*iii*) **Receiver**, which receives the signal from communication channel, demodulates it and then converts it back into its original form.

Q. 15. What is an antenna? What role does it play in a communication system? What should be the length of a dipole antenna?

Ans. Antenna in a transmitter which radiates electromagnetic waves into the free space and in a receiver it picks up the transmitted signal from free space.

Antenna plays an important role in communication channel. At the tranmitter stage, it helps in radiating energy in the form of *em* waves. At the receiver end it picks up *em* waves and these waves supply electrical input signal to the receiver.

Q. 16. Why are short waves used into long distance radio broadcasts?

OR

Long distance radio broadcasts use short wave bands. Why?

Ans. The short waves are the waves of wavelength less than 200 m or frequency greater than 1.5 MHz. They are absorbed by the earth due to their high frequency. These waves are reflected from ionosphere. These waves, after reflection from ionosphere, reach the surface of the earth at a large distance from the place of transmission. It means attenuation is less for short waves. It is due to this reason, the short waves are used in long distance broadcasts.

Q. 17. A transmitting antenna at the top of tower has a height 32 m and that of the receiving antenna is 50 m. What is the maximum distance between them for satisfactory communication in line of sight mode? Given radius of earth is 6.4×10^6 m.

Ans. Here, $h_T = 32$ m, $h_R = 50$ m, $R = 6.4 \times 10^6$ m

We have,
$$d_m = \sqrt{2R\,h_T + 2R\,h_R}$$
$$= \sqrt{2 \times 6.4 \times 10^6 \times 32 + 2 \times 6.4 \times 10^6 \times 50}$$
$$= 45.5 \times 10^3 \text{ m} = 45.5 \text{ km}$$

Q. 18. Why does the electrical conductivity of earth's atmosphere increase with altitude?

Ans. We know that, with an increase in altitudes, the atmospheric pressure decreases. The high energy particles (*i.e.*, γ-rays and cosmic rays) coming from outer space and entering our eye's atmosphere cause ionisation of the atoms of the gases present there. The ionising power of these radiations decreases rapidly as they apporach the earth, due to increase in number of collisions with the gas atoms. It is due to reason that the electrical conductivity of earth's atmosphere increases with altitude.

SHORT ANSWER TYPE QUESTIONS (SA-II)

(Carrying 3 marks)

Q. 1. What is meant by the term 'modulation'? Explain with the help of a block diagram, how the process of modulation is carried out in radio broadcasts?

Ans. Modulation is the process of super imposing the AF base band message or information signals (called the modulating signals) on high frequency wave or pulse (called the carrier wave or pulse) such that some specific property of carrier wave (or pulse) is varied in accordance with the information or message signal.

The block diagram showing process of modulation is shown in Fig. 10.1.

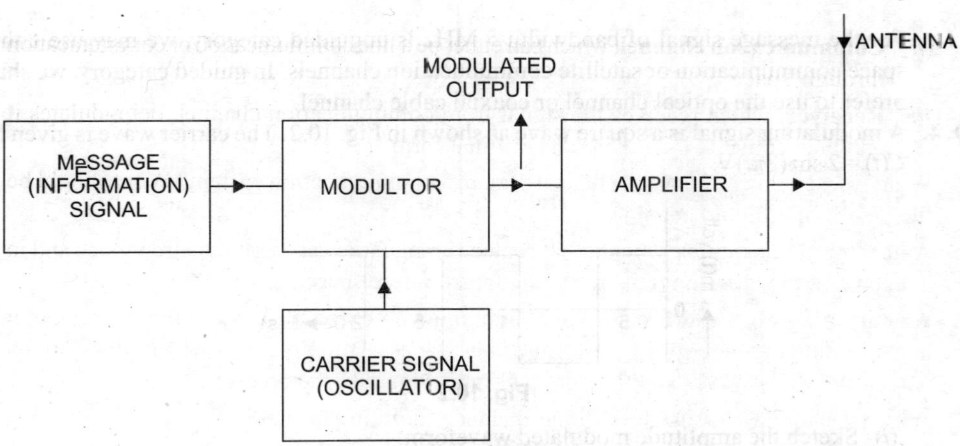

Fig. 10.1

Q. 2. In a diode AM detector, the output circuit consits of $R = 1\text{k}\Omega$ and $C = 10$ pF. A carrier signal of 100 kHz is to be detected. Is it good? If yes, then explain why. If not, what value of C would you suggest?

Ans. Here,

$$R = 1\text{ k}\Omega = 10^3\Omega,\ C = 10\text{ pF} = 10 \times 10^{-12}\text{ F} = 10^{-11}\text{F}$$

$$\therefore \quad RC = 10^3 \times 10^{-11}\text{s} = 10^{-8}\text{s}$$

and

$$\frac{1}{\nu_c} = \frac{1}{100 \times 10^3}\text{s} = 10^{-5}\text{s}$$

We find that $\frac{1}{\nu_c}$ is not less than RC, as is required for demodulation. Therefore, the arragement is no good. For the satisfactory arragement, let us try

$$C = 1\ \mu\text{F} = 10^{-6}\text{F}$$

$$\therefore \quad RC = 10^3 \times 10^{-6}\text{ s} = 10^{-3}\text{s}$$

Now,

$$\frac{1}{\nu_c} = (10^{-5}\text{ s}) << \text{RC } (=10^{-3}\text{ s})$$

∴ The condition is satified. This is good enough for demodulation.

Q. 3. How do we make the choice of a communication channel? A message signal has a bandwidth of 5 MHz. Suggest a possible communication channel for its transmission.

Ans. The physical medium between the transmitter and receiver of a commuication system, through which signals propagate, is referred to as the communication channel. Communication channels are broadly classified into following two broad categories:

(i) **Line communication**

In this mode, the signal is guided and it travels along a conducting physical path (or line) to the receiver. Two wire transmission lines, coaxial cables and optical communication method come in this category.

(*ii*) **Space communication**

In this method, the signal is freely transmitted in space by using an antenna and is received at the other end by intercepting the signal with the help of another antenna. Space communication is an unguided mode of communication. Ground waves propogation, sky waves, space waves and satellite communication are some examples of space communication channels.

The choice of communication channel depends on (*i*) whether we want guided or unguided communication channel, (*ii*) the frequency of carrier wave and the frequency bandwidth and (*iii*) the range of transmission.

For the message signal of bandwidth 5 MHz is unguided category, we may use either space communication or satellite communincation channels. In guided category, we shall prefer to use the optical channel or coaxial cable channel.

Q. 4. A modulating signal is a square wave as shown in Fig. 10.2. The carrier wave is given by $C(f) = 2 \sin (8\pi t)$ V.

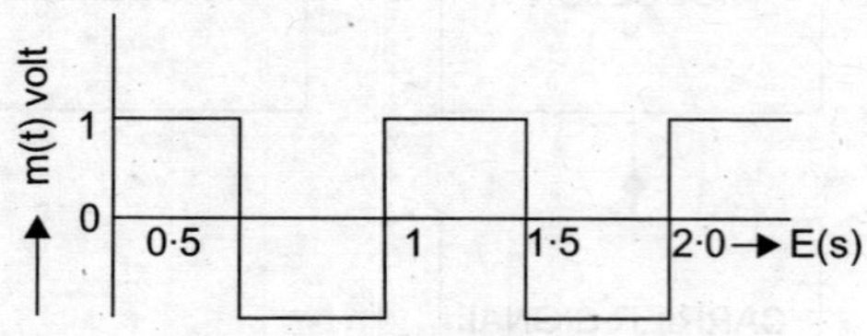

Fig. 10.2

(*i*) Sketch the amplitude modulated waveform.
(*ii*) What is the modulation index?

Ans. (*i*) Here,
$$A_m = 1\text{V}, A_c = 2\text{V},$$
$$w_m = \frac{2\pi}{T_m} = \frac{2\pi}{1} \text{ rads}^{-1}$$
$$w_c = 8\pi = 4w_m$$

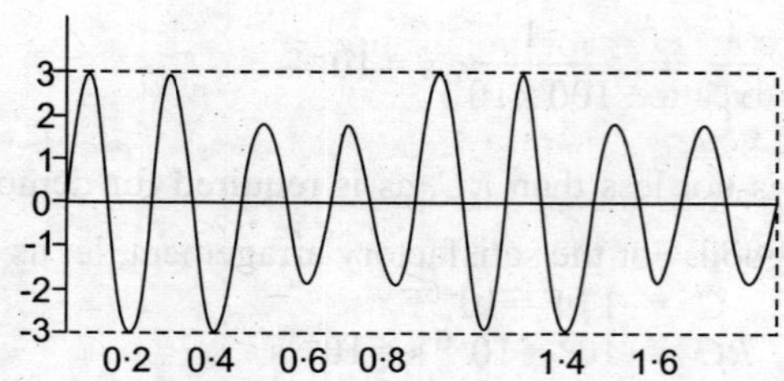

Fig. 10.3

Superimposition of modulating signal on carrier wave is given in the waveform.

(*ii*)
$$\mu_a = \frac{A_m}{A_c} = \frac{1}{2} = 0.5$$

Q. 5. Mention the frequency at which TV signals are transmitted. Derive an expression for the range up to which signals transmitted by a TV tower can be received.

Ans. TV signals in VHF band are transmitted at frequency bands 54-72 MHz, 76-88 MHz and 174-216 MHz. In UHF band, the frequency range is from 420 to 890 MHz. In satellite communication mode, TV signals frequency band for uplinking is 5.925-6.425 GHz and for downlinking the frequency band is 3.7-4.2 GHz.

Let, at a place P on the earth, a TV tower antenna PQ of height h be installed. By space wave (line of sight method) transmitted signal from TV tower can at the most cover a maximum distance d up to points S and Z. Beyond these points, the signal cannot reach due to the curvature of the earth.

Let $OP = OZ = OS = R$ be the radius of the earth.

Then from the triangle OZQ, we have
$$OQ^2 = OZ^2 + ZQ^2$$
$$\therefore \quad (R+h)^2 = R^2 + d^2$$
$$\Rightarrow \quad d^2 = (R+h)^2 - R^2 = 2hR + h^2$$

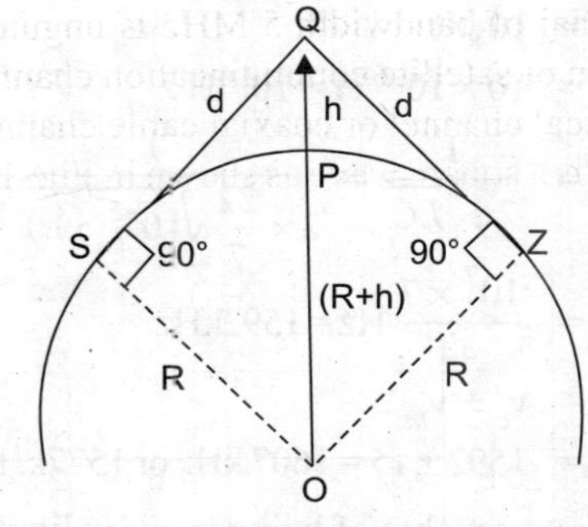

Fig. 10.4

As $h << R$, hence the term h^2 can be neglected as compared to $2hR$, and, hence, $d^2 = 2hR$

or transmission range $d = \sqrt{2hR}$

Thus, the range depends upon the height of TV tower (or the transmitting antenna). The greater the height of TV tower the greater is the transmission range.

In general, if height of transmitting antenna is h_T and that of receiving antenna be h_R, the maximum distance, up to which signal can be received, will be given by:

$$d_m = \sqrt{2h_T.R} + \sqrt{2h_R.R}\,.$$

Q. 6. What does the term 'LOS communication' mean? Name the types of waves that are used for this communication. With the help of a suitable figure give typical examples of communication systems that use space wave mode propagation.

Ans. 'LOS communication' means Line-of-Sight communication system, in which the wave travels in a straight line from the transmitting antenna to the receiving antenna.

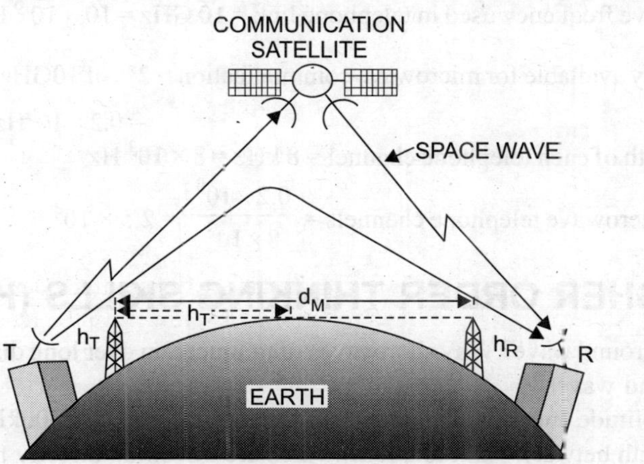

Fig. 10.5

For LOS communcation, space waves are used. Space waves consist of electromagnetic radiowaves of frequencies more than 50 MHz sent directly from the transmitting antenna to the receiving antenna.

Terrestrial TV telecast, Radar and communication satellite systems make use of space waves as shown in Fig. 10.5.

Q. 7. An audio signal of 15000 Hz modulates a carrier generated by a tank circuit containing 1nF capacitor and 10 μH inductor. Calculate the frequencies of first pair of side bands.

Ans. Here

$$\nu_m = 15000\,\text{Hz} = 15\,\text{kHz}$$
$$C = 1\,\text{nF} = 10^{-9} F, \nu_{SB} = ?$$

$$L = 10\,\mu H$$
$$= 10 \times 10^{-6}\,H = 10^{-6}H$$

We know that
$$\nu_c = \frac{1}{2\pi\sqrt{LC}} = \frac{1}{2 \times \frac{22}{7}\sqrt{10^{-5} \times 10^{-9}}}$$
$$= \frac{10^7 \times 7}{44}\,Hz = 1592kHz$$
$$\nu_{SB} = \nu_c \pm \nu_m$$
$$= 1592 \pm 15 = 1607\,kHz \text{ or } 1577kHz$$

Q. 8. Estimate the fastest bit rate capable of being used by light of wavelength 1.3 µm. How many phone calls could be carried at this bit rate? Bandwidth of optical fibre = 2GHz.

Ans. Here, $\lambda = 1.3 \times 10^{-6}m$,

We have, $$\nu = \frac{c}{\lambda} = \frac{3 \times 10^8}{1.3 \times 10^{-6}} = 2.3 \times 10^{14}Hz$$

Max. bit rate $= 2\nu = 2 \times 2.3 \times 10^{14} = 4.6 \times 10^{14}Hz$

For optical fibre, bandwidth $= 2GHz = 2 \times 10^9Hz$

No. of phone calls $= \frac{4.6 \times 10^{14}}{2 \times 10^9} = 2.3 \times 10^5$

Q. 9. A microwave telephone link operating at the central frequency of 10GHz has been established. If 2% of this is available for microvave communication channel, then how many telephone channels can be simultaneously granted if each telephone is alloted a bandwidth of 8 kHz.

Ans. Microwave frequency used in telephone link $= 10$ GHz $= 10 \times 10^9$ Hz $= 10^{10}$Hz

Frequency available for microwave communication = 2% of 10GHz $= \frac{2}{100} \times 10^{10}$

$= 0.2 \times 10^9$Hz

Bandwidth of each telephone channel = 8 kHz $= 8 \times 10^3$ Hz

No. of microwave telephone channels $= \frac{0.2 \times 10^9}{8 \times 10^3} = 2.5 \times 10^4$

HIGHER ORDER THINKING SKILLS (HOTS)

Q. 1. What is ground wave? Why shortwave communication over long distance is not possible via ground waves?

Ans. The amplitude modulated radiowaves having frequency 1500kHz upto 40MHz (or wavelength between 7.5m to 200m) which are travelling directly following the surface of earth are known as ground waves. The shortwave communication over long distance is only possible via sky waves. It is not possible via ground waves because the ground waves can bend round the corners of the objects on earth and, hence, their intensity falls with distance. Moreover, the ground wave transmission becomes weaker as frequency increases.

Q. 2. A transmitter transmits a power of 25kW, when modulation is 40%. Calculate the power of carrier waves.

Ans. Here, $P_t = 25kW, \mu = \frac{40}{100} = 0.4, P_c = ?$

Now $$P_c = \frac{P_t}{\left(1+\frac{\mu^2}{2}\right)} = \frac{25}{1+\frac{(0.4)^2}{2}} = \frac{25}{1.08} = 23.14\text{ kW}$$

Q. 3. A radio can tune any station in the 6MHz to 12MHz band. What is the corresponding wavelength band?

Ans. The wavelength of the corresponding to a frequency of 6MHz is

$$\lambda_1 = \frac{c_1}{v_1} = \frac{3\times10^8}{6\times10^6} = 50\text{ m}$$

The wavelength of the corresponding to a frequency of 12MHz is

$$\lambda_2 = \frac{c}{v_2} = \frac{3\times10^8}{12\times10^6} = 25\text{ m}$$

$\therefore$ The coresponding wavelength band in question is 25 m to 50 m band.

Q. 4. A TV tower has height 100 m. By how much the height of tower be increased to triple its coverage range?

Ans. We have $d = \sqrt{2hR}$

So that $3d = 3\sqrt{2hR}$

If new height is h' then

$$\sqrt{2h'R} = 3d = 3\sqrt{2hR}$$

or $$h' = 9h = 9\times100 = 900\text{ m}$$

Increase in height of tower = 900 – 100 = 800m.

Q. 5. An AM transmitter records an antenna current 10.5 A. The antenna's current drops to 10 A when only carrier is transmitted. Determine the modulation index.

Ans. Here $I_t = 10.5\text{ A and } I_c = 10\text{ A}, \mu = ?$

As $$\sqrt{1+\frac{\mu^2}{2}} = \frac{I_t}{I_c} = \frac{10.5}{10} = \frac{21}{20}$$

$$\therefore \quad 1+\frac{\mu^2}{2} = \frac{441}{400} = 1+\frac{41}{400},$$

$$\Rightarrow \quad \mu^2 = \frac{82}{400} = 0.205$$

$$\mu = \sqrt{0.205} = 0.453 = 45.3\%$$

Q. 6. For sky wave propogation of a 15MHz signal, what should be the minimum electron density in ionosphere?

Ans. Here $v_c = 15\text{ MHz} = 15\times10^6\text{ Hz}, N_{max} = ?$

As, $v_c = 9(N_{max})^{1/2}$

or $$N_{max} = \left(\frac{v_c}{9}\right)^2 = \frac{v_c^2}{81} = \frac{\left(15\times10^6\right)^2}{81} = 2.78\times10^{12}\text{ m}^{-3}$$

Q. 7. Why is ground wave transmission of signals restricted to a frequency of 1500kHz?

Ans. In ground wave propogation, the loss in energy due to interaction with matter increases with the increase in frequency of wave. Therefore, the waves of frequency above 1500kHz get heavily damaged in ground wave propogation. Hence, the ground wave propogation is restricted to a frequency of 1500kHz.

Q. 8. In a detector, output circuit consists of $R = 10\text{k}\Omega$, $C = 100\text{pF}$. Calculate the frequency of carrier signal it can detect.

Ans. Here, $R = 10\text{k}\Omega = 10^4\Omega$, $C = 100\text{pF} = 10^{-10}\text{F}$

$\therefore$ Time constant of the circuit, $t = RC = 10^4 \times 10^{-10} = 10^{-6}\text{s}$

For demodulation, $\frac{1}{\nu_c} << RC$

or $\quad \nu_c >> \frac{1}{RC}$ or $\nu_c >> \frac{1}{10^{-6}} = 10^6\text{ Hz} = 1\text{MHz}$

$\therefore$ Frequency of carrier signal must be much greater than 1MHz.

❑❑❑

VALUE BASED QUESTIONS (SOLVED)

Q. 1. Mohan and his friends visited a Hospital. There, they were taken into the operating room and were asked to wear special shoes. Some of his friends did not want to change their shoes. An argument broke out between the ward boy and his friends. Mohan explained to his friends why these shoes were necessary. He gave them the details of what would happen if they walked into that area with their shoes on. His friends were convinced and wore the shoes given by the ward boy before entering the operation room.

(*a*) What according to you might be the reason behind wearing those special shoes?

(*b*) What values are displayed by Mohan and his friends?

Ans. (*a*) The shoes are made of special conducting material. When we walk with our ordinary shoes in the carpeted region of the operation theater, shoes get charged. There while discharging will give out sparks. This may ignite the oxygen present near the oxygen cylinders and lead to a mishap. The special conducting shoes connect earth with any charge produced on your body, thereby avoiding an accidental fire.

(*b*) Concern for the safety of others, logical reasoning and leadership quality.

Q. 2. The immediate cause of many deaths is ventricular fibrillation, an uncoordinated quivering of the heart as opposed to proper beating. An electric shock to the chest can cause momentary paralysis of the heart muscle, after which the heart will sometimes start organized beating again. Rohini's father suddenly loses consciousness. He is rushed to the emergency ward of a hospital. There the doctors find that his heart had uncoordinated quivering. They approach for taking consent of the family members for using a defibrillator to revive the heart. Rohini's mother refuses to grant permission. When Rohini comes to know about this she at once talks to her mother and convinces her that it was vital. She explains, in detail, to her how this device works and convinces her to give consent for its use. Her mother agrees. This saves the life of Rohini's fate. What values are imbibed by Rohini?

A defibrillator is a device that applies a strong electric shock to the chest over a time interval of a few millisecond. The device contains a capacitor of several microfarad, charged to several thousand volts. Electrodes called paddles, about 8 cm across and coated with conducting paste, are held against the chest on both sides of the heart. Their handles are insulated to prevent injury to the operator, who calls "Clear!" and pushes a button on one paddle to discharge the capacitor through the patient's chest. Assume that energy of 300 J is to be delivered from a 30.0 pF capacitor. To what potential difference must it be charged?

Ans. The values imbibed by Rohini are

(*i*) Prompt decision making

(*ii*) Up to date knowledge

Given $U = 300$ J,

$C = 30\,pF = 30 \times 10^{-12}\,F, V = ?$

Using the expression

$$U = \frac{1}{2}CV^2, \text{ we have}$$

$$V = \sqrt{\frac{2U}{C}} = \sqrt{\frac{2 \times 300}{30 \times 10^{-12}}} = 4.47 \times 10^6\,V$$

Q. 3. Divya and her family visited Shanghai. There they wanted to visit a nearby town. They bought tickets for a railway train between the two cities. Divya's mother refused to board the train when she came to know that the train does not have wheels. This created a problem. It was necessary for the family to board the train and reach the other city. Seeing her family in quandary Divya talked to her mother by giving her complete details of how the train will move. This convinced her mother. The family boarded the train and reached their destination safety.

(*a*) What is such train without wheels called? How does it move?

(*b*) Which value do you think is shown by Divya?

Ans. (*a*) Such a train is called Maglev (Magnetic levitation). Electromagnets are mounted on the magnetic levitation vehicle, and a series of propulsion coils are placed along the side of the track. The polarity of the magnets on the vehicle remains constant. An electrical signal is passed through the coils such that each magnet on the vehicle "sees" a coil with opposite polarity ahead of it and a coil with the same polarity behind it. As a result, the vehicle experiences an attractive force from the coil ahead of it and a repulsive force from the coil behind it, both forces pushing the vehicle in the forward direction. This propels the train which does not require wheels.

(*b*) Concern for her family and good use of fundamentals learnt.

Q. 4. Zaheen found a child playing with a convex lens. Time and again the child pointed the lens towards the sun to view it. She at once stopped the child, took the lens from him and reported the matter to the child's mother. The child's mother began beating the child for his mistake. Zaheen stopped the mother from doing so. She told the mother that it was not the fault of the child but her fault.

(*a*) According to you what are the values displayed by Zaheen?

(*b*) What do you think is the reason for Zaheen to stop the child from pointing the lens towards the sun?

Ans. (*a*) Presence of mind, High degree of general awareness, caring.

(*b*) A convex lens converges a parallel beam of high falling on it. When the child uses it to watch the sun, the sun's rays are focused on his retina. Due to the heat this might have damaged the retina of the child and the child would have lost his sight.

Q. 5. On a trip to the cold tundra region a group of friends find themselves stranded in the scorching bright sun. The match sticks they had brought with them had been spoiled by the ice. They were hungry but they could not cook as they could not light a fire although they had paper and dry wood. Just then Oshin and her friends were passing by. Seeing the stranded group she thought of helping them. She cut a piece of ice and gave it a convex shape. Staking the pieces of paper and dry wood she allowed the rays of the sun to pass through the convex shaped ice. By adjusting the distance of the convex ice piece from the pieces of paper she was able to light a fire. The group thanked her and relished the cooked food which they then made.

(*a*) How could Oshin light up a fire with the help of ice?

(*b*) What values do you attribute to Oshin?

Ans. (*a*) If a piece of ice is given a convex shape, it will behave as a convex lens. When rays from the sun at infinity entered the convex lens they collect at the focus. This generates a large amount of heat which startes the fire.

(*b*) Helping nature and high degree of awareness about her subject.

Q. 6. Albert Swank Jr., a civil engineer in Anchorage, Alaska wants to install a nuclear particle accelerator - or cyclotron - in his home. He wants to use it to produce radioactive isotopes that can be used in treating cancer patients. But neighbors and the city council think it's a bad idea. Swank grew up in this house and was a science whiz as a kid, building mall-model cyclotrons with the help of his father, who died of cancer. Now Swank wants to give something back to Alaska in his father's name. He wants to manufacture isotopes used in PET scans to screen cancer patients and allow school children to watch the process. A PET scan is like a highly detailed X-ray. There's growing demand for the isotopes used in the process, which have a short shelf life and currently come from out of state. Swank wants to meet that demand and cut down the lag time during delivery. He says it's safe.

(*a*) What according to you are the values displayed by Swank?

(*b*) What is the principle of a cyclotron?

(*c*) Is Swank right in saying that it is safe?

Ans. (*a*) The values displayed are concern for fellow human beings and his desire to help them.

(*b*) It is based on the principle that the positive ions can be accelerated to high energies with a comparatively smaller alternating potential difference by making them to cross electric field again and again, by making use of a strong magnetic field.

(*c*) Cyclotrons are safe, but because they may emit low levels of radiation, they're typically shielded with concrete walls and lead sheets. And there are strict requirements for operation, security, waste disposal and transportation. Most are operated in highly equipped laboratories or on site in hospitals. So Swank is only partly right in saying the cyclotrons are safe.

Q. 7. Mobile communications would not be possible without radio waves; however, some people are concerned that radio waves from mobile phones and base stations may cause health problems. A substantial number of scientific studies conducted by various research bodies have indicated that electromagnetic fields, at levels within the limits prescribed by public health authority safety standards and recommendations, cause no adverse effects to human health. Yasmine always tells her parents to make the minimum use of the mobile phone and switch it off during the night she also tells them not to keep the phone close to the heart.

(*a*) What according to you are the values displayed by Yasmine?

(*b*) Why is a mobile phone a hazard to health?

Ans. (*a*) Concern for the well being of her parents. Adequate knowledge of the ill effects of the mobile phone.

(*b*) Wireless cell phones transmit signals via radio frequency (RF), the same kind of low-frequency radiation used in microwave ovens and AM/FM radios. Scientists have known for years that large doses of high frequency radiation-the kind used in X-rays-causes cancer, the same is possible true for low radiations also.

Q. 8. At one of the blind ends of a road in a colony lot of accidents used to take place. One day Kunwar moved into a house near the blind end. On a certain day he saw an accident take place at the blind end. He at once rushed to the spot and helped the victims with first aid. He then telephoned for an ambulance. Later on he met the President of the welfare committee of the colony and requested him to install huge convex mirrors at both ends of the blind end. After the installation of the mirrors the accident rates suddenly dropped.

(*a*) What accroding to you are the values displayed by Kunwar?

(*b*) Why did Kunwar advise the installation of convex mirrors?

Ans. (*a*) Concern for others, correct use of knowledge.

(*b*) A convex mirror has a wide range of view. As a result it is capable of showing the traffic on the other side of the blind end. Since Kunwar was aware of this fact, therefore he advised for their installation.

Q. 9. Rhea and harnoor were at the dining table having their dinner. An argument broke out between them about convex and concave mirrors as to which mirror forms an inverted image. Losing no time Rhea took a highly polished spoon. She made Harnoor look into the depressed surface of the spoon and then the bulging surface. The images formed in the two cases were different. In the first case the image formed was inverted while in the second case it was correct. Then she explained to Harnoor about the two surfaces acting as mirrors and also which formed an inverted image. This at once stopped the argument.

(*a*) Which of the two mirrors forms an inverted image; concave or convex.

(*b*) What are the values shown by Rhea and Harnoor?

(*c*) Give once use of a concave mirror.

Ans. (*a*) A concave mirror forms an inverted image.

(*b*) Rhea : concern for her brother and correct knowledge.
Harnoor : Ability to learn and understand, respect for elders.

(*c*) Used as a shaving mirror.

Q. 10. On a picnic Zabeen and her friend Chahat went fishing. Instead of using the fishing rod they thought of using the methods used by their ancestors; fishing with a spear. Chahat tried a lot but could not get her spear on target. Zaheen who was watching came to her rescue by telling her to hit the spear slightly below the point where she seen the fish. Heeding her advice Chahat tried again and this time she was successful. They roasted the fish and enjoyed their picnic. While coming back they gathered all the waste in a bag and disposed it off in the dustbin.

(*a*) Why Zaheen advised her friend to hit the spear slightly below the point where she saw the fish?

(*b*) What value was shown by Zaheen?

(c) What value was shown by the two girls before they left the picnic spot?

Ans. (a) Due to refraction of light an object placed in water appears to be raised and above its actual depth. This phenomenon was known to Zaheen therefore she advised her friend.

(b) Zaheen attributed the value of concern for her friend and her helping nature.

(c) Both showed the value of keeping their surroundings clean.

Q. 11. Simran's aunt has an eyesight problem. She visits a doctor for the same. The doctor advises her to get herself operated for the cataract which she has developed. Her aunt was reluctant to go through the operation due to two reasons: (i) She was not aware of the details and the outcome of the surgery and (ii) She thought that the surgery was too expensive for her to bear. When Simran learnt of this she decided to do something for her aunt. She took the help of her friends and arranged the required money. She also explained to her aunt the benefit of the operation and the negligible rate of failure. She told her that the operation was expensive due to the costly operating equipment and the eye lens which is to be planted in place of the clouded lens. Her aunt was convinced and the operation was successful. Her aunt later on thanked Simran for her timely help.

(a) What according to you are the values displayed by Simran and her friends?

(b) What is cataract?

Ans. (a) The values displayed by Simran. (i) Concern for her aunt (ii) Ability to take decisions.

The values displayed by Simran's friends. (i) Helping nature (ii) Faith in Simran.

(b) Cataract in the clouding of the eye lens. Due to this visibility becomes poor. This is an age related defect of the eye.

Q. 12. Two students were asked to study the variation of resistance of the two conductors A and B with temperature. They set up a suitable apparatus for the same and projected their results in the form of the plots as given below.

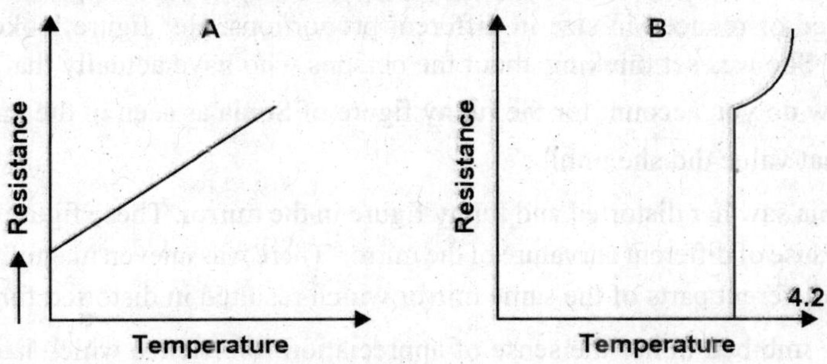

(a) Which of the two conductors A and B is ohmic?

(b) Which of the two conductors A and B is a superconductor?

(c) Which of the two can be used for producing strong magnetic field required in particle accelerator and other devices like high speed computer and also in power transmission?

(d) What is the value imbibed by the students?

Ans. (a) The conductor A is ohmic.

(b) The conductor B is a superconductor as it has a zero resistance up to 4.2 K which is the critical temperature for the conductor B.

(c) The conductor B i.e., superconductor is used for producing strong magnetic fields required in particle accelerator, high speed computers.

(d) In depth knowledge of their subject.

Q. 13. Surinder, one fine evening after the rainfall, was happy to observe coloured concentric arcs hanging in the sky. The sight of what we now call rainbow was spectacular and his heart leapt up with joy because he had seen it for the first time. In his heart of heart he looked at it as nature's gift. Two rainbows were visible to him, one above the other. The inner one called the primary rainbow has the outer edge red and the inner edge violet and was brighter than the outer one called the secondary rainbow. The outer rainbow had violet outer edge and the red inner edge and was comparatively fainter. Surinder's father wanted to explain to him the formation of the rainbow but he was in no mood to listen and lose the charm of the rainbow. However, he finally agreed.

(a) Explain the formation of rainbow in the sky.

(b) What did Surinder feel after the formation of the rainbow was explained to him?

Ans. (a) The rainbow appears on the earth after the rainfall to a person who has his back towards the sun. It is formed due to dispersion of light suffering refraction primary rainbow; there is only one total internal reflection but two refractions whereas in the case of the secondary rainbow there take place two refractions and two internal reflections. That is why the order of the colour is reversed in the secondary rainbow i.e., violet colour is on the inner side and red colour on the outer side.

(b) Surinder was happy to know the scene behind the formation of the rainbow but was sad to feel that his heart no longer leaps up with joy. He had thus the mixed feelings.

Q. 14. Sonia went to Pushpa Gujral Science city and saw the different sections. It was her first exposure to the world of science. Among other exhibits she saw a number of curved mirrors installed at a place. When she looked at her image in different mirrors, she was amused. Do I really look like this, she asked her friend? Different parts of the body were magnified or reduced in size in different proportions. Her figure looked funny in the mirrors. She was set thinking about the persons who have actually that type of figure.

(a) How do you account for the funny figure of Sonia as seen in the mirror?

(b) What value did she imbibe?

Ans. (a) Sonia saw her distorted and funny figure in the mirror. These figures were distorted because of different curvature of the mirror. There was uneven magnification produced by different parts of the same mirror which resulted in distorted funny figures.

(b) She imbibed in her the sense of appreciation for science which had made our life funny and enjoyable.

Q. 15. Richa's father, after retirement, went regularly both for long morning and evening walks. He enjoyed these long walks because they kept him slim and trim. During the summer break, Richa also joined him. She enjoyed the red colour of the sun both at sunrise and sunset. She would wait long enough to watch sunset and sunrise. "Why is the sun not red" all the day long? Finally, she asked her father one day. Her father explained to her the redness of sun both at sunset and sunrise.

(a) Explain how her father satisfied her curiosity about the red colour of the sunset and sunrise.

(b) What ideas did Richa imbibe in her about nature?

Ans. (*a*) The sun appears red at sunrise and sunset. Richa was confused as to why this phenomenon was observed only in the morning and in the evening and not throughout the day. Her father argued with her that both at sunset and sunrise, light has to travel a longer distance as compared to the distance at noon. Light in passing through the atmosphere is scattered. Since blue colour of smaller wavelength is scattered much more than the red colour of longer wavelength, blue colour fails to reach the observer and hence the sun appears to be reddish.

(*b*) Richa, started appreciating nature and became much closer to it. She started seeing nature in all activities.

Q. 16. Energy is required for the development of a nation. Non-renewable sources of energy are limited and will be exhausted sooner or later. Nuclear energy is said to be the ultimate source of energy. Countries like China, Japan and America have enough Nuclear power plants.

Nuclear power is the use of sustained nuclear fission to generate heat and electricity.

There is, however, an ongoing debate about the use of nuclear power after the disaster of Fukushima in Japan in 2011.

(*a*) Do you recommend that India must also go in for setting up in Nuclear Plants? Keep in mind that China has 25 nuclear plants and is in the process of setting more such plants.

(*b*) Why do we not use fusion as a source of energy although it releases much more energy? Give logical reasoning for a thermonuclear reaction as a source of energy.

Ans. (*a*) All nations both developed and developing require energy. Most nations are using the fossil fuels to meet their energy needs. Fossil fuels like coal, petroleum etc. are limited and will be exhausted soon.

Nuclear plants must he installed to meet the growing energy needs of the people. This is the only sustainable source of energy. India's energy needs are colossal and can be met only by nuclear energy. The disaster of Fukushima in Japan in 2011 should not deter us. We must observe stringent safety measures while installing these plants. Simultaneously, research projects aiming at discovering new sources of energy must be encouraged.

(*b*) Nuclear fusion reactor or thermonuclear reactors are difficult to install because fusion nuclear reaction start at a very high temperature $\sim 10^7$°C, a temperature difficult to produce and maintain.

□□□

SAMPLE PAPER – I

PHYSICS (THEORY)

Class XII

Time: 3hours **M.M.: 70**

GeneralInstructions:

(i) All questions are compulsory.

(ii) There are 30 questions in total. Questions 1 to 8 are very short answer type questions and carry one mark each.

(iii) Questions 9 to 18 carry two marks each, questions 19 to 27 carry three marks each and questions 28 to 30 carry five marks each.

(iv) There is no overall choice. However, an internal choice has been provided in one question of two marks, one question of three marks and all three questions of five marks each. You have to attempt only one of the given choice in such questions.

(v) Use of calculators is not permitted. However, you may use log tables if necessary.

(vi) You may use the following values of physical constants wherever necessary.

$c = 3 \times 10^8$ m/s

$h = 6.63 \times 10^{-34}$ Js

$e = 1.6 \times 10^{-19}$ C

$\mu_o = 4\pi x 10^{-7}$ TmA^{-1}

$$\frac{1}{4\pi \in_o} = 9x10^9 \frac{Nm^2}{C^2}$$

1. A ray of light, incident on an equilateral glass prism $\left(\mu_{glass} = \sqrt{3}\right)$ moves parallel to the base of the prism, inside it.
   What is the angle of incidence for this ray?

2. A capacitor, of capacitance C, is being charged up by connecting it across a d.c voltage source of voltage V. How do the conduction and displacement currents, in this set up compare with each other
   (a) during the charging up process?
   (b) after the capacitor gets fully charged?

3. Two electrically charged particles, having charges of different magnitude, when placed at a distance 'd' from each other, experience a force of attraction 'F'. These two particles are put in contact and again placed at the same distance from each other.
   What is the nature of new force between them?
   Is the magnitude of the force of interaction between them now more or less than F?

4. A resistance R is connected across a cell, of emf E, and internal resistance r. A potentionter now measures the p.d, between the terminals of the cell, as V. State the expression for 'r' in terms of E, V and R.

5. Show, on a graph, the nature of variation, of the (associated) de-Broglie wavelength (λ_B), with the accelerating potential (V), for an electron initially at rest.

6. The mean life of a radioactive sample is T_m. What is the time in which 50% of this sample would get decayed?

7. A narrow stream, of protons and deuterons, having the same momentum values, enter a region of a uniform magnetic field directed perpendicular to their common direction of motion. What would be the ratio of the radii of the circular paths, described by the protons and deuterons?

8. A proton, and an alpha particle, both initially at rest, are (suitably) accelerated so as to have the same kinetic energy. What is the ratio of their de - Broglie wavelengths?

9. Find the amount of work done in rotating an electric dipole, of dipole moment 3×10^{-8} Cm, from its position of stable equilibrium, to the position of unstable equilibrium, in a uniform electric field of intensity 10^4 N/C

10. Find the magnitude of the force on each segment of the wire shown below, if a magnetic field of 0.30 T, is applied parallel to AB and DE. Take the value of the current, flowing in the wire, as1 ampere.

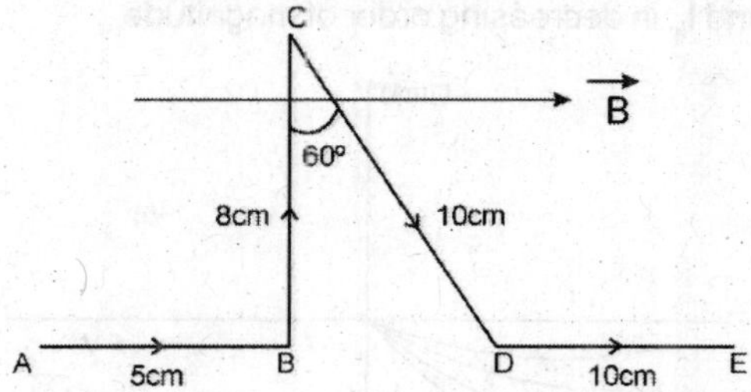

11. The intensity, at the central maxima (O) in a Young's double slit set up is I_o. If the distance OP equals one third of the fringe width of the pattern, show that the intensity, at point P, would equal $I_o/4$.

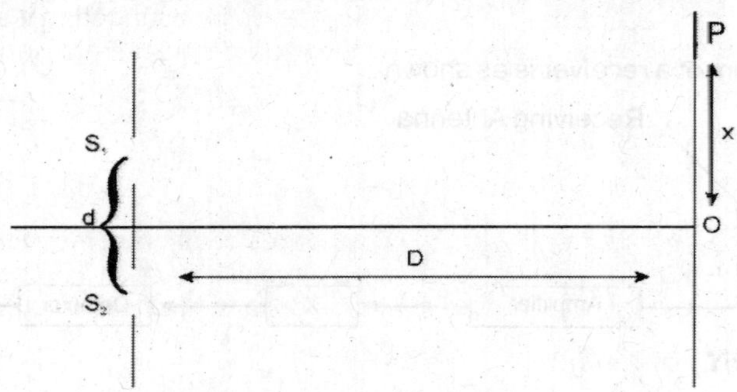

12. An electric heater is connected, turn by turn, to a d.c and a.c sources of equal voltages. Will the rate of heat production be same in the two cases? Explain.

13. Two students A and B prepare the following table about the electromagnetic waves. Rewrite this table in its corrected form.

	Direction of			Peak Value of	
Student	Electric field	Magnetic field	Propagation	Electric field	Magnetic field
A	Along X-axis	Along X-axis	Along Y-axis	E	B=cE
B	Along Y-axis	Along Z-axis	Along X-axis	E=cB	B

14. Light, of wavelength 2000 A°, falls on a metal surface of work function 4.2 eV. What is the kinetic energy (in eV) of (i) the fastest and (ii) the slowest photo electrons emitted from the surface?

15. Why is a photodiode operated in reverse bias mode? Figure shows reverse bias current, under different illumination intensities I_1, I_2, I_3 and I_4, for a given photodiode. Arrange the intensities I_1, I_2, I_3 and I_4, in decreasing order of magnitude.

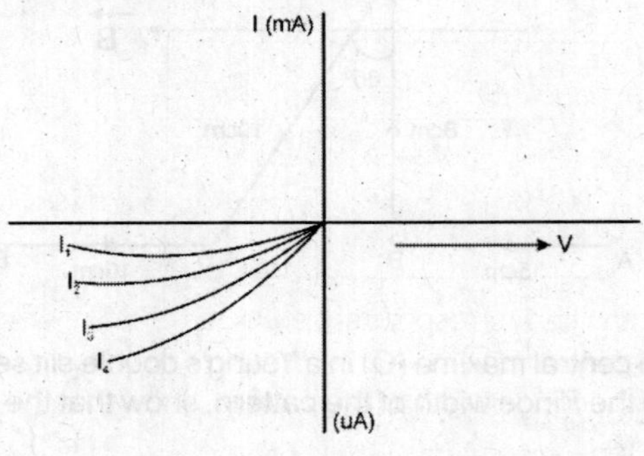

16. Block diagram of a receiver is as shown :-

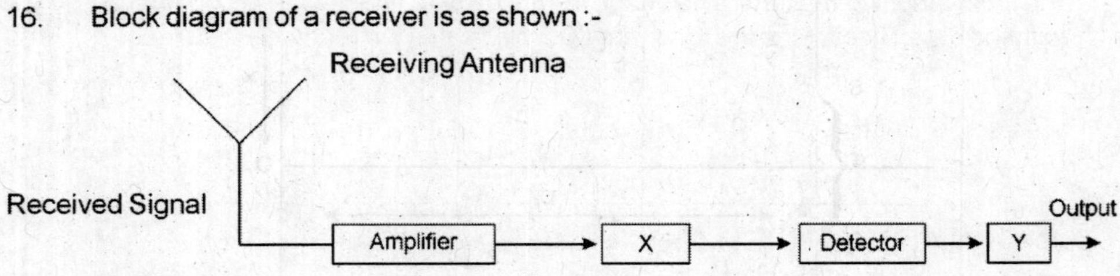

Identify X and Y.

State their function.

17. Name the physical quantity whose S.I Unit is becquerel (Bq): How is this quantity related to (i) disintegration constant, (ii) half life, and (iii) mean life of the radioactive element.

OR

Write the equations for the two types of β-decay. Why is it very difficult to detect the neutrino?

18. Draw the output wave form at X, using the given inputs A,B for the logic circuit shown below. Also identify the (equivalent) gate.

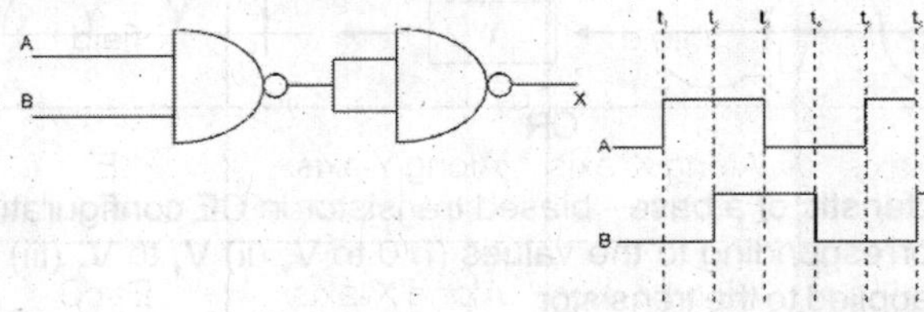

19. A resistor of resistance 400Ω, and a capacitor of reactance 200Ω, are connected in series to a 220V, 50Hz. a.c source. If the current in the circuit is 0.49 ampere find the (i) voltage across the resistor and capacitor (ii) value of inductance required so that voltage and current are in phase.

20. The energy levels of a hypothetical atom are as shown below. Which of the shown transitions will result in the emission of a photon of wavelength 275 nm?

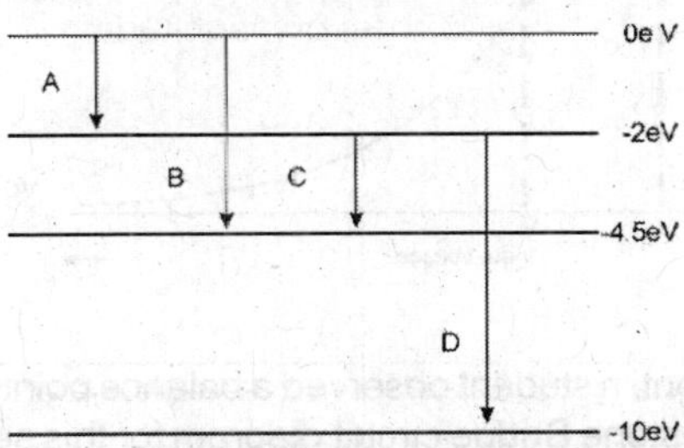

Which of these transition corresponds to emission of radiation of (i) maximum and (ii) minimum wavelength?

21. An object is placed at a distance of 15cm from a convex lens of focal length 10cm. On the other side of the lens, a convex mirror is placed such that its distance, from the lens, equals the focal length of the lens. The image formed by this combination is observed to coincide with the object itself. Find the focal length of the convex mirror.

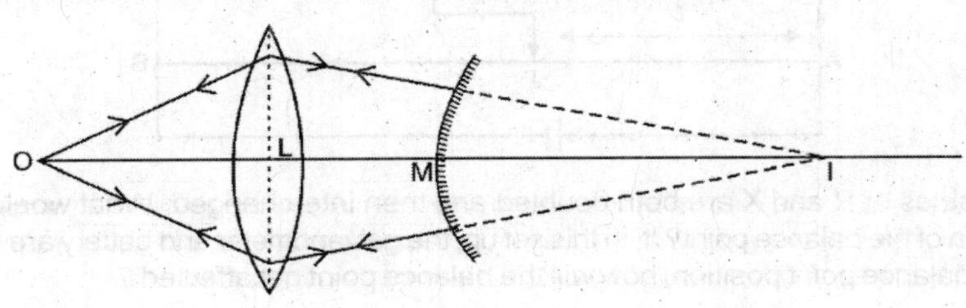

22. An a.c. signal is fed into two circuits X and Y and the corresponding output in the two cases have the waveforms shown below. Name the circuits X and Y. Also draw their detailed circuit diagrams.

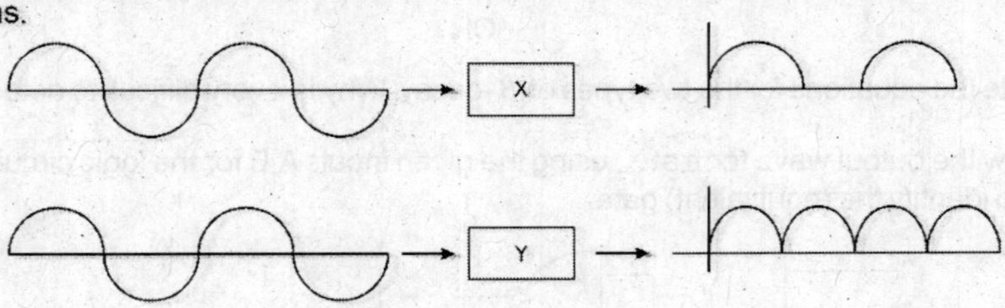

OR

The transfer characteristic of a base - biased transistor in CE configuration is as shown. Name the region corresponding to the values (i) 0 to V_1 (ii) V_1 to V_2 (iii) greater than V_2 of the input voltage applied to the transistor.

Identify the voltage range that should not be used if the transistor has to work as a switch. What is the practical use of transistor, when it is operated in this voltage range? Name the source that results in a higher energy of the output of a transistor operated in this range?

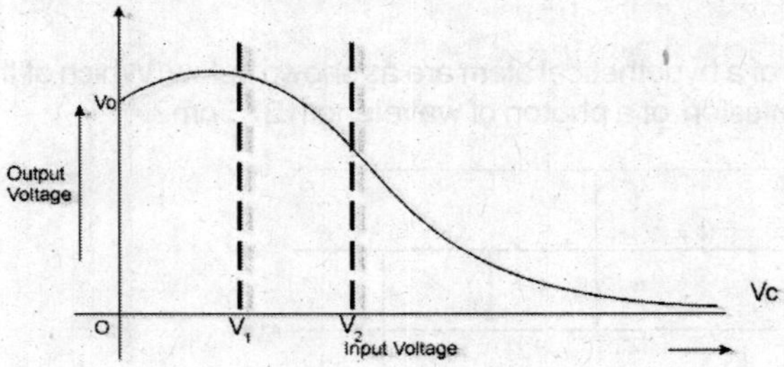

23. In the meter bridge experiment, a student observed a balance point at the point J, where AJ=l. Draw the equivalent Wheat stone Bridge circuit diagram for this set up.

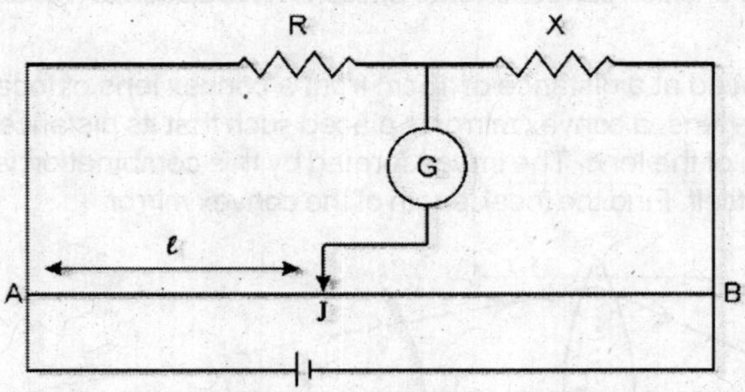

The values of R and X are both doubled and then interchanged. What would be the new position of the balance point? If, in this set up, the galvanometer and battery are interchanged at the balance point position, how will the balance point get affected ?

24. A rectangular loop and a circular loop are moving out of a magnetic field to a field free region with a constant velocity. It is given that the field is normal to the plane of both the loops.

(a) (b)

Draw the expected shape of the graphs, showing the variation of the flux, with time, in both the cases.

What is the cause of the difference in the shape of the two graphs?

25. Two convex lenses, of equal focal length, but of aperture A_1 and A_2 $(A_2<A_1)$, are used as the objective lenses in two astronomical telescopes having identical eyepieces.

Compare the ratio of their (i) resolving power (ii) (normal) magnifying power and (iii) intensity of images formed by them. Which one of the two telescopes should be preferred? Why?

26. Give reasons for the following:-

(i) For ground wave transmission, size of antenna (ℓ) should be comparable to wave-length of signal i.e $\ell \simeq \lambda/4$

(ii) Audio Signals, converted into an emwave, are not directly transmitted as such.

(iii) The amplitude of modulating signal is kept less than the amplitude of carrier wave.

27. Find the potential difference across each cell and the rate of energy dissipation in R

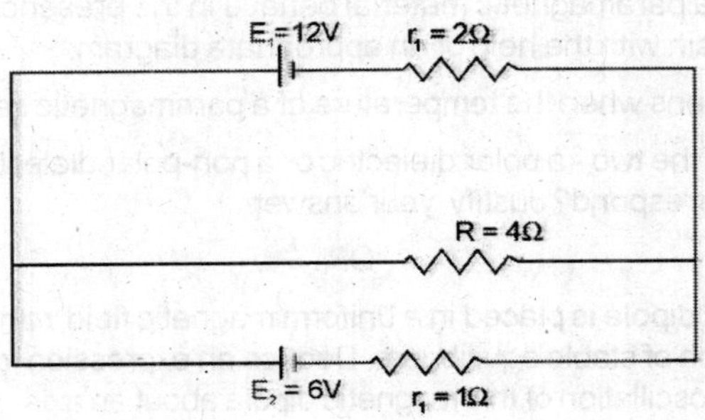

28. State the principle of a machine that can build up high voltages of the order of a few million volts. Also explain the construction and working of this machine.

OR

Three identical parallel plate (air) capacitors C_1, C_2 C_3 have capacitances C each. The space between their plates is now filled with dielectrics as shown. If all the three capacitors, still have equal capacitances, obtain the relation between the dielectric constants K, K_1, K_2, K_3 and K_4.

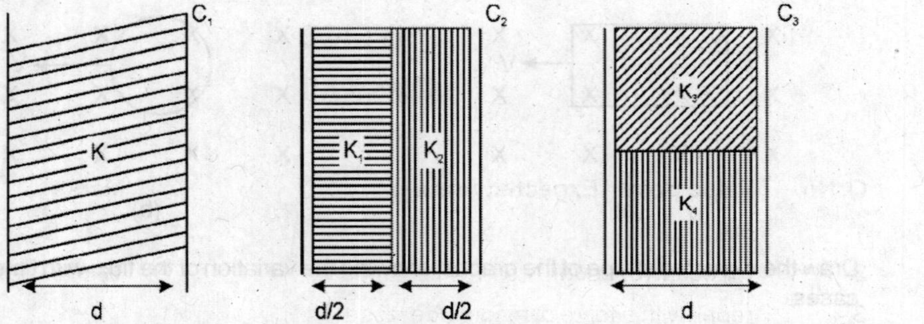

29. (a) A plane wave front approaches a plane surface separating two media. If medium one is (optically) denser and medium two is (optically) rarer, construct the refracted wave front using Huygens's principle.

Hence prove Snell's law.

(b) Draw the shape of the refracted wave front when a plane wave front is incident on (i) prism and (ii) convex mirror. Give a brief explanation for the construction.

OR

(a) State the essential condition for the diffraction of light to take place.

A parallel beam of monochromatic light falls normally on a narrow slit and light coming out of the slit is obtained on the screen. Derive an expression for the angular width of the central bright maxima obtained on the screen.

(b) 'Diffraction defines the limit of the ray optics'. Give a brief explanation of this statement.

30. (a) How does a paramagnetic material behave in the presence of an external magnetic field? Explain with the help of an appropriate diagram.

(b) What happens when the temperature of a paramagnetic sample is lowered?

(c) To which of the two - a polar dielectric or a non-polar dielectric - does a paramagnetic material correspond? Justify your answer.

OR

(a) A magnetic dipole is placed in a uniform magnetic field with its axis tilted with respect to its position of stable equilibrium. Deduce an expression for the time period of (small amplitude) oscillation of this magnetic dipola about an axis, passing through its centre and perpendicular to its plane.

(b) If this bar magnet is replaced by a combination of two similar bar magnets, placed over each other, how will the time period vary?

SAMPLE PAPER - I

MARKING SCHEME

(THEORY)

PHYSICS

Class XII

Q. No.	Value point / Expected Answer	Marks	Total
1.	60°	1	1
2.	(a) equal (b) equal	½ + ½	1
3.	repel, with a force of magnitude less than F	½ +½	1
4.	$r = \left(\frac{E}{V} - 1\right)R$	1	1
5.	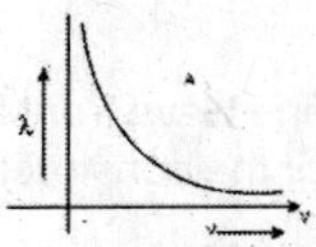	1	1
6.	Time needed = Half life = $0.693T_m$	1	1
7.	1:1	1	1
8.	2:1	1	1
9.	$w = pE(1 - \cos\theta)$	½	
	$\theta = 180^\circ$	½	
	$W = pE(-(-1))$		
	$= 2pE$		
	$= 2 \times 3.2 \times 10^{-8} \times 10^4 J$	½	
	$= 6.4 \times 10^{-4} J$		
	$= 0.64$ mJ	½	2
10.	AB and DE are II to the magnetic field		
	$F = 0 \; (F = IB\ell \sin\theta)$	½ + ½	
	$F_{BC} = I\ell_{BC} B \sin 90^\circ$	½	
	$= 0.024N$		
	$F_{CB} = I\ell_{CD} B \sin 30^\circ$	½	2
	$= 0.015$ N		

11. $x=\frac{1}{3}\beta$(given)

$\Rightarrow x=\frac{\lambda D}{3d}$ ½

$\Delta p=\frac{xd}{D}$

$\Rightarrow \Delta\Phi=\frac{2\pi\Delta p}{\lambda}=\frac{2\pi}{3}$ ½

$I=I_o\cos^2\frac{\Phi}{2}$ ½

$=I_o\cos^2\left(\frac{2\pi}{3}\right)=I_o/4$ ½ 2

12. The element of the heater is a coil having inductance L and resistance R. Hence, for a. c, its effective ½

resistance (impedance) $\left(=\sqrt{R^2+(\omega L)^2}\right)$ will be greater than its resistance R for d.c ½

Hence rate of heat production, for the same voltage, for a.c will be less. 1 2

13. Correction for student 'A'

Electric field	Magnetic field	Peak Value of	
		Electric Field	Magnetic Field
Along X-axis or Along Z-axis	Along Z-axis or Along X-axis	E	$B=\frac{E}{c}$

1

No Correction for student B 1 2

14. $E_{photon}=\Phi_o+\frac{1}{2}mV_{max}^2$ → for fastest electron

$\frac{1}{2}mV_{max}^2=\frac{hc}{\lambda}-\Phi_o$ ½

$$= \left[\frac{6.63 \times 10^{-34} \times 3 \times 10^{8}}{2000 \times 10^{-10} \times 1.6 \times 10^{-19}} - 4.2 \right] eV$$ ½

$= 1.99\ eV$ ½

The K.E of the slowest emitted electron is zero ½ 2

15. Fractional change, due to the photo effects, on the minority carrier dominated reverse bias current, is more easily measurable than the fractional change in the forward bias current. 1

$$I_4 > I_3 > I_2 > I_1$$ 1 2

16. X = IF Stage ½

Y = Amplifier ½

IF Stage - Carrier frequency is usually changed to a (standard) lower frequency ½

Amplifier - The detected signal may not be strong enough to be made use of and is hence required to be amplified. ½ 2

17. Activity or decay rate ½

$R = \lambda N$ | where λ is the decay constant ½

$R = \left(\frac{0.693}{T_{1/2}}\right) N$ | $T_{1/2}$ is the half life ½

$R = \left(\frac{1}{T_m}\right) N$ | T_m is the mean life ½ 2

OR

β^- decay $\quad {}^{A}_{Z}X \rightarrow {}^{A}_{Z+1}Y + {}^{0}_{-1}e + \bar{\nu}$ ½

β^+ decay $\quad {}^{A}_{Z}X \rightarrow {}^{A}_{Z-1}Y + {}^{0}_{+1}e + \nu$ ½

Neutrino is an uncharged particle which interacts very weakly with matter and hence escapes undetected. 1 2

18.

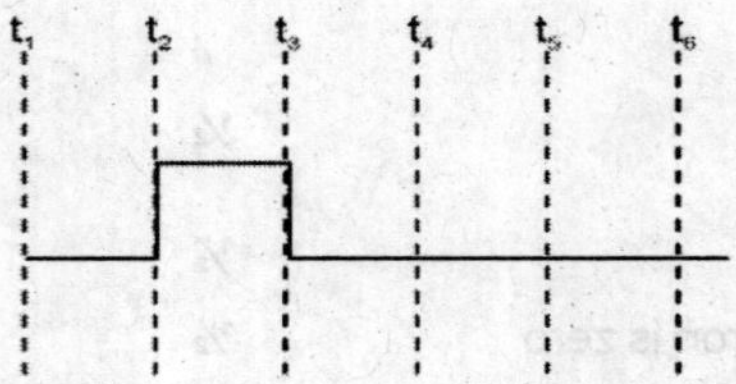

1 2

AND Gate 1

19. (i) $V_R = I R$

$= 0.49 \times 400V = 196\ V$ ½

$V_C = IX_C$

$= 0.49 \times 200V = 98V$ ½

(ii) V and I are in phase

$\Rightarrow \omega L = \frac{1}{\omega C}$

$\Rightarrow L = \frac{1}{\omega^2 C}$ 1

$= 0.64H$ 1 3

20. $E = \frac{hc}{\lambda}$ ½

$E = \left[\frac{6.63 \times 10^{-34} \times 3 \times 10^{8}}{275 \times 10^{-9} \times 1.6 \times 10^{-19}}\right] eV = 4.5eV$ 1

Therefore transition B corresponds to

the emission of a photon of $\lambda = 275nm$ ½

Transition A emits maximum wavelength ½

Transition D emits minimum wavelength ½ 3

21. The image of the combination

coincides with the object itself

This implies that 'I' is the centre

of curvature of the convex mirror ½

$\Rightarrow$ focal length of mirror

$f_m = \frac{MI}{2}$ ½

For lens $\frac{1}{f} = \frac{1}{v} - \frac{1}{u}$ ½

u = -15 cm

f = +10 cm ½

$\Rightarrow$ v = 30cm

$\Rightarrow$ MI = (30-10)cm =20cm ½

$f_m = \frac{MI}{2} = \frac{20}{2} = 10cm$ ½ 3

22. X - Half wave rectifier ½

Y - Full wave rectifier ½

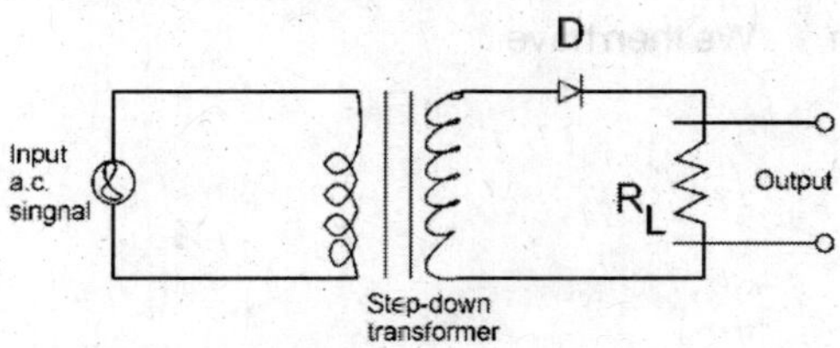

1

Circuit diagram of
Half wave rectifier

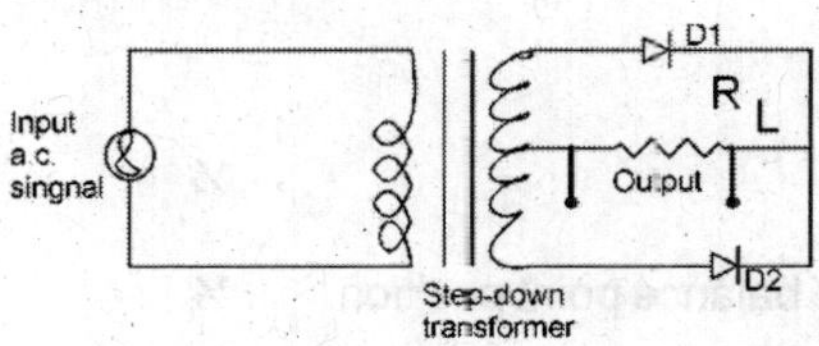

1

Circuit diagram of
Full wave rectifier 3

OR

(i) O to V_1 Cut off region ½

(ii) V_1 to V_2 Active region ½

(iii) greater than V_2 Saturation region

For transistor to work as a switch, it should not remain in active region, i.e., from V_1 to V_2 ½

Transistor works as an amplifier in the active region (V_1 to V_2) ½

The energy, for the higher a.c power at
the output is supplied by the biasing battery. 1 3

23.

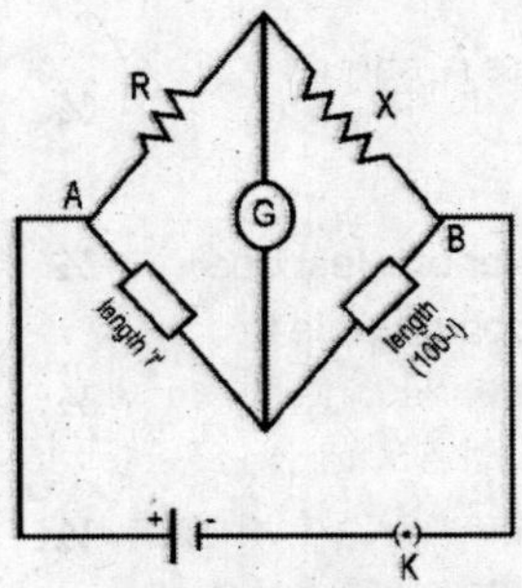

After doubling R and X, and interchanging, let the new balance point be at length ℓ^1. We then have

$$\frac{2X}{2R} = \frac{\ell^1}{\left(100-\ell^1\right)}$$ ½

Also $\frac{R}{X} = \frac{\ell}{100-\ell}$ ½

It fellows that

$\ell^1 = (100-\ell)$ ½

No there will be no change in the balance point position. ½ 3

24.

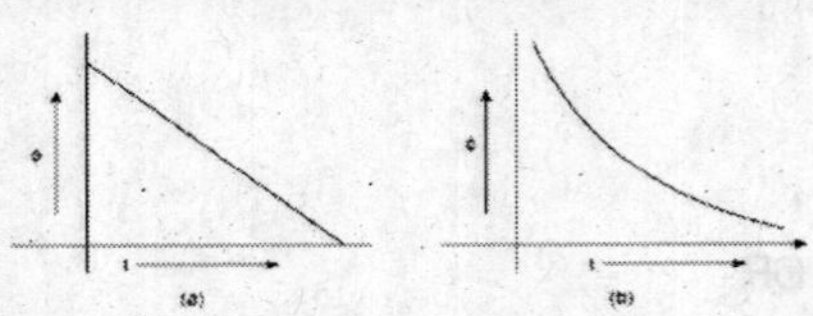

(a) (b)

1+1

In case of circular loop the rate of change of area during
its passage out of the field, is not a constant 1 3

25. $R.P = \frac{a}{1.22\lambda} \Rightarrow \frac{(R.P)_1}{(R.P)_2} = \frac{A_1}{A_2}$ ½

$M.P = \frac{f_o}{f_e}$ (normal adjustment)

= 1:1 ½

$$\frac{I_1}{I_2} = \left(\frac{A_1}{A_2}\right) > 1$$ ½

The telescope with objective of aperture A_1 should ½
be prefered for viewing as this would ½

(i) give a better resolution. ½

(ii) have a higher light gathering power of telescope. ½ 3

26. (i) When the size of the antenna is comparable to wave length of the signal the time variation of the signal is properly sensed by the antenna 1

(ii) An e.m. wave, of audio signal frequency, would have a very high wavelength. It would, therefore, need an antenna, whose size would be practically unattainable. 1

(iii) The amplitude of modulating signal is kept less than the amplitude of carrier wave to avoid distortion. 1 3

27. Applying Kirchoff's Laws

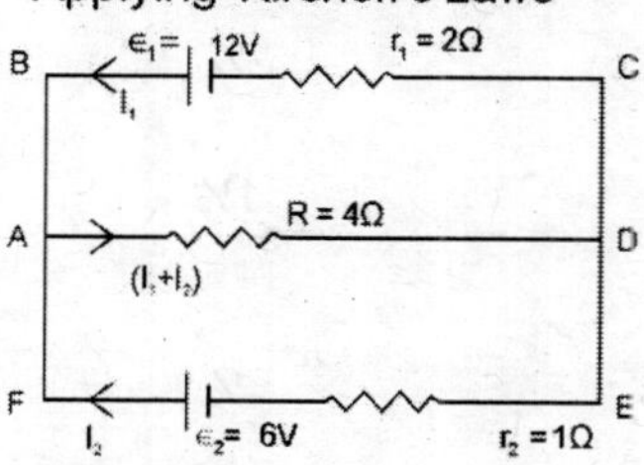

For closed loop ABCDA

$$12 = 4(I_1+I_2) + 2I_1$$

$$= 6I_1 + 4I_2 \qquad \text{(i)}$$ ½

For closed loop ADEFA

$$6 = 4(I_1+I_2) + I_2$$

$$= 4I_1 + 5I_2 \qquad \text{(ii)}$$ ½

Solving (i) & (ii)

$$I_1 = \frac{18}{7}\text{A and } \quad I_2 = \frac{-6}{7}\text{A}$$

p.d across R = V= (I_1+I_2) R

$$= \left(\frac{18-6}{7}\right) \times 4 \text{ volt} = \frac{48}{7} \text{volt}$$ ½

p.d across each cell = p.d across R ½

Energy dissipated in R = 4Ω

$$= (I_1 + I_2)^2 R = \left(\frac{12}{7}\right)^2 \text{ x4J}$$

$$= \frac{576\text{J}}{49} = 11.75\text{ J}$$ 1

28. The machine is the Van de - Graff generator ½

Principle of Vande graff generator 1½

construction 1

working 2

OR

New Capacitance of $C_1 = \frac{k\varepsilon_o A}{d}$ ½

New Capacitance of C_2

= Series Combination of two Capacitors ½

$$= \frac{\varepsilon_o A}{d}\left(\frac{2k_1k_2}{k_1+k_2}\right)$$ 1½

New Capacitance of C_3

= Parallel Combination of two Capacitors ½

$$\frac{\varepsilon_o A}{d}\left(\frac{k_3+k_4}{2}\right)$$ 1½

$$\therefore K = \frac{2k_1k_2}{k_1+k_2}$$

$$= \frac{k_3+k_4}{2}$$ ½ 5

29. (a) Construction of refracted wave front 1

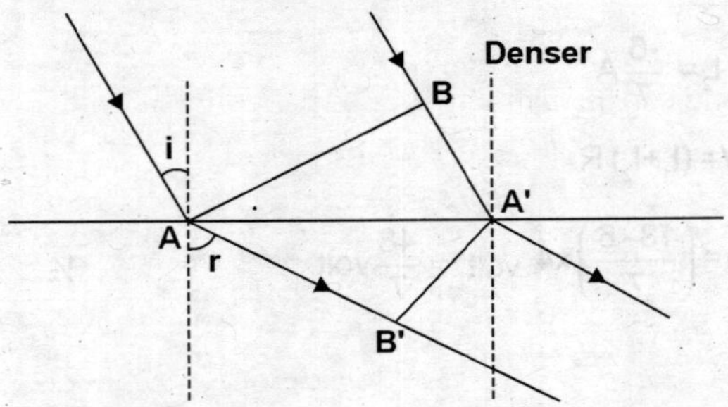

$\sin r = \dfrac{c_1 t}{\text{base}}$ ½

$\sin i = \dfrac{c_2 t}{\text{base}}$ ½

$\dfrac{\sin i}{\sin r} = \dfrac{c_1}{c_2}$ ½

or

${}_r^d\mu = \dfrac{c_1}{c_2}$ ½

(b)

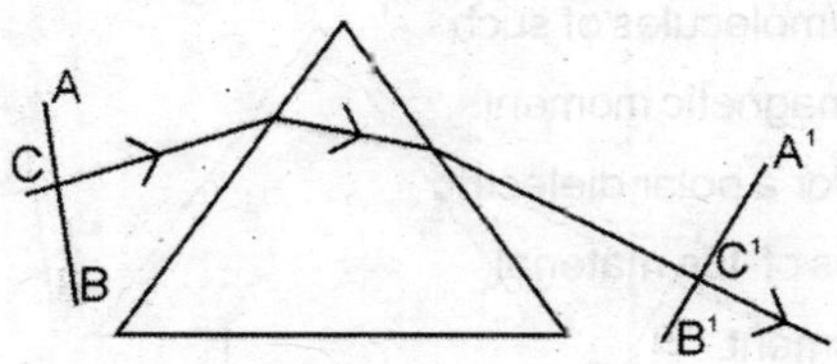

½

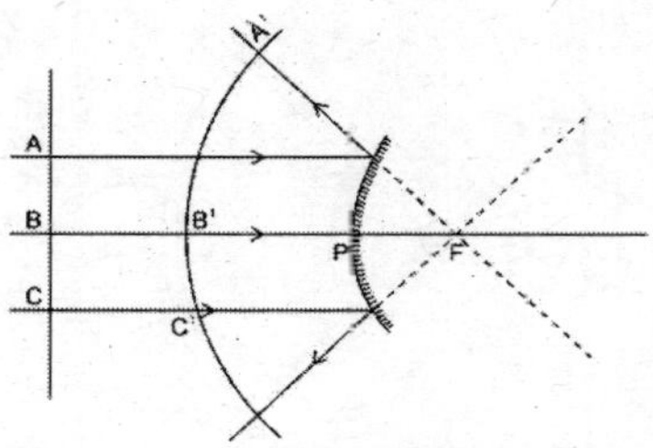

½

Explanation - time taken by any disturbance to travel from incident wave front to the refracted wave front is same 1

5

OR

Essential Condition for diffraction - size of aperture / obstacle comparable to the wave length of light 1

Derivation of angular width of central maxima = $\left(\dfrac{\lambda}{a}\right)$ 2

Explanation of the limit

$\lambda \to o$ for ray optics to be valid 2 5

30. (a) Explanation of parallel alingment of atomic dipoles. Net dipole moment non - zero 2½

(b) As the temprature is lowered, the magnetisation increases until it reaches the saturation value at which point all the dipoles are perfectly alinged with the field 1

(c) Paramagnetic material correspond to a polar dielectric. ½

This is because the atoms/molecules of such a material have non-zero magnetic moment. A similar statement holds for a polar dielectric where the atoms/molecules of the material, have a non-zero dipole moment. 1 5

OR

(a)

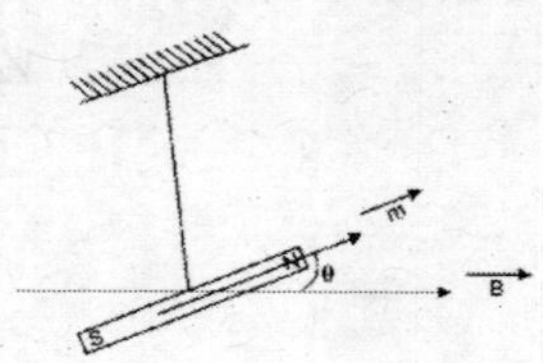

$\sin\theta \simeq \theta$

$\therefore \tau = m B \sin\theta \simeq m\ B\ \sin\theta$

This torque is in the nature of a restoring torque ½

Hence equation of motion, for the oscillatory motion, of the magnet is

$I\frac{d^2\theta}{dt^2} \simeq -mB\theta$ ½

This is the equaion of a S.H.M

$$\frac{d^2\theta}{dt^2} + \omega^2\theta = 0$$

where $\omega^2 = \frac{mB}{I}$ ½

Hence the time period of oscillaiton of the magnet,

is given by

$$T = \frac{2\pi}{\omega}$$

$$= 2\pi\sqrt{\frac{I}{mB}}$$ 1

(b)

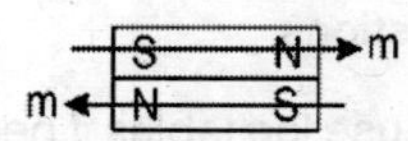

$m_{net} = o$, $I_{net} = 2I$ ½

$\Rightarrow T \to \infty$ ½

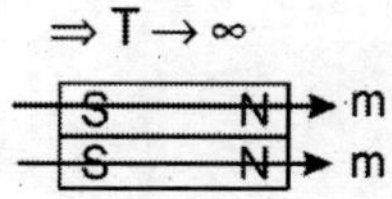

$m_{net} = 2m$, ½

$I_{net} = 2I$

$\Rightarrow$ T will remain same ½ 5

SAMPLE PAPER – II
PHYSICS (THEORY)
Class XII

Time: 3hours **M.M.: 70**

General Instructions:

(i) All questions are compulsory.

(ii) There are 30 questions in total. Questions 1 to 8 are very short answer type and carry one mark each.

(iii) Questions 9 to 18 carry two marks each, questions 19 to 27 carry three marks each and questions 28 to 30 carry five marks each.

(iv) There is no overall choice. However, an internal choice has been provided in one question of two marks, one question of three marks and three question of five marks. You have to attempt only one of the choice in such questions.

(v) Use of calculators is not permitted. However, you may use log tables if necessary.

(vi) You may use the following values of physical constants, wherever necessary.

$c = 3x10^8 m/s$

$h=6.63 \times 10^{-34} Js$

$e= 1.6x10^{-19}C$

$\mu_o = 4\pi x 10^{-7} Tm A^{-1}$

$$\frac{1}{4\pi\varepsilon_o} = 9x10^9 \frac{Nm^2}{C^2}$$

1. The velocity of propagation (in vaccum) and the frequency of (i) x rays and (ii) radio waves are denoted by (ϑ_x, n_x) and (ϑ_R, n_R) respectively.

   How do the values of

   (a) ϑ_x and ϑ_R

   (b) n_x and n_R

   compare with each other?

2. How will the intensity of maxima and minima, in the Young's double slit experiment change, if one of the two slits is covered by a transparent paper which transmits only half of the light intensity?

3. The most probable kinetic energy of thermal neutrons at a temperature of T kelvin, may be taken as equal to kT, where k is Boltzmann constant. Taking the mass of a neutron and its associated de-Broglie wavelength as m and λ_B respectively, state the dependence of λ_B on m and T.

4. The short wavelength limits of the Lyman, Paschen and Balmer Series, in the hydrogen spectrum, are denoted by λ_L , λ_P and λ_B respectively. Arrange these wavelengths in increasing order.

5. Charges of magnitudes 2 Q & - Q are located at points (a,o,o) and (4a,o,o). Find the ratio of the flux of electric field, due to these charges, through concentric spheres of radii 2a and 8a centered at the origin.

6. A parallel combination of two cells of Emf's E_1 & E_2 ,and internal resistances r_1 and r_2 ,is used to supply current to a load of resistance R. Write the expression for the current through the load in terms of E_1, E_2 r_1 and r_2.

7.

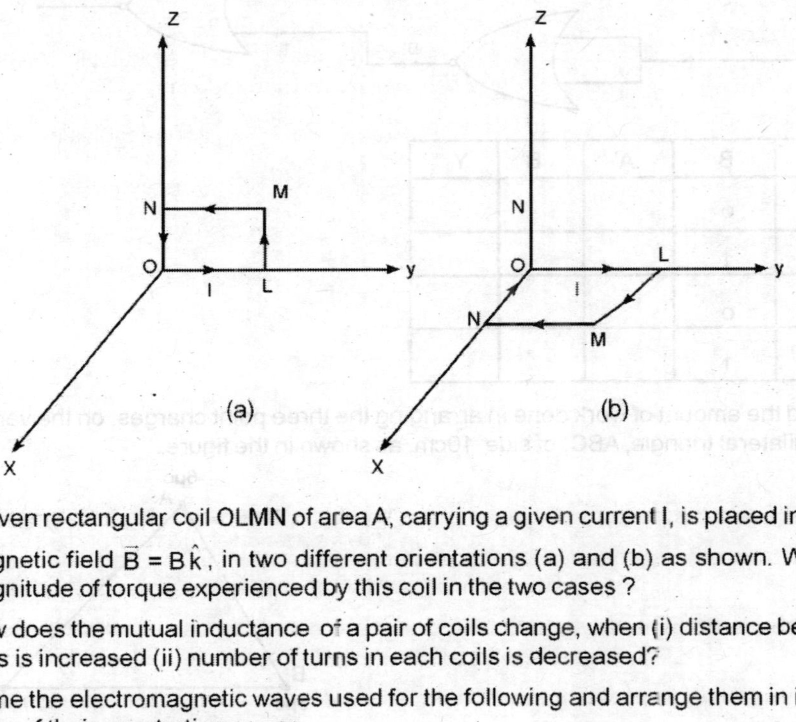

A given rectangular coil OLMN of area A, carrying a given current I, is placed in a uniform magnetic field $\bar{B} = B\hat{k}$, in two different orientations (a) and (b) as shown. What is the magnitude of torque experienced by this coil in the two cases ?

8. How does the mutual inductance of a pair of coils change, when (i) distance between the coils is increased (ii) number of turns in each coils is decreased?

9. Name the electromagnetic waves used for the following and arrange them in increasing order of their penetrating power.

(a) Water purification

(b) Remote Sensing

(c) Treatment of cancer

10. A light beam is incident on the boundary between two transparent media. At a particular angle of incidence the reflected ray is perpendicular to the refracted ray. Obtain an expression for this angle of incidence. Does this angle depend on the wavelength of light used?

11. Calculate the half life period of a radioactive substance if its activity drops to $\frac{1}{16}$ th of its initial value in 30 years.

12. Inputs A & B are applied to the logic gate set up as shown below. Complete the truth table given below, and name the equivalent gate formed by this 'set-up'.

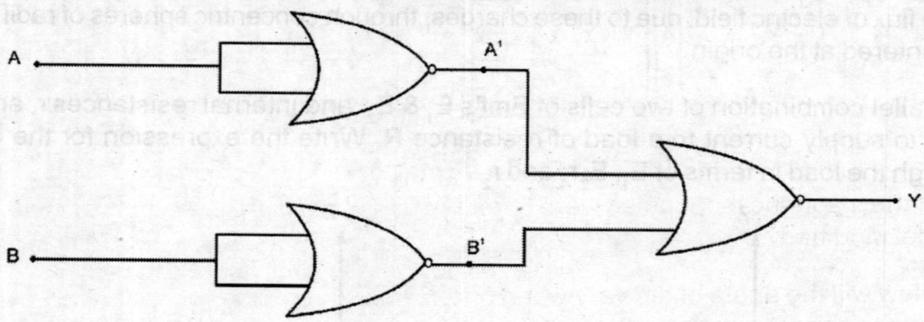

A	B	A'	B'	Y
o	o			
o	1			
1	o			
1	1			

13. Find the amount of work done in arranging the three point charges, on the vertices of an equilateral triangle, ABC, of side 10cm, as shown in the figure.

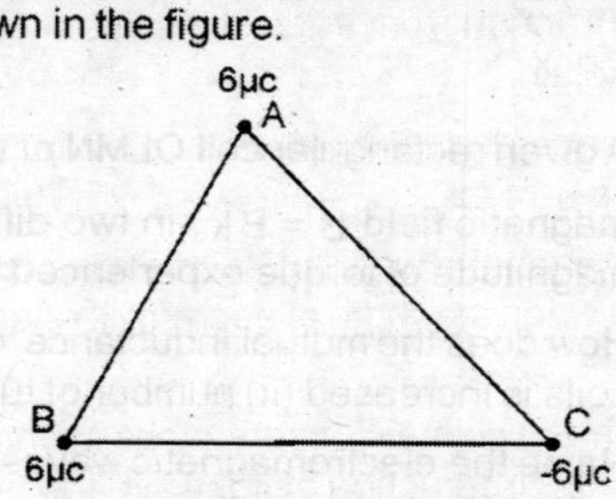

14. Write the relation for current sensitivity and voltage sensitivity of a moving coil galvanometer. Using these relations, explain the fact that increasing the current sensitivity may not necessary increase the voltage sensitivity.

OR

Using the relation for potential energy of a current carrying planar loop, in a uniform magnetic field, obtain the expression for the work done in moving the planar loop from its unstable (equilibrium) position to its stable (equilibrium) position.

15. A straight conductor PQ is moving in a uniform and time independent magnetic field as shown below. Assuming that there is no loss of energy due to friction, deduce an expression for the power spent by an external agency to move the arm PQ, with a constant speed v, in terms of the magnetic field, the length PQ, and speed v.

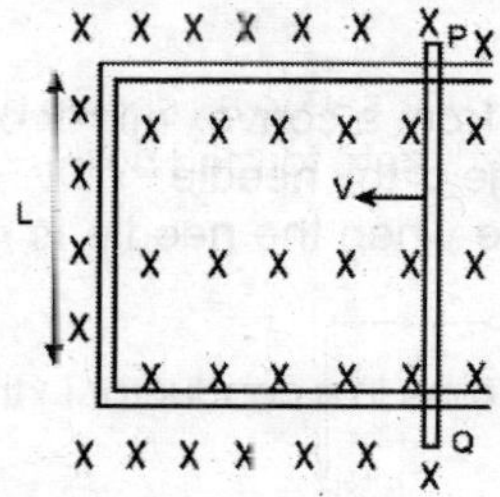

16. (a) If the magnetic monopoles were to exist, how would the Gauss's law of magnetism get modified?

(b) How will the angle of dip vary when one goes from a place, where the acceleration due to gravity is maximum, to a place where it is minimum, on the surface of earth?

17. A long solenoid, with 20 turns per cm, has a small loop of area $4cm^2$ placed inside the solenoid normal to its axis. If the current carried by the solenoid changes steadily from 4A to 6A in 0.2 second, what is the (average) induced emf in the loop while the current is changing?

18. Draw a plot of the variation of 'amplitude' versus 'ω' for an amplitude modulated wave. Hence explain the need for keeping the broadcast frequencies sufficiently spaced out?

19. In the double slit experiment, the pattern on the screen is actually a superposition of single slit diffraction from each slit and the double slit interference pattern. In what way is the diffraction from each slit related to the interference pattern in a double slit experiment? Explain.

Hence draw the intensity distribution curve, obtained on the screen, in the double slit experiment

(i) when the width of each slit is comparable to wavelength of monochromatic light used
(ii) when the width of each slit is relatively large compared to wave length of monochromatic light.

20. Which two main observations in photoelectricity led Einstein to suggest the photon theory for the interaction of light with the free electrons in a metal? Obtain an expression for the threshold frequency for photoelectric emission in terms of the work function of the metal.

21. Derive the expression for the radius of the nth orbit of hydrogen atom using Bohr's postulates. Show graphically the (nature of) variation of the radius of orbit with the principal quantum number, n.

OR

What is the frequency of radiation emitted when a hydrogen atom de-excites from level x to level (x-1).? For large x, show that this frequency equals the classical frequency of revolution of the electron in the orbit.

22. State various modes of propagation of electromagnetic waves. Explain using a proper diagram, the mode of propagation used in the frequency range from a few MHz upto 40MHz.

23. A 5cm long needle is placed 10cm from a convex mirror of focal length 40cm. Find the position, nature and size of the image of the needle.
What happens to the size of image when the needle is moved farther away from the mirror?

24. Write the nature of path of free electrons in a conductor in the

(i) presence of electric field

(ii) absence of electric field.

Between two successive collisions each free electron acquires a velocity from o to V where $V=\frac{eE}{m}\tau$. What is the average velocity of a free electron in the presence of an electric field? Do all electrons have the same average velocity?
How does this average velocity of the free electrons, in the presence of an electric field, vary with temperature?

25. A wire AB is carrying a current of 12A and is lying on the table. Another wire CD, carrying a current of 5A, is arranged just above AB at a height of 1mm. What should be the weight, per unit length of this wire so that CD remains suspended at its position? Indicate the direction of current in CD and the nature of force between the two wires.

26. A series LCR circuit is connected to an a-c source of voltage V and angular frequency ω. When only the capacitor is removed, the current lags behind the voltage by a phase angle 'ϕ' and when only the inductor is removed, the current leads the voltage by the same phase angle. Find the current flowing and the average power dissipated in the LCR circuit.

27. A potentiometer circuit is set up as shown. The potential gradient across the potentiometer wire is 0.025 V/cm and the ammeter present in the circuit reads 0.1 A, when the two way key is completely switched off. The balance points, when the key between the terminals (i) 1 & 2 (ii) 1 & 3, is plugged in, are found to be at lengths 40cm and 100cm respectively. Find the values of R and X.

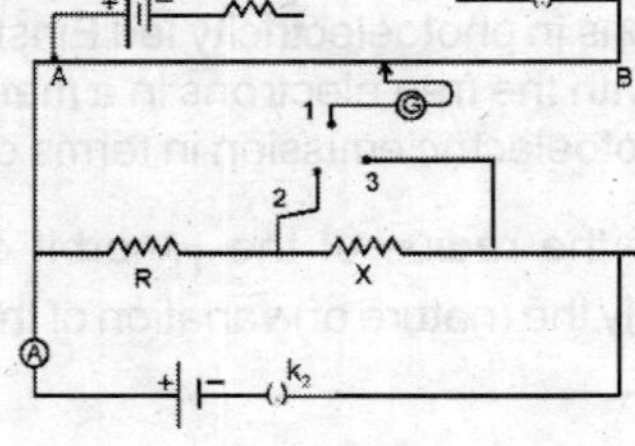

28. Find the expression for the electric field intensity, and the electric potential, due to a dipole at a point on the equiatorial line. Would the electric field be necessarily zero at a point where the electric potential is zero? Give an example to illustrate your answer.

OR

Find the expression for the capacitance of a parallel plate capacitor of area A and plate separation d if (i) a dielectric slab of thickness t, and (ii) a metallic slab of thickness t, where (t<d) are introduced one by one between the plates of the capacitor. In which case would the capacitance be more and why?

29. Draw a ray diagram for a compound microscope. Derive an expression for the magnifying power when the final image is formed at the least distance of distinct vision. State the expression for the magnifying power when the image is formed at infinity. Why is the focal length of the objective lens of a compound microscope kept quite small?

OR

Derive the lens formula giving the relation between u, v and f for a thin convex lens. Define the term 'linear magnification' and draw a graph showing the variation of linear mangin fication with image distance for a thin convex lens. How can this graph be used for finding the focal length of the lens?

30. The set up, shown below, can produce an a-c output without any external input signal. Identify the components X and Y of this set up. Draw the circuit diagram for this set up and briefly describe its working.

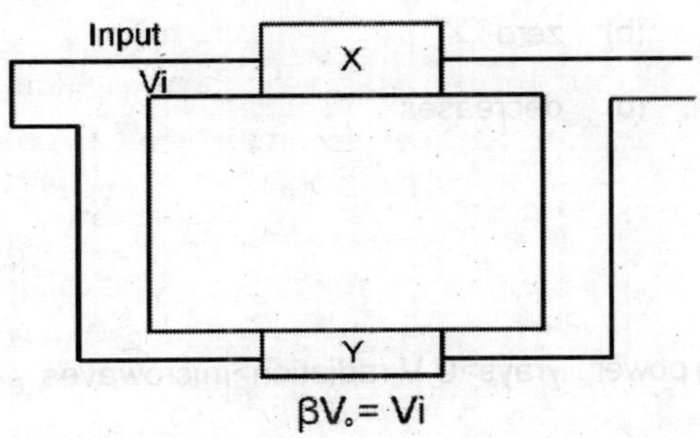

OR

Explain the formation of the depletion region for a P-N Juntion. How does the width of this region change when the junction is

(i) forward biased, and (ii) reverse based.

(iii) How does an increase in the doping concentration affect the width of the depletion region?

SAMPLE PAPER - II
MARKING SCHEME
(THEORY)
PHYSICS
Class XII

Q No.	Value point / expected points	Marks	Total
1.	(a) equal (b) $n_X > n_R$	½ + ½	1
2.	Intensity of maxima decreases and that of minima increases	½ + ½	1
3.	$\lambda_B \alpha \frac{1}{\sqrt{mT}}$	1	1
4.	$\lambda_L, \lambda_B, \lambda_P$.		1
5.	2 : 1	1	
6.	$I = \frac{E_1 r_2 + E_2 r_1}{R\,(r_1 + r_2) + r_1 r_2}$	1	1
7.	(a) BIA (b) zero	½ + ½	1
8.	(a) decreases (b) decreases	½ + ½	1
9.	(a) U. V radiation	½	
	(b) Microwaves	½	
	(c) γ rays	½	
	In order of penetrating power : γrays>U.V radiation>microwaves	½	2
10.	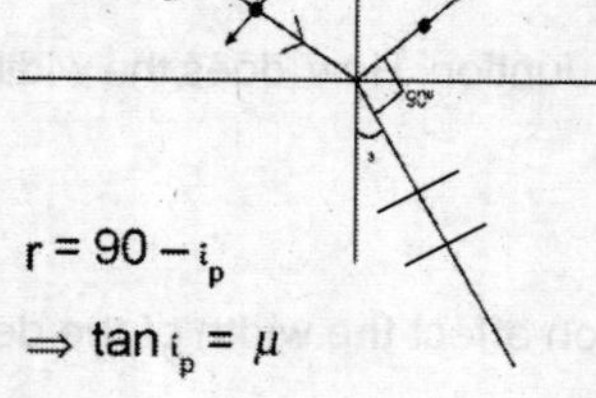	½	
	$r = 90 - i_p$	½	
	$\Rightarrow \tan i_p = \mu$	½	
	yes ; $\left(\mu \alpha \frac{1}{\lambda}\right)$	½	2

		Marks	Total
11.	$N = \frac{N_o}{16}$ where t = 30 years	½	
	$N = N_o\left(\frac{1}{2}\right)^n$		
	$\frac{N}{No} = \left(\frac{1}{2}\right)^4$	½	
	No. of half lives $n = 4 = \frac{\text{Time of disintegration}}{\text{half life period}}$	½	
	$\Rightarrow \frac{30\text{years}}{4} = \text{half life period}$		2
	$\Rightarrow$ half life period = 7.5 years	½	
12.	A' B' Y 1 1 0 1 0 0 0 1 0 0 0 1	1	
	AND Gate	1	2
13.	P.E of a pair of charges :		
	$U = \frac{kq_1q_2}{r}$	½	
	∵ Total work done W		
	$= W_1 + W_2 + W_3$		
	Calculation of W and result	½	
	(in J) W = -3.24 J	1	2
14.	Relation for Current Sensitivity	½	
	Relation for Voltage Sensitivity	½	
	Explantion	1	2
	OR		
	Relation for P.E	½	
	Calculation of work done		
	Work done = -2mB		
	= -2IA B	1½	2

15. $P = Fv$ ½

$= BI\ell v$ ½

$= B\left(\frac{BV\ell}{R}\right)\ell v$ ½

$= \frac{B^2v^2\ell^2}{R}$ ½ 2

16. (a) $\oint \vec{B}.\vec{ds} = \mu_\circ q_m$ where q_m is the net (magnetic) charge enclosed by the closed surface. 1

(b) from 90° to 0° 1 2

17. $\phi = \vec{B}.\vec{A} = \mu_\circ nIA$ ½

$|E| = \frac{d\phi}{dt} = \frac{d}{dt}(\mu_o nIA) = \mu_\circ nA\frac{dI}{dt}$ ½

Substituting values, we get

$E = 50.24 \times 10^{-5}$ V 1

18. 1

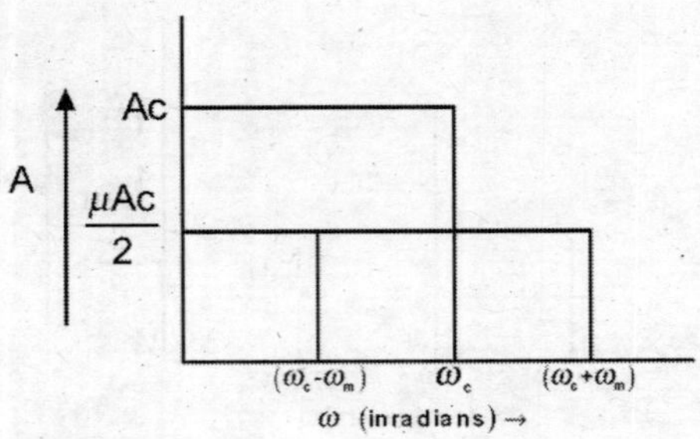

When the broadcast frequencies are spaced out, the different stations can operate without interference. 1

19. The pattern shows a broader diffraction peak in which there appear several fringes of smaller width due to the double slit interference.

The number of interference fringes depends upon the ratio of the distance between the two slits to the width of a slit.

In the limit of width of a slit becoming very small, the diffraction pattern will become very flat and we will observe the two slit interference pattern. 1

(i) 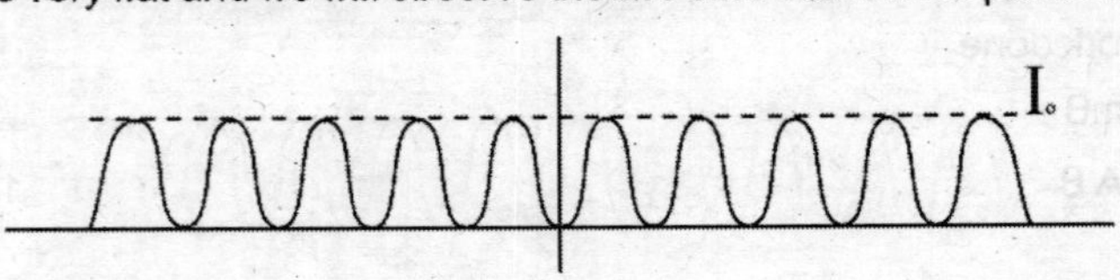

1

(ii) 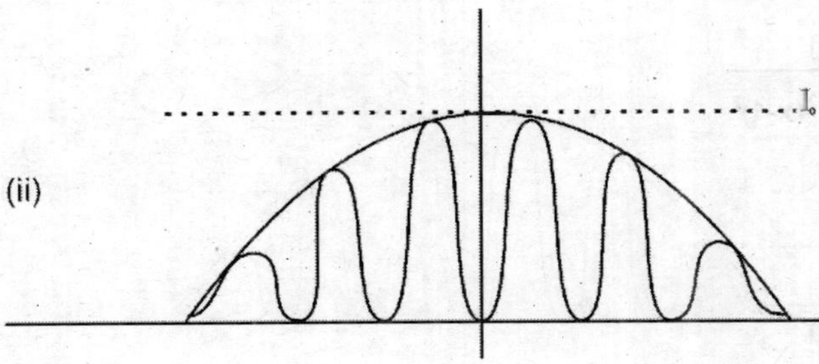

1 3

20. Two main observations :-

(i) The maximum kinetic energy of the emitted photoelectrons is independent of the intensity of light. 1

(ii) For each photoemitter, there exist a threshold frequency (of incident light) below which no emission takes place. 1

Relation $h\vartheta = \phi_{\circ} + \frac{1}{2}mV^2 \max$

$\Rightarrow h\vartheta_{\circ} = \phi_{\circ}$ when $V_{max} = O$ 1 3

21. $\frac{mV^2}{r} = \frac{Kq_1q_2}{r^2}$ ½

$L = mVr = \frac{nh}{2\pi}$ ½

$r = \frac{n^2h^2\mathcal{E}_o}{\pi mZe^2}$ 1

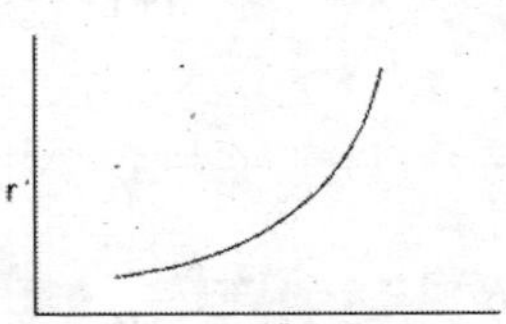

1 3

OR

$$\vartheta = \frac{me^4}{(4\pi)^3 \mathcal{E}_o{}^2}\left[\frac{1}{(x-1)^2} - \frac{1}{x^2}\right]$$ ½

$$=\frac{me^4(2x-1)}{(4\pi)^3\mathcal{E}_o^2\left(\frac{h}{2\pi}\right)x^2(x-1)^2}$$ ½

for large x,

$$\upsilon=\frac{me^4}{32\pi^3\mathcal{E}_o^2\left(\frac{h}{2\pi}\right)^3x^3}$$ ½

orbital frequency $\upsilon=\frac{V}{2\pi r}$ ½

where $V=\frac{nh}{2\pi mr}$

and $r=\frac{4\pi\varepsilon_o\left(\frac{h}{2\pi}\right)^2x^2}{me^2}$ ½

This leads to -

$$\upsilon=\frac{me^4}{32\pi^3\varepsilon_o^2\left(\frac{h}{2\pi}\right)^3x^3}$$ ½ 3

which is same as ϑ for large x

22. (a) Different modes of propagation. 1

(b) mode of propagation used–sky wave propagation (explanation and diagram). 1+1 3

23. u = -10cm

f = + 40cm ½

$\frac{1}{f}=\frac{1}{v}+\frac{1}{u}$ ½

v = 8cm ½

$m=\frac{-v}{u}=0.8<1$ ½

When the needle is farther away from the convex mirror, its image moves farther behind the mirror towards the focus and its size goes on decreasing.

When it is far off, it appears almost as a point image at the focus. 1 3

24. (i) Curved path ½

(ii) Straight lines ½

(iii) average velocity $= \frac{eE}{m}\tau$ ½

(iv) No, there is a variation in the velocity for individual electrons. ½

(v) Explanation 1 3

25. As magnetic force is balanced by the weight of wire

$$\frac{W}{\ell} = \frac{F}{\ell} = \frac{\mu_o i_1 i_2}{2\pi r}$$ 1

Substitution and result

$$\frac{W}{\ell} = 12 \times 10^{-2} \text{ N/m}$$ 1

Direction of current in CD is opposite to that of in AB ½

Nature of force - repulsive ½ 3

26. $\tan \phi = \frac{X_L - X_C}{R}$

$$\frac{\omega L - \frac{1}{\omega C}}{R}$$

When capacitor is removed

$\tan \phi = \frac{\omega L}{R}$ ½

When inductor is removed

$\tan \phi = \frac{-\frac{1}{\omega C}}{R}$ ½

— ve sign indicates that current leads the voltage

$\therefore \omega L = \dfrac{1}{\omega C}$ ½

$\omega = \dfrac{1}{\sqrt{LC}}$ ½

$\Rightarrow$ LCR circuit is in resonance.

$i_{rms} = \dfrac{V_{eff}}{R}$ ½

Pav = $V_{rms}\ i_{rms}$ ½ 3

V_{rms}^2/R

27. $R \times 0.1 = k\ell_1$ and $\dfrac{R}{R+X} = \dfrac{\ell_1}{\ell_2}$ 1

Solving we get

Value of R	=	10 Ω	1	
Value of X	=	15 Ω	1	3

28. Derivation $\vec{E} = \dfrac{K\,\vec{P}}{\left(r^2 + a^2\right)^{3/2}}$ 2½

Derivation of V = O 1½

No, illustrative example ½ + ½ 5

OR

Derivation of Capacitance of parallel plate capacitor

(i) with dielectric slab 2

(ii) with metal slab 2

Reason 1 5

29. Ray diagram of compound microscope 1

Derivation of magnifying power 2

Formula of magnifying power for image formed at infinity 1

Reason 1 5

OR

Ray diagram of thin convex lens ½

	Derivation of $\frac{1}{f}=\frac{1}{v}-\frac{1}{u}$	2	
	Definition of m	½	
	graph	1	
	Finding focal length from graph	1	5
30.	X - Amplifier circuit	½	
	Y - Feed back circuit	½	
	Circuit Diagram	2	
	Working	2	5
	OR		
	Formation of Depletion layer	2	
	Explanation of each case	2	
	Effect of increase in doping concentration on width of depletion region	1	5

SAMPLE PAPER – III
PHYSICS (THEORY)
Class XII

Time: 3hours **M.M.: 70**

General Instruction:

(i) All questions are compulsory

(ii) There are 30 questions in total. Questions 1 to 8 are very short answer type and carry one mark each.

(iii) Questions 9 to18 carry two marks each, questions 19 to 27 carry three marks each and questions 28 to 30 carry five marks each.

(iv) There is no overall choice. However, an internal choice has been provided in one question of two marks, one question of three marks and all the questions of five marks. You have to attempt only one of the given choices in such questions.

(v) Use of calculators is not permitted. You may, however, use log tables if necessary. You may use the following values of physical constants wherever necessary:

$c = 3 \times 10^8\ ms^{-1}$

$h = 6.63 \times 10^{-34} Js$

$e = 1.6 \times 10^{-19}\ C$

$\mu_o = 4\pi \times 10^{-7}\ TmA^{-1}$

$$\frac{1}{4\pi\varepsilon_o} = 9x10^9 \frac{Nm^2}{C^2}$$

1. Let the wavelengths of the electromagnetic waves used quite often for

(i) killing germs in household water purifiers.

(ii) remote sensing

(iii) treatment of cancer

be labelled as λ_1, λ_2 and λ_3. Arrange λ_1, λ_2 and λ_3 in increasing order.

2. The motion of a copper plate is damped when it is allowed to oscillate between the pole pieces of a magnet. State the cause of this damping.

3. Two circular loops, of radii r and 2r, have currents I and I/2 flowing through them in clockwise and anticlockwise sense respectively. If their equivalent magnetic moments are $\overline{M_1}$ and $\overline{M_2}$ respectively, state the relation between $\overline{M_1}$ and $\overline{M_2}$.

4. What is the equivalent capacitance, C, of the five capacitors, connected as shown ?

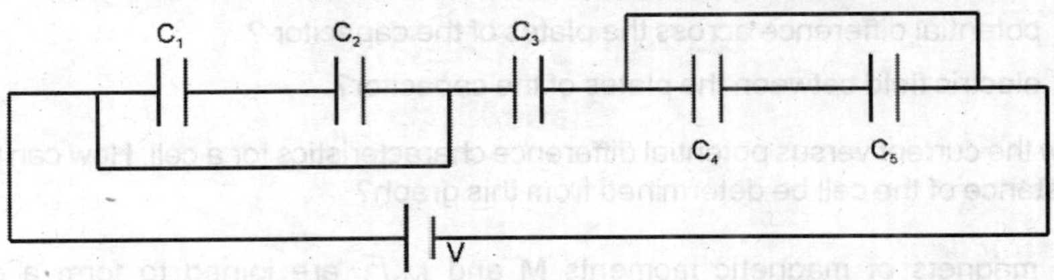

5. A plane wave front, of width X, is incident on an air-water interface and the corresponding refracted wavefront has a width Z as shown. Express the refractive index of air with respect to water, in terms of the dimension shown.

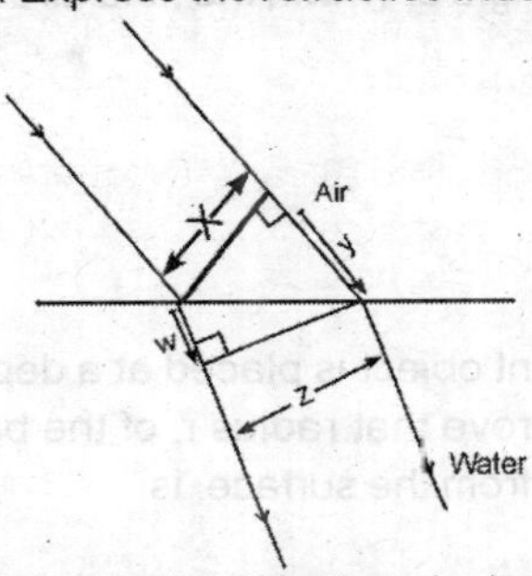

6. A device X can convert one form of energy into another. Another device Y can be regarded as a combination of a transmitter and a receiver. Name the devices X and Y.

7. The maximum velocity of electrons, emitted from a metal surface of negligible work function, is 'V', when frequency of light falling on it is 'f'. What will be the maximum velocity when the incident light frequency is made '4f' ?

8. An audio signal of frequency υ_a is to be transimitted as an electromagnetic wave

(i) directly as such,

(ii) through its use as the modulating signal on a carrier wave of frequency υ_c.

State the ratio of the size of the transmitting antenna, that can properly sense the time variation of the signal, in terms of υ_a and υ_c.

9. A plane electromagnetic wave, of angular frequency ω, is propagating with velocity c along the Z-axis. Write the vector equations, of oscillating electric and magnetic fields, and show these fields diagramatically.

10. Justify that the electrostatic potential is constant throughout the volume of a charged conductor and has the same value on its surface as inside it.

OR

A capacitor is charged with a battery and then its plate separation is increased without disconnecting the battery. What will be the change in

(a) charge stored in the capacitor?

(b) energy stored in the capacitor?

(c) potential difference across the plates of the capacitor ?

(d) electric field between the plates of the capacitor?

11. Draw the current versus potential difference characteristics for a cell. How can the internal resistance of the cell be determined from this graph?

12. Two magnets of magnetic moments M and $M\sqrt{3}$ are joined to form a cross. The combination is suspended in a uniform magnetic field B. The magnetic moment M now makes an angle of θ with the field direction. Find the value of angle θ.

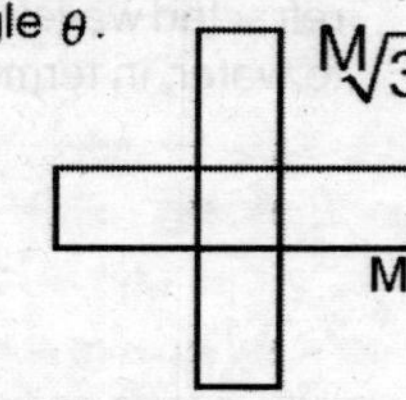

13. A luminiscent object is placed at a depth 'd' in a (optically) denser medium of refractive index 'μ'. Prove that radius r, of the base of the cone of light, from the object, that can emerge out from the surface, is

$$r = \frac{d}{\sqrt{\mu^2 - 1}}$$

14. A certain n - p - n transistor has the common emitter output characteristics as shown

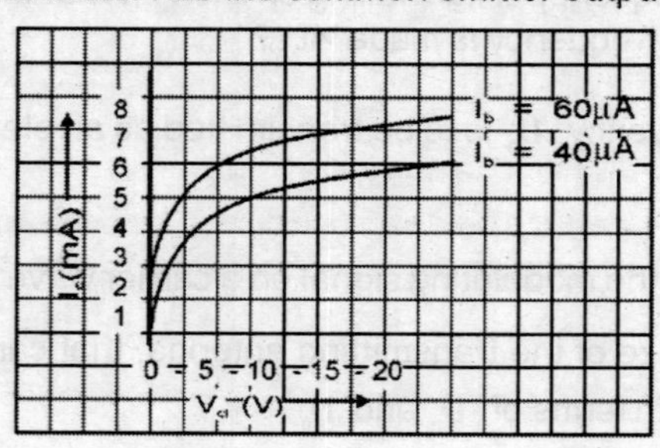

(a) find the emitter current at V_{cc} = 10V and I_b = 60 μ A.

(b) find β at this point.

15. Using Gauss law establish that the magnitude of electric field intensity, at a point, due to an infinite plane sheet, with uniform charge density σ is independent of the distance of the field point.

OR

Define an electric field line. Draw the pattern of the field lines around a system of two equal positive charges separated by a distance.

16. An average induced emf of 0.4V appears in a coil when the current in it is changed from 10A in one direction to 10 A in opposite direction in 0.40 second. Find the coefficient of self induction of the coil.

17. A conducting U tube can slide inside another U tube maintaining electrical contact between the tubes. The magnetic field is perpendicular to the plane of paper and is directed inward. Each tube moves towards the other at a constant speed V. Find the magnitude of induced emf across the ends of the tubes in terms of magnetic field B, velocity v and width ℓ of the tube.

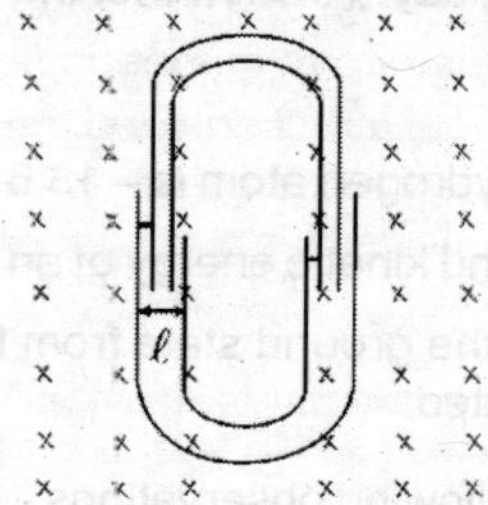

18. For the given combination of gates, Find the values of outputs Y_1 and Y_2 in the table given below. Identify the gates G_1 and G_2.

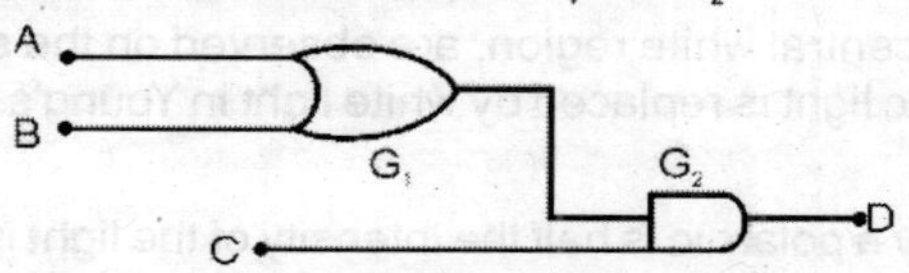

A	B	C	D
O	O	O	Y_1
1	1	O	Y_2

19. A small magnet, of magnetic moment M, is placed at a distance r from the origin O with its axis parallel to x-axis as shown. A small coil, of one turn, is placed on the x-axis, at the same distance from the origin, with the axis of the coil coinciding with x-axis. For what value of current in the coil does a small magnetic neddle, kept at origin, remains undeflected? What is the direction of current in the coil?

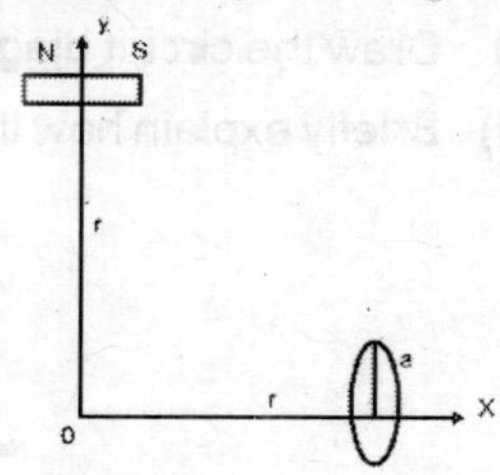

20. A slit of width 'd' is illuminated by white light. For what value of 'd' is the first minimum, for red light of λ = 650 nm, located at point P ? For what value of the wave length of light will the first diffraction maxima also fall at P?

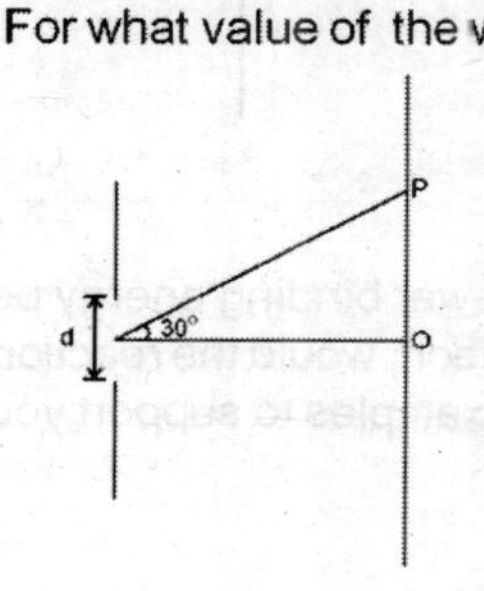

21. A charged particle, of charge 2 μ C and mass 10 milligram, moving with a velocity of 1000 m/s entres a uniform electric field of strength 10^3 NC^{-1} directed perpendicular to its direction of motion. Find the velocity, and displacement, of the particle after 10s.

22. What reasoning led de- Broglie to put forward the concept of matter waves? The wavelength, λ, of a photon, and the de - Broglie wave length associated with a particle of mass 'm', has the same value, say λ. Show that the energy of photon is $\frac{2\lambda mc}{h}$ times the kinetic energy of the particle.

23. The ground state energy of hydrogen atom is – 13.6 eV.

(i) What are the potential and kinetic energy of an electron in the 3rd excited state?

(ii) If the electron jumps to the ground state from the third excited state, calculate the frequency of photon emitted.

24. Give reason for each of the following observations :

(i) The resultant intensity at any point on the screen varies between zero and four times the intensity due to one slit, in Young's double slit experiment.

(ii) A few coloured fringes, around a central white region, are observed on the screen, when the source of monochromatic light is replaced by white light in Young's double slit experiment.

(iii) The intensity of light transmitted by a polaroid is half the intensity of the light incident on it.

25. The figure below shows the V – I characteristics of a semiconductor device.

(i) Identify the semiconductor device used here.

(ii) Draw the circuit diagram to obtain the given charactersitics of this diode.

(iii) Briefly explain how this device is used as a voltage regulator.

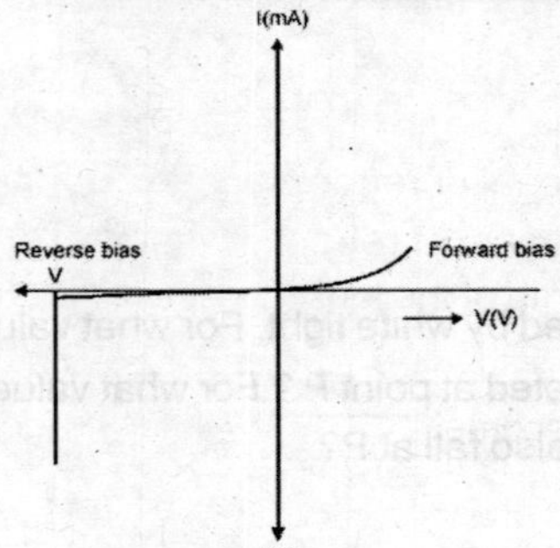

(b)

26. If nuclei, with lower binding energy per nucleon, transform to nuclei with greater binding energy per nucleon, would the reaction be exothermic or endothermic? Justify your answer and write two examples to support your answer.

27. Complete the following block diagram depicting the essential elements of a basic communication system.

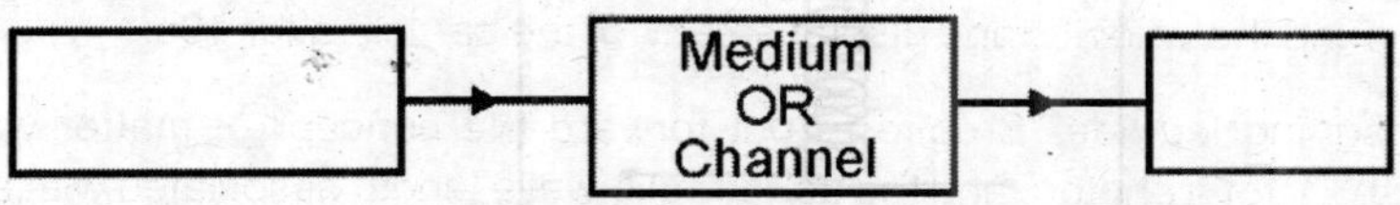

Name the two basic modes of communication. Which of these modes is used for telephonic communication?

OR

Is it necessary for the transmitting antenna and the receiving antenna to be of the same height for line of sight communication? Find an expression for maximum line of sight distance d_m between these two antennas of heights h_T and h_R.

28. A plot, between the angle of deviation (δ) and angle of incidence (i), for a triangular prism is shown below.

Explain why any given value of 'δ' corresponds to two values of angle of incidence? State the significance of point 'P' on the graph. Use this information to derive an expression for refractive index of the material of the prism.

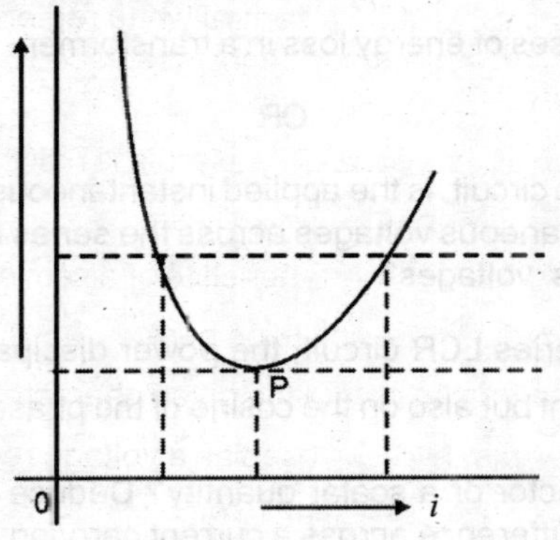

OR

A thin lens, made of a material of refractive index μ, has a focal length 'f'. If the lens is placed in a transparent medium of refractive index 'n' ($n<\mu$), obtain an expression for the change in the focal length of the lens. Use the result to show that the focal length of a lens of the glass ($\mu = \mu_g$) becomes $\dfrac{\mu_w(\mu_g-1)}{(\mu_g-\mu_w)}$ times its focal length in air, when it is placed in water ($\mu=\mu_w$).

What happens when $n > \mu$. Explain using appropriate ray diagram.

29. (a) Out of the two arrangements, given below, for winding of primary and secondary coil in a transformer, which arrangement do you think will have higher efficiency and why?

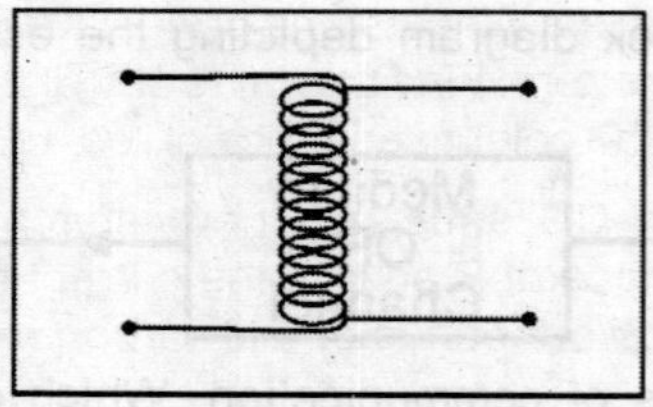

(a)

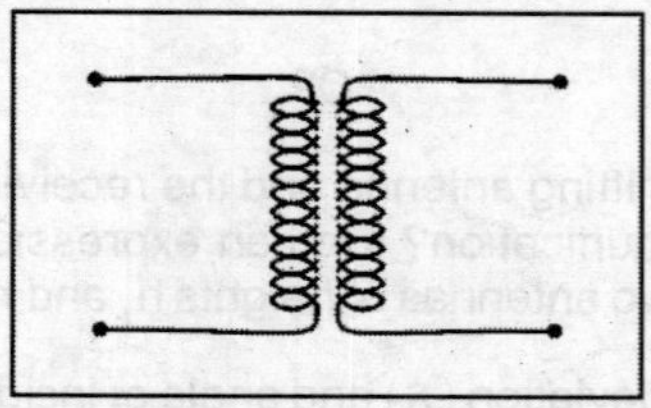

(b)

(b) Show that, in an ideal transformer, when the voltage is stepped up by a certain factor, the current gets stepped down by the same factor.

(c) State any two causes of energy loss in a transformer.

OR

(a) In a series LCR ac circuit, is the applied instantaneous voltage equal to the algebric sum of the instantaneous voltages across the series elements of the circuit? Is the same true for r.m.s. voltages?

(b) Prove that in a series LCR circuit, the power dissipated depends not only on the voltage and current but also on the cosine of the phase angle ϕ between these two.

30. Is current density a vector or a scalar quantity? Deduce the relation between current density and potential difference across a current carrying conductor of length l, area of cross-section A, and number density of free electrons n. How does the current density, in a conductor vary with

(a) increase in potential gradient?

(b) increase in temperature?

(c) increase in length?

(d) increase in area of cross-section?

(Assume that the other factors remain constant in each case.)

OR

Write the condition of balance in a Wheatstone bridge. In the given Wheatstone bridge, the current in the resistor 3R, is zero. Find the value of R, if the carbon resistor, connected in one arm of the bridge, has the colour sequence of red, red and orange.

The resistances, of BC and CD arms, are now interchanged and another carbon resistance is connected in place of R so that the current through the arm BD is again zero. Write the sequence of colour bands of this carbon resistor. Also find the value of current through it.

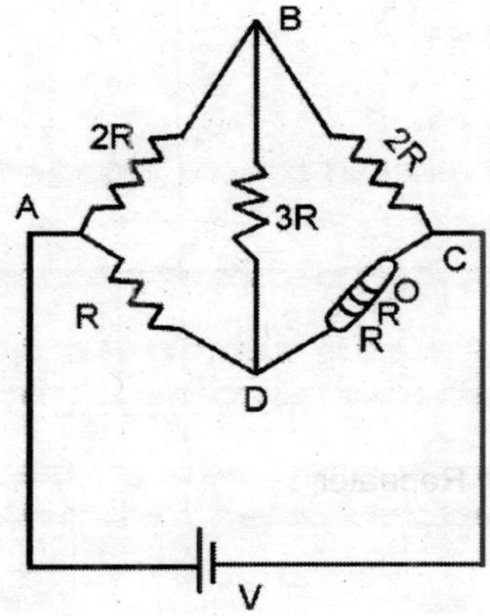

SAMPLE PAPER - III
MARKING SCHEME
PHYSICS (THEORY)
Class XII

Q No.	Value point / expected points	Marks	Total
1.	$\lambda_3 < \lambda_1 < \lambda_2$	1	1
2.	eddy currents	1	1
3.	$\overline{M_1} = -\frac{1}{2}\overline{M_2}$	1	1
4.	$C = C_3$	1	1
5.	${}_w^a\mu = \frac{\sin r}{\sin i} = \frac{w}{y}$	$\frac{1}{2}+\frac{1}{2}$	1
6.	(a) Transducer (b) Repeater	$\frac{1}{2}+\frac{1}{2}$	1
7.	2ν	1	1
8.	υ_c / υ_a	1	1
9.	$\vec{E} = E_o \sin\omega t\,\hat{i}$	½	
	$\vec{B} = B_o \sin\omega t\,\hat{j}$	½	
	OR	OR	
	$\vec{E} = E_o \sin\omega t\,\hat{j}$	½	
	$\vec{B} = B_o \sin\omega t\,\hat{i}$	½	
	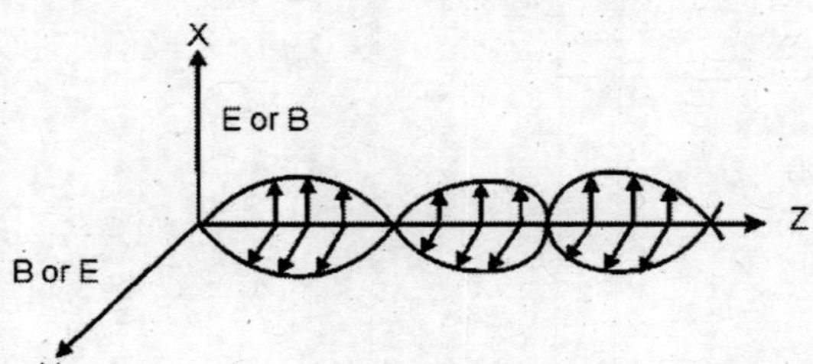	1	2

10. Since electric field inside the conductor is zero and has no tangential component on the surface, no work is done in moving a small test charge within the conductor or on its surface. 1

This means that, there is no potential difference between any two points inside or on the surface of the conductor. Hence the potential is constant through out the volume of the conductor and has the same value on its surface. 1 2

OR

(a) decreases (b) decreases ½+½

(c) remains same (d) decreases ½+½ 2

11.

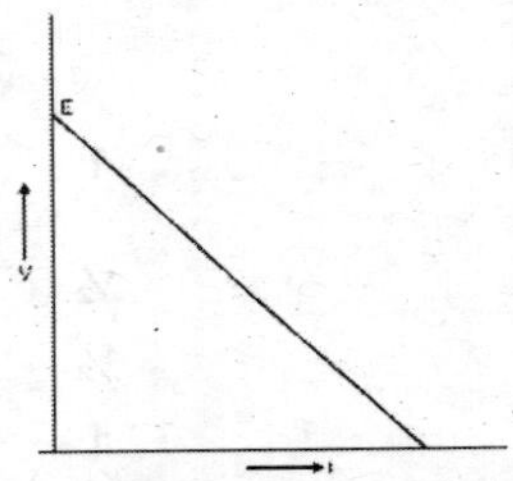

1

Since $V = E - ir$, the internal resistance equals the negative of the slope of this graph 1 2

12. $MB \sin\theta = \sqrt{3}\, MB \sin(90° - \theta)$ 1

$= \sqrt{3}\, MB \cos\theta$

$\Rightarrow \tan\theta = \sqrt{3}$

i.e $\theta = 60°$ 1 2

13.

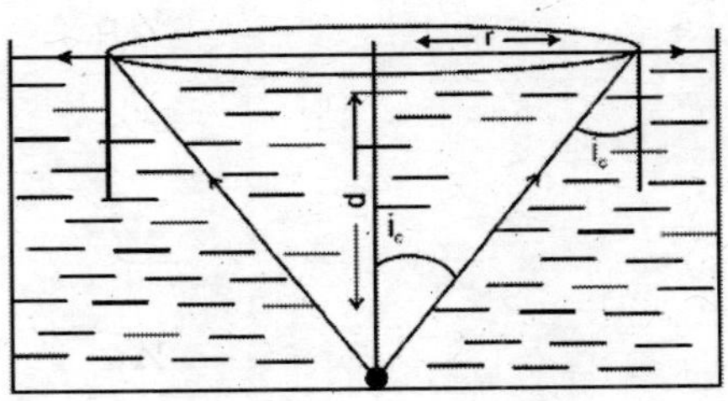

For total internal reflection

$\sin i_c = \dfrac{1}{\mu}$ ½

also, from the figure,

$\tan i_c = \dfrac{r}{d}$ ½

$\therefore \frac{\sin i_c}{\sqrt{1-\sin^2 i_c}} = \frac{r}{d}$ ½

$\therefore r = \frac{d}{\sqrt{\mu^2 - 1}}$ ½ 2

14. (a) For $V_{cc} = 10$ V and $I_b = 60$ μA

$I_c = 6$ mA 1

$I_e = I_c + I_b = 6\text{mA} + 60\,\mu\text{A} = 6.06$ mA

(b) $\beta = \frac{I_c}{I_b} = \frac{6\text{mA}}{6\mu\text{A}} = 1000$ 1 2

15. Statement of Gauss law ½

Diagram ½ 2

Derivation 1

OR

Definition of field lines 1

Diagram 1 2

16. $\frac{dI}{dt} = \frac{I_2 - I_1}{at} = \frac{-10-10}{40} = \frac{-20}{40}$ ½

$= -50\ \text{As}^{-1}$ ½

$E = -L\frac{dI}{dt}$ ½

$0.4 = -L\ (-50)$

$L = \frac{0.4}{50}$

$= 0.008\text{H}$ ½ 2

$= 8\text{mH}$

17. Relative velocity

$= v - (-v) = 2\ v$ 1

$\therefore E = B\ell(2v)$

$= 2v\ B\ \ell$ 1 2

18. $G_1 \to OR$ $G_2 \to AND$ $\frac{1}{2}+\frac{1}{2}$ 2

$Y_1 = O$ $Y_2 = O$ 1

19. This happens when magnetic field of bar magnet is equal and opposite to the magnetic field of coil $\Rightarrow |\overrightarrow{B_m}| = |\overrightarrow{B_c}|$ 1

$$\frac{\mu_o M}{4\pi r^3} = \frac{\mu_o I a^2}{2r^3}$$ 1

$$\Rightarrow I = \frac{2M}{4\pi a^2}$$ ½ 3

Current is in anticlockwise sense, as seen from the origin. ½

20. At first minimum n=1

$d \sin 30^o = n\lambda$ ½

or $\frac{d}{2} = 1 \times 650\,nm$

or $d = 1300\,nm$ 1

For 1st maxima to lie at P:

$$d \sin\theta = \frac{3}{2}\lambda^1$$ ½

$$\text{or } \lambda^1 = \frac{2d\sin\theta}{3} = \frac{2x1300 \times \sin 30^o}{3}\,nm$$

$= \quad 433.3\,nm$ 1 3

21. The velocity of the particle, normal to the direction of field, $\vartheta_x = 1000ms^{-1}$, is constant. ½

The velocity of the particle, along the direction of field, after 10s, is given by

$\vartheta_y = u_y + a_y$

$$= 0 + \frac{qE_y}{m}t$$

$$= \frac{2x10^{-6}x10^3x10}{10x10^{-6}} = 2000ms^{-1}$$ ½

The net velocity after 10s

$$\vartheta = \sqrt{\vartheta_x^2 + \vartheta_y^2}$$

$$= \sqrt{(1000)^2 + (2000)^2}\ \text{m s}^{-1}$$

$$= 1000\sqrt{5}\ \text{m s}^{-1}$$ ½

Displacement, along the x-axis, after 10s

X=1000 x 10m = 10000 m

Displacement along y - axis (in the direction of field) after 10s, ½

$$y = U_y t + \frac{1}{2}a_y t^2$$

$$= (0)t + \frac{1}{2}\frac{qE_y}{m}t^2$$

$$= \frac{1}{2} \times \frac{2\times10^{-6}\times10^{3}}{10\times10} \times (10)^2$$

$$= 10000\ \text{m}$$ ½

Net displacement

$$r = \sqrt{x^2 + y^2}$$

$$= \sqrt{(10000)^2 + (10000)^2}$$

$$= 10000\sqrt{2}\ \text{m}$$ ½ 3

22. de-Broglie put forward the bold hypothesis that moving particles of matter should display wave-like properties under suitable conditions. He reasoned that nature was symmetrical and that the two basic physical entities, matter and energy, must have symmetrical character. If radiation shows a dual nature, so should matter. 1

$$K = \frac{p^2}{2m} \text{ and } p = \frac{h}{\lambda}$$ ½

$$\therefore K = \frac{h^2}{2m\lambda^2}$$ ½

$$\text{Also } E_{photon} = \frac{hc}{\lambda}$$ ½

$$\therefore \frac{K}{E} = \frac{h}{2mc\lambda}$$

$$\therefore E_{photon} = \left(\frac{2\lambda mc}{h}\right)K$$ ½ 3

23. $E_n = \frac{-13.6}{n^2} eV$ ½

For third excited state, n=4

$$\therefore E_4 = \frac{-13.6}{16} eV = -0.85 eV$$

$\therefore$ KE= 0.85eV ½

and PE = 2E = -1.7eV ½

$\Delta E = E_4 - E_1 = [-0.85 - (-13.6)] eV$

= 12.75 eV ½

and $v = \frac{\Delta E}{h} = \frac{12.75 x 1.6 x 10^{-19}}{6.63 x 10^{-34}} \simeq 3 x 10^{15} Hz$ 1 3

24. (i) The resultant intensity, at any point on the screen, is given by

$$I = 4I_o \cos^2 \frac{\phi}{2}$$

For constructive interference:

$\varphi = 0, 2\pi, 4\pi$ and so on

For destructive interference:

$\phi = \pi, 3\pi, 5\pi$ and so on

$\Rightarrow I = 0$ for minimum intersity,

and $I = 4I_o$ for maximum intensity 1

Thus, intensity varies between zero and four times the intensity, due to each slit, in Young's double slit experiment.

(ii) The interference pattern due to different colours of white light overlap incoherently. The central bright fringes for different colours are at the same position. Therefore the central fringe is white and the fringes closest, on either side of central white fringe, are red and the farthest will appear blue. After a few fringes no clear fringe pattern is seen. 1

(iii) A polaroid consists of a long chain of molecules aligned in a particular direction. The electric vector (associated with the propagating light wave) along the direction of the aligned molecules get absorbed. Thus, if the light, from an ordinary source, pases through a polaroid, it is observed that its transmitted intensity gets reduced by half. 1 3

25. (i) Zener diode ½

(ii) Circuit diagram in forward bias and reverse bias

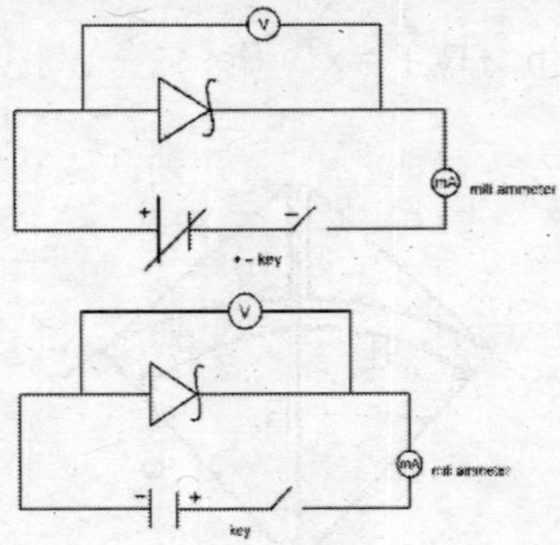

½

½

(iii)

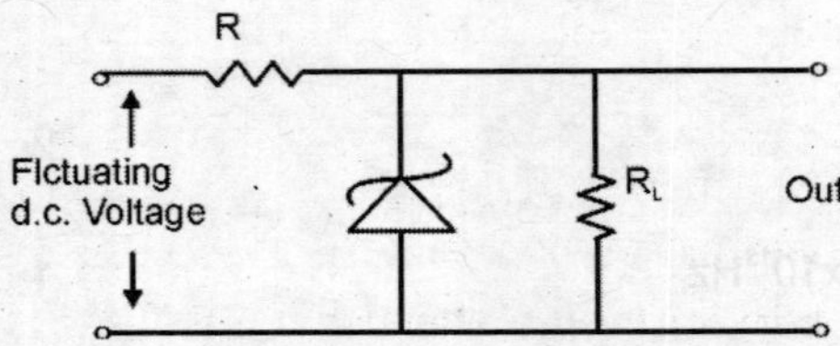

½

If the input voltage increases, the current through R and Zener diode also increases. This increases voltage drop across R without any change of voltage across the Zener diode. 1 3

26. Greater the binding energy, less is the total mass of a bounded system, such as a nucleus. Consequently, if a nucleus, with less binding energy per nucleon, transforms to nuclei with greater binding energy per nucleon, there will be a net energy release. Reaction will be exothermic. 1

For example in case of fission, when a heavy nucleus decays into two or more intermediate mass fragments or in fusion, when light nuclei fuse into a heavier single nucleus, energy is released 2 3

27.

1

Two basic modes of transmission are (i) point-to-point and (ii) broad cast mode. $\frac{1}{2}+\frac{1}{2}$

Point-to-point mode is used for Telephonic communication. 1 3

OR

No, it is not necessary to have the same height. ½

For transmitting antenna of height $h_T (h_T + R_e)^2 = x^2 + Re^2$

$\because \quad h_r << Re \qquad \therefore \qquad x = d_T$

or

$(h_T + R_e)^2 = d_T^2 + R_e^2$ ½

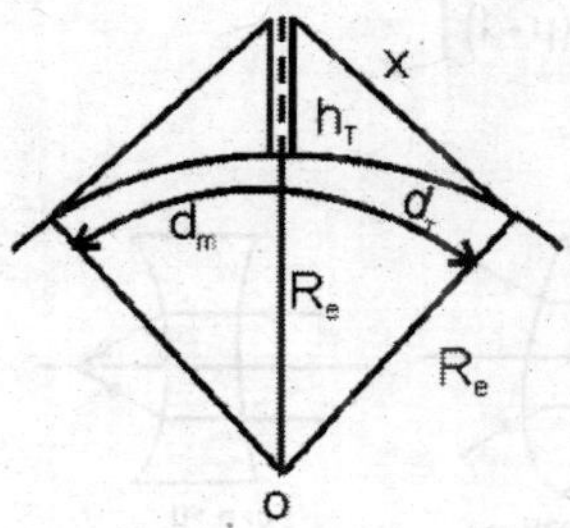

$h_T^2 + R_e^2 + 2h_T R_e$

$= \quad d_T^2 + R_e^2$

(h_T^2 is negligible) ½

$\Rightarrow d_T = \sqrt{2R_e h_T}$

d_T is also called the radio horizon of the transmiting antenna. ½

The maximum line-of-sight distance d_m between the two antennae is

$d_m = \sqrt{2R_e h_T} + \sqrt{2R_e h_R}$ 1 3

where h_R is the height of the receiving antenna.

28. In general, any given value of δ, except for i = e, corresponds to two values i and e This, in fact, is expected from the symmetry of i and e as $\delta = i + e - A$, i.e, δ remains the same if i and e are interchanged. 1

Point P is the point of minimum deviation. This is related to the fact that the path of the ray, as shown in figure, can be traced back resulting in the same angle of deviation. At the minimum deviation D_m, the refracted ray inside the prism becomes parallel to the base. 1

For $\delta = D_m, i = e \Rightarrow r_1 = r_2$ 1

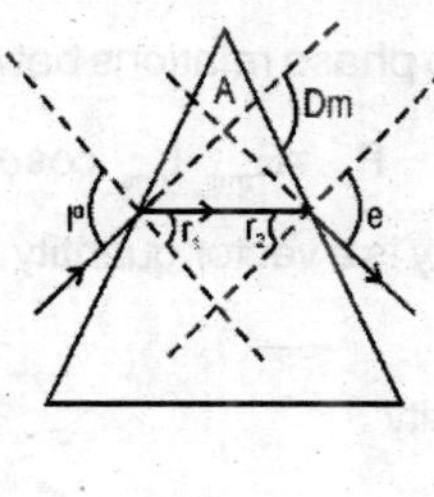

or $2r = A$ or $r = A/2$

In the same way

$D_m = 2i - A$ or $i = \dfrac{A + D_m}{2}$ 1

$\therefore$ The refractive index of the prism is

$\mu = \dfrac{\sin (A + D_m)/2}{\sin A/2}$ 1 5

OR

Derivation of

$$\Delta f = \frac{R_1R_2}{R_2 - R_1}\left[\frac{n}{\mu - n} - \frac{1}{(\mu - 1)}\right]$$ 2

Proof of

$$f_w = \frac{\mu_w(\mu_g - l)}{\mu_g - \mu_w} f_w$$ 1

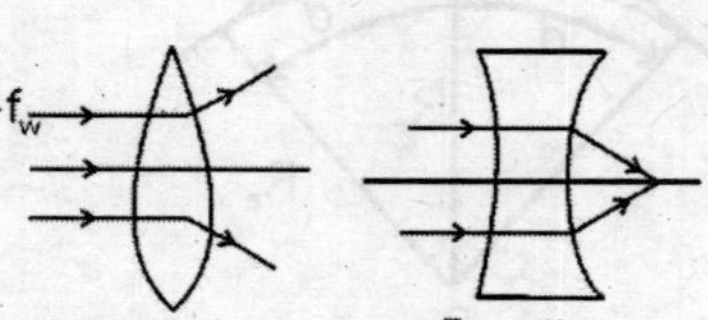

For n>μ Convex lens

For n >μ Concave lens 1

1 5

Explanation

29. Arrangment (a): because leakage of flux is minimum (almost zero.) 1

For an ideal transformer–Input power = output power

$$\Rightarrow \frac{E_S}{E_P} = \frac{I_P}{I_S}$$ 2

$\therefore$ when E_s increases, I_s decrease in the same ratio

Any two correct causes 2 5

OR

(a) Yes, $V = V_L + V_C + V_R$ for instantaneous values

It is not true for r.m.s values. For r.m.s value $V = \sqrt{(V_L \sim V_C)^2 + V_R^{\,2}}$ 2

This is due to phase relations between the different voltages.

(b) Proof of : $P_{AV} = E_{rms}\ I_{rms}\ \cos\phi$ 3 5

30. Yes, current density is a vector quantity ½

$\therefore$ $I = neAV_d$

$\therefore$ Current density ½

$$\frac{I}{A} = neV_d = ne\frac{eE}{m}\tau$$ 1

or

$$J = \frac{ne^2V}{ml}.\tau = \left(\frac{ne^2\tau}{m}\right)\frac{V}{\ell}$$ 1

(a) increases

(b) decreases

(c) decreases

(d) remains same ½ x 4 = 2 5

OR

The balance condition is–

$P/Q = R/S$ or $P/R = Q/S$ ½

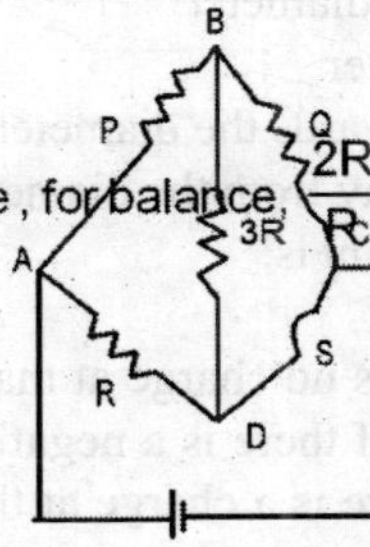

In the given Wheatstone bridge, we have, for balance, $\frac{2R}{R} = \frac{2R}{S}$ ½

$\therefore$ R = S = resistance of carbon resistor

$= 22x10^3\,\Omega$

= 22 k Ω 1

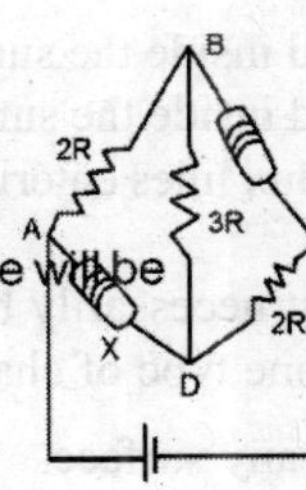

When the resistances are intercharged, the bridge will be a balanced one if

$$\frac{2R}{X} = \frac{22x10^3}{2x22x10^3} = \frac{1}{2}$$

$\therefore$ X = 4R = 88kΩ ½

$\therefore$ The sequence of colours will be grey, grey and orange. 1

Also equivalent resistance,of the balanced wheatstone bridge, is given by

$$\frac{1}{R_{eq}} = \frac{1}{3R} + \frac{1}{6R} = \frac{2+1}{6R}$$

$\therefore R_{eq} = 2R$ ½

$\therefore$ Current through the (new) carbon resistor $= \frac{1}{3} x \frac{V}{2R}$

$= \frac{V}{6R}$ 1 5

MCQs

1. A hemisphere is uniformly charged positively. The electric field at a point on a diameter away from the centre is directed.
(a) perpendicular to the diameter.
(b) parallel to the diameter.
(c) at an angle tilted towards the diameter.
(d) at an angle tilted away from the diameter.

2. The Electric field at a point is:
(a) always continuous.
(b) continuous if there is no charge at that point.
(c) discontinuous only if there is a negative charge at that point.
(d) discontinuous if there is a charge at that point.

3. If $\oint_s \mathrm{E.dS} = 0$ over a surface, then:
(a) the electric field inside the surface and on it is zero.
(b) the electric field inside the surface is necessarily uniform.
(c) the number of flux lines entering the surface must be equal to the number of flux lines leaving it.
(d) all charges must necessarily be outside the surface.

4. If there were only one type of charge in the universe, then
(a) $\oint_s \mathbf{E.dS} \neq 0$ on any surface.
(b) $\oint_s \mathbf{E.dS} = 0$ if the charge is outside the surface.
(c) $\oint_s \mathbf{E.dS}$ could not be defined.
(d) $\oint_s \mathbf{E.dS} = \frac{q}{E_0}$ if charges of magnitude q were inside the surface.

5. Consider a region inside which there are various types of charges but the total charge is zero. At points outside the region:
(a) the electric field is necessarily zero.
(b) the electric field is due to the dipole moment of the charge distribution only.
(c) the dominant electric field is $\propto \frac{1}{r^3}$, for large r, where r is the distance from an origin in this region.
(d) the work done to move a charged particle along a closed path, away from the region, will be zero.

6. A positively charged particle is released from rest in an uniform electric field. The electric potential energy of the charge:

(a) remains constant because the electric field is uniform.
(b) increases because the charge moves along the electric field.
(c) decreases because the charge moves along the electric field.
(d) decreases because the charge moves opposite to the electric field.

7. The electrostatic potential on the surface of a charged conducting sphere is 100V. Two statements are made in this regard:
S_1: At any point inside the sphere, electric intensity is zero.
S_2: At any point inside the sphere, the electrostatic potential is 100V.
Which of the following is a correct statement?
(a) S_1 is true but S_2 is false.
(b) Both S_1 & S_2 are false.
(c) S_1 is true, S_2 is also true and S_1 is the cause of S_2.
(d) S_1 is true, S_2 is also true but the statements are independent.

8. Equipotentials at a great distance from a collection of charges, whose total sum is not zero, are approximately:
(a) spheres. (b) planes.
(c) paraboloids. (d) ellipsoids.

9. Consider a uniform electric field in the $\hat{z}$ direction. The potential is a constant:
(a) in all space. (b) for any x for a given z.
(c) for any y for a given z. (d) on the x-y plane for a given z.

10. Equipotential surfaces:
(a) are closer in regions of large electric fields compared to regions of lower electric fields.
(b) will be more crowded near sharp edges of a conductor.
(c) will be more crowded near regions of large charge densities.
(d) will always be equally spaced.

11. Consider a current carrying wire (current I) in the shape of a circle. Note that as the current progresses along the wire, the direction of **j** (current density) changes in an exact manner, while the current I remains unaffected. The agent that is *essentially* responsible for this is:
(a) source of emf.
(b) electric field produced by charges accumulated on the surface of wire.
(c) the charges just behind a given segment of wire which push them just the right way by repulsion.
(d) the charges ahead.

12. A resistance R is to be measured using a meter bridge. A student chooses the standard resistance S to be 100Ω. He finds the null point at $l_1 = 2.9$ cm. He is told to attempt to improve the accuracy. Which of the following is a useful way?
(a) He should measure l_1 more accurately.
(b) He should change S to 1000Ω and repeat the experiment.
(c) He should change S to 3Ω and repeat the experiment.
(d) He should give up hope of a more accurate measurement with a meter bridge.

13. Two cells of emf's approximately 5V and 10V are to be accurately compared using a potentiometer of length 400cm.
(a) The battery that runs the potentiometer should have voltage of 8V.
(b) The battery of potentiometer can have a voltage of 15V and R adjusted so that the potential drop across the wire slightly exceeds 10V.
(c) The first portion of 50 cm of wire itself should have a potential drop of 10V
(d) Potentiometer is usually used for comparing resistances and not voltages.

14. Kirchhoff's junction rule is a reflection of:
(a) conservation of current density vector.
(b) conservation of charge.

(c) the fact that the momentum with which a charged particle approaches a junction is unchanged (as a vector) as the charged particle leaves the junction.
(d) the fact that there is no accumulation of charges at a junction.

15. Temperature dependence of resistivity $\rho(T)$ of semiconductors, insulators and metals is significantly based on the following factors:
(a) number of charge carriers can change with temperature T.
(b) time interval between two successive collisions can depend on T.
(c) length of material can be a function of T.
(d) mass of carriers is a function of T.

16. A current carrying circular loop of radius R is placed in the x-y plane with centre at the origin. Half of the loop with $x > 0$ is now bent so that it now lies in the y-z plane.
(a) The magnitude of magnetic moment now diminishes.
(b) The magnetic moment does not change.
(c) The magnitude of **B** at $(0.0.z)$ $z>>R$ increases.
(d) The magnitude of **B** at $(0.0.z)$ $z>>R$ is unchanged.

17. An electron is projected with uniform velocity along the axis of a current carrying long solenoid. Which of the following is true?
(a) The electron will be accelerated along the axis.
(b) The electron path will be circular about the axis.
(c) The electron will experience a force at 45° to the axis and, hence, execute a helical path.
(d) The electron will continue to move with uniform velocity along the axis of the solenoid.

18. In a cyclotron, a charged particle:
(a) undergoes acceleration all the time.
(b) speeds up between the dees because of the magnetic field.
(c) speeds up in a dee.
(d) slows down within a dee and speeds up between dees.

19. The gyro-magnetic ratio of an electron in an H-atom, according to Bohr model, is:
(a) independent of which orbit it is in. (b) negative.
(c) positive. (d) increases with the quantum number n.

20. Consider a wire carrying a steady current, I placed in a uniform magnetic field **B** perpendicular to its length. Consider the charges inside the wire. It is known that magnetic forces do no work. This implies that:
(a) motion of charges inside the conductor is unaffected by **B** since they do not absorb energy.
(b) some charges inside the wire move to the surface as a result of **B**.
(c) if the wire moves under the influence of **B**, no work is done by the force.
(d) if the wire moves under the influence of **B**, no work is done by the magnetic force on the ions assumed fixed within the wire.

21. The magnetic field of Earth can be modelled by that of a point dipole placed at the centre of the Earth. The dipole axis makes an angle of 11.3° with the axis of Earth. At Mumbai, declination is nearly zero. Then:
(a) the declination varies between 11.3° W and 11.3° E.
(b) the least declination is 0°.
(c) the plane defined by dipole axis and Earth axis passes through Greenwich.
(d) declination averaged over Earth must be always negative.

22. In a permanent magnet at room temperature:
(a) magnetic moment of each molecule is zero.
(b) the individual molecules have non-zero magnetic moment which are all perfectly aligned.

(c) domains are partially aligned.
(d) domains are all perfectly aligned.

23. S is the surface of a lump of magnetic material.
(a) Lines of **B** are necessarily continuous across *S*.
(b) Some lines of **B** must be discontinuous across *S*.
(c) Lines of **H** are necessarily continuous across *S*.
(d) Lines of **H** cannot all be continuous across *S*.

24. The primary origin(s) of magnetism lie(s) in:
(a) atomic currents.
(b) Pauli exclusion principle.
(c) polar nature of molecules.
(d) intrinsic spin of electron.

25. Let the magnetic field on earth be modelled by that of a point magnetic dipole at the centre of the earth. The angle of dip at a point on the geograhical equator:
(a) is always zero.
(b) can be zero at specific points.
(c) can be positive or negative.
(d) is bounded.

26. The self-inductance L of a solenoid of length l and area of cross-section A, with a fixed number of turns N increases as:
(a) l and A increase.
(b) l decreases and A increases.
(c) l increases and A decreases.
(d) both l and A decrease.

27. A metal plate is getting heated. It can be because
(a) a direct current is passing through the plate.
(b) it is placed in a time varying magnetic field.
(c) it is placed in a space varying magnetic field, but does not vary with time.
(d) a current (either direct or alternating) is passing through the plate.

28. An e.m.f. is produced in a coil, which is not connected to an external voltage source. This can be due to:
(a) the coil being in a time varying magnetic field.
(b) the coil moving in a time varying magnetic field.
(c) the coil moving in a constant magnetic field.
(d) the coil being stationary in external spatially varying magnetic field, which does not change with time.

29. The mutual inductance M_{12} of coil 1 with respect to coil 2:
(a) increases when they are brought nearer.
(b) depends on the current passing through the coils.
(c) increases when one of them is rotated about an axis.
(d) is the same as M_{21} of coil 2 with respect to coil 1.

30. A circular coil expands radially in a region of magnetic field and no electromotive force is produced in the coil. This can be because:
(a) the magnetic field is constant.
(b) the magnetic field is in the same plane as the circular coil and it may or may not vary.
(c) the magnetic field has a perpendicular (to the plane of the coil) component, whose magnitude is decreasing suitably.
(d) there is a constant magnetic field in the perpendicular (to the plane of the coil) direction.

31. To reduce the resonant frequency in an LCR series circuit with a generator:
(a) the generator frequency should be reduced.
(b) another capacitor should be added in parallel to the first.
(c) the iron core of the inductor should be removed.
(d) dielectric in the capacitor should be removed.

32. An inductor of reactance 1Ω and a resistor of 2 Ω are connected in series to the terminals of a 6 V (rms) a.c. source. The power dissipated in the circuit is:

(a) 8 W. (b) 12 W.
(c) 14.4 W. (d) 18 W.

33. As the frequency of an a.c. circuit increases, the current first increases and then decreases. What combination of circuit elements is most likely to comprise the circuit?
(a) Inductor and capacitor. (b) Resistor and inductor.
(c) Resistor and capacitor. (d) Resistor, inductor and capacitor.

34. In an alternating current circuit consisting of elements in series, the current increases on increasing the frequency of supply. Which of the following elements are likely to constitute the circuit?
(a) Only resistor. (b) Resistor and inductor.
(c) Resistor and capacitor. (d) Only capacitor.

35. Electrical energy is transmitted over large distances at high alternating voltages. Which of the following statements is (are) correct?
(a) For a given power level, there is a lower current.
(b) Lower current implies less power loss.
(c) Transmission lines can be made thinner.
(d) It is easy to reduce the voltage at the receiving end using step-down transformers.

36. One requires 11eV of energy to dissociate a carbon monoxide molecule into carbon and oxygen atoms. The minimum frequency of the appropriate eletromagnetic radiation to achieve the dissociation lies in:
(a) visible region. (b) infrared region.
(c) ultraviolet region. (d) microwave region.

37. Light with an energy flux of 20 W/cm^2 falls on a non-reflecting surface at normal incidence. If the surface has an area of 30 cm^2, the total momentum delivered (for complete absorption) during 30 minutes is:
(a) 36 10^{-5} kg m/s. (b) 36 10^{-4} kg m/s.
(c) 108 10^{4} kg m/s. (d) 1.08 10^{7} kg m/s.

38. A charged particle oscillates about its mean equilibrium position with a frequency of 10^9 Hz. The electromagnetic waves produced:
(a) will have frequency of 10^9 Hz. (b) will have frequency of 2×10^9 Hz.
(c) will have a wavelength of 0.3 m. (d) fall in the region of radiowaves.

39. The source of electromagnetic waves can be a charge:
(a) moving with a constant velocity. (b) moving in a circular orbit.
(c) at rest. (d) falling in an electric field.

40. An EM wave of intensity I falls on a surface kept in vacuum and exerts radiation pressure p on it. Which of the following are true?
(a) Radiation pressure is I/c if the wave is totally absorbed.
(b) Radiation pressure is I/c if the wave is totally reflected.
(c) Radiation pressure is $2I/c$ if the wave is total reflected.
(d) Radiation pressure is in the range $I/c<p<2I/c$ for real surfaces.

41. A ray of light incident at an angle θ on a refracting face of a prism emerges from the other face normally. If the angle of the prism is 5° and the prism is made of a material of refractive index 1.5, the angle of incidence is:
(a) 7.5° (b) 5°
(c) 15° (d) 2.5°

42. A short pulse of white light is incident from air to a glass slab at normal incidence. After travelling through the slab, the first colour to emerge is:
(a) blue. (b) green.
(c) violet. (d) red.

43. An object approaches a convergent lens from the left of the lens with a uniform speed of 5 m/s and stops at the focus. The image:
(a) moves away from the lens with an uniform speed of 5 m/s.
(b) moves away from the lens with an uniform accleration.
(c) moves away from the lens with a non-uniform acceleration.
(d) moves towards the lens with a non-uniform accleration.

44. A passenger in an aeroplane shall:
(a) never see a rainbow.
(b) may see a primary and a secondary rainbow as concentric circles.
(c) may see a primary and a secondary rainbow as concentric arcs.
(d) shall never see a secondary rainbow.

45. The phenomena involved in the reflection of radiowaves by ionosphere is similar to:
(a) reflection of light by a plane mirror.
(b) total internal reflection of light in air during a mirage.
(c) dispersion of light by water molecules during the formation of a rainbow.
(d) scattering of light by the particles of air.

46. Consider sunlight incident on a slit of width 10^4 A. The image seen through the slit shall:
(a) be a fine sharp slit white in colour at the center.
(b) a bright slit white at the center diffusing to zero intensities at the edges.
(c) a bright slit white at the center duffusing to regions of different colours.
(d) only be a diffused slit white in colour.

47. In a Young's double slit experiment, the source is white light. One of the holes is covered by a red filter and another by a blue filter. In this case:
(a) there shall be alternate interference patterns of red and blue.
(b) there shall be an interference pattern for red distinct from that for blue.
(c) there shall be no interference fringes.
(d) there shall be an interference pattern for red mixing with one for blue.

48. Consider sunlight incident on a pinhole of width 10^3A. The image of the pinhole seen on a screen shall be:
(a) a sharp white ring.
(b) different from a geometrical image.
(c) a diffused central spot, white in colour.
(d) diffused coloured region around a sharp central white spot.

49. Consider the diffraction patern for a small pinhole. As the size of the hole is increased:
(a) the size decreases.
(b) the intensity increases.
(c) the size increases.
(d) the intensity decreases.

50. For light diverging from a point source:
(a) the wavefront is spherical.
(b) the intensity decreases in proportion to the distance squared.
(c) the wavefront is parabolic.
(d) the intensity at the wavefront does not depend on the distance.

51. A particle is dropped from a height H. The de Broglie wavelength of the particle as a function of height is proportional to:
(a) H
(b) $H^{1/2}$
(c) H^0
(d) $H^{-1/2}$

52. The wavelength of a photon needed to remove a proton from a nucleus, which is bound to the nucleus with 1 MeV energy, is nearly:
(a) 1.2 nm
(b) 1.2 10^{-3} nm
(c) 1.2 10^{-6} nm
(d) 1.2 10^{1} nm

53. A proton, a neutron, an electron and an α-particle have same energy. Then their de Broglie wavelengths compare as:

(a) $\lambda_p = \lambda_n > \lambda_e > \lambda_\alpha$ (b) $\lambda_\alpha < \lambda_p = \lambda_n > \lambda_e$

(c) $\lambda_e < \lambda_p = \lambda_n > \lambda_\alpha$ (d) $\lambda_e = \lambda_p = \lambda_n = \lambda_\alpha$

54. Two particles A_{1s} and A_2 of masses m_1, m_2 $(m_1 > m_2)$ have the same de Broglie wavelength. Then:

(a) their momenta are the same.

(b) their energies are the same.

(c) energy of A_1 is less than the energy of A_2.

(d) energy of A_1 is more than the energy of A_2.

55. Photons absorbed in matter are converted to heat. A source emitting n photon/sec of frequency v is used to convert 1 kg of ice at 0° C to water at 0° C. Then, the time T taken for the conversion:

(a) decreases with increasing n, with v fixed.

(b) decreases with n fixed, v increasing.

(c) remains constant with n and v changing such that nv = constant.

(d) increases when the product nv increases.

56. Taking the Bohr radius as $a_0 = 53$ pm, the radius of Li^{++} ion in its ground state, on the basis of Bohr's model, will be about:

(a) 53 pm (b) 27 pm

(c) 18 pm (d) 13 pm

57. The simple Bohr model cannot be directly applied to calculate energy levels of an atom with many electrons. This is because:

(a) of the electrons not being subject to a central force.

(b) of the electrons colliding with each other.

(c) of screening effects.

(d) the force between the nucleus and an electron will no longer be given by Coulomb's law.

58. Two H atoms in the ground state collide inelastically. The maximum amount, by which their combined kinetic energy is reduced, is:

(a) 10.20 eV (b) 20.40 eV

(c) 13.6 eV (d) 27.2 eV

59. An ionised H-molecule consists of an electron and two protons. The protons are separated by a small distance of the order of angstrom. In the ground state:

(a) the electron would not move in circular orbits.

(b) the energy would be $(2)^4$ times that of an H-atom.

(c) the electrons, orbit would go around the protons.

(d) the molecule will soon decay in a proton and an H-atom.

60. The Bohr model for the spctra of an H-atom:

(a) will not be applicable to hydrogen in the molecular form.

(b) will not be applicable as it is for an He-atom.

(c) is valid only at room temperature.

(d) predicts continuous as well as discrete spectral lines.

61. Suppose we consider a large number of containers, each containing initially 1000 atoms of a radioactive material with a half life of 1 year. After 1 year:

(a) all the containers will have 5000 atoms of the material.

(b) all the containers will contain the same number of atoms of the material but that number will only be approximately 5000.

(c) the containers will, in general, have different numbers of the atoms of the material but their average will be close to 5000.

(d) none of the containers can have more than 5000 atoms.

62. When a nucleus in an atom undergoes a radioactive decay, the electronic energy levels of the atom:

(a) do not change for any type of radioactivity.

(b) change for α- and β-radioactivity but not for γ-radioactivity.

(c) change for α-radioactivity but not for others.

(d) change for β-radioactivity but not for others.

63. Heavy stable nuclei have more neutrons than protons. This is because of the fact that:

(a) neutrons are heavier than protons.

(b) electrostatic force between protons is repulsive.

(c) neutrons decay into protons through beta decay.

(d) nuclear forces between neutrons are weaker than that between protons.

64. In a nuclear reactor, moderators slow down the neutrons which come out in a fission process. The moderators used have light nuclei. Heavy nuclei will not serve the purpose because:

(a) they will break up.

(b) elastic collision of neutrons with heavy nuclei will not slow them down.

(c) the net weight of the reactor would be unbearably high.

(d) substances with heavy nuclei do not occur in liquid or gaseous state at room temperature.

65. Fusion processes, like combining two deuterons to form an He nucleus, are impossible at ordinary temperatures and pressure. The reasons for this can be traced to the fact that:

(a) nuclear forces have short range.

(b) nuclei are positively charged.

(c) the original nuclei must be completely ionized before fusion can take place.

(d) the original nuclei must first break up before combining with each other.

66. The conductivity of a semiconductor increases with increase in temperature because:

(a) number density of free current carriers increases.

(b) relaxation time increases.

(c) both number density of carriers and relaxation time increase.

(d) number density of current carriers increases, relaxation time decreases but effect of decrease in relaxation time is much less than increase in number density.

67. Hole is:

(a) an anti-particle of electron.

(b) a vacancy created when an electron leaves a covalent bond.

(c) absence of free electrons.

(d) an artificially created particle.

68. When an electric field is applied across a semiconductor:

(a) electrons move from lower energy level to higher energy level in the cunduction band.

(b) eletrons move from higher energy level to lower energy level in the conduction band.

(c) holes in the valence band move from higher energy level to lower energy level.

(d) holes in the valence band move from lower energy level to higher energy level.

69. In an npn transistor circuit, the collector current is 10 mA. If 95 percent of the electrons emitted reach the collector, which of the following statements are true?

(a) The emitter current will be 8 mA. (b) The emitter current will be 10.53 mA.

(c) The base current will be 0.53 mA. (d) The base current will be 2 mA.

70. What happens during regulation action of a Zener diode?

(a) The current in and voltage across the Zener remains fixed.

(b) The current through the series Resistance (R_s) changes.

(c) The Zener resistance is constant.

(d) The resistance offered by the Zener changes.

71. A speech signal of 3 kHz is used to modulate a carrier signal of frequency 1 MHz, using amplitude modulation. The frequencies of the side bands will be:

(a) 1.003 MHz and 0.997 MHz. (b) 3001 kHz and 2997 kHz.

(c) 1003 kHz and 1000 kHz. (d) 1 MHz and 0.997 MHz.

72. A male voice after modulation-transmission sounds like that of a female to the receiver. The problem is due to:

(a) poor selection of modulation index (selected $0 < m < 1$)

(b) poor bandwidth selection of amplifiers.

(c) poor selection of carrier frequency

(d) loss of energy in transmission.

73. An audio signal of 15kHz frequency cannot be transmitted over long distances without modulation because:

(a) the size of the required antenna would be at least 5 km which is not convenient.

(b) the audio signal cannot be transmitted through sky waves.

(c) the size of the required antenna would be at least 20 km, which is not convenient.

(d) effective power transmitted would be very low, if the size of the antenna is less than 5 km.

74. Audio sine waves of 3 kHz frequency are used to amplitude modulate a carrier signal of 1.5 MHz. Which of the following statements are true?

(a) The side band frequencies are 1506 kHz and 1494 kHz.

(b) The bandwidth required for amplitude modulation is 6 kHz.

(c) The bandwidth required for amplitude modulation is 3 MHz.

(d) The side band frequencies are 1503 kHz and 1497 kHz.

75. A TV transmission tower has a height of 240 m. Signals broadcast from this tower will be received by LOS communication at a distance of (assume the radius of earth to be 6.4×10^6 m):

(a) 100 km. (b) 24 km.

(c) 55 km. (d) 50 km.

ANSWERS

1. (a) **2.** (b), (d) **3.** (c), (d)

4. (b), (d) **5.** (c), (d) **6.** (c)

7. (c) **8.** (a) **9.** (b), (c), (d)

10. (a), (b), (c) **11.** (b) **12.** (c)

13. (b) **14.** (b), (d) **15.** (a), (b)

16. (a) **17.** (d) **18.** (a)

19. (a), (b) **20.** (b), (d) **21.** (a)

22. (c) **23.** (a), (d) **24.** (a), (d)

25. (b), (c), (d) **26.** (b) **27.** (a), (b), (d)

28. (a), (b), (c) **29.** (a), (d) **30.** (b), (c)

31. (b) **32.** (c) **33.** (a), (d)

37. (c), (d) **35.** (a), (b), (d) **36.** (c)

37. (b) **38.** (a), (c), (d) **39.** (b), (d)

40. (a), (c), (d)	**41.** (a)	**42.** (d)
43. (c)	**44.** (b)	**45.** (b)
46. (a)	**47.** (c)	**48.** (b), (d)
49. (a), (b)	**50.** (a), (b)	**51.** (d)
52. (b)	**53.** (b)	**54.** (a), (c)
55. (a), (b), (c)	**56.** (c)	**57.** (a)
58. (a)	**59.** (a), (c)	**60.** (a), (b)
61. (c)	**62.** (b)	**63.** (b)
64. (b)	**65.** (a), (b)	**66.** (d)
67. (b)	**68.** (a), (c)	**69.** (b), (c)
70. (b), (d)	**71.** (a)	**72.** (b)
73. (a), (b), (d)	**74.** (b), (d)	**75.** (b), (c), (d)

❑❑❑

CBSE XII

SOLVED QUESTION PAPER

Q. 1. Define the term 'Mobility' of charge carriers in a conductor. Write its S.I. unit.

Q. 2. The carrier wave is given by $C(t) = 2\sin(8\pi t)$ volt.

The modulating signal is a square wave as shown. Find modulation index.

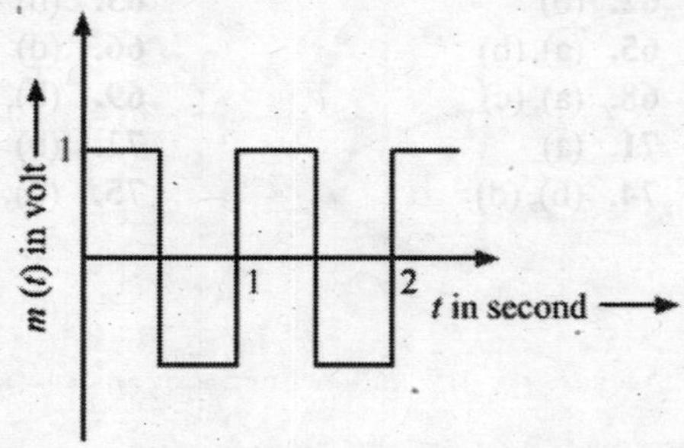

Q. 3. "For any charge configuration, equi-potential surface through a point is normal to the electric field." Justify.

Q. 4. Two spherical bobs, one metallic and the other of glass, of the same size are allowed to fall freely from the same height above the ground. Which of the two would reach earlier and why?

Q. 5. Show variation of resistivity of copper as a function of temperature in a graph.

Q. 6. A convex lens is placed in contact with a plane mirror. A point object at a distance of 20 cm on the axis of this combination has its image coinciding with itself. What is the focal length of the lens?

Q. 7. Write the expression, in a vector form, for the Lorentz magnetic force $\vec{F}$ due to a charge moving with velocity $\vec{V}$ in a magnetic field $\vec{B}$. What is the direction of the magnetic force?

Q. 8. The figure given below shows the block diagram of a generalized communication system. Identify the element labelled 'X' and write its function.

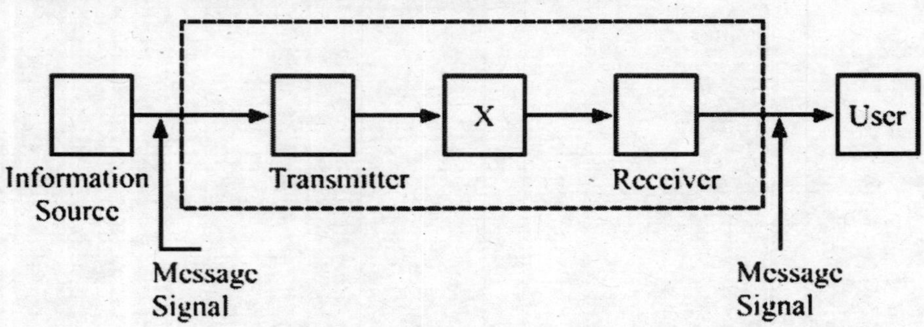

Q. 9. Out of the two magnetic materials, 'A' has relative permeability slightly greater than unity while 'B' has less than unity. Identify the nature of the materials 'A' and 'B'. Will their susceptibilities be positive or negative?

Q. 10. Given a uniform electric field $\vec{E} = 5 \times 10^3 \hat{i}$ N/C, find the flux of this field through a square of 10 cm on a side whose plane is parallel to the y-z plane. What would be the flux through the same square if the plane makes a 30° angle with the x-axis?

Q. 11. For a single slit of width "a", the first minimum of the interference pattern of a monochromatic light of wavelength λ occurs at an angle of $\frac{\lambda}{a}$. At the same angle of $\frac{\lambda}{a}$, we get a maximum for two narrow slits separated by a distance "a". Explain.

Q. 12. Write the truth table for the combination of the gates shown. Name the gates used.

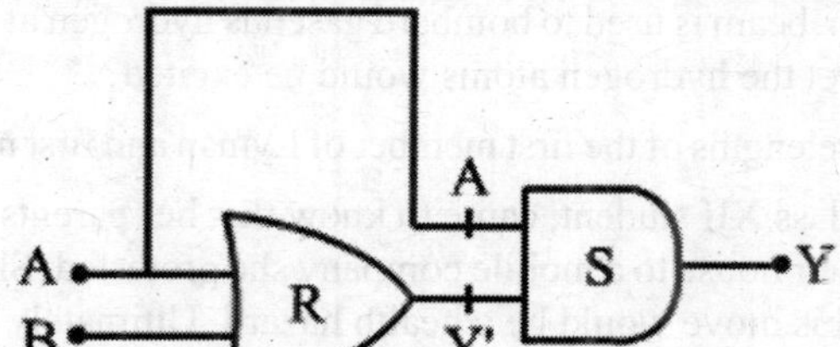

OR

Identify the logic gates marked 'P' and 'Q' in the given circuit. Write the truth table for the combination.

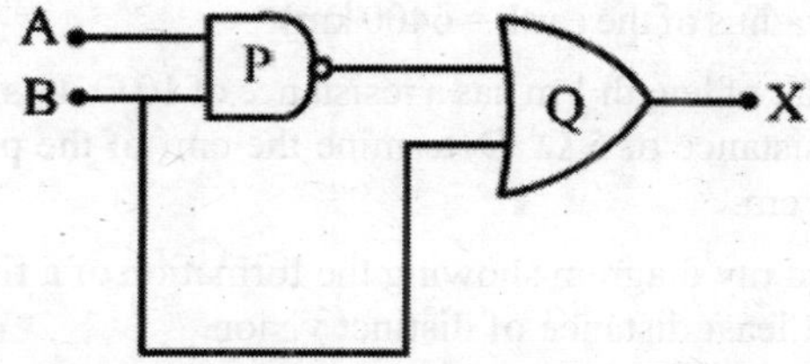

Q. 13. State Kirchhoff's rules. Explain briefly how these rules are justified.

Q. 14. A capacitor 'C', a variable resistor 'R' and a bulb 'B' are connected in series to the ac mains in circuit as shown. The bulb glows with some brightness. How will the glow of the bulb change if (i) a dielectric slab is introduced between the plates of the capacitor, keeping resistance R to be the same; (ii) the resistance R is increased keeping the same capacitance?

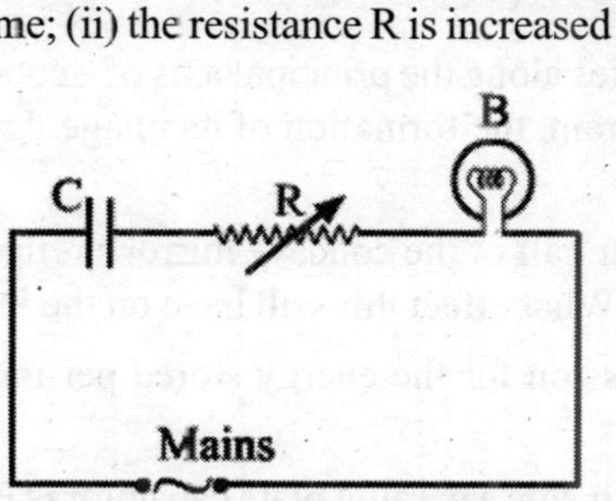

Q. 15. State the underlying principle of a cyclotron. Write briefly how this machine is used to accelerate charged particles to high energies.

Q. 16. An electric dipole of length 4 cm, when placed with its axis making an angle of 60° with a uniform electric field, experiences a torque of $4\sqrt{3}$ Nm. Calculate the potential energy of the dipole, if it has charge ± 8 nC.

Q. 17. A proton and a deuteron are accelerated through the same accelerating potential. Which one of the two has:

(a) greater value of de-Broglie wavelength associated with it, and

(b) less momentum?

Give reasons to justify your answer.

Q. 18. (i) Monochromatic light of frequency 6.0×10^{14} Hz is produced by a laser. The power emitted is 2.0×10^{-3} W. Estimate the number of photons emitted per second on an average by the source.

(ii) Draw a plot showing the variation of photoelectric current versus the intensity of incident radiation on a given photosensitive surface.

Q. 19. A 12.5 eV electron beam is used to bombard gaseous hydrogen at room temperature. Upto which energy level the hydrogen atoms would be excited?

Calculate the wavelengths of the first member of Lyman and first member of Balmer series.

Q. 20. When Sunita, a class XII student, came to know that her parents are planning to rent out the top floor of their house to a mobile company she protested. She tried hard to convince her parents that this move would be a health hazard. Ultimately her parents agreed.

(1) In what way can the setting up of transmission tower by a mobile company in a residential colony prove to be injurious to health?

(2) By objecting to this move of her parents, what value did Sunita display?

(3) Estimate the range of e.m. waves which can be transmitted by an antenna of height 20 m. (Given radius of the earth = 6400 km).

Q. 21. A potentiometer wire of length 1 m has a resistance of 10 Ω. It is connected to a 6 V battery in series with a resistance of 5 Ω. Determine the emf of the primary cell which gives a balance point at 40 cm.

Q. 22. (a) Draw a labeled ray diagram showing the formation of a final image by a compound microscope at least distance of distinct vision.

(b) The total magnification produced by a compound microscope is 20. The magnification produced by the eye piece is 5. The microscope is focused on a certain object. The distance between the objective and eyepiece is observed to be 14 cm. If least distance of distinct vision is 20 cm, calculate the focal length of the objective and the eye piece.

Q. 23. (a) A mobile phone lies along the principal axis of a concave mirror. Show with the help of a suitable diagram, the formation of its image. Explain why magnification is not uniform.

(b) Suppose the lower half of the concave mirror's reflecting surface is covered with an opaque material. What effect this will have on the image of the object? Explain.

Q. 24. (a) Obtain the expression for the energy stored per unit volume in a charged parallel plate capacitor.

(b) The electric field inside a parallel plate capacitor is E. Find the amount of work done in moving a charge q over a closed loop a b c d a.

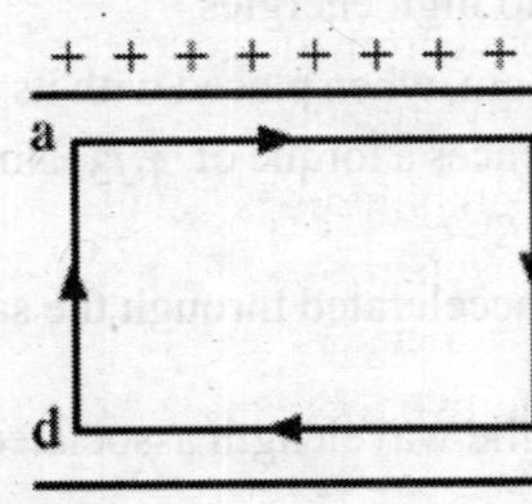

OR

(a) Derive the expression for the capacitance of a parallel plate capacitor having plate area A and plate separation d.

(b) Two charged spherical conductors of radii R_1 and R_2 when connected by a conducting wire acquire charges q_1 and q_2 respectively. Find the ratio of their surface charge densities in terms of their radii.

Q. 25. (a) State Ampere's circuital law, expressing it in the integral form.

(b) Two long coaxial insulated solenoids, S_1 and S_2 of equal lengths are wound one over the other as shown in the figure. A steady current "I" flow thought the inner solenoid S_1 to the other end B, which is connected to the outer solenoid S_2 through which the same current "I" flows in the opposite direction so as to come out at end A. If n_1 and n_2 are the number of turns per unit length, find the magnitude and direction of the net magnetic field at a point (i) inside on the axis and (ii) outside the combined system.

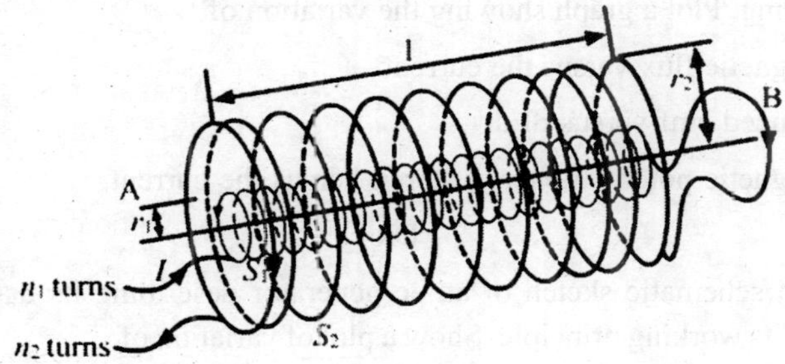

Q. 26. Answer the following:

(a) Name the em waves which are suitable for radar systems used in aircraft navigation. Write the range of frequency of these waves.

(b) If the earth did not have atmosphere, would its average surface temperature be higher or lower than what it is now? Explain.

(c) An em wave exerts pressure on the surface on which it is incident. Justify.

Q. 27. (a) Deduce the expression, $N = N_0 e^{-\lambda t}$, for the law of radioactive decay.

(b) (i) Write symbolically the process expressing the β^+ decay of $^{22}_{11}Na$. Also write the basic nuclear process underlying this decay.

(ii) Is the nucleus formed in the decay of the nucleus $^{22}_{11}Na$, an isotope or isobar?

Q. 28. (a) (i) 'Two independent monochromatic sources of light cannot produce a sustained interference pattern'. Give reason.

(ii) Light waves each of amplitude "a" and frequency "ω", emanating from two coherent light sources superpose at a point. If the displacements due to these waves is given by $y_1 = a \cos \omega t$ and $y_2 = a \cos (\omega t + \phi)$ where ϕ is the phase difference between the two, obtain the expression for the resultant intensity at the point.

(b) In Young's double slit experiment, using monochromatic light of wavelength λ, the intensity of light at a point on the screen where path difference is λ, is K units. Find out the intensity of light at a point where path difference is $\lambda/3$.

OR

(a) How does one demonstrate, using a suitable diagram, that unpolarised light when passed through a Polaroid gets polarised?

(b) A beam of unpolarised light is incident on a glass-air interface. Show, using a suitable ray diagram, that light reflected from the interface is totally polarised, when $\mu = \tan i_B$, where μ is the refractive index of glass with respect to air and i_B is the Brewster's angle.

Q. 29. (a) Describe a simple experiment (or activity) to show that the polarity of emf induced in a coil is always such that it tends to produce a current which opposes the change of magnetic flux that produces it.

(b) The current flowing through an inductor of self inductance L is continuously increasing. Plot a graph showing the variation of

(i) Magnetic flux versus the current

(ii) Induced emf versus dI/dt

(iii) Magnetic potential energy stored versus the current.

OR

(a) Draw a schematic sketch of an ac generator describing its basic elements. State briefly its working principle. Show a plot of variation of

(i) Magnetic flux and

(ii) Alternating emf versus time generated by a loop of wire rotating in a magnetic field.

(b) Why is choke coil needed in the use of fluorescent tubes with ac mains?

Q. 30. (a) State briefly the processes involved in the formation of p-n junction explaining clearly how the depletion region is formed.

(b) Using the necessary circuit diagrams, show how the V-I characteristics of a p-n junction are obtained in

(i) Forward biasing

(ii) Reverse biasing

How are these characteristics made use of in rectification?

OR

(a) Differentiate between three segments of a transistor on the basis of their size and level of doping.

(b) How is a transistor biased to be in active state?

(c) With the help of necessary circuit diagram, describe briefly how n-p-n transistor in CE configuration amplifies a small sinusoidal input voltage. Write the expression for the ac current gain.

SOLUTIONS

1. Magnitude of the drift velocity of charge carrier per unit applied = Electric field is called mobility.

$$\text{Mobility, } \mu = \frac{Drift\,Velocity}{Electric\,Field}$$

$$\mu = \frac{|V_d|}{E}$$

$$\text{SI unit} = \frac{m^2}{(Volt\,second)} \text{ or } ms^{-1}N^{-1}C$$

2. The generalised equation of a carrier wave is:

$c(t) = A_c \sin \omega_c t$

The generalised equation of a modulating wave is:

$c_m(t) = A_c \sin \omega_c t + \mu A_c \sin \omega_m t \sin \omega_c t$

Modulation Index μ is defined as $\frac{A_m}{A_c}$

On comparing this with the equations of carrier wave and modulating wave, we get:

Amplitude of modulating signal, $A_m = 1$ V

Amplitude of carrier wave, $A_c = 2$ V

$$\mu = \frac{A_m}{A_c} = \frac{1}{2} = 0.5$$

3. We know that the work done (W) in moving a test charge along an equipotential surface is zero. This is because an equipotential surface is a surface with a constant value of potential at all the points on the surface.

If Electric field is not normal, it will have non-zero component along the surface. In that case, work would be done in moving a charge on an equipotential surface which is not possible.

4. A glass bob is non-conducting, while a metallic bob is conducting. Due to the non-conducting nature of the glass bob, it will only experience the Earth's gravitational pull. In glass there is no effect of electromagnetic induction, due to presence of Earth's magnetic field, unlike in the case of metallic ball. So, the glass bob will reach the ground earlier.

5. The variation of resistivity of copper with temperature is parabolic in nature.

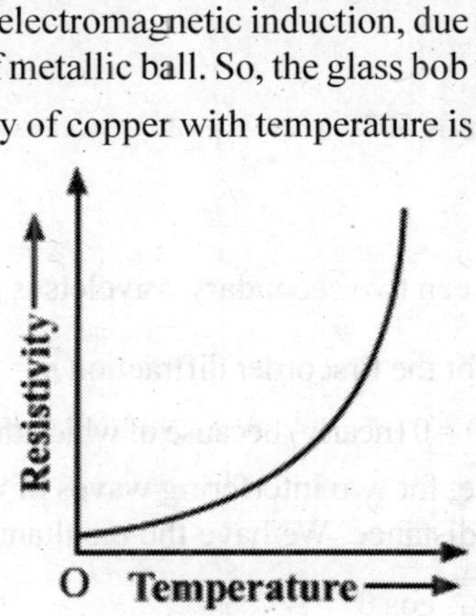

6. Here, the convex lens is in contact with a plane mirror and the image distance is equal to the object distance. This is possible only when the point object is placed at the centre of the curvature of the lens.

$$f = \frac{R}{2}$$

Focal length of the lens $= \frac{20}{2} = 10\,\text{cm}$

7. The Lorentz magnetic force is given by the following relation:

$$\vec{F} = q\left(\vec{V} \times \vec{B}\right)$$

The direction of the magnetic force is perpendicular to the plane containing the velocity vector ($\vec{V}$) and the magnetic field vector ($\vec{B}$).

8. The element labelled 'X' is called 'channel'. The function of the channel is to connect the transmitter and the receiver.

9. For a paramagnetic material, the relative permeability lies between $1 < \mu_r < 1 + \varepsilon$ and its susceptibility lies between $0 < \chi < \varepsilon$.

Hence, 'A' is a paramagnetic material and its susceptibility is positive.

For a diamagnetic material, the relative permeability lies between $0 \le \mu_r < 1$ and its susceptibility lies between $-1 \le \chi < 0$.

Hence, 'B' is a diamagnetic material and its susceptibility is negative. This is because its relative permeability is less than unity.

Here, μ_r and χ refer to the relative permeability and susceptibility.

10. Electric flux, $\phi = \vec{E}.\vec{A}$

$$\vec{E} = 5 \times 10^3\,\hat{i}\,\frac{N}{C}$$

$$\vec{A} = (10cm)^2\,\hat{i} = 10^{-2}\,\hat{i}\,m^2$$

$$\phi = \left(5 \times 10^3\,\hat{i}\right).\left(10^{-2}\,\hat{i}\right)$$

$\therefore \quad \phi = 50$ Weber

When the plane makes a 30° angle with the x-axis, the area vector makes 60° with the x-axis.

$$\phi = EA\cos\theta$$

$$= (5 \times 10^3)(10^{-2})\cos 60°$$

$$= \frac{50}{2} = 25 \text{ weber}$$

11. The path difference between two secondary wavelets is given by $n\lambda = a\sin\theta$. Since, θ is very small $\sin\theta = \theta$. So, for the first order diffraction $n = 1$, the angle is $\frac{\lambda}{\alpha}$. Now we know that θ must be very small $\theta = 0$ (nearly) because of which the diffraction pattern is minimum. Now for interference case, for two interfering waves of intensity I_1 and I_2 we must have two slits separated by a distance. We have the resultant intensity,

$$I = I_1 + I_2 + 2\sqrt{I_1 I_2}\,\cos\theta$$

Since, $\theta = 0$, so $\cos\theta = 1$ (nearly)

$\Rightarrow \quad I = I_1 + I_2 + 2\sqrt{I_1 I_2}$

We see the resultant intensity is sum of the two intensities, so there is a maxima corresponding to the angle $\frac{\lambda}{a}$. This is why, at the same angle of $\frac{\lambda}{a}$, we get a maximum for two narrow slits separated by a distance "a".

12. R - OR GATE

S - AND GATE

A	B	Y' = A + B	Y = Y'.A
0	0	0	0
0	1	1	0
1	0	1	1
1	1	1	1

OR

P - NAND GATE

Q - OR GATE

$X' = \overline{A.B}$

A	B	$X' = \overline{A.B}$	X
0	0	1	1
0	1	1	1
1	0	1	1
1	1	0	1

13. **Junction rule:** At any junction, the sum of the currents entering the junction is equal to the sum of currents leaving the junction.

Alternatively, $\sum i = 0$

Justification : Conservation of charge

Loop rule: The Algebraic sum of changes in the potential around any closed loop involving resistors and cells in the loop is zero.

Alternatively, $\Sigma\Delta V = 0$, where ΔV is the changes in potential

Justification : Conservation of energy

14. (i) As the dielectric slab is introduced between the plates of the capacitor, its capacitance will increase. Hence, the potential drop across the capacitor will decrease $\left(V = \frac{Q}{C}\right)$.

As a result, the potential drop across the bulb will increase (since both are connected in series). So, its brightness will increase.

(ii) As the resistance (R) is increased, the potential drop across the resistor will increase. As a result, the potential drop across the bulb will decrease (since both are connected in series). So, its brightness will decrease.

15. The underlying principle of a cyclotron is that an oscillating electric field can be used to accelerate a charge particle to high energy.

A cyclotron involves the use of an electric field to accelerate charge particles across the gap between the two D-shaped magnetic field regions. The magnetic field is perpendicular to the paths of the charged particles that makes them follow in circular paths within the two Ds. An alternating voltage accelerates the charged particles each time they cross the Ds. The radius of each particle's path increases with its speed. So, the accelerated particles spiral toward the outer wall of the cyclotron.

Square wave electric fields are used to accelerate the charged particles in a cyclotron. The accelerating electric field reverses just at the time the charge particle finishes its half circle so that it gets accelerated across the gap between the Ds. The particle gets accelerated again and again, and its velocity increases. Therefore, it attains high kinetic energy.

16. $\tau = pE \sin\theta$

$4\sqrt{3} = pE \sin 60°$

$\Rightarrow$ Potential Energy, $pE = 8$

$U = -pE \cos\theta$

$= -8 \times \cos 60° = -4J$

17. (a) de Broglie wavelength is given by

$$\lambda = \frac{h}{\sqrt{2mqV}}$$

Mass and charge of a proton are m_p and e respectively, and, mass and charge of a deutron are $2m_p$ and e respectively;where, e is the charge of an electron

$$\frac{\lambda_P}{\lambda_D} = \sqrt{\frac{m_D q_D}{m_p q_p}} = \sqrt{\frac{(2m_p)(e)}{(m_p)(e)}} = \sqrt{2}$$

Thus, de-broglie wavelength associated with proton is $\sqrt{2}$ times of the de-broglie wavelength of deutron and hence it is more.

(b) Momentum,

$$p = \frac{h}{\lambda} \quad \text{or} \quad p \propto \frac{1}{\lambda}$$

As the wavelength of a proton is more than that of deutron thus, the momentum of a proton is lesser than that of deutron. Hence, the momentum of proton is less.

18. (i) Power = $nh\nu$, where n = no. of photons per second

$$2.0 \times 10^{-3} = n \times 6.6 \times 10^{-34} \times 6 \times 10^{14}$$

$$\Rightarrow \quad n = \frac{2.0 \times 10^{-3}}{6.63 \times 10^{-34} \times 6 \times 10^{14}}$$

$$= 5.03 \times 10^{15} \text{ photons/second}$$

(ii)

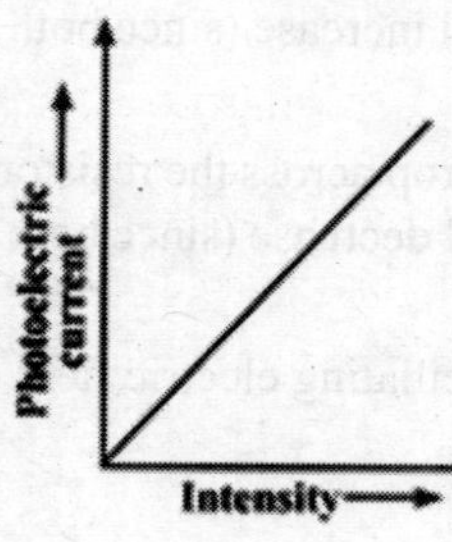

19. $E_n = -\frac{13.6}{n^2} eV$

Energy required to excite an atom from the initial state (n_i) to the final state (n_f)

$$= -\frac{13.6}{n_f^2} + \frac{13.6}{n_i^2} eV$$

$$\Rightarrow \quad -\frac{13.6}{n_f^2} + \frac{13.6}{n_i^2} = 12.5$$

Energy of the electron in the ground state $= -\frac{13.6}{1^2} = -13.6eV$

Therefore, $13.6 - 12.5 = \frac{13.6}{n_f^2}$

$\Rightarrow \quad n_f = 3.5$, but State cannot be a fraction number. So $n_f = 3$

Hence, hydrogen atom would be excited up to 3rd energy level.

Rydberg formula for the spectrum of the hydrogen atom is given below:

$$\frac{1}{\lambda} = R\left[\frac{1}{n_1^2} - \frac{1}{n_2^2}\right]$$

$R = 1.097 \times 10^7 \text{ m}^{-1}$

For the first member of the Lyman series:

$n_1 = 1$ and $n_2 = 2$

Therefore $\lambda = 1215$ A°

For the first member of Balmer series:

$n_1 = 2$ and $n_2 = 3$

Therefore $\lambda = 6563$ A°

20. (1) A transmitting tower makes use of electromagnetic waves such as microwaves, exposure to which can cause severe health hazards like tumour and cancer. Also, the transmitting antenna operates on a very high power, so the risk of someone getting severely burnt in a residential area increases.

(2) By objecting to this move of her parents, Sunita has displayed awareness towards the health and environment of her society.

(3) Range of the transmitting antenna, $d = \sqrt{2hR}$

$R = 6400 \text{ km} = 64 \times 10^5 \text{ m}$

$d = \sqrt{2 \times 20 \times 64 \times 10^5} = 16000 \text{ m}$

21. Current flowing in Potentiometer wire,

$$I = \frac{V}{R + R'}$$

$$= \frac{6}{10 + 5} = 0.4 \text{ A}$$

Potential drop across the potentiometer wire

V = IR

$= 0.4 \times 10 = 4.0$ V

Potential Gradient $k = \frac{V}{l} = 4.0 \ V/m$

Therefore, unknown EMF of Cell $= k \,.\, l' = 4.0 \times 0.4 = 1.6$ V

22. (a)

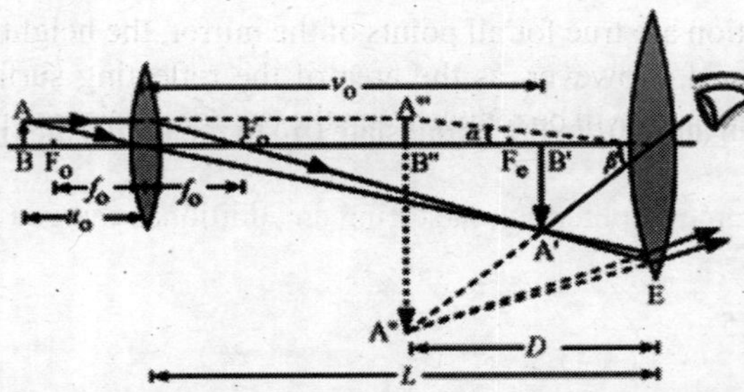

Where, AB = object, A'B' = image formed by objective and A"B" = image formed by eyepiece

f_0 = focal length of objective,

u_0 = object distance from objective

v_0 = image distance from objective

D = distance of least distinct vision

L = length of the microscope

(b) For the least distance of clear vision, the total magnification is given by:

$$-\frac{L}{f_0}\left(1+\frac{D}{f_e}\right) = m_0 . m_e \quad ...(1)$$

Also, the given magnification for the eyepiece:

$$m_e = 5 = \left(1+\frac{D}{f_e}\right)$$

$\Rightarrow \quad f_e = 5$ cm (since D = 20 cm)

Substituting the value of m and m_e in equation (1), we get:

$$m = m_0 . m_e$$

$$\Rightarrow \quad m_0 = \frac{m}{m_e} = \frac{20}{5} = 4$$

Also, $\quad m_0 = \frac{L}{|f_0|}$

So, $\quad f_0 = \frac{14}{4} = 3.5\,\text{cm}$

23. (a)

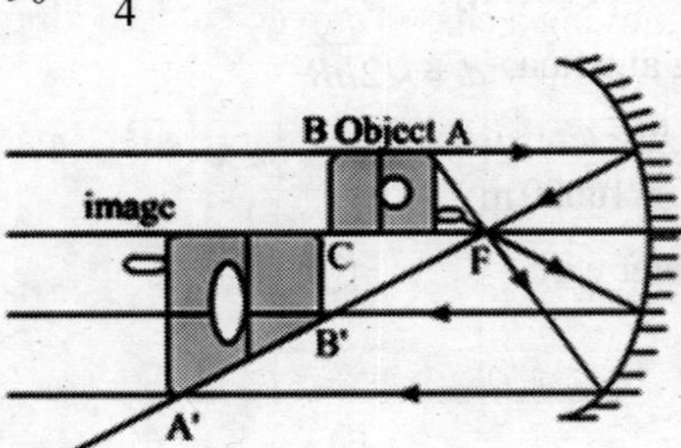

The image of the mobile phone formed by the concave mirror is shown in the above figure. The part of the mobile phone that is at C will form an image of the same size only at C. In the figure, we can see that B'C = BC. The part of the mobile phone that lies between C and F will form enlarged image beyond C as shown in the figure. It can be observed that the magnification of each part of the mobile phone cannot be uniform on account of different locations. That is why the image formed is not uniform.

(b) As the laws of reflection are true for all points of the mirror, the height of the whole image will be produced. However, as the area of the reflecting surface has been reduced, the image intensity will be reduced. In other words, the image produced will be less bright.

24. (a) Work done by the source of potential, in storing an additional charge (dq), is

$$dW = V \, . \, dq$$

But $\quad V = \dfrac{q}{C}$

$\Rightarrow \quad dW = \dfrac{q}{C} dq$

Total work done in storing the charge Q,

$$\int dW = \int_O^Q \frac{q}{C} dq$$

$$\Rightarrow \quad W = \frac{1}{C}\left(\frac{q^2}{2}\right)_O^Q = \frac{Q^2}{2C}$$

This work is stored as electrostatic energy in the capacitor.

$\because \quad Q = CV, \quad \therefore \quad U = \dfrac{1}{2} CV^2$

Energy stored per unit volume $= \dfrac{1}{2}\dfrac{CV^2}{Ad}$

$$= \frac{\frac{1}{2}\left(\frac{\epsilon_0 A}{d}\right)(Ed)^2}{Ad}$$

$$= \frac{1}{2} \epsilon_0 E^2$$

(b) Work done in moving the charge q from a to b, and from c to d is zero because Electric field is perpendicular to the displacement.

Work done from b to c = – Work done from d to a

$\therefore$ Total work done in moving a charge q over a closed loop = 0

OR

(a) A parallel plate capacitor consists of two large plane parallel conducting plates separated by a small distance.

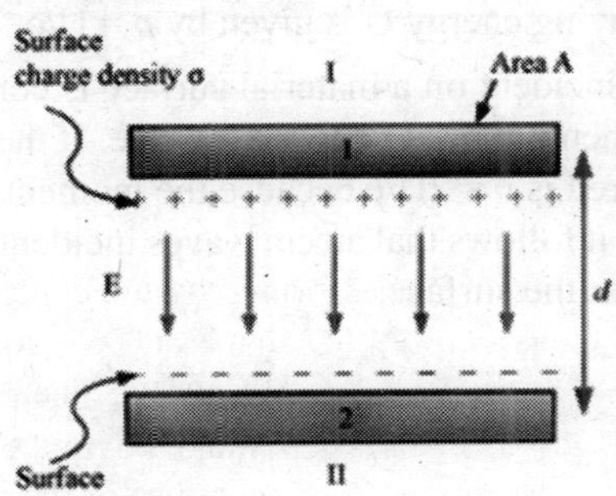

Electric field between the plates of capacitor $E = \dfrac{\sigma}{\varepsilon_0} = \dfrac{Q}{A\varepsilon_0}$

$\therefore$ potential difference $V = Ed = \dfrac{Qd}{A\varepsilon_0}$

Capacitance $C = \dfrac{Q}{V} = \dfrac{\varepsilon_0 A}{d}$

(b) When the two charged spherical conductors are connected by a conducting wire, they acquire the same potential

i.e., $\dfrac{Kq_1}{R_1} = \dfrac{Kq_2}{R_2} \Rightarrow \dfrac{q_1}{q_2} = \dfrac{R_1}{R_2}$

Hence, ratio of surface charge densities

$$\frac{\sigma_1}{\sigma_2} = \frac{\dfrac{q_1}{4\pi R_1^2}}{\dfrac{q_2}{4\pi R_2^2}}$$

$$= \frac{q_1 R_2^2}{q_2 R_1^2}$$

$$= \frac{R_1}{R_2} \times \frac{R_2^2}{R_1^2} = \frac{R_2}{R_1}$$

25. (a) Ampere's Circuital Law states that the circulation of the resultant magnetic field along a closed, plane curve is equal to μ_0 times the total current crossing the area bounded by the closed curve, provided the electric field inside the loop remains constant.

$$\oint \vec{B}.\vec{dl} = \mu_0 i$$

Magnitude of net magnetic field inside the combined system on the axis,

$$\mathrm{B} = \mathrm{B}_1 - \mathrm{B}_2$$

$\Rightarrow$ $\mathrm{B} = m_0 (n_1 - n_2)\,1$

(iii) Outside the combined system, the net magnetic field is zero.

26. (a) Microwaves are suitable for radar systems used in aircraft navigation. The range of frequency for these waves is 10^9 Hz to 10^{12} Hz.

(b) In the absence of atmosphere, there would be no greenhouse effect on the surface of the Earth. As a result, the temperature of the Earth would decrease rapidly, making it difficult for human survival.

(c) An em wave carries a linear momentum with it. The linear momentum carried by a portion of wave having energy U is given by p = U/c.

Thus, if the wave incident on a material surface is completely absorbed, it delivers energy U and momentum p = U/c to the surface. If the wave is totally reflected, the momentum delivered is p = 2U/c because the momentum of the wave changes from p to $-p$. Therefore, it follows that an em waves incident on a surface exert a force and hence a pressure on the surface.

27. (a) $\dfrac{dN}{dt} = -\lambda N$

$$\int_{N_0}^{N} \frac{dN}{N} = \int_0^t -\lambda dt$$

$$[\log_e N]_{N_0}^{N} = -\lambda[t]_0^t$$

$$\log_e \frac{N}{N_0} = -\lambda t$$

$$N = N_0 e^{-\lambda t}$$

(b) (i) $^{22}_{11}Na \rightarrow ^{22}_{10}Ne + e^{+} + \nu$

Basic process

$p \rightarrow n + e^{+} + \nu$

(ii) The nucleus so formed is an isobar of $^{22}_{11}$Na because the mass number is same, but the atomic numbers are different.

28. (a) (i) Light waves, originating from two independent monochromatic sources, will not have a constant phase difference. Therefore, these sources will not be coherent and, therefore, would not produce a sustained interference pattern.

(ii) Let the displacement of the waves from the sources S_1 and S_2 at point P on the screen at any time t be given by:

$y_1 = a \cos \omega t$ and $y_2 = a \cos (\omega t + \phi)$

$y = y_1 + y_2$

$= a \cos \omega t + a \cos (\omega t + \phi)$

$$= 2a \cos\frac{\phi}{2}.\cos\left(\omega t + \frac{\phi}{2}\right)$$

Amplitude of resultant displacement is $2a \cos \frac{\phi}{2}$

$\therefore$ Intensity $I = 4a^2 \cos^2 \frac{\phi}{2}$

(b) A path difference of λ, corresponds to a phase difference of 2π

$\therefore$ The intensity, $K = 4a^2$

$$\Rightarrow \quad a^2 = \frac{K}{4}$$

A path difference of $\frac{\lambda}{3}$, corresponds to a phase difference of $\frac{2\pi}{3}$

$$\therefore \quad \text{Intensity} = 4 \times \frac{K}{4}.\cos^2\frac{2\pi}{3} = \frac{K}{4}$$

OR

(a)

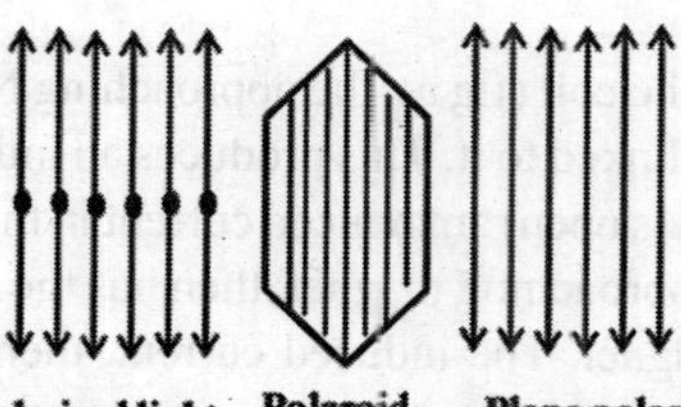

The components of electric vector associated with light wave, along the direction of aligned molecules of a polaroid, get absorbed. As a result after passing through it, the components perpendicular to the direction of aligned molecules will be obtained in the form of plane polarised light.

(b)

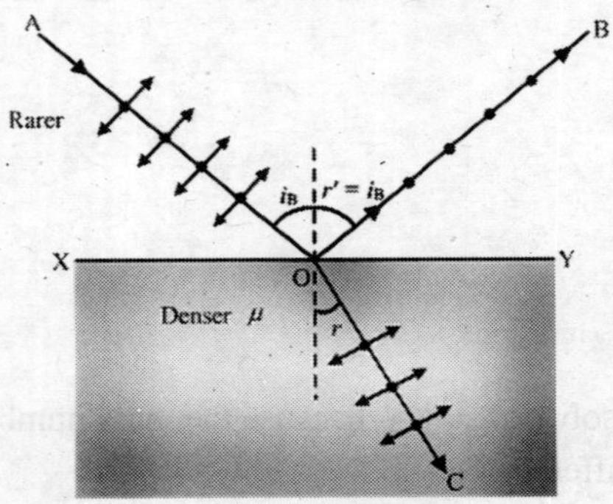

When unpolarised light is incident on the glass-air interface at Brewster angle i_B, then reflected light is totally polarised. This is called Brewster's Law. When light is incident at Brewster angle, the reflected component OB and the refracted component OC are mutually perpendicular to each other.

$$\angle BOY + \angle YOC = 90^\circ$$

$$(90^\circ - i_B) + (90^\circ - r) = 90^\circ$$

Where, r is angle of refraction

$$90^\circ - i_B = r$$

According to the Snell's law:

$$\mu = \frac{\sin i}{\sin r}$$

$$i = i_B \text{ and } r = (90^\circ - i_B)$$

$$\mu = \frac{\sin i_B}{\sin(90^\circ - i_B)} = \frac{\sin i_B}{\cos i_B}$$

$$\mu = \tan i_B \qquad \text{Hence proved.}$$

29. (a)

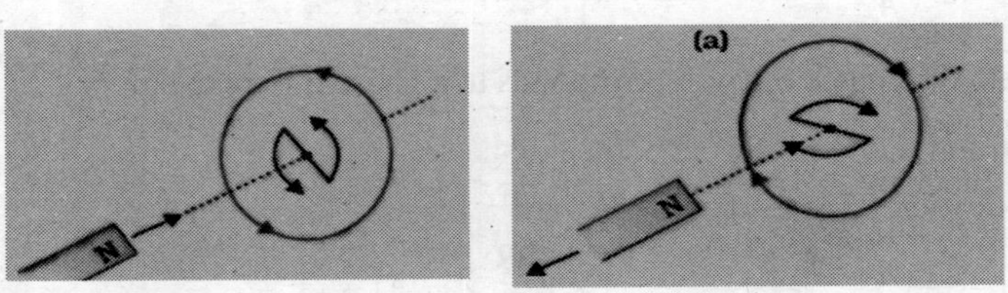

When a bar magnet is brought close to the coil (fig a), the approaching North Pole of the bar magnet increases the magnetic flux linked to it. This produces an induced emf which produces (or tends to produce, if the coil is open) an induced current in the anti-clockwise sense. The face of the coil, facing the approaching magnet, then has the same polarity as that of the approaching pole of the magnet. The induced current, therefore, is seen to oppose the change of magnetic flux that produces it.

(b) (i) *p-n* junction diode under forward bias

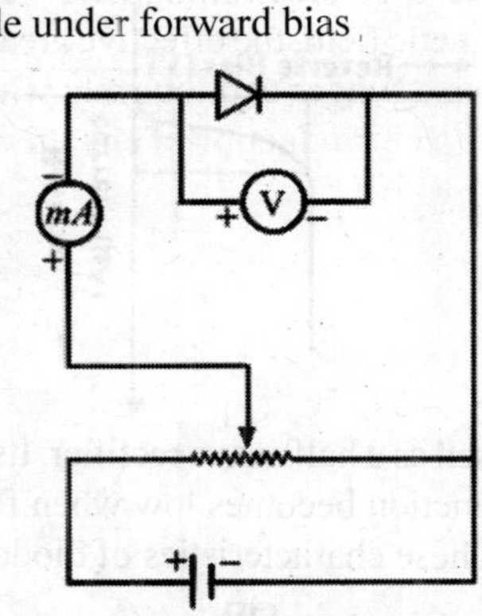

p-side is connected to the positive terminal and *n*-side to the negative terminal. Applied voltage drops across the depletion region. Electron in *n*-region moves towards the *p-n* junction and holes in the *p*-region move towards the junction. The width of the depletion layer decreases and hence, it offers less resistance. Diffusion of majority carriers takes place across the junction. This leads to the forward current.

The V-I characteristics of p-n junction in forward bias is shown below:

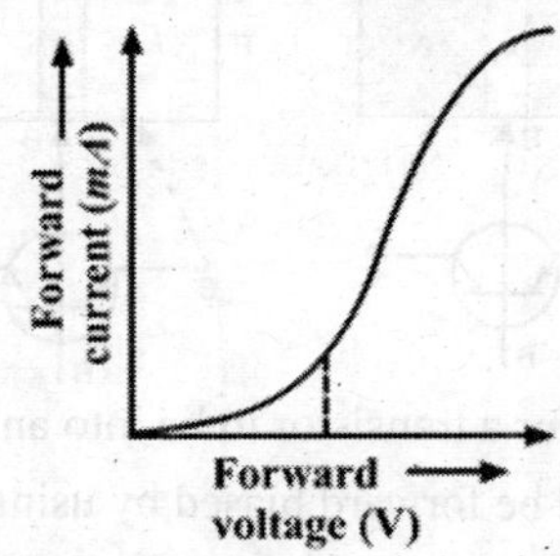

(ii) *p-n* junction diode under reverse bias

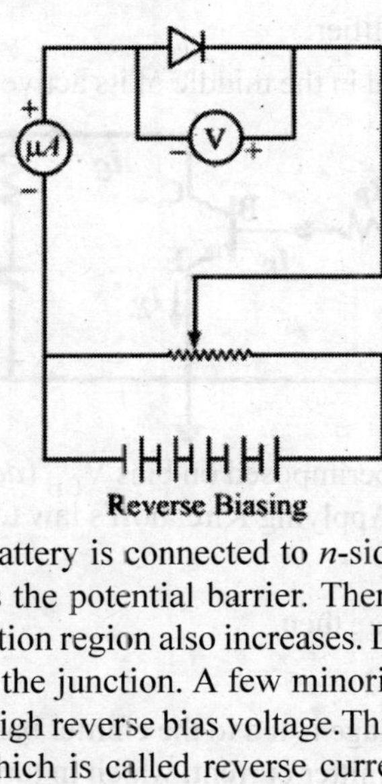

Reverse Biasing

Positive terminal of battery is connected to *n*-side and negative terminal to *p*-side. Reverse bias supports the potential barrier. Therefore, the barrier height increases and the width of depletion region also increases. Due to the majority carriers, there is no conduction across the junction. A few minority carriers cross the junction after being accelerated by high reverse bias voltage. This constitutes a current that flows in opposite direction, which is called reverse current. The V-I characteristics of *p-n* junction diode in reverse bias is shown below:

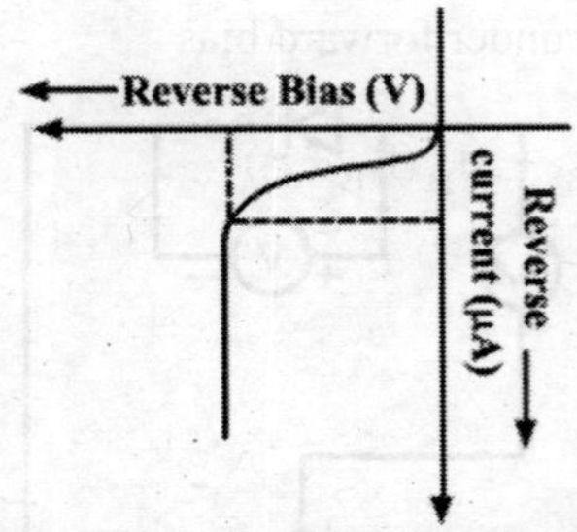

p-n junction diode is used as a half-wave rectifier. Its working is based on the fact that the resistance of *p-n* junction becomes low when forward biased and becomes high when reverse biased. These characteristics of diode is used in rectification.

OR

(a) Emitter (E) - It is the left hand side thick layer of the transistor, which is heavily doped.

Base (B) - It is the central thin layer of the transistor, which is lightly doped.

Collector (C) - It is the right hand side thick layer of the transistor, which is moderately doped.

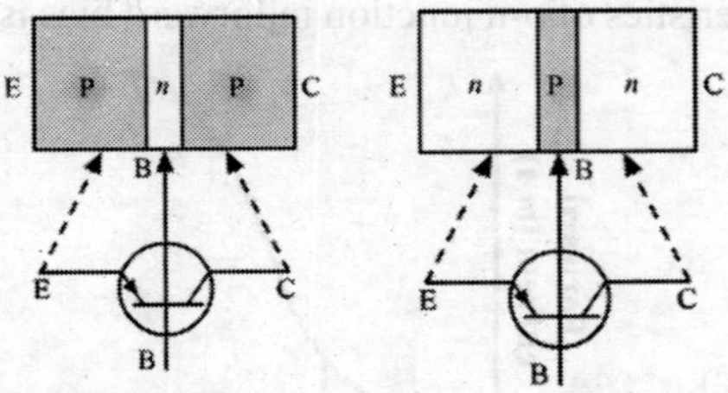

(b) There are two conditions for a transistor to be into an active region.

1. The input circuit should be forward biased by using a low voltage battery.
2. The output circuit should be reverse biased by using a high voltage battery.

(c) *n-p-n* Transistor as an amplifier:

The operating point is fixed in the middle of its active region.

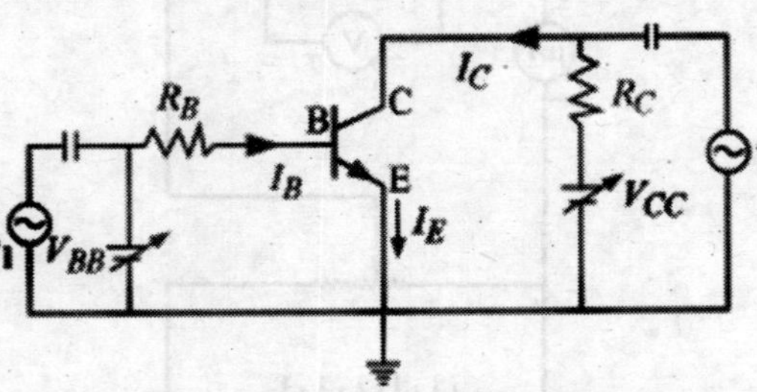

An ac input signal v_i is superimposed on bias V_{BB} (*dc*). The output is taken between the collector and the ground. Applying Kirchhoff's law to the output loop:

$$V_{CC} = V_{CE} + I_C R_C$$

If V_C is the collector voltage then,

$$V_C = V_{CE} - I_C R_C \quad ...(A)$$

When the input signal voltage is fed to the emitter base circuit, it will change the emitter voltage and hence to the emitter current, which in turn will change the collector current. Due to this the collector voltage V_C will vary in accordance with relation (A). This variation in collector voltage appears as amplified output.

$$V_{BB} = V_{BE} + I_B R_B$$

$$v_i \neq O$$

Then, $V_{BB} + v_i = V_{BE} + I_B R_B + \Delta I_B (R_B + r_i)$

$$\because \quad r_i = \left(\frac{\Delta V_{BI}}{\Delta I_B}\right)_{V_{CE}}$$

$$\therefore \quad v_i = \Delta I_B (R_B + R_i)$$

$$= r \Delta I_B$$

$$\beta_{AC} = \frac{\Delta I_C}{\Delta I_B} = \frac{i_c}{i_b}$$

□□□